MEDIA BURN

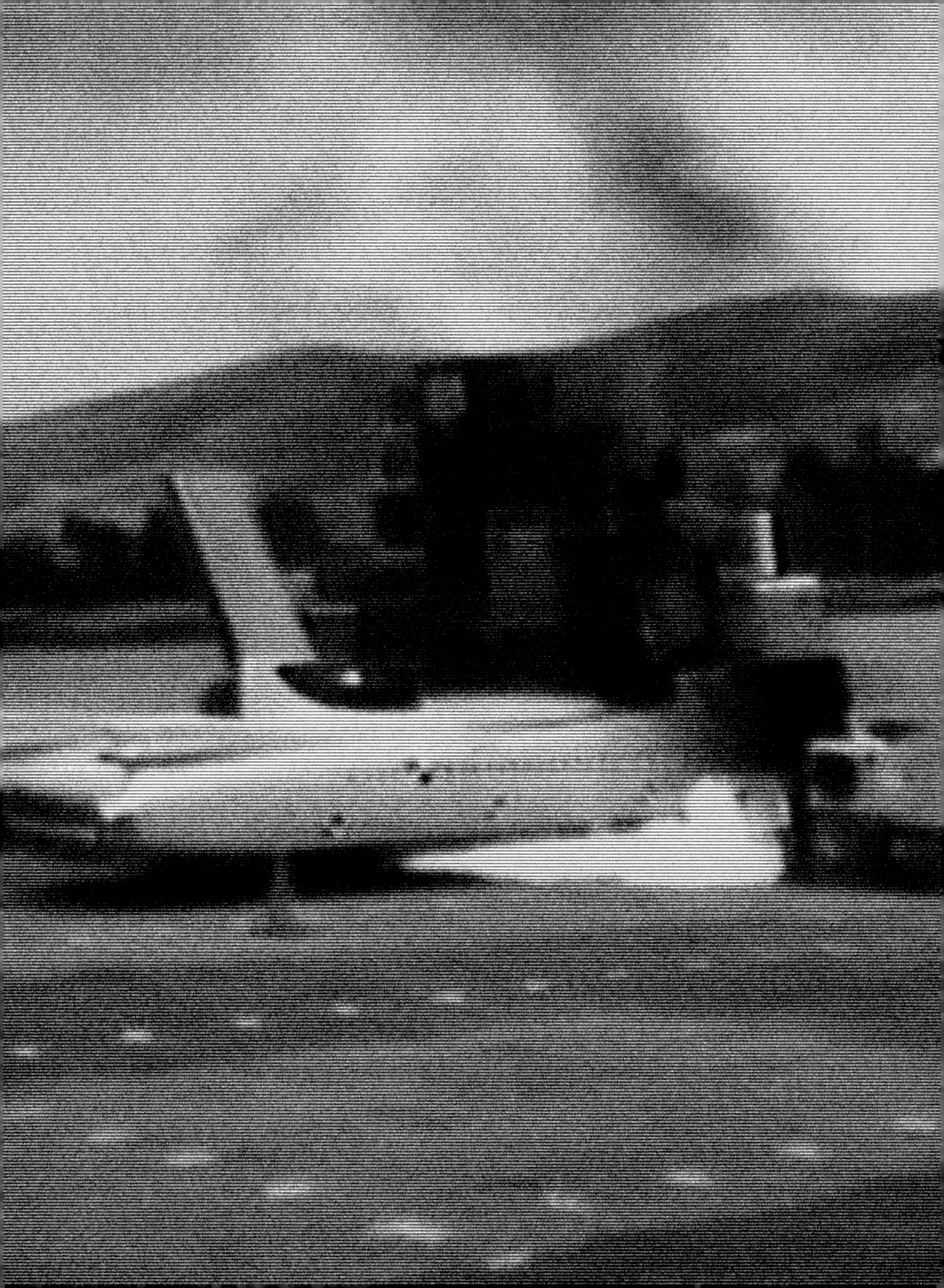

INVENTORY PRESS

MEDIA BURN

ANT FARM AND THE MAKING OF AN IMAGE

STEVE SEID

RITE Editions.

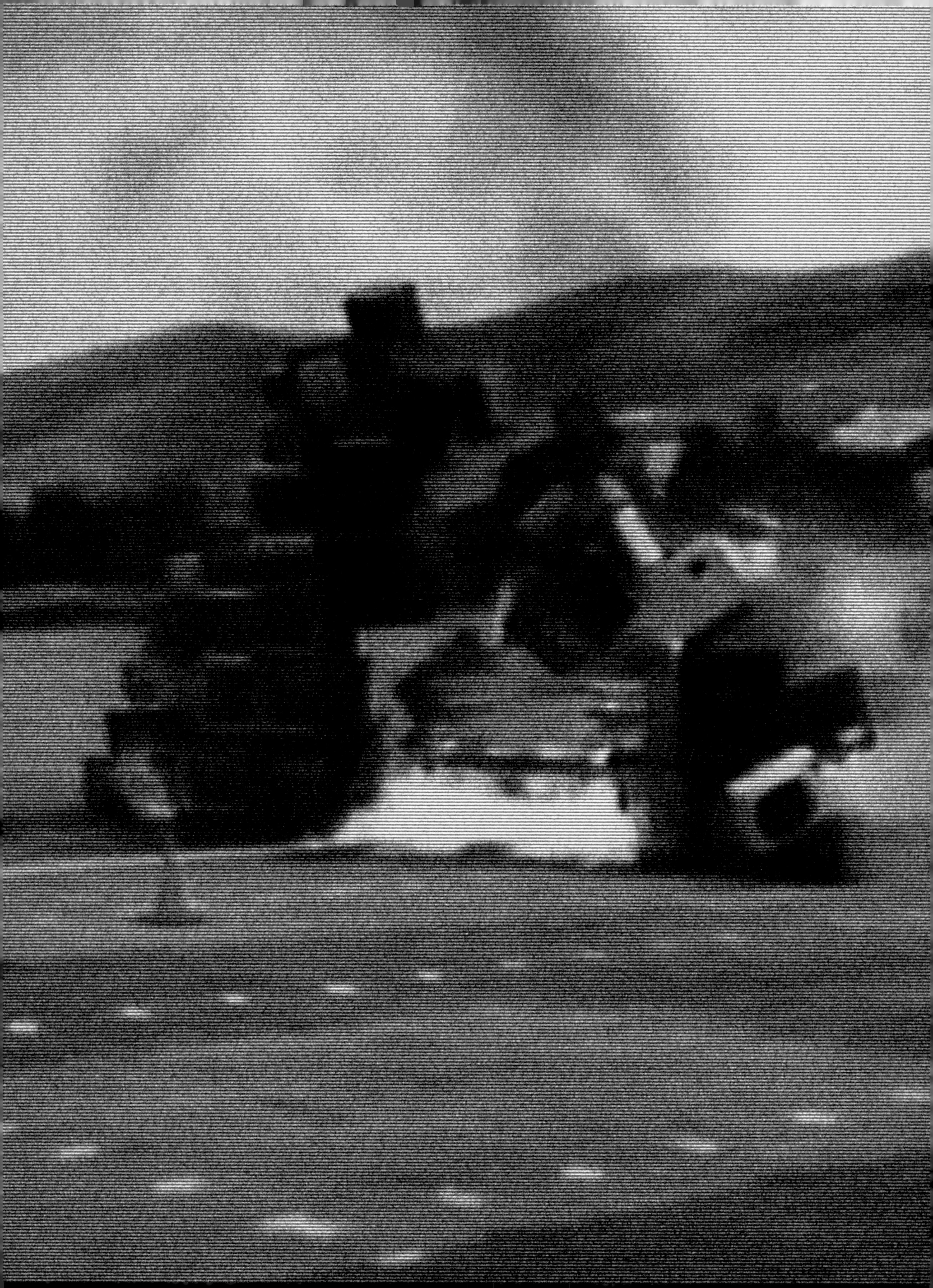

FOREWORD
CHIP LORD

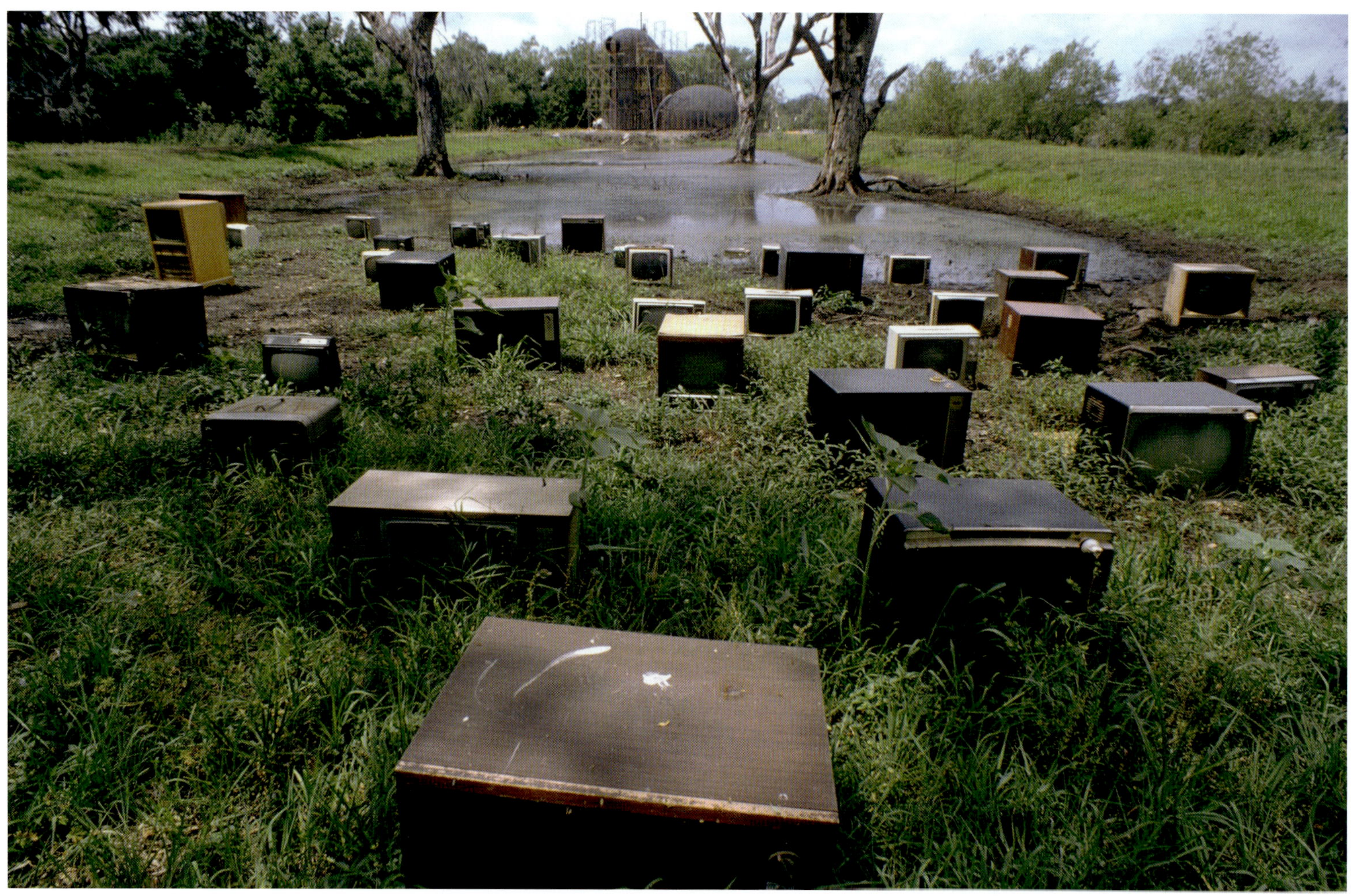

A prepared landscape, *100 Television Sets* (1972), emerging from Mojo Lake, near Angleton, Texas. House of the Century can be seen under construction in the background. Photograph courtesy Chip Lord.

In 1972, two-thirds of Ant Farm—Doug Michels and I—were living in Angleton, Texas, building a futuristic ferro-cement house, the House of the Century (so named by our client's husband). This is rural Texas, forty miles southeast of Houston, and there wasn't much to do there, so we invented side projects to stave off boredom. One of these was an environmental sculpture, *100 Television Sets*, installed in a swampy marsh in front of the construction site. We never made it to a hundred televisions, but we came close.

Around the same time at the Cow Palace, near our home base of San Francisco, the professional daredevil Evel Knievel made a successful motorcycle jump over more than a dozen cars, but suffered a broken back and concussion after getting thrown off and run over by his own Harley-Davidson. This greatly influenced Doug Michels, who made the first drawing of a similarly spectacular event—a "late model sedan" being driven through a wall of TV sets (see pp. 20–21). What would become *Media Burn* was first imagined in Angleton, Texas, and Michels (who died in 2003) should be remembered and thanked for imagining it and getting it down on paper.

Doug was always the first one to the drawing board, but back in the Bay Area, Ant Farmer Curtis Schreier was busy sketching a crude drawing of a cathode-ray tube (CRT) tearing down the highway on smoking tires. After some refinements, this daydream doodle would become the *Media Burn* logo.

When the *Media Burn* event took place at the Cow Palace, on July 4, 1975, it was the culmination of a year of preparation and planning by the three partners of Ant Farm and Tom Weinberg. An even longer period of gestation had informed the basic idea—to drive a customized vehicle through a wall of burning televisions in order to produce a singular image of a moment of truth that we believed would have a political power all its own. On the appointed day, I was there in my "Uncle Buddie" business suit, playing the role of the producer/director. This meant I was the one who poured kerosene on the TVs and lit the match!

With that image in hand—and its dispersal via the mainstream media ongoing—what better way to further distribute it to the world than a postcard—an inexpensive advertising medium that had developed in the first half of the twentieth century into a full-blown industry, morphing not-so-quietly into a discrete art medium of its own. The *Media Burn* postcard was produced through Dexter Press of Nyack, New York, from a 35mm

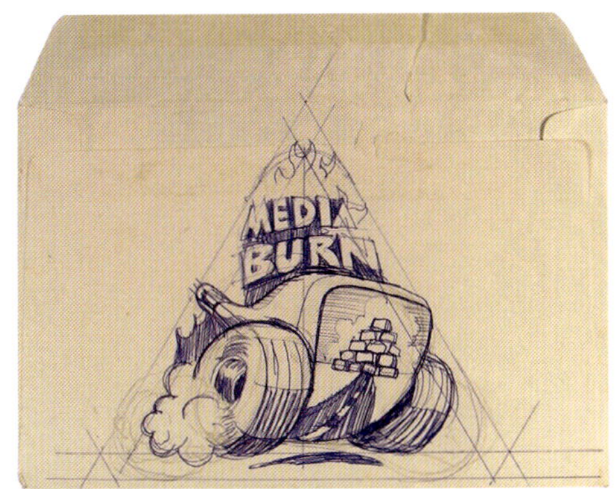

A rendering of the *Media Burn* logo (c. 1974–75), sketched on an envelope by Curtis Schreier.

slide shot by John F. Turner, one of several artist/photographer friends who had been invited into the "press area" of the *Media Burn* performance.

Over the next few years, the *Media Burn* postcard was distributed by Fotofolio, New York; Quantity Postcards in San Francisco; and Untitled, a store on Spring Street in Soho that sold nothing but artists' postcards. Eventually there were more than 120,000 *Media Burn* postcards circulating—making it perhaps the best-selling artist postcard of all time!

The *Media Burn* event was covered by four local television news programs and numerous print outlets. Television news anchors in the Bay Area could only mock what was reported by their crews, but the countercultural press was another story. *The Berkeley Barb* ran it as a cover story; Jon Carroll wrote a piece for the *Village Voice*; and Paul Krassner for *Crawdaddy*. Francis Ford Coppola's *City* magazine used the image as a centerfold to accompany Jerry Mander's excerpt from his forthcoming book, *Four Arguments for the Elimination of Television*.

Over the years, the *Media Burn* image would surface in unexpected places: In 1980, filmmaker Les Blank would use it as the backdrop to an anti-TV rant by none other than Werner Herzog; a few years later, MTV featured *Media Burn* as a central image for the Video Music Awards marketing campaign; Roman Coppola directed a faithful reenactment of *Media Burn* in a music video for British band Supergrass' "We Still Need More (Than Anyone Can Give)." Bruce Springsteen delved back into the Ant Farm repertoire of images for "57 Channels (and Nothin' On)" and Kendrick Lamar's 2015 single "Alright" paid tribute to *Media Burn* with a wall of boom boxes and a tire-spinning muscle car.

Where did the idea for *Media Burn* come from and how was it developed? Was it part of the larger Conceptual art movement that transformed contemporary art and culture in California in the

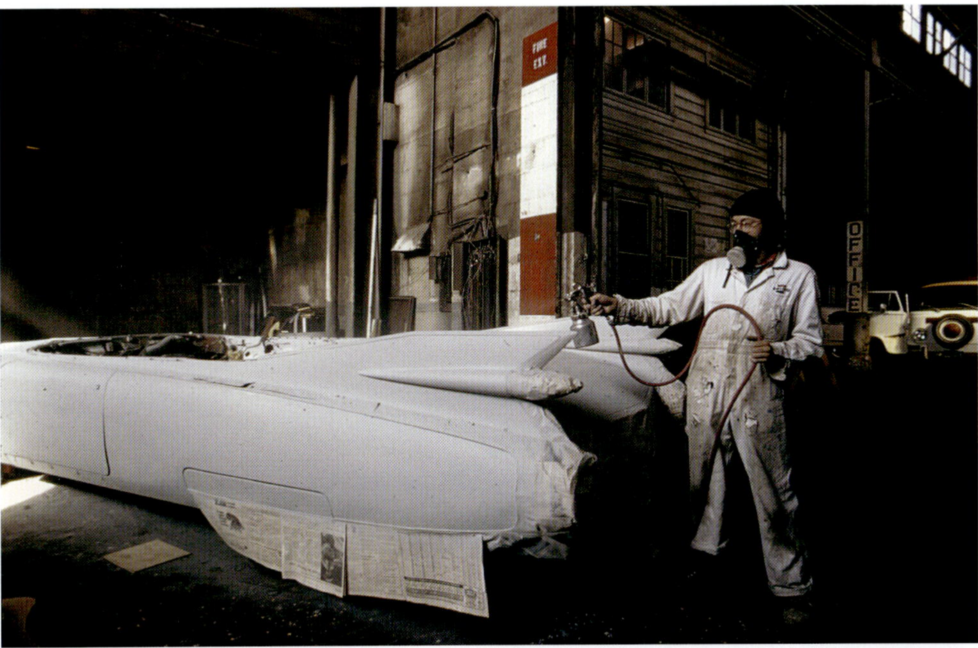

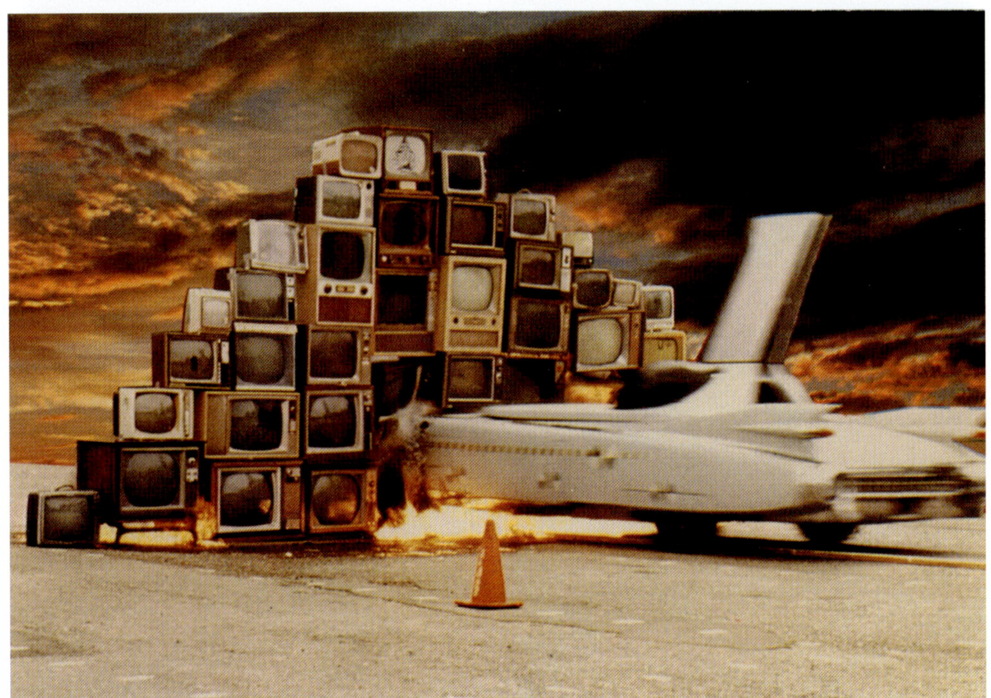

A masked Chip Lord sprays a fresh coat of primer on the Ant Farm work-in-progress, the Phantom Dream Car. Photograph by Ant Farm.

Bottom: One of three official postcards of *Media Burn* issued by Ant Farm. This card shows John F. Turner's now classic photo with a heavily manipulated sky. Distributed by Dexter Press, mid-1970s.

1970s? How was it that young architects would create such a spectacularly influential performance/video event without an actual building involved? The pages that follow come about as close to answering these questions as anyone's going to get.

Thank you to Robin M. Wright of RITE Editions and Adam Michaels and Shannon Harvey of Inventory Press for recognizing that Ant Farm's *Media Burn* deserves a full telling, forty-five years after it was made.

PART I
BEFORE THE BURN

OH, SAY, CAN YOU SEE

These artists are pioneers. They are pioneers as surely as were Lewis and Clark when they explored uncharted territory.
—Artist-President, performed by Doug Hall

Modern alert
The danger is near
Burn your TV
Eliminate fear
—Doug Michels, "Media Burn," the song

On July 4, 1975, the *real* U.S. bicentennial, an art performance was staged on the sweltering tarmac at San Francisco's Cow Palace. This auspicious intervention was not encumbered by the celebratory hype of the official bicentennial, still a year off, but to the 400 or so observers it stood out as its own renegade declaration of independence, even adopting the trappings of patriotism in its display of tricolored bunting, a blaring "Star-Spangled Banner," and a rousing send-off speech delivered by a fake president. But if it was not an outright disruption of patriotism, or a defiant fist raised against jingoistic loyalties, then why this overdetermined day and its garniture of patriotic provenance?

On the blacktop the intensity of the performance was palpable. Audience members craned and gawked, the media made their baffled pronouncements, and the artist-participants carried out their assigned actions with premeditated precision. Again, it wasn't patriotism contained within this favored day that was the objective, but something removed, at least from sight, from the very structures of meaning that stood behind it all, pushing forth the folderol we all followed—the devolving and dispersing images that encased the everyday.

This performance had a name, *Media Burn*, but it was divorced from sundry other (reactionary) burns that ignited banned books, condemned saints, land, plague bodies, and fetid cows, to name a few. This burn was radical, and it was a daring to-do: an accumulation of aesthetic incentives, media theories, and cultural complaints that aspired toward a single outcome: the generation of a lone image, remarkably peculiar and supremely potent, that would go "viral" years before the phrase became common currency.

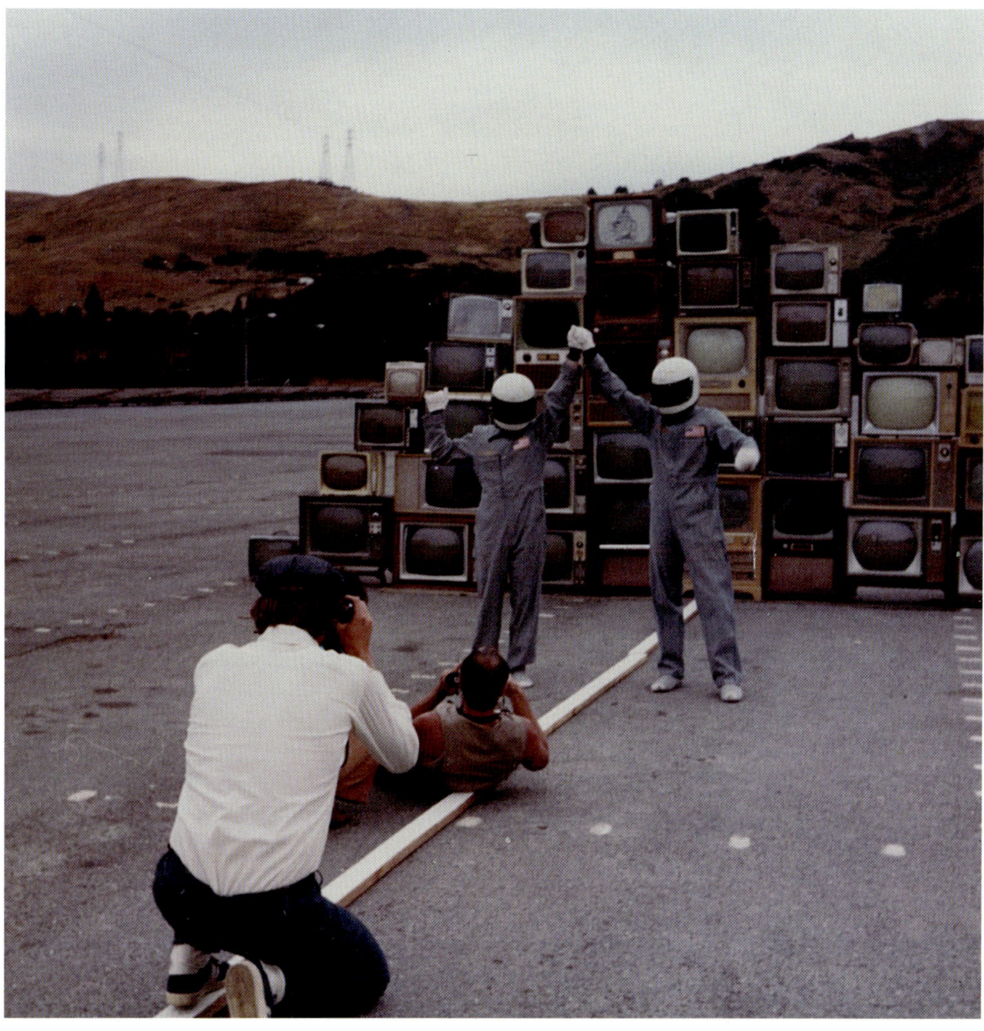

The pre-victory pose by Artist-Dummies Doug Michels and Curtis Schreier. Note the white-painted two-by-fours that were used to guide the Phantom Dream Car. Photograph by Ant Farm.

The result was a distillation of sixties utopianism tempered by seventies realpolitik as embodied by the art collective known as Ant Farm, three "hippie architects" who morphed into Conceptual artists.

The unforgettable image of a customized Cadillac bursting through a wall of blazing television sets, then, is the end point of an experiential algorithm: a compression scheme of Pop influences, architectural renunciations, activist aesthetics, and democratic critiques that, once creatively decompressed, encapsulates the dynamic and telling act of its making. The world contained in a grain of sand, or at least the underground substrate of an ant farm.

The endeavor here is to reverse engineer *Media Burn*, tracking such elusive influences as guerilla television, American mythopoeia, media theory, car culture, architectural pedagogy, and contemporary art. A lossy effort that sheds much, yet still retains a facsimile of the whole, returning the overlooked and discarded bits to their rightful place: the last authentic image.

After a three-year period of reinventions, postponements, and re-entrenchments, Ant Farm staged *Media Burn* in the parking lot of the Cow Palace—a WPA-era arena built with agricultural expos in mind. The performance consisted of four distinct facets: a speech presented by the "Artist-President," which mimicked the delivery style of John F. Kennedy; a customized 1959 Cadillac Eldorado Biarritz driven at high speed through a pyramid of forty-four flame-engulfed television sets; video documentation that incorporated

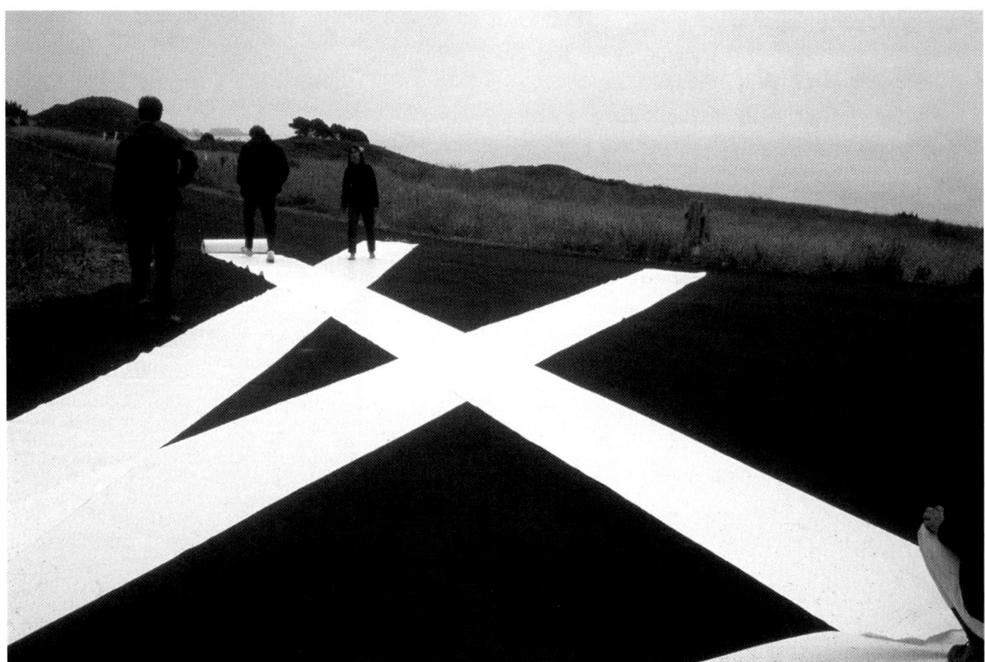

Participants in Lawrence Halprin's Experiments in Environment workshop manipulating the landscape of Northern California sometime in the late 1960s.

Ant Farm–produced footage, mainstream televised news coverage, and commentary by viewers; and the strategic distribution of a resonant still image of the premeditated crash.

Ant Farm's performance (and subsequent videowork, also called *Media Burn*) set on a literal collision course two American icons: the automobile and the television set. The motion was both intrinsic, the car being built to move, and extrinsic, the television set's inertia broken, propelled forth by the collision. The image, gleaned from many sources, captured the impact, thrust, and dematerialization as these two symbolic objects were joined in mutual destruction.

What strange hybrid, forged in fire and fury, might be born from this artful act?

It's hard to stay below ground when what you're doing takes place above it. But that was the chosen metaphor when a hirsute trio of recent transplants to the fog-shrouded city of San Francisco, circa '68, were asked what it was they did. "We are underground architects," they would routinely reply.[1] One day, a friend, Sharon Skolnick, riposted, "Oh, you mean like an Ant Farm?" The name stuck, and sometime later, with the inducement of psychedelics, nuance was attached to it:

An Ant Farm is a self-contained community, its workers are all equals and they accomplish things not possible individually. The Ant Farm is literally a slice of a larger reality, it is plastic on the outside, but natural on the inside, and it breaks down into component parts like portable architecture … It has traditional buildings above ground and free form spaces below ground.[2]

The core of the shape-shifting collective called Ant Farm comprised Charles "Chip" Lord (b. 1944; Cleveland, OH), Doug Michels (1943–2003; Seattle, WA), and Curtis Schreier (b. 1944; Philadelphia, PA), architect-trained visionaries all.[3] The commonality here, for there must be one, is that they were boisterous boys of the 1950s who found themselves entering academia in the midst of the turmoil of the mid-1960s. Things were coming apart: the Civil Rights Movement, soon followed by Free Speech, would test the righteous mettle of the nation's youth. The draft for an escalating war in Vietnam increased the vulnerability of every able-bodied male. And the cultural backlash from the conformist fifties inspired a massive recoil that generated shockwaves of rethinking, rejection, and reinvention. Or as Chip Lord would say, "It seemed that the social structure in America was ruthless and headed for collapse."[4]

Things were coming apart, and architecture was no safe haven. Decades of severe Brutalist style had found a waiting body of young dissenters favoring the scale and softness of human need over the monolithic indifference of corporate design. At Yale, for instance, Charles Moore, late of UC Berkeley, took over the deanship of the School of Architecture, where Doug Michels had recently enrolled. A chief designer of Northern California's environmentally provocative Sea Ranch, Moore replaced Paul Rudolph, an advocate of hulking concrete structures and the heavy-handed gestures that accompanied them. But this upheaval took on more than design. Pedagogical style, specialization of skills, the social theories underpinning human enclosures—everything was up for grabs.[5]

While at Yale (Michels; graduated 1967), Tulane (Lord; graduated 1968), and the Rhode Island School of Design (Schreier; graduated 1967) each thrived as dissident students enriched by the tumult of new possibilities. Lord recalled: "If there is a need for what we do it can probably be best related to research and experimentation in living patterns."[6] Buildings had lost their primacy, with social behavior driving the occupancy theories.

In 1968, the siren call of Northern California was soundly seductive.[7] The Haight-Ashbury had already slipped into communal legend, *Rolling Stone* magazine consolidated a new hip culture while Stewart Brand's *Whole Earth Catalog* advocated DIY self-sufficiency. Composers like Terry Riley and Steve Reich signaled the arrival of new aesthetics while Robert Crumb's *Fritz the Cat* became the comic to the counterculture. The Bay Area was also a haven to pursuits of the spirit, whether it be the Zen Buddhism of Alan Watts, Fritz Perls' Gestalt therapy, or the metalogues of Gregory Bateson. There was a convergence of creativity that shunned the gray flannel of the East Coast establishment.[8]

---

1 Pre-Ant Farm, Chip Lord had declared in the October 1968 issue of *Progressive Architecture* that "the first generation of hippie architects has come of age."

2 From the complete Ant Farm timeline (originally published in 1976) found in Felicity Scott, *Living Archive 7: Ant Farm* (Barcelona: ACTAR, 2008), p. 201.

3 Other notable Ant Farm members were Hudson Marquez, Doug Hurr, and Joe Hall.

4 Scott 2008, p. 200.

5 A simple example of this radical shift could be seen in Charles Moore's "Yale Building Project," which he initiated in 1967. First-year architecture students were obligated to go into the community and work on housing. This would demystify the process of construction while inspiring social responsibility.

6 Scott 2008, p. 203.

7 Lord had already been to San Francisco, in 1966. As a student, he interned at the architectural practice Anshen + Allen, who would have been in the midst of constructing the Space Sciences Lab at UC Berkeley.

8 This countercultural shopping list should also include the experimental film and video

But what was perhaps the principal attractant for our westbound tyro architects was Experiments in Environment, a creative process workshop led by noted landscape architect Lawrence Halprin and his equally noted wife, radical choreographer Anna Halprin.[9] The month-long workshop was an experiential immersion in what would be formalized as the "RSVP Cycles," a methodology for collaboration summarized in the Halprins' 1970 book of the same name. Four components—resources, score, valuation, and performance—comprised a successive exploration of a relationship to space and those within it. For Anna Halprin this might engender expanded choreography addressing both the environment and the audience; for Lawrence Halprin, a community of collaborators could be rallied to develop the beneficial uses of an architectural site. Regardless of application, the intention of RSVP was to encourage deep engagement through inspired collectivity. And in an even more radical departure, Experiments in Environment shunned the limitation of goals in favor of spontaneous process, creativity, and human interaction. People, not buildings, came to the fore.

This was heady stuff for some green architects more interested in "living patterns" than the hard structures around them. Lord graduated in June 1968 and made a beeline for the Bay Area. Schreier, one year his senior, had already been part of Lawrence Halprin's studio for a year and was tasked with documenting the workshop. It was here that the two future Farmers met.

As Experiments in Environment was coming to a close, Michels was speeding across the U.S. in a "drive-away" Cadillac convertible, fresh from his own workshop, Crash City. Co-designed by partner Bob Feild,[10] this experimental context for "responsive learning" gave the participants access to "a large loft, a communal house, a darkroom, a workshop, a pickup truck, and the city of Washington D.C." Crash City was intended to erode the predetermined goals of most architectural pedagogy. For Michels, "the normal boundaries between work/play/learning were eliminated."[11]

An anarchist at heart, Michels had incorporated similar theories into his first teaching assignment at Catholic University in D.C. the previous year. (To reinforce his rebellious credibility, Michels would often label his design documents with the phrase "Not-A-Plan.") Finding chaos as a design goal unacceptable for their curriculum, the university administrators shut down his course. Encouraged by his former dean, Charles Moore, Michels and fellow graduate Feild instead organized a college tour, lecturing about contemporary modes of architectural practice, a surprising accomplishment considering the inexperience of these designers. One of the sixteen colleges they visited was Tulane, where Lord was on the School of Architecture's student committee.[12]

In San Francisco, August 1968, the elements of a new creative collaboration were converging: a triumvirate of young architects drawn to sensory awakening, pedagogical pluralities, and the understanding that countercultural design was holistic, open-ended, and guided by the primacy of people, not property. Lord and Michels formally established Ant Farm. (Curtis Schreier continued at the Halprin architectural practice until 1970, before officially joining Ant Farm.)

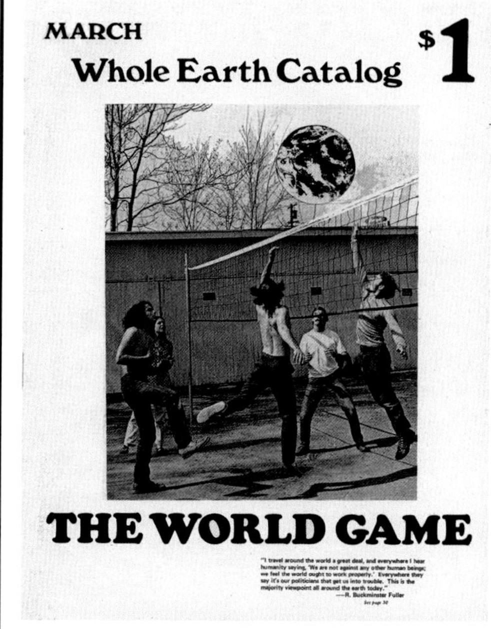

The cover of *Whole Earth Catalog,* March 1970. This is an image associated with the first Earth Day, celebrated on April 22, 1970. Note the inclusion of the pioneering photograph of Earth taken in 1967 by the ATS-3 satellite, then repurposed for the inaugural issue of the *Whole Earth Catalog* in 1968.

---

community of the greater Bay Area that was thriving during this period, but it wasn't a particularly strong enticement for Ant Farm. Nonetheless, they would have encountered film artists Bruce Baillie, Jordan Belson, Bruce Conner, Lawrence Jordan, Gunvor Nelson, Chick Strand, and others, alongside early practitioners such as Bill Gwin, Allen Rucker, Loren Sears, and Skip Sweeney, from the nascent video side.

9   According to Anna Halprin, Dr. Paul Baum, a Gestalt therapist, also helped conduct the workshop. See Halprin, *Moving Toward Life: Five Decades of Transformational Dance* (Middletown, CT: Wesleyan University Press, 1995).

10   The October 1968 issue of *Progressive Architecture* called the duo "the Bonnie and Clyde of Archiworld."

11   Ibid. Lord claims that Crash City was directly influenced by an article about Experiments in Environment published the year before in *Progressive Architecture.*

12   It was this same tour that took Michels to the University of Houston, where he was invited to teach the following year. This cemented an ongoing association between Michels, Ant Farm, and Texas.

BACKGROUND NOISE

They imagined an architectural practice that would operate more like a rock band than a corporate business.
—Ken Johnson, *New York Times*, June 21, 2003

It was strangely prescient that Doug Michels should arrive in San Francisco in a Cadillac. That American icon would bring Ant Farm ample notoriety in the mid-seventies with the creation of *Cadillac Ranch*, soon followed by *Media Burn*, but there was much to be explored in the years preceding 1975. The expansive practice that characterized Ant Farm encompassed ambitiously heaped installations (such as *Space Cowboy Meets Plastic Businessman* and *Electronic Oasis*, both 1969), trippy time capsules (*Citizen's Time Capsule*, 1975), freewheeling happenings (*Time Slice*, 1969; *Freestone Conference*, 1970), shape-shifting inflatables (*50 × 50′ Pillow* and *Clean Air Pod*, both 1970), nomadic journeys (*The Truckstop Network*, 1971), exuberant publications (*The Inflatocookbook*, 1970), rough-hewn videoworks (*The World's Longest Bridge*, 1970 and *The Eternal Frame*, 1975), speculative architectural developments (*Freedomland*, 1973; *Convention City*, 1976; *The Dolphin Embassy*, 1977), open-air sculptures (*Cadillac Ranch*, 1974), and the occasional built structure like House of the Century (1973) and the Antioch Art Building (1971).

Ant Farm's architectural practice became an aesthetic investigation, with communities replacing clients and interventions replacing assignments. The "underground architects" abandoned the strict construction of hard spaces for a more spacious architectonics of the everyday. How does form prescribe behavior? Why must environment embody power? How can design liberate rather than encase function? These structural queries could be observed in such disparate mediums as an organically extruded residence, a cultural mapping of roadways, or a fleet and ever-circulating moving image.

Key to *Media Burn* is the notion that its end product, an image, will not just circulate, but will become an integral part of a cultural lexicon of free-floating, mediated, and hollowed-out signifiers. In the closing line from the speech delivered by Doug Hall (as the Artist-President) during *Media Burn* (and most likely penned by Chip Lord), he says, "The world may never understand what was done here today, but it shall not forget the image created here." Prior to *Media Burn*, images were different. Or at least our relationship to them was different.

Five months before the performance of *Media Burn*, Sony's Betamax VCR was introduced to the U.S. market. A year later, RCA would introduce the VHS VCR. Though portable video formats had existed since the latter part of the sixties, no format geared to the consumer market had yet been developed. Sony's ½-inch open-reel format and their subsequent ¾-inch (or U-matic) format were intended for the educational and industrial markets—they were cumbersome and expensive.[13] *Media Burn* itself was a product of these huskier formats as evidenced by photographic documentation of Ant Farm's partners, Optic Nerve, for example, lugging Sony Portapaks around the performance site.[14]

The above is not an attempt to recount a history of video technology, but to consider the implications of that technology. In the years preceding the introduction of convenient, accessible, and reasonably priced home video systems, media images were elusive. But more than elusive, they were generally the exclusive property of mass media producers. Viewers were kept in lockstep with the strategic desires of large-scale, highly financed image disseminators. Whether newsworthy, popular, or just plain entertaining, images were set adrift at the convenience of the (mainly) corporate owners, to be passively consumed at their discretion. Rare was it that an average citizen could capture and replay, much less manipulate, a mass

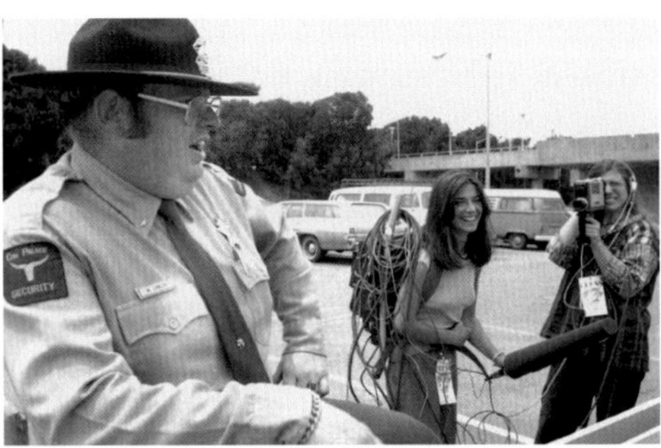

Optic Nerve members Sherrie Rabinowitz (with the Sony record deck in a backpack) and Mya Shone (with the Portapak camera) interview a Cow Palace security guard at the *Media Burn* performance. Photograph by Lynn Adler.

media image; outside of a small market in 8mm and 16mm prints, there was little trade beyond mass appeal imagery[15] and much of that was unauthorized.

Media images in continual recirculation could be purposeful, potent, but rarely private. History came to us as a preselected provocation: the Zapruder footage,[16] the Watts Riots, the entire Vietnam War, the Apollo 11 moon landing, and, much later, the Challenger explosion and 9/11.

Ant Farm was not alone in their aggressive reconsideration of the image. The proliferation of media images was met by an equal upsurge in speculative writing about the occupation of the cultural unconscious by free-floating images. If it wasn't the departure of "aura" as described in Walter Benjamin's "The Work of Art in the Age of Mechanical Reproduction,"[17] it was the impregnable surround of Guy Debord's *Society of the Spectacle*.[18] If it

---

13   In 1972, the Sony AV-3400 Portapak sold for $1,650. By comparison, a Volkswagen Beetle cost only a few hundred dollars more.

14   The final edit of *Media Burn*, the videotape, would be rendered on a broadcast standard format: 2-inch Quad videotape developed by Ampex.

15   Home movies on 8mm and S-8 were plentiful and a hobbyist sector flourished with 16mm, but these practices were dominated by self-expression and not the appropriation of culturally and historically important images.

16   Just a few months after staging *Media Burn*, Ant Farm would regroup in Dallas to reenact the Kennedy assassination in Dealey Plaza. The resulting tape, *The Eternal Frame*, made with T. R. Uthco, was a vertiginous critique of the image and the abdication of meaning and is discussed later here.

17   Written in 1936, but first published in English in *Illuminations* (New York: Harcourt, Brace, 1968).

18   Written in 1967, but first published in English in 1970 (Detroit: Black & Red).

wasn't Roland Barthes' interrogation of how signifiers were infused with cultural meaning in *Mythologies*,[19] it was the manner in which culture employs simulations and false appearance as noted in Daniel Boorstin's *The Image: A Guide to Pseudo-Events in America*.[20]

Perhaps creating its own all-enveloping context was Marshall McLuhan's notion that electronic media would push aside traditional text-based culture only to replace it with a more fluid, visually driven counterpart.[21] His "global village"[22] would simulate consciousness itself through the instantaneous global exchange of information, often in the form of images. These global transactions would extend our reach and our responsibility as we were networked into a pseudo-tribal unity. But in these early McLuhan formulations we were still conduits and consumers, not creators of information or images. And a principal purveyor of this exchange, perhaps with ever-heightening status, was television itself. To some this might be an instance of technological evolution; to others it could constitute colonization by a not-so-benign image supplier. McLuhan's much-vaunted slogan, "The medium is the message," clearly resonates within *Media Burn*. That one's chosen medium is of equal or greater value than the message itself throws unexpected weight upon the television set (as icon), which becomes a domestic portal to a corporate cornucopia of images.

In May 1961, Newton Norman Minow, chairman of the Federal Communications Commission (FCC), topped T. S. Eliot by calling television a "vast wasteland." Minow declared that if you spend the day with television, you'll "see a procession of game shows, formula comedies about totally unbelievable families, blood and thunder, mayhem, violence, sadism, murder, western bad men, western good men, private eyes, gangsters, more violence, and cartoons. And endlessly, commer-

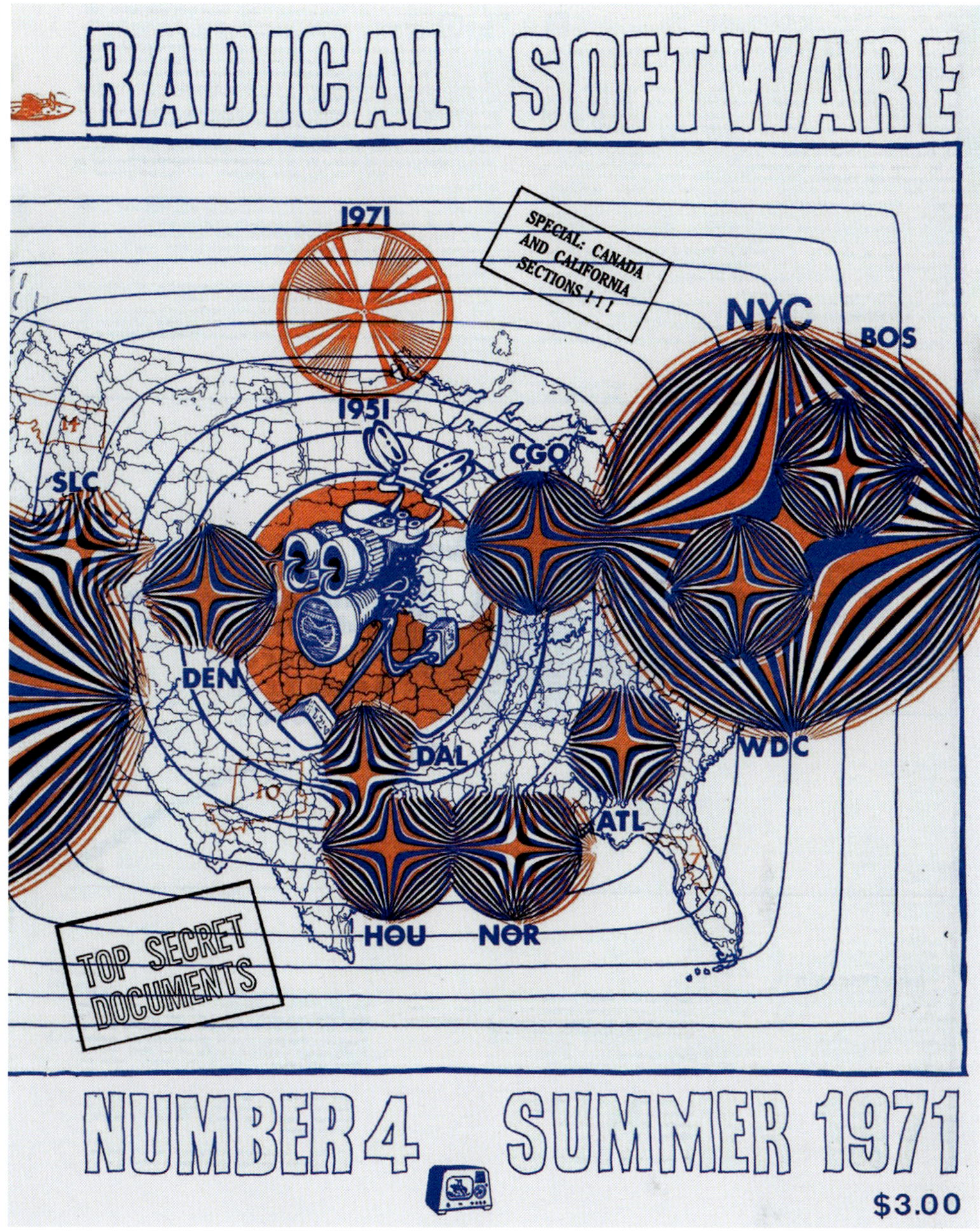

The fourth issue of *Radical Software* (Summer 1971), published by the Raindance Corporation, features a cover concept by Ant Farm, drawn by Curtis Schreier.

cials—many screaming, cajoling, and offending. And most of all, boredom."[23]

The so-called Golden Age of Television was thoroughly tarnished. But the sentiments Minow held were not his alone. A groundswell of dissatisfaction with mainstream television had inspired ire from both the Left and the Right, and from the great public in between.

In 1967, the Rockefeller Foundation, for instance, began funding TV Labs at major public stations as an antidote to poisonous network programming. Artists at these Labs[24] turned the technology of television toward unexpected means, creating hybrid programming in which dance, contemporary music, poetry, and other art forms found their reinvention through temporal manipulation, image processing, and nonnarrative explication.

Access to non-broadcast grade video technology encouraged another tier of alternative practices that embraced art-specific approaches and what came to be known as guerrilla television. In particular, guerrilla television enabled artists, activists, and average citizens to make their own images to, in effect, finally talk back to television.

An emblematic early performance by Nam June Paik at 1963's Fluxus Yam Festival in upstate New York evokes this early desire to fell, at least symbolically, the giant of media. A TV set, still plugged in, was wrapped with barbed wire and then buried in a pasture—a primitive, yet not premature, gesture. Subsequent

---

19   Written in 1957, but first published in English in 1972 (London: Jonathon Cape).

20   Published in 1962 by Atheneum.

21   This discussion began in *The Gutenberg Galaxy: The Making of Typographic Man* (Toronto: University of Toronto Press, 1962) and continued in *Understanding Media* (New York: McGraw-Hill, 1964) and elsewhere.

22   A prominent New York City–based media group, Global Village, adopted McLuhan's term as a utopian ideal in the late sixties. Ant Farm members would have certainly been aware of this group.

23   Minow's speech was titled "Television and the Public Interest" and was delivered at the annual convention of the National Association of Broadcasters. The complete text and audio can be found at AmericanRhetoric.com.

24   They were sited at KQED in San Francisco, WNET in New York, and WGBH in Boston.

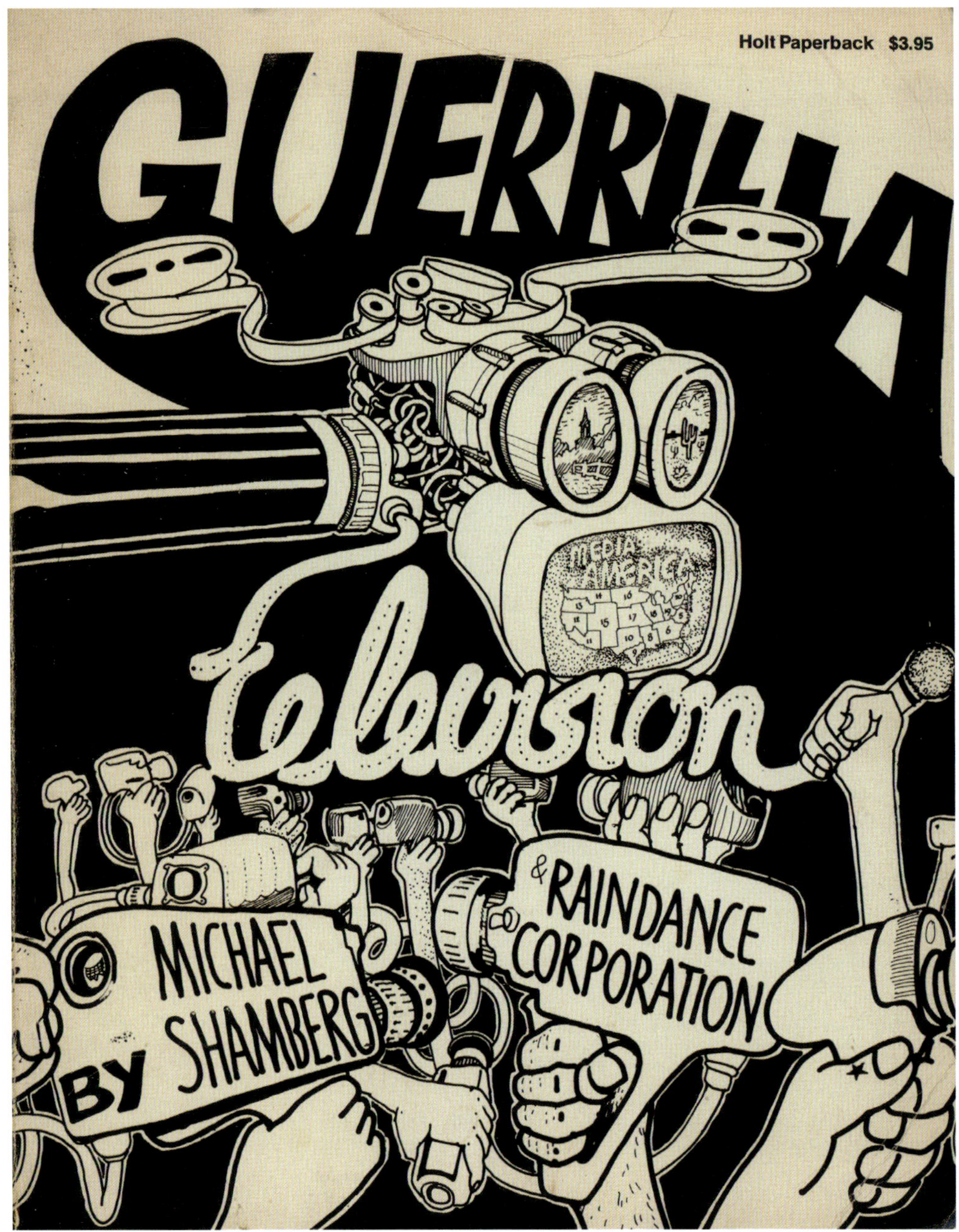

Michael Shamberg's *Guerrilla Television* (1971), designed by Ant Farm, with a cover illustration by Curtis Schreier. Shortly after its publication, Shamberg formed the video collective Top Value Television (TVTV).

interventions by Paik would include picture tube distortions caused by the strategic placement of large magnets, and eventually a deeper insurgency when, as Paik declared, "thirteen sets suffered thirteen sorts of variations … in their inner circuits."[25] These aesthetic defacements of the TV console (and circuitry) would continue even after Paik had acquired the means, through small-format video, to make his own electronic images.[26]

Eventually, Paik's subversive cooptation of the television set would proliferate as the essential tropes of video sculpture and installation.

The pyramid of flaming television sets central to *Media Burn* seems like a logical extension of Paik's more contained and Zen-like gestures.[27] Yet Ant Farm's seminal work distinguishes itself from Paik through its more overt political demolition. It is here that Ant Farm links up with the more socially radical and independent,

activist videomakers who, fueled with a distrust of mainstream media, held a utopian desire to create alternative cultural spaces, and with their recently gained access to small-format video, initiated a grassroots movement of guerrilla television. Theirs was a response to a centralized media industry that ignored regional cultures, advocated a corporate ideology, and ultimately shaped political and social realities. Needless to say, the individual was deleted from this equation. Instead, television advanced a sort of generic facsimile, i.e., shallow stereotypes and colorless stand-ins for the populace. For many television viewers, their televisual equivalence simply did not exist. You could not see yourself in this supposed mirror of culture.

The radical media movement had two distinct modes: the localized producers of community programming and those with ambitions to create nationally viable alternatives. The first could be represented by the likes of Videofreex or the People's Video Theater; the second by Top Value Television (TVTV) or Raindance Corporation. Many prominent groups were collective in structure and their members often filled in the ranks of other media collectives when the scale of a project required it. Members of TVTV and Videofreex (particularly Skip Blumberg and David Cort) routinely expanded Ant Farm's resources with participation in such performances as *Media Burn* and *The Eternal Frame*.

Where Nam June Paik commandeered television by turning it into an art object, the video guerrillas had something a bit more populist in mind. Formed in 1969, Videofreex,[28] perhaps the quintessential media collective, ventured to Lanesville, a hamlet in upstate New York, and rented a former boardinghouse. There they built a quasi-television studio, jerry-rigged a transmitter, and began pirate broadcasts on channel 3 of the spectrum. Videofreex programs were a mix of off-the-cuff, regionally interesting topical coverage of the nearby community, phone-in gab, edited programs (often political in nature) brought back from their travels, and spoofs of mainstream television. Undeterred by the need for FCC approval,[29] Videofreex

---

25   "Videa, Vidiot, Videology," found in one iteration in *New Artists Video*, Gregory Battcock, ed. (New York, E. P. Dutton, 1978).

26   In 1969 Paik, along with engineer Shuya Abe, introduced the Paik/Abe video synthesizer. Within the next few years, a handful of other video synthesizers would be designed by artist/techies. These included the Beck Direct Video Synthesizer (1970/71), the Rutt/Etra Video Synthesizer (1972), and the Sandin Image Processor (1971/73). These

represented an early and serious attempt to circumvent conventional image production by creating unique processing tools.

27   Presented in 1972, Ant Farm's *100 Television Sets*, a scattering of assorted sets that appear to be rising out of a swampy shoreline located near their House of the Century, beat out Paik's TV Garden (1974) by a few seasons.

28   The essential members of Videofreex were Skip Blumberg, Nancy Cain, David Cort, Bart Friedman, Davidson Gigliotti, Chuck Kennedy, Curtis Ratcliff, Parry Teasdale, Carol Vontobel, and Ann Woodward.

29   In 1972, the FCC issued its "Third Report and Order," which required all cable systems in the top 100 U.S. television markets to offer three access channels, one each for public, educational, and

persisted from 1972 to 1977, leaving behind 258 programs in all. But more than just amassing their visual data bank, they left behind a model (not necessarily sustainable but a model nonetheless) that connected media production to its site, so that, in essence, the producers resembled the audience in both culture and concerns.

You could call the Videofreex model "farm to cable." Top Value Television,[30] on the other hand, wanted to make it in the big city or, more accurately, subvert it. Provisionally led by Michael Shamberg, author of the highly influential *Guerrilla Television*[31] and co-publisher of *Radical Software*, TVTV went straight for the mainstream, albeit through a low-fi, self-reflexive, and iconoclastic critique of mass communications. Their opening televisual salvos were loud and clear: *The World's Largest TV Studio* (1972) and *Four More Years* (1972), serving up, respectively, the Democratic and Republican National Conventions, covered the coverage, and uncovered the overlooked, in a fashion that was irresistibly irreverent. Without the politically charged cachet of being network reps, TVTV's spontaneous Portapak crews seemed to find easy passage through the conventions, capturing behind-the-scenes conniving, clueless enthusiasm, and unguarded frankness on the part of delegates, volunteers, and high-powered newscasters like Dan Rather, Walter Cronkite, and Mike Wallace. These two prototypical docs were rewarded with substantial public broadcast airings and are touted as the first ½-inch open-reel works to be granted such exposure.

TVTV continued in this ironic vein, producing *The Lord of the Universe* (1974), *Adland* (1974), *TVTV Goes to the Super-bowl* (1976), *TVTV Looks at the Oscars* (1976), and other programs tempered by restrained sarcasm, intentionally suspect production values, and a dash of non-authoritarian verité. By the late 1970s, their countercultural irreverence had lost its political edge and TVTV disbanded. Within three years, Michael Shamberg would produce *The Big Chill* (1983).

Ant Farm pursued a third path that skirted the borders of performance, Conceptual art, anthropology, the diaristic, and media critique.[32] For them, video was a pliable medium that could be turned toward a multiplicity of uses: installation elements, populist how-tos, enhanced documentation, conceptual marketing, and other applications. Ant Farm acquired its first Sony Portapak in the summer of 1970, though they had already incorporated prerecorded images in *The Electronic Oasis*, made the previous year.[33]

Mention of a few videotapes will illustrate the gamut of their practice. First up might be *Dirty Dishes* (1970). This is a rough, day-in-the-life glimpse of Ant Farm and extended family hanging out in their Sausalito studio.[34] Best is the capture of straight-on portraits of the artists, all slightly glazed from some inhaled sensory enhancement, around a communal table. Many of these collectively diaristic "scrapbook" excerpts are recorded by a camera on a lazy Susan, which affords perfect, machinelike pans in stark contrast to the spontaneity of the subjects.

Early the next year, 1971, Ant Farm embarked on the Truckstop Network tour,[35] a lengthy drive across the South in the Media Van, a late-model Chevy van tricked out with multiple skylights, bubble windows, and a custom-built video viewing station inside the passenger compartment. Visiting college campuses, the tour was a lecture, performance, and

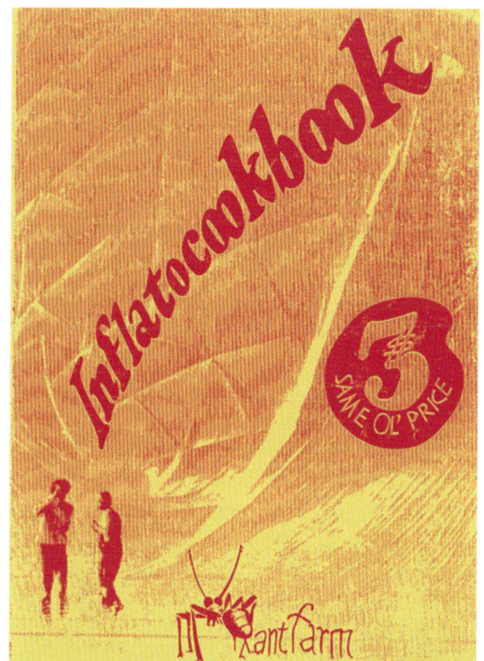

Top: The *Inflatocookbook* (1970) was a large-format, fourteen-page publication with "recipes" for assembling inflatable structures.

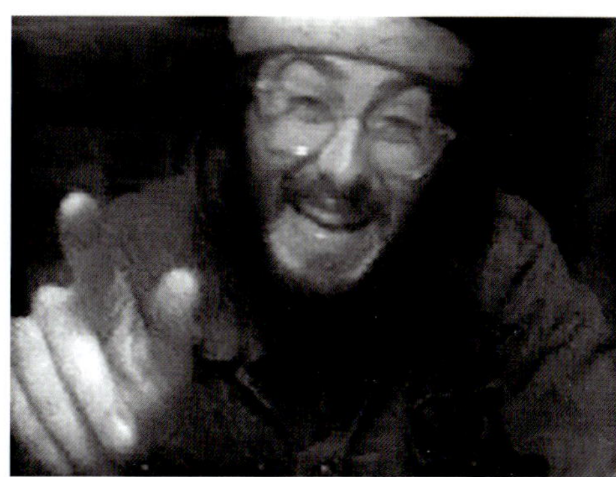

Bottom: Chip Lord as featured in the early Ant Farm videotape *Dirty Dishes* (1970), shot in their studio space in Sausalito, California.

---

local government use. Further legislation enacted in 1984 brought the era of public access television to a halt. But during that earlier unrestricted decade, the outpouring of community and alternative programming through local access was remarkable for its cultural diversity, idiosyncratic subject matter, and antidotal intentions.

30   TVTV was an offshoot of the Raindance Corporation, an East Coast video collective. The principal members of TVTV were Allen Rucker, Michael Shamberg, Tom Weinberg, and Megan Williams. Other important collaborators included Ant Farm, Wendy Appel, Skip Blumberg, Nancy Cain, Hudson Marquez, Elon Soltes, and Parry Teasdale.

31   Published in late 1971, *Guerrilla Television* (New York: Henry Holt and Co.) was designed by Ant Farm, principally Chip Lord and Curtis Schreier. Ant Farm had already contributed the cover design for *Radical Software*'s fourth issue, in 1971, the seminal Raindance publication.

32   This completely excludes their earlier architectural projects and such latter-day efforts as the Dolphin Embassy.

33   A photograph documenting the performance of *Space Cowboy Meets Plastic Businessman* in Houston in 1969 shows Doug Michels clutching a Sony Portapak.

34   The studio was located at 247 Gate 5 Road, Sausalito.

35   See Scott 2008. It is clear from both Ant Farm's statements and Scott's critique that "nomadism" was a driving force behind much of Ant Farm's early efforts. This was a nomadism that theorized a post-architectural society, not of homelessness but of fluidity created by a McLuhanesque connectivity. The need for place, for site, would be replaced by access to nodes of information. Automotive nomadism as seen in the Media Van was merely an interim state before the Information Network replaced the Truckstop Network.

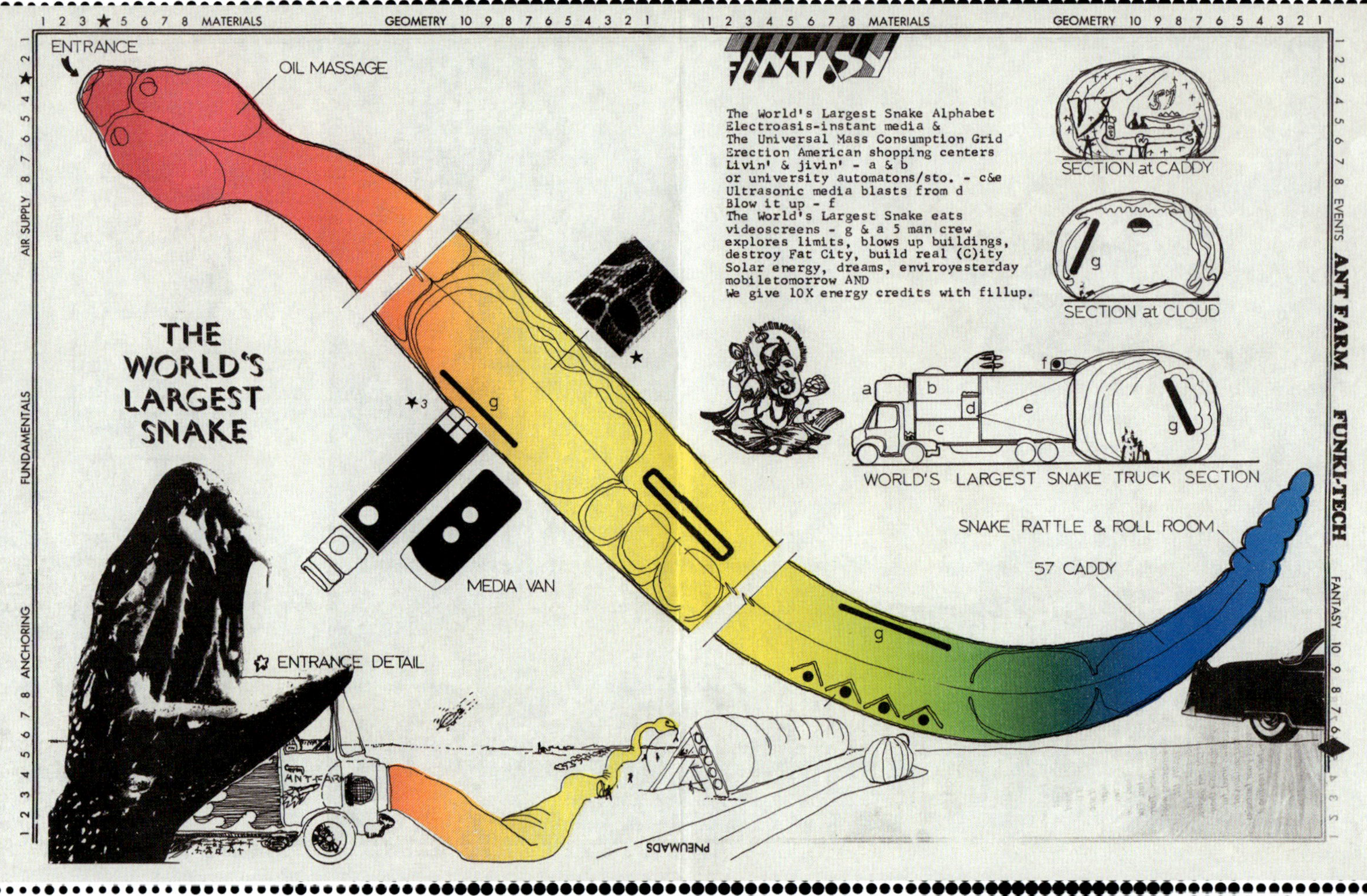

Above: *The World's Largest Snake,* an amusement park ride designed by Chip Lord, Hudson Marquez, and Doug Michels, first appeared in the *Inflatocookbook* (1970). Three years later, it would be a component of *Freedomland,* a shopping mall for teenagers.

Facing page: The *Truckstop Network* was a Happening on wheels. Touring colleges throughout the country, Ant Farm—in its customized Chevy *Media Van*—conducted interactive performances and showed off *ICE-9,* an inflatable structure. The above graphic mimics a stereotypical roadside diner placemat.

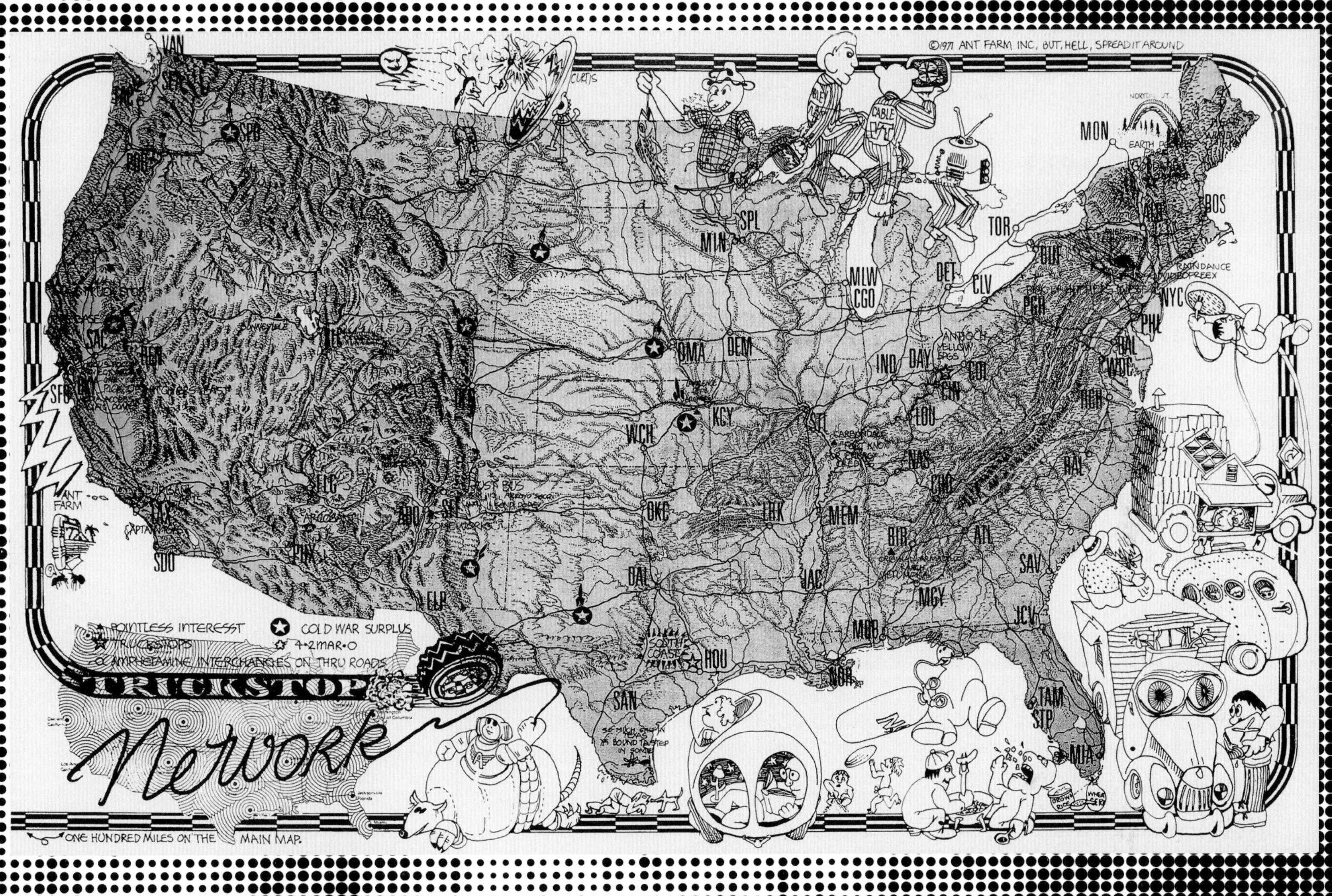

©1971 ANT FARM INC, BUT, HELL, SPREAD IT AROUND
TRICKSTOP
Network
POINTLESS INTERESST
TRUCKSTOPS
AMPHETAMINE INTERCHANGES ON THRU ROADS
COLD WAR SURPLUS
4+2 MAR•O
ONE HUNDRED MILES ON THE MAIN MAP.
CABLE VT
MON
EARTH PEOPLE PARK
CURTIS

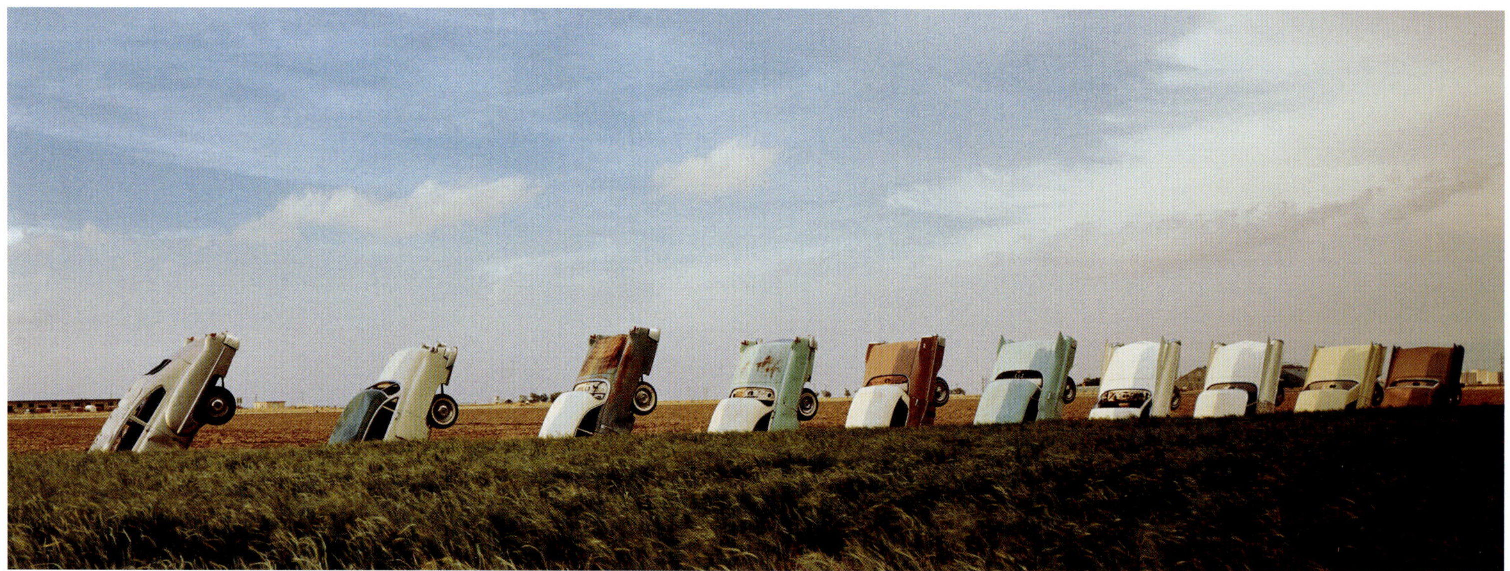

An early (1976) image of *Cadillac Ranch*, near Amarillo, Texas, when the individual cars were still intact. Photograph by Wyatt McSpadden.

happening drive-by with their ICE-9[36] inflatable in tow. This was perhaps the first condensed confluence of Ant Farm's principal preoccupations: architecture, the car, and television. The apotheosis of this union is seen in *World's Longest Bridge* (1971), which captures the crossing of the Lake Pontchartrain Causeway in Louisiana in a single take, executed by Doug Michels. With Hudson Marquez at the wheel, the Media Van slips into the monotony of the featureless road, keeping a steady sixty miles per hour on the nearly twenty-four-mile-long span. With the elevated highway revealing its endless homogeny against the unbroken lake, this real-time gaze undercuts the exhilaration of the road. Instead of constantly changing landscape markers signifying time elapsed, the view from within[37] seems to glorify stasis, as though the outer world were a mere projection upon the windshield, refreshed moment by moment.

In one of their finest gestures of populist architecture, Ant Farm released the *Inflatocookbook* (1970), a $3 handbook for the construction of easy-to-make inflatables. The "cookbook" included gorgeous collage-style how-to graphics, along with a clippable "energy credit" as reward for your conservation efforts. As a follow-up Curtis Schreier and TVTV's Allen Rucker slapdashed *Inflatables Illustrated* (1971), a breezy twenty-one-minute look at DIY inflatable architecture. Bracketed by footage of Ant Farm's more ambitious inflatables, the tutorial has Curtis in his kitchen preparing household materials for their reinvention as a human-size inflatable. An iron, some plastic bags, and a knife are about all you need to construct your own inflated chamber. The utter informality of *Inflatables Illustrated* sets it against the stultifying manners of industrial and educational instructional films of the seventies while anticipating the endless like-minded how-tos surging through YouTube today.

"Freedomland" was a speculative leisure zone to be built in Houston. The impossibility of the project, its sardonic notions and improbable structures, made it unlikely for development, but the pitch was part of the ploy. In the video *Freedomland* (1973), a bearded Doug Michels, wearing a ten-gallon hat, describes the futuristic joys of this proposed amusement mall. The details of a tabletop model are shown as Michels describes the bubble roof–enclosed park occupied with restaurants, shops, a cable TV studio, and the "World's Largest Snake," a walk-through reptile of mammoth proportions. In teaming with Fast Track Builders, their fictive contractors company, even the engineering obstacles would be overcome. Keyed over many of the sequences, Michels is a dryly funny caricature of the corporate spokesperson, now inhabiting video space.

The prodigious project that accelerated *Media Burn* was Ant Farm's seminal sculpture *Cadillac Ranch*, executed a year prior in 1974.[38] Ten vintage 1948 to 1963 Cadillacs were installed tail fins to the sky in a Texas plain owned by local millionaire Stanley Marsh 3.[39] The high-profile placement, along Route 66[40] outside Amarillo, Texas, solidified their interest in manufacturing a powerful image that could infiltrate the cultural imagination—in other words, go viral. *Cadillac Ranch*, a videowork that is reedited every decade or so, fits neatly within the self-perpetuating promo genre.

The startling image reads as a study of the rise and fall of the tail fin, a cipher for the exaggerated objects of consumerist desire.[41] In the video, Cadillac commercials are interspersed with the antics of Ant Farm, stressing both the inflated luxury embodied by these upscale autos and their design inspiration, the fuselage of a jet fighter. The technologic, the modern, and the lethal converge in the elegant luxury car.

---

36   Ice-9, or more properly "ice-nine," is a reference to a literary invention from Kurt Vonnegut's novel *Cat's Cradle*, in which an alternative structure is created for water. Solid at room temperature, ice-nine crystallizes liquid water upon contact. You might consider the Ice-9 inflatable a catalyzer of structural change.

37   Charissa N. Terranova in her book *Automotive Prosthetic* (2014) describes two states of automobile perception, "looking-at and looking-through." *World's Longest Bridge* is a definitive instance of looking-through in which the distancing features of steel and window glass, fuel and rubber conspire in a form of amiable alienation from the land traversed.

38   At this point in Ant Farm history, Curtis Schreier was more a silent partner. Fellow artist Hudson Marquez stepped in, co-creating *Cadillac Ranch*.

39   A great patron of Ant Farm, Stanley Marsh 3 has a cameo in the video as Leo Wyoming in which he shoots "Ant Farm" into the side of a Cadillac with a six- shooter and sings a parody of "Magical Mystery Tour."

40   In 1985, the Route 66 designation was replaced by Interstate 40.

41   There are a multitude of overlapping readings of *Cadillac Ranch*, an obvious one being the replacement of cattle on the "ranch" by cars in a state whose primary industry was now oil extraction. To that we could add the vanishing cowboy and the literal mechanization of horsepower, the rugged and authentic individual made anachronistic by technological advancements.

DRIVEN TO DISTRACTION

By the early twentieth century, the mythologies of cars and cinema commingled and became potent inhabitants of the popular imaginary about mobility and independence. Where venturing out into the American landscape was once an arduous, risky, but almost limitless exercise, the colonization of the wilds by civil development made this journey more a mediated practice. Yet the American spirit could not digest the notion of the unregulated pioneer confronted by a vanishing frontier. As if in compensation, this unsettled space was now to be experienced as a mobile view accessed through the automobile's windscreen or thrown directly upon the silvered screen as a virtual reclamation of landscape, displaced at twenty-four frames per second: a journey registered through degrees of visuality. Both mediums—film and car—were intimately tied up in America's manifest sense of independence, precarious earlier conquests now turned toward touristic ends, but let us consider only the automobile as it relates to the cultural canopy arching over Ant Farm. The symbology here permeates all things: one's driveway extending from front door to curb becomes a personal link in a vast network connecting everything to everything, rural and citified.[42] Back your car onto the roadbed and you gain access to the unlimited possibilities of travel, and as the highway emits its hypnotic hum, you might experience a curious communion with the world at large. Boundless escapades and untethered independence await. Thus, the blacktop becomes a networked circuit—asphalt as medium and automobile as message.

And what is that message?

In this metal pellet propelled down the road, an implicit celebration occurs—a celebration of the foundational freedom to roam, to explore, to conquer, to settle, nostalgically reenacted in a mass-produced vehicle, iterating independence. This is the insinuated folklore of the automobile, the adoration of which is intuitively sourced.

"See the U.S.A. in your Chevrolet."[43]

Hot rod culture did this one better. Here the dream is announced and modified. What better way to advance the fantastical notion of American self-sufficiency than by personalizing a mass-produced object. Unexpected interventions in the car's intended use (or at least formal design) declare the obdurate individuality of the owner. But there is that great leveler: eventually the rubber must meet the road, and the road is communal.

World War II gave hot rod culture a real boost. Returning GIs found an abundance of affordable heaps from the 1930s, matched perfectly to their new mechanical skills, meager budgets, and idle time. Chopped, lowered, souped-up jalopies became the signature objects of a newfangled youth scene. Not that everyone had (or wanted) a roadster, but pumped by rising affluence and effective ad campaigns by auto manufacturers, the car itself came to be an entry into coveted autonomy, cultural mobility, and chrome-plated modernity.

Coming of age postwar—as Chip Lord, Doug Michels, and Curtis Schreier did—was bound to be a four-barreled boyhood. This was confirmed by Lord himself in his paean to the auto industry, *Automerica*.[44] In the midst of its idiosyncratic history telling, Lord's book, a qualified adoration, reveals a youth intimately entwined with the mounting myth of the automobile. From early bicycles modified to emulate custom rods through tales of driving the family car, to his ownership, finally, of a Model A Ford (won in a contest at the local Ford dealership), he recounts his fascination with all things auto, a fascination still driving his way in the world.[45] "Once it was

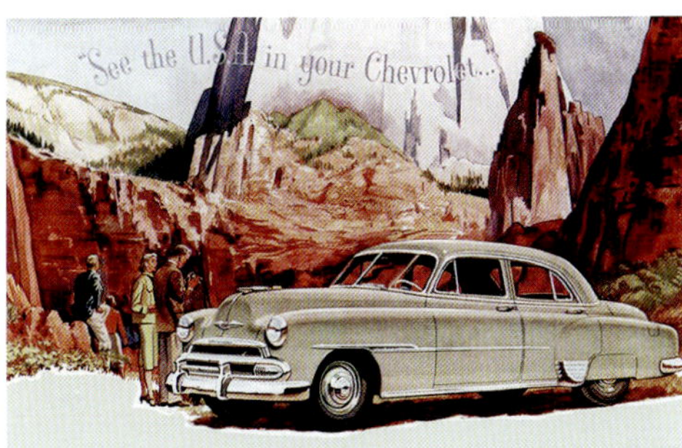

Top: An early 1950s print advertisement for Chevrolet. "See the U.S.A. in Your Chevrolet" was Chevrolet's jingle, popularized by Dinah Shore in television advertisements that aired between 1956 and 1963.

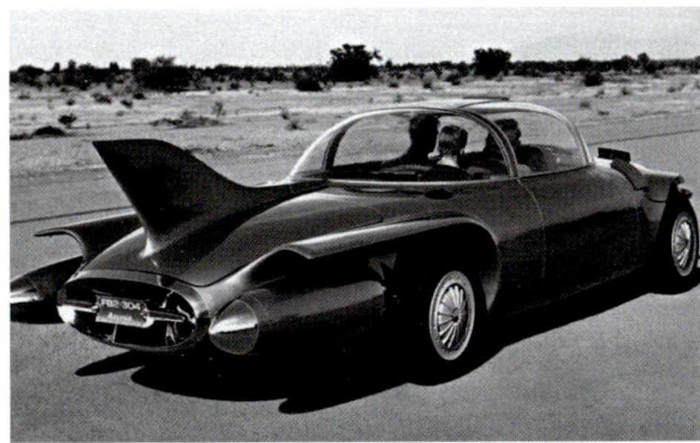

Bottom: The GM Firebird II was designed as a "concept car" in 1956. It had a titanium body, was fueled by kerosene, and had disc brakes on all four wheels. The large vertical tail fin is echoed in the Phantom Dream Car.

a gadget," he says of his adored subject, "now it is a way of life, in the future it may be merely a strange anachronism."[46]

Doug Michels was susceptible to the same mythology, having owned thirty cars by the time *Automerica* was published, his "last" car being a Triumph TR-3. Michels was a bit of an entrepreneur, buying his first car, a 1949 Ford Tudor, at age fifteen, then flipping successive rods, sometimes retaining them for only weeks. It is rumored that when Michels first came to San Francisco in the early seventies, he supported Ant Farm by working at a local body shop.

The second (and, really, the central) chapter of *Automerica*, "I Dream

---

42 Eisenhower's Federal-Aid Highway Act of 1956 alone created 41,000 miles of new roadway.

43 A commercial jingle first used in 1949 and written for General Motors. Later popularized by Dinah Shore and Pat Boone.

44 *Automerica: A Trip Down U.S. Highways from World War II to the Future* (New York: E. P. Dutton & Co., 1976).

45 Lord associates important life events with paired autos: "I drove a Corvair Monza to architectural school at Tulane University. I graduated in a Volkswagen … I became a registered architect in Ant Farm's media van. I became an artist in a '56 Cadillac Sedan de Ville."

46 After Ant Farm disbanded, Lord would go on to create *The Motorist*, a featurette from 1989 about a 1962 T-Bird being driven to Los Angeles so that it could be shipped to a Japanese collector. The monologue voiced by the "motorist" is a sorrowful personal story of the automobile's formative but fading influence on American culture.

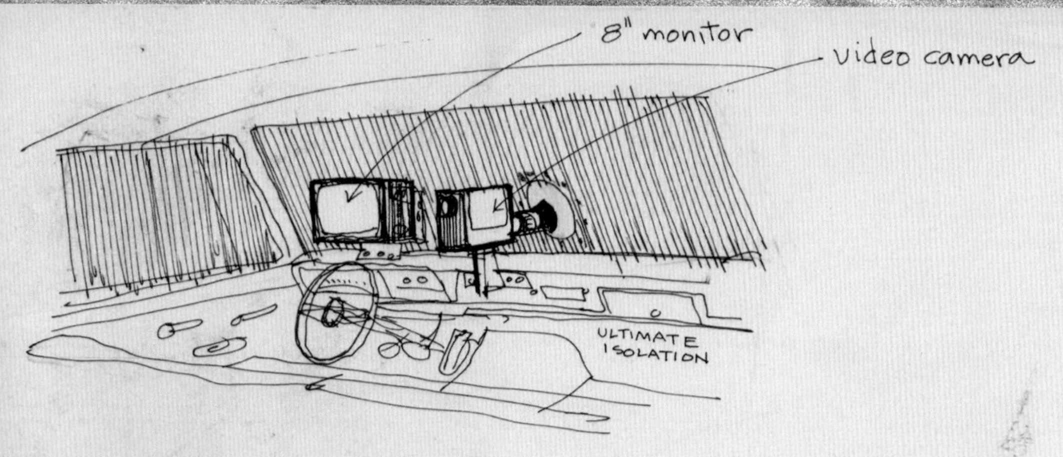

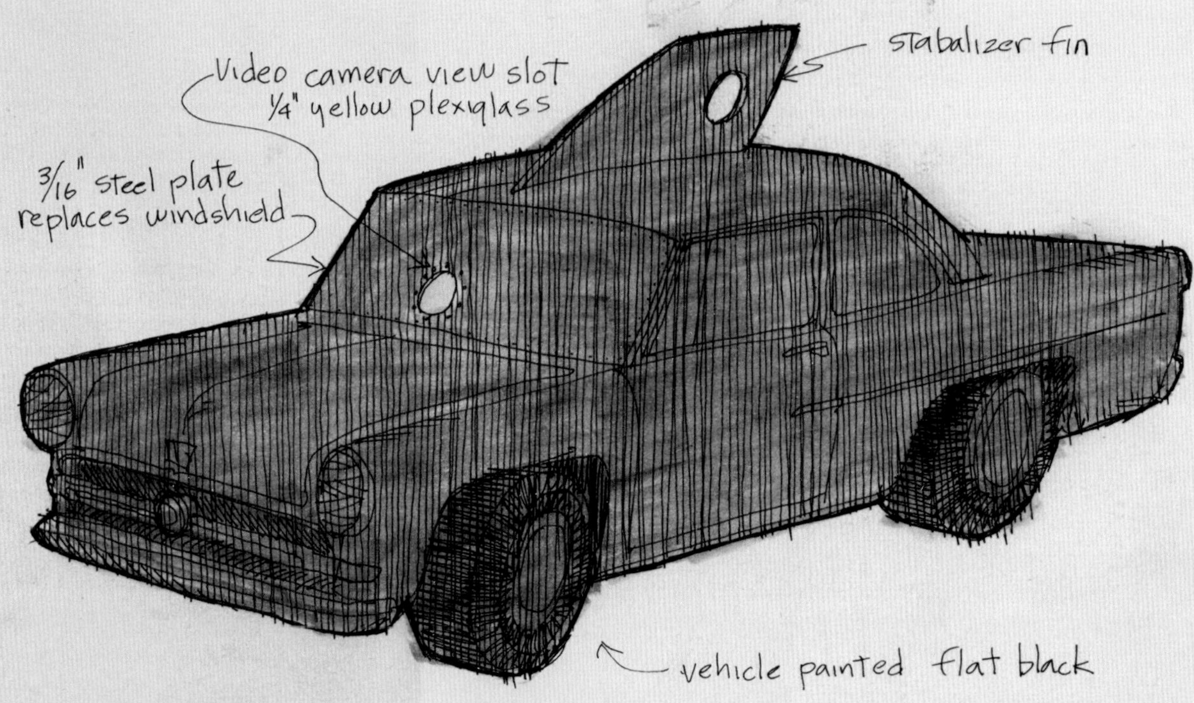

A drawing of *Media Vision* by Doug Michels, dated January 1973, is the earliest known depiction of what would become *Media Burn*. Note the "firewall" of functioning television sets.

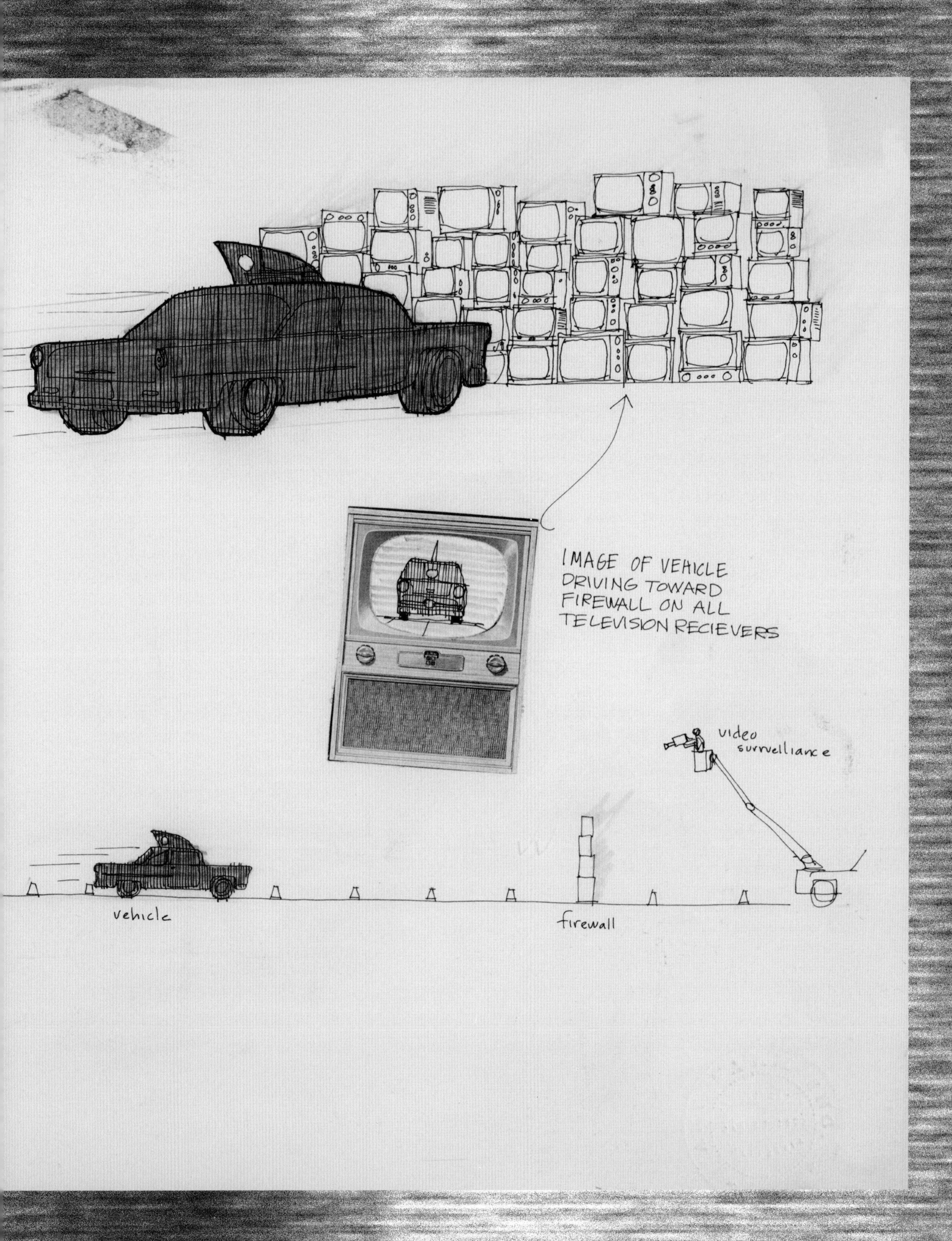

IMAGE OF VEHICLE
DRIVING TOWARD
FIREWALL ON ALL
TELEVISION RECIEVERS
video
surveillance
vehicle
firewall

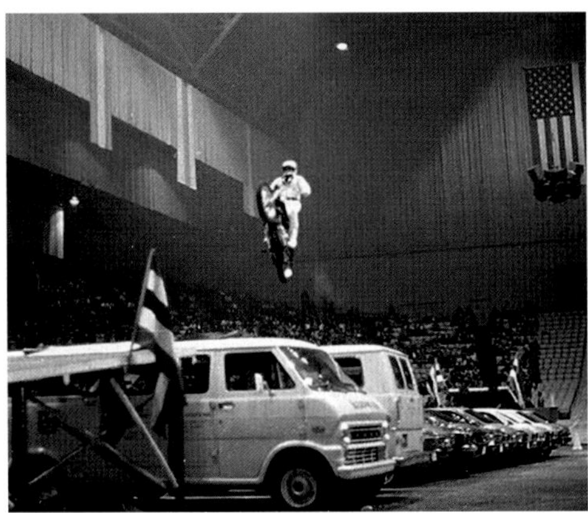

Evel Knievel jumping fifteen vehicles at the Cow Palace in Daly City, California, March 3, 1972.

Automobiles," begins with an encomium to the patron saint of car design, Harley J. Earl, the man responsible for putting progressively larger tail fins on the Cadillac. It was Earl who oversaw the design and promotion of much of General Motors' output in the forties and fifties. Of his innovations at GM, the fantastical prototypes known as the dream cars were his chief breakthrough. More *Jetsons* than *Father Knows Best*, these futuristic automobiles with impractical but seductive features were designed and exhibited as mind-boggling examples of American know-how. According to Lord, the 1949 Le Sabre was Harley's most famous prototype. "It represented the romance and high-speed, streamlined styling of a fast fighter plane," wrote Lord, "yet it clearly rested on a large and heavy automobile chassis." The dream car's manifold purpose was to offer up a dazzling glimpse of the future while declaring the obsolescence of the present, and to show off an exaggerated model from which more practical features could be extracted for production cars. These prototypes were then toured throughout the U.S. in what were known as Motoramas, highly polished trade shows, held from 1949 to 1961, that juxtaposed a utopian and affluent future with glamorously styled cars that could take you there.

Introduced in 1956, the much-lauded GM Firebird II prototype was "a four-passenger family car" clearly based on the design of a jet fighter. Its unearthly styling—with its tapered nose, bubble-shaped passenger cockpit, and prominent single tail fin—promised flight. Other prototypes, such as the Ford Mystere and the Oldsmobile Golden Rocket, reinforced the jet age link. These were cars that would erase the restrictions of the road through their subtle suggestion of aerial escape and offer entry into the technologically advanced trajectory of the future.

Twenty years after these dream cars were introduced, Ant Farm reverse engineered their own version, the Phantom Dream Car.[47] Using a 1959 Cadillac Biarritz as the departure point, they altered the passenger compartment, attached dome-like windows to the extended roof, and erected an enormous tail fin with an embedded video camera. A standard production model was now enhanced with the exaggerated features of a jet-inspired vehicle. All this dream car needed were a few "Artist-Dummies" to pilot the prototype and a destination worthy of its design.

The auto industry doesn't have exclusive say in the mythopoeic majesty of their product. Outside the industry exists a kind of folkloric culture organized around motor vehicle fetishism, ritual, and connoisseurship. Grand Prix racing offers a highbrow alternative to the roar of the NHRA drag strip; the Pebble Beach Concours d'Elegance faces off with the rice rocket and rat rod; Rat Fink vies for position with the ascot and beret; the soapbox derby is the flat-footed answer to the Bonneville Salt Flats; the polished perfection of "America's Most Beautiful Roadster" gives way to the damage done at the demolition derby. Class is often the distinguishing factor—the beleathered audience at figure 8 racing versus the chardonnay crowd at Le Mans—but there is an equivalent adoration for burned rubber, high compression, and straining suspension.

The need for speed found its early expression in the time trials that emerged even before the internal combustion engine began puttering. Land speed records were being sought with steam- and electric-powered cars, and finally, in 1902, a fossil fuelie pulled its payload all the way to seventy-six miles per hour. Daytona Beach was the first pit stop of choice with a gas-guzzler going 200 mph in 1927, adding another 100 mph by 1935. But things really picked up at the Bonneville Salt Flats when the ever-daring Mickey Thompson pushed the Challenger 1 all the way up to 406 mph.

This was 1960, and Thompson would not hold on for long—in 1963, the revered Craig Breedlove would crank his Spirit of America to 407 mph, then 526 mph in 1965, almost achieving lift off when the Spirit propelled forward at 600 miles per hour later that same year.[48] This speed freak was a full-on celebrity throughout the sixties, dressed in a jumpsuit, a crash helmet gripped in one hand, wraparound sunglasses above his ever-present smile, and behind him, the three-wheeled Spirit of America with its enormous tail fin, cramped cockpit, and absolutely aerodynamic styling. It should be noted that Breedlove's racer was jet powered. This was no gas- or nitro-fed speedster, but a turbojet engine originally intended for aircraft. The Spirit of America never left the ground, but its intention was to harness the power of a sky-bound vehicle for maximum overdrive on the salt. What was only suggested by Harley Earl's flighty concept cars of the fifties was embraced with full throttle forward at Bonneville in the sixties. Another decade along and the Phantom Dream Car would overtly embody the spirit of a new America.

But Evel Knievel also dreamed of flying (as Werner Herzog might say). His first real notoriety came in 1967 when he attempted to jump the fountain at Caesar's Palace in Las Vegas. The failed 141-foot jump left Knievel with a crushed pelvis and femur, fractures to his hip, wrist, and both ankles, and a major concussion. The cringe-producing footage of him skidding into the Dunes parking lot was aired by ABC-TV and successfully launched his career. A succession of jumps—over thirteen Cadillacs in Atlanta, seven Greyhound buses in Seattle, a tank with thirteen sharks in Chicago, a fifty-car pile-up in Los Angeles, among others—had him in and out of the hospital but always in the limelight, where he thrived. His most outrageous stunt was the attempted jump of the Snake River Canyon in Idaho, a distance of about three-fourths of a mile, using the X-2 Skycycle, a steam-powered rocket. With its sleek fuselage and tail-fin stabilizers, the X-2 Skycycle forsook wheels for a vertical launch ramp, a devolutionary stage in man's quest for flight and fancy.

For our purposes, though, there is a more important stunt, which occurred on March 3, 1972. That is the day Evel Knievel attempted to jump fifteen cars, botched his landing, and slid under the utility door into the parking lot of the Cow Palace.

---

47   This was 1975. But the concept can already be seen percolating in Ant Farm's "Dream Cars" panels for *20:20 Vision*, an exhibition at the Contemporary Art Museum in Houston, 1973. The exhibition was organized around four utopian moments, each of which was represented by a different car: a 1939 Cord, a 1959 Cadillac, the Media Van for 1984, and for the future, 2020, a Lunar Rover borrowed from NASA. All vehicles were to be displayed in a section of the exhibition called the "Avenue of Progress."

---

48   Breedlove held on to his land speed record until 1970, when Gary Gabelich went 622 mph.

EASY MONEY, HARD LANDING

Always a doodler, in 1972 Curtis Schreier threw open his ever-present notebook and hastily drew a cathode-ray tube, but not just any CRT—this one had no television console encasing it, yet it had two wheels and, just visible beyond its curved back, an engine block with a gear shift pointing skyward, and a flared exhaust pipe. On the CRT's screen was a representation of the road before it.

At first, the drawing hints at the world of Big Daddy Roth and other car cartoonists who drew custom rods with monstrous proportions and an often grotesque driver protruding from the hood. Schreier's take was tame, though the V-8 was off-size and the action lines around the fat tires were a tad Road Runner. But the union of media and mobility was present in this simple sketch, and the image shown on the phosphor screen complicated the accelerating matter: was the CRT displaying the road ahead in real time, traveling a prerecorded patch, or was the road represented summoned from the interlaced imaginary of the CRT itself? If the last scenario was true, then the CRT was just spinning its wheels and the road ahead had been replaced by its televisual double. A few refinements and Schreier's CRT doodle would become the official *Media Burn* logo—even if it was three years until its public emergence.

But first we must make a not-so-restful stop outside Houston, where an early vision, *Media Vision* (see pp. 20–21), emanates from the miasmic shallows of Mojo Lake.[49] In the first few months of 1973, Ant Farm put the finishing touches on House of the Century, a bit of ferrocement futurism built along a swampy shoreline near Angleton, Texas.[50] They spent an enormous amount of time around Houston while the fifteen-month

building project unfolded. And like all Ant Farmers, they got antsy.

In what Chip Lord called an "idea session," he and Doug Michels formulated a wholly new project, a performative piece in which a car would be driven through a wall of television sets. To conceptualize the affair, Michels made a diptych drawing,[51] the lower half titled *Media Vision*, the upper, *Artificial Consumption*. A customized "late model sedan"[52] is rendered in three different aspects: a perspective drawing has the sedan "painted flat black," a "stabilizer fin," very much in the form of a shark fin, on the roof, and an armored windshield with a small, single circular viewing port. A more active drawing has the flat black sedan rushing toward a wall of about forty television sets, stacked four high with dim flames visible; a final side view has the sedan driving headlong down a course toward the wall of TV sets while, behind the wall, a crane holds a camera operator aloft.

Most important, though, are two details: a rendering of the car's interior with the dashboard and surrounding windshield featured. A small video camera is mounted on the dashboard and is aimed at the circular aperture in the windshield. Beside it an eight-inch monitor (the small TV embedded in the dash) fills the view that the driver would have. From this drawing, it is clear that the "late model sedan" is navigated via mediated control, the video image representing the image of the road. A machine view for a machine, the driver once removed from the physicality of the car hurtling forward. *Media Vision* reified.

The second detail is a drawing of a classic television console. The explanatory text reads: "image of vehicle driving toward firewall on all television receivers."[53] On the screen is a head-on drawing of the

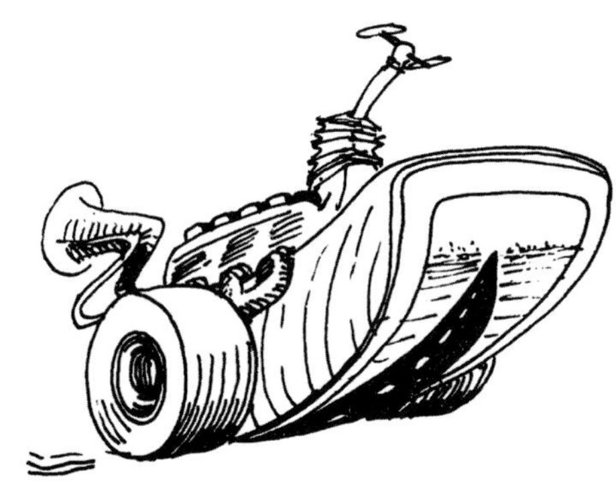

An early prototype of the *Media Burn* logo found in a sketchbook belonging to Curtis Schreier.

sedan. Obviously, this image is captured by the elevated camera just beyond the wall of flaming TV sets. As the sedan nears its target the image would be displayed on some forty sets with the image growing in scale and intensity, moment by moment. The driver would experience the eventual collision as a self-consuming bit of perverse narcissism as flame, impact, and general destruction converge in one grand decomposing image.

If, as in the final *Media Burn*, a single image of the collision was selected and circulated, *Media Vision* would have had a doubling image, an image of a car colliding with an image of itself. Is this self-destruction or self-perpetuation?

Media Vision was illustrated, in 1973, as a means of clarifying its components. There was no funding source, no specified site, no commissioning institution panting in anticipation, no use-by date. Then *Cadillac Ranch* reared its ugly fins and Ant Farm headed for Amarillo. But let us leap forward to the next iteration, *Easy Money* (see pp. 30–31), and a busy stretch of the Lloyd Bentsen Highway as it runs through Houston.

Having completed *Cadillac Ranch* on June 21, 1974, Ant Farm was a hot property in Texas. The sculpture had garnered attention in the national art press, and the Lone Star State was pumped. A letter, dated July 8, arrived at Ant Farm's San Francisco headquarters inviting them to be the "Project Artist" at Houston's upcoming Main Street '74, a Chamber of Commerce–sponsored public arts festival. Their attention was directed to

---

49   The location of House of the Century is generally listed as Mojo Lake, near Angleton, but Mojo does not exist. Chenango Lake seems to be the correct body of water. It is on property owned by Marilyn and Alvin Lubetkin.

50   A preliminary drawing for House of the Century, dated 1971, has a mid-1950s Ford Fairlane elevated on a large column in front of the main structure.

51   The drawing is dated January 1973. The verso of the drawing reveals an illustration from the *Inflatocookbook*, which would have a second printing in July 1973. Possibly a discarded proof?

52   According to Lord, a 1953 Ford coupe. From an email to the author, October 9, 2014.

53   This would require all televisions being in working order. Later renditions used broken and discarded sets.

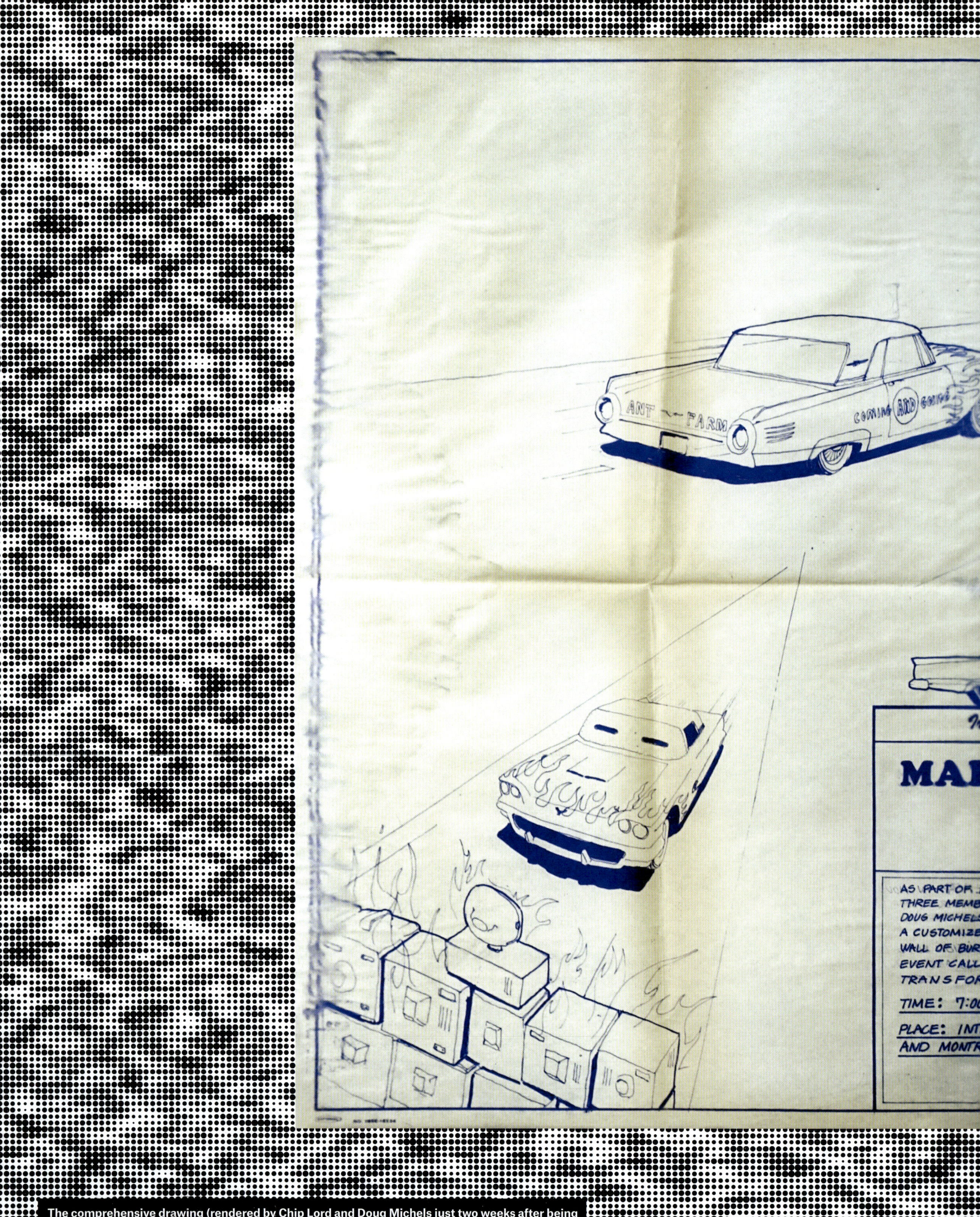

The comprehensive drawing (rendered by Chip Lord and Doug Michels just two weeks after being invited to participate) of Ant Farm's Autorama contribution, here called "Coming and Going: Transformational Access."

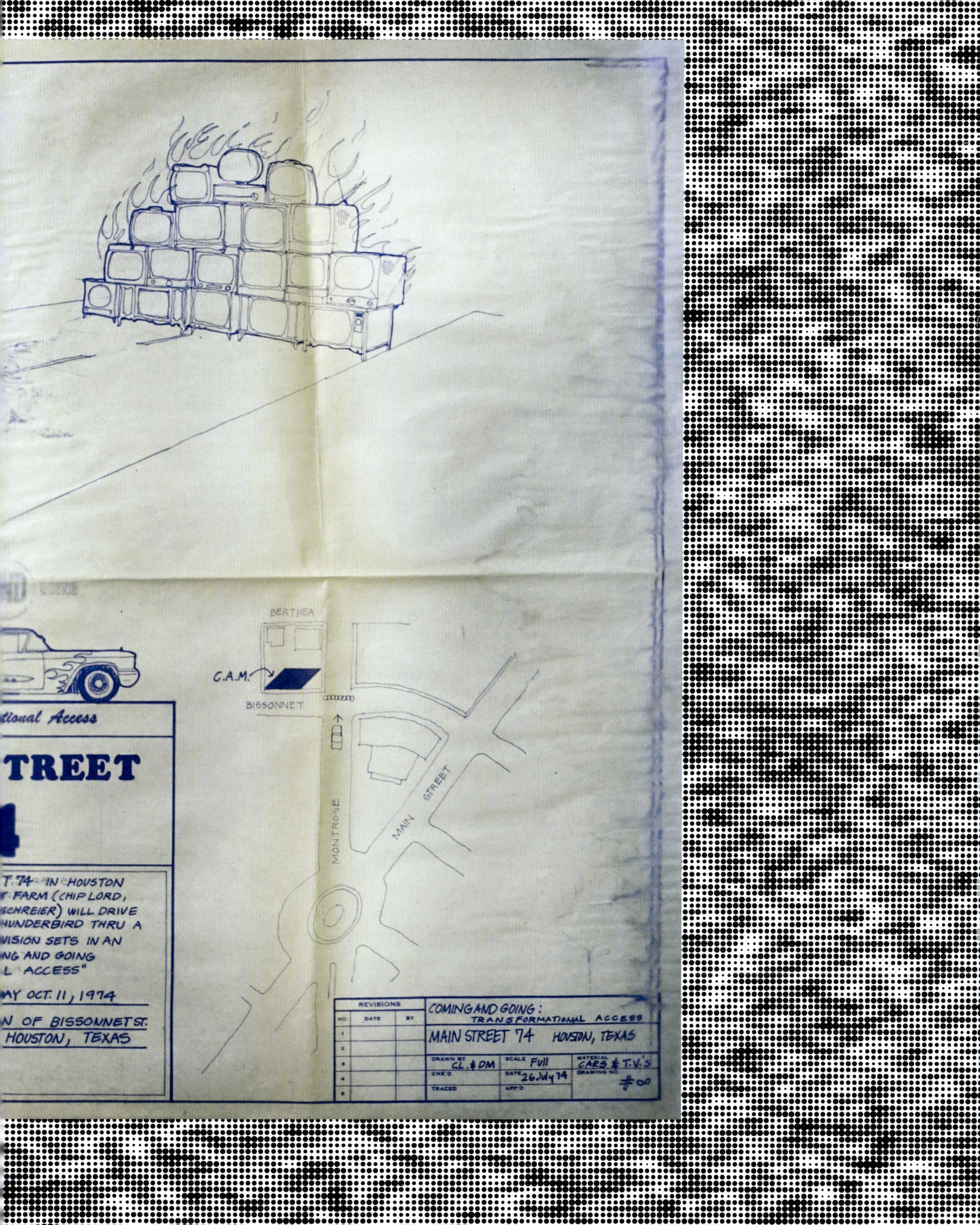

...tional Access

...TREET

4

...T. 74... IN HOUSTON
...FARM (CHIP LORD,
...SCHREIER) WILL DRIVE
...HUNDERBIRD THRU A
...VISION SETS IN AN
...NG AND GOING
...L ACCESS"

...AY OCT. 11, 1974

...N OF BISSONNET ST.
...HOUSTON, TEXAS

BERTHEA
C.A.M.
BISSONNET
MONTROSE
MAIN STREET

REVISIONS
NO   DATE   BY

COMING AND GOING:
TRANSFORMATIONAL ACCESS
MAIN STREET 74   HOUSTON, TEXAS

DRAWN BY CL. & DM   SCALE Full   MATERIAL CARS & T.V.S
CHK'D   DATE 26 July 74   DRAWING NO # ∞
TRACED   APP'D

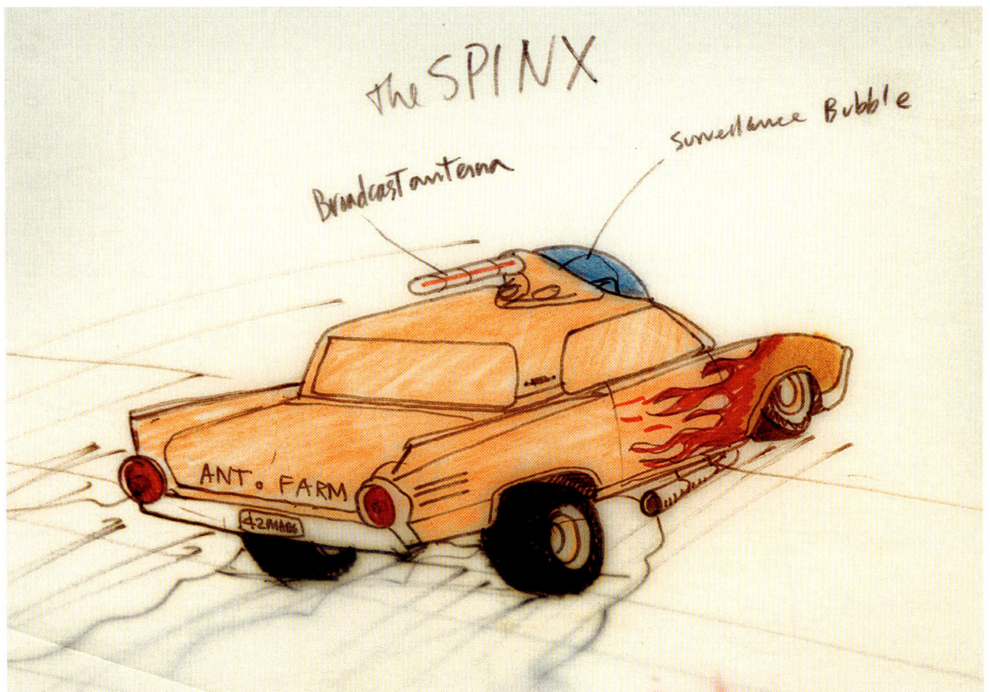

"The Spinx" [sic] was a customized early 1960s Ford Thunderbird to be deployed as part of *Easy Money* in Houston, Texas. This design is from autumn 1974. Note also the license plate number, "4·2 MARO," a reference to a 1973 video anthology. Drawing by Doug Michels.

a sub-event called Autorama,[54] which was "envisioned as an effort to capture some of the aesthetic, as well as social impact of the automobile on our lives, forming a moving sculpture." Charles T. Landsden, manager of the event, continued: "Hopefully, it can be an imaginative, pleasing experience for participants and viewers."[55]

The remuneration for participation in the October 12 Autorama was rather paltry. It included transportation, lodging, approved expenses, and a $100 honorarium. They were requested to submit a project proposal "outlining the artistic concept and anticipated expenses and/or requirements for its execution prior to July 30." Perhaps it was the bountiful honorarium that inspired Ant Farm's proposal title, *Easy Money*.

Houston's Main Street Art Happening had started in 1971 along a retail strip with several department stores. By 1974, the Happening had moved to Hermann Park, a sizable green space bordering Main Street, a half mile to the south of the original event site. Bifurcating those two sites was the Southwest Freeway, which Ant Farm proposed to jump in a customized 1958 Ford Thunderbird. Not just jump but end its trajectory by plunging through a pyramid of burning television sets. Six lanes of elevated freeway, a

one-mile run-up, thirty seconds in the air, and the mass of TV sets hit at seventy-five miles per hour. This, thankfully, would never happen.[56]

Doug Michels created a detailed drawing of *Easy Money*[57] to aid in the pitch. This included a rendering of the modified '59 Thunderbird with painted flames and a small Plexiglas dome where a sunroof might have been. In his brief description of the event, Michels volunteered all three Ant Farmers as occupants during the jump. Needless to say, both Lord and Schreier agree that the extremity of the proposal was really to "get their attention."

A revised but still controversial proposal eliminated the jump and concentrated on the collision.[58] Retitled *Transformational Access: Coming and Going*,[59] the performance would "realize

the age-old fantasy of driving a car thru a wall of burning television sets." Michels was also strategic in his appropriation of the official event language. In his letter, he described the outcome as "forming a moving sculpture," an exact quote from Charles T. Landsden's original invitation. Michels was aware that the project was endangered. The official project manager assigned by the Chamber of Commerce, one Alan S. Finger of the Finger Furniture Co., categorically refused to assist with the proposal. *Easy Money* had become hardscrabble as Houston-based sponsorships and fundraising proved to be unexpectedly difficult.

Doug Michels tagged the souped-up '59 T-Bird he designed "The Sphinx." The car would crash through a "pyramid" of televisions. But what is this Sphinx, this guardian of the pyramids, telling us? A riddle? Perhaps it was to affix what Michels called "the age-old fantasy" in antiquity. Or perhaps it was to equate the prototypical pyramids with a contemporary pyramid of television sets and thus to intimate that the image created from the death-defying act was a sort of reincarnation, an iconic rebirth of image into eternity. As *Easy Money* would morph into *Media Burn* in the coming months, the intentions would detach and drift into the future.

According to Schreier, Michels also "proposed using a deuce coupe," a 1932 Ford two-door, "for *Easy Money* the Houston predecessor to *Media Burn*."[60] Schreier has drawings from fall 1974 with the notation "1932 deuce," showing major modifications, most aggressively a single wheel on the rear axle and the car being driven backwards. One such drawing has TV sets being deflected off the tapered trunk. What is interesting is that the three-wheeled deuce coupe with its rounded squat features resembles Buckminster Fuller's 1933 Dymaxion car. As avid fans of this futurist,[61] Ant Farm was well aware of his innovative vehicle, abandoned before it could be fully developed. Attaching *Media Burn* to this Fuller concept car would have placed the Phantom Dream Car in a prematurely aborted future rather than in the ironic reaches of the Jet Age.

---

54   When GM launched their concept car cavalcade Motorama, competing events adopted the generic Autorama.

55   Letter found in BAM archives.

56   "We were not in it for being daredevils," Chip Lord said. Email to the author, October 6, 2014.

57   This drawing is dated September 1974 and includes such notations as a $300 songwriting fee for The Tubes, an outrageous San Francisco rock band best remembered for "White Punks on Dope," and government auto safety crash footage.

58   An architectural drawing, signed by both Lord and Michels, dated July 26, includes a small map detail with the exact location of the performance at the corner of Montrose and Bissonnet. The car would rush up Montrose and collide with the TV sets in front of the Contemporary Art Museum, which had opened in 1972.

59   *Transformational Access* was the name given to a sub-division of the *20:20 Vision* exhibition. It was to contain a "history of image processing appliances." This performance title also recalls Peter d'Agostino's video series *Comings and*

Goings, though that series did not surface until 1977. D'Agostino's trilogy dealt broadly with complex systems of urban transit, including Bay Area Rapid Transit (BART).

60   Email to the author, August 21, 2014.

61   Buckminster Fuller came to Houston in 1969 to deliver a lecture. Ant Farm was also in Houston and, upon hearing that Fuller would soon arrive, decided to "kidnap" him at the airport. After waylaying Fuller they took him to Rice University, where a Dymaxion car was on display.

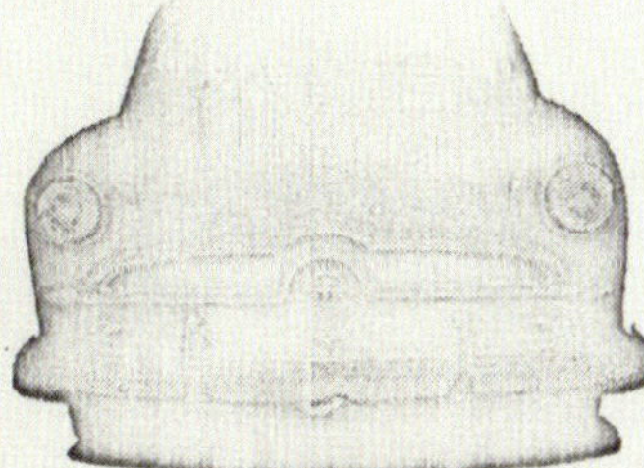

UNCLE BUDDIE'S

USED CARS

PIER 40
P. O. BOX 471
SAN FRANCISCO, CALIF. 94101
(415) 788-1424

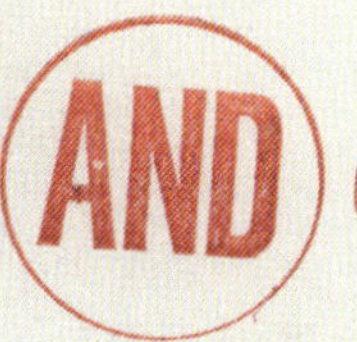

ANT FARM

MAIN STREET 74 ,houston,texas

"autorama"

ANT FARM (chip lord,curtis schreier,doug michels)

project description; ant farm will drive a car thru a
wall of burning t.v. sets.

requirements;100 television sets.(need not be in working order,
however the screens must not be broken)most of
the tv sets can be collected free from tv repair
shops.use of large van or truck will be needed.

one car.$300 will be plenty to buy the automobile.
ant farmers will perform the necessary modifications
to the car.(ie attaching metal shield over windshield,etc. cost of modifications approx.$200.

time line;three members of ant farm will arrive in houston on
tuesday oct.8,1974.ant farm will have responsibility
to find and collect the 100 tv sets.ant farm will
also purchase the car and alter it for safety.
the event will be ready for execution on oct.12,1974.
due to the nature of the artistic conception,the
event will be executed once only.

contract;this document will serve as a contract between the
houston chamber of commerce and ant farm when signed
by both parties.we accept your $100 honorarium plus
transportation and lodging for three members of ant
farm in return for our participation in MAIN STREET 74

___________________________   ___________________________
houston chamber of commerce   ant farm

CASH FOR CARS

The unsigned contract for Ant Farm's participation in Main Street '74. As featured on the letter-head, Uncle Buddie was a fictional used car salesman whose persona was often "performed" by Chip Lord.

"Conceived of as a very entertaining and funnier than shit tv show," Michels' description of *Easy Money* also (unintentionally) contradicts Chip Lord's recent remark that "we were not in it for being daredevils."

What Uncle B was proposing was a fake television program about daredevils who have come to Houston at the behest of a "greasy new york promoter" to jump the Southwest Freeway in "a 58 ford T-bird." All the preparations for the spectacular jump would be conducted with the utmost sincerity—the jump ramp would be built, the T-Bird tricked out, press releases issued, test runs staged for the press. "The reality of the actual event would slip and slide." In effect, Michels wanted to roil the mercurial surface of reality, creating what he called "psychic dada."[64]

The New York promoter, an agent for "top drawer inc.," would "put up the big BIG millions" for a television spectacle that Ant Farm actually budgeted at "8 Gs" and which included a thirty-minute final videotape ready for distribution. The hybrid event would culminate in driving The Sphinx through the wall of burning TVs, but they would "probably not jump the sw freeway." Still, the run-up to the daring jump and its aborted execution would cause a formidable "confusion" that would be the actual "essence" of the performance—the muddling of the line between the authenticated real and the reliably fictive, between ample veracity and sleight of hand, between crude media and general hoax.

Michels' (and/or Ant Farm's) deep distrust of mass media led him to relish its subversion. His strategically deployed "psychic dada" was an attempt to inoculate the viewer with a systemic skepticism. In this sense, the hoax of *Easy Money* falls away and is replaced by spectatorial alienation. A viewer alienated is a viewer no longer under the sway of Big Brother.

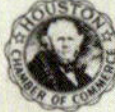

HOUSTON CHAMBER of COMMERCE

Chartered by the Republic of Texas 1840

CHAMBER OF COMMERCE BUILDING
P. O. BOX 53600 · HOUSTON, TEXAS 77052
TELEPHONE 227-5111, AREA CODE 713

July 8, 1974

The Ant Farm
P.O. Box 471
San Francisco, California 94101

Dear Persons:

    Mr. Tom Morey of our Cultural Affairs Committee's MAIN STREET '74 project group has requested us to extend to you an invitation to participate in this major Houston arts event as Project Artist for an activity we have termed "Autorama".

    You may recall participation in the committee's first Main Street Art Happening back in October of 1971, but as background, our committee has sponsored an annual public arts festival each October for the past three years on Main Street in downtown on the second Sunday in October. MAIN STREET '74, which is scheduled for October 11, 12 and 13, is a continuation of this effort to bring the arts and the people together in a dramatic and enjoyable way. Besides expanding it from a Sunday afternoon event into the full weekend this year, the committee has moved it to the South Main-Montrose-Bissonnet area near the two art museums and Hermann Park. Enclosed is a street plan and brief description of the visual and performing arts concept for 1974.

    As you will note on the enclosed material, "Autorama" is envisioned as an effort to capture some of the aesthetic, as well as social impact of the automobile on our lives, forming a moving sculpture. Hopefully, it can be an imaginative, pleasing experience for participants and viewers.

    As we envision your participation as Artist for "Autorama", you and the project's Coordinator (or Director), Mr. Alan S. Finger, would develop and submit for review by our Art Steering Committee a proposal outlining the artistic concept and anticipated expenses and/or requirements for its execution prior to July 30. Upon its approval, you would work with Mr. Finger in assuring its proper execution on October 12 (and possible replay on the 13th). Mr. Finger's contact information is as follows: Mr. Alan S. Finger, Vice President, Finger Furniture Co., P.O. Box 194, Houston, Texas 77001 (phone - 713/228-3441).

    Our MAIN STREET '74 committee, in turn, offers you air transportation to and from the October event, offers to supply you with lodging and approved expenses, and agrees to pay you the admittedly token honorarium of $100.00.

(Continued)

The Houston Chamber of Commerce's invitation to Ant Farm to participate in Main Street '74, an annual public arts festival. The invitation is specific to a thematic exhibition, Autorama, which will "capture some of the aesthetic, as well as social impact of the automobile."

Continuing to promote *Easy Money* from their Pier 40 studio in San Francisco, Ant Farm experienced the steady decline of Houston-based support for the project. Slowly *Easy Money* would break loose from the Main Street Art Fair and become first an independently staged event in Houston (abandoned) and then a fully transplanted extravaganza at San Francisco's Cow Palace (achieved). In a hasty letter to TVTV co-founder Tom Weinberg,[62] dated October 1, 1974, it was declared that *Easy Money* would now take place on December 25, or "ONLY 86 DAYS LEFT TILL CHRISTMAS (X-MA$ DAY)." The intended vehicular projectile was a 1959 Cadillac convertible; the location, the Cow Palace. But neither the Phantom Dream Car customization nor formal access to the Cow Palace had been realized at this time. Christmas Day would prove to be impossible, even if a gift of unexpected financial support were to appear.

In early September, Doug Michels (now signing off as "Uncle B") sent a somewhat detailed letter to Tom "$core" Weinberg attempting to get financial and production support from him. The slapdash note has a typo-riddled description of *Easy Money* that veers drastically from the final aspects of *Media Burn*, but it offers a prescient idea for what now would be called reality TV and essentially abandons the focus on generating a singular media image in favor of a localized hoax.[63]

---

62   The letter to Weinberg is signed "Doug 'swami sez' Michels." *Media Burn* Archive, Chicago.

63   *Easy Money* would be bracketed by several examples of this kind of faux reality: Luis Buñuel's *Land Without Bread* (1933), a counterfeit documentary, sets the stage. *Candid Camera*'s lengthy run, starting in 1948, established the popular affection for the hoax. Jim McBride's fabricated autobiography, *David Holzman's Diary* (1967), further undermines the trustworthiness of the moving image. By the eighties, popular manifestations of mock documentaries would surface, *This Is Spinal Tap* (1984) and *It's Garry Shandling's Show* (1985) being two influential examples.

64   An early example of media creating a mass confusion might be Orson Welles' radio broadcast from 1938, "The War of the Worlds." "Psychic dada" was certainly an outcome of this hoax without an actual invasion.

HOUSTON, WE HAVE A PROBLEM

Though *Cadillac Ranch* had made Ant Farm a notable art group, particularly in Texas, the great oil state was not hospitable to such an unctuous, risky, and iconoclastic concoction as *Easy Money*. After Alan Finger gave their Autorama proposal the figurative finger, no one stepped in to replace him. Houston arts patron Bobby Gerry, a petroleum executive, was approached to no avail. Soon, other Texan supporters followed suit: Marilyn Lubetkin (House of the Century) and Stanley Marsh 3 (*Cadillac Ranch*). By mid-September Ant Farm was seeking greener pastures, namely in San Francisco.

Only a few things were missing for this hastily arranged (re)launch and location: Ant Farm didn't have adequate sponsorship, the 1959 Cadillac Biarritz convertible was owned but not modified, the Cow Palace site hadn't been secured, and the entire production and promotion of the event would have to transpire within the next "86 DAYS." But the pedal was to the metal anyway.

Tom Weinberg, their "pay-tron" from Chicago as Doug Michels called him,[65] was on board the rapidly accelerating event. But those of more sober sensibility could not be coaxed to embark: in late September, San Francisco Museum of Modern Art curator Suzanne Foley turned down a request for sponsorship, then the Walker Art Center said no, followed closely by a rejection from David Ross at the Long Beach Museum of Art.[66]

Actually, there was some progress; at least a budget compiled in late November[67] lists three sources of the $7,000 total funding, an unholy trinity: Tom "Score" Weinberg was in for $3,000; Environmental Communications, a Venice-based publisher of art and architecture books who also worked with TVTV, donated $2,000; and San Francisco's Schroeder Gallery, a short-lived gallery exhibiting media art, would pay for the forty-odd television sets, the Cow Palace rental, some of the merchandising materials, and a percentage of the Phantom Dream Car modification. For their support, they were granted a pre-impact Ant Farm exhibition at their space from March 7 to April 1. This exhibition never materialized and later letters from Ant Farm would demand reimbursement for monies already spent.

A second revised budget exists, also dated November 20, 1974, but with one line item deleted, "launch vehicle modification: $500," bringing the sum total to $6,500. What really distinguishes this document from all others is the art project's alternative title, *Petroleum Paradise*, a telling and short-lived label that would have taken the project on to rockier terrain. Though the tarmac at the Cow Palace would reek of gasoline-infused exhaust spewed from the Phantom Dream Car, commingling with the additional reek of kerosene poured on the assembled TV sets, *Media Burn*, the eventual performance, was not about the politics of fossil fuel—though certainly the ethos of mobility and a quirky critique of technologic affluence were part of the general combustion. *Media Burn* was out to burn the media, not mount an ironic gesture in opposition to the well-fueled fantasies of American culture. It's all in the image and the image would be unforgettable.

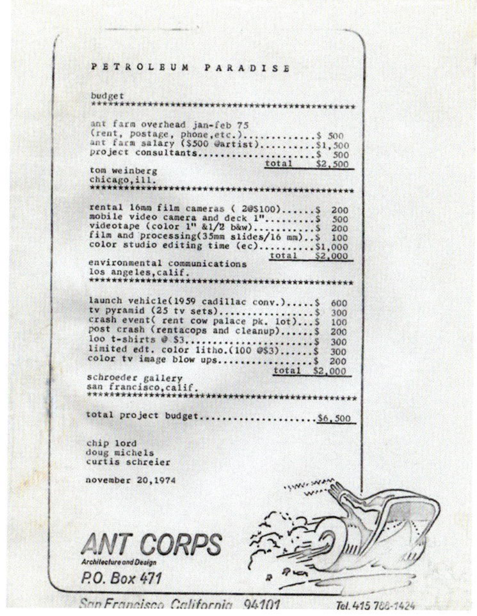

PETROLEUM PARADISE

budget
****

ant farm overhead jan-feb 75
(rent, postage, phone,etc.)..............$ 500
ant farm salary ($500 @artist)..........$1,500
project consultants.....................$ 500
                                   total $2,500
tom weinberg
chicago,ill.
****

rental 16mm film cameras (2@$100)......$ 200
mobile video camera and deck 1".........$ 500
videotape (color 1" &1/2 b&w)...........$ 200
film and processing(35mm slides/16 mm)..$ 100
color studio editing time (ec).........$1,000
                                   total $2,000
environmental communications
los angeles,calif.
****

launch vehicle(1959 cadillac conv.).....$ 600
tv pyramid (25 tv sets).................$ 300
crash event(rent cow palace pk. lot)...$ 100
post crash (rentacops and cleanup)......$ 200
loo t-shirts @ $3.......................$ 300
limited edt. color litho.(100 @$3)......$ 300
color tv image blow ups.................$ 200
                                   total $2,000
schroeder gallery
san francisco,calif.
****

total project budget....................$6,500

chip lord
doug michels
curtis schreier

november 20,1974

ANT CORPS
Architecture and Design
P.O. Box 471
San Francisco California 94101   Tel. 415 788-1424

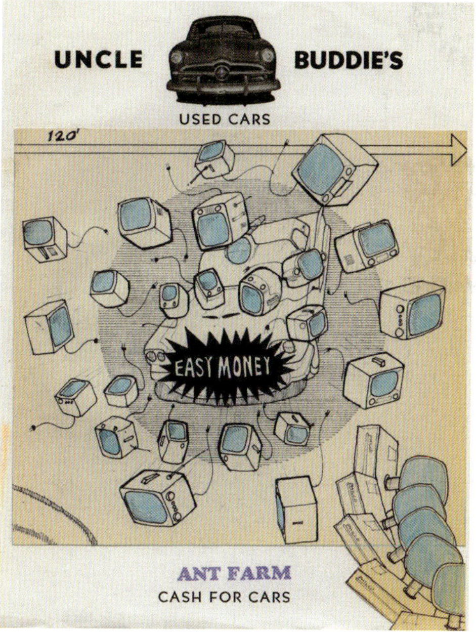

Top: "Petroleum Paradise" was a short-lived title for what would become *Media Burn*. Here, the location has moved to San Francisco ("rent cow palace pk. lot") and three funding sources are listed: Tom Weinberg, Environmental Communications, and the Schroeder Gallery.

Bottom: A promotional flyer recycling a graphic element from the larger *Easy Money* drawing.

Following spread: A radical revision of the first proposed "Coming and Going" street-based performance. Here, "The Sphinx" is not simply colliding with a pyramid of TV sets, but jumping the Southwest Freeway. Doug Michels rendered this complex *Easy Money* drawing.

---

65   From a letter dated October 1, 1974.

66   SFMOMA letter, September 26, 1974; Walker Art Center, January 30, 1975; Long Beach Museum of Art, March 13, 1975.

67   This budget is dated November 20, 1974.

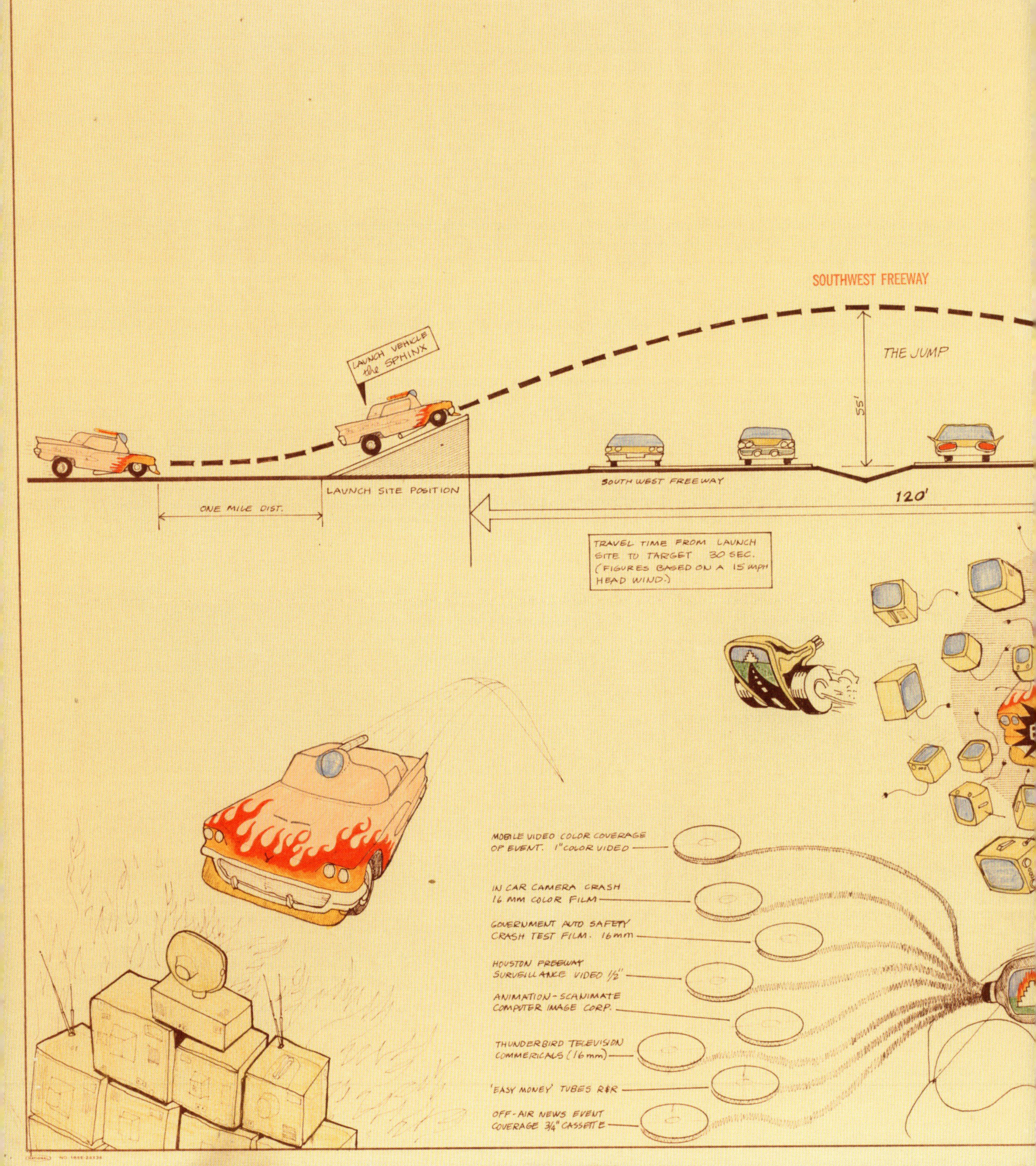

SOUTHWEST FREEWAY
THE JUMP
55'
LAUNCH VEHICLE the SPHINX
ONE MILE DIST.
LAUNCH SITE POSITION
SOUTH WEST FREEWAY
120'
TRAVEL TIME FROM LAUNCH SITE TO TARGET 30 SEC. (FIGURES BASED ON A 15 MPH HEAD WIND.)
MOBILE VIDEO COLOR COVERAGE OF EVENT. 1" COLOR VIDEO
IN CAR CAMERA CRASH 16 MM COLOR FILM
GOVERNMENT AUTO SAFETY CRASH TEST FILM. 16mm
HOUSTON FREEWAY SURVEILLANCE VIDEO 1/2"
ANIMATION - SCANIMATE COMPUTER IMAGE CORP.
THUNDERBIRD TELEVISION COMMERCIALS (16mm)
'EASY MONEY' TUBES R&R
OFF-AIR NEWS EVENT COVERAGE 3/4" CASSETTE

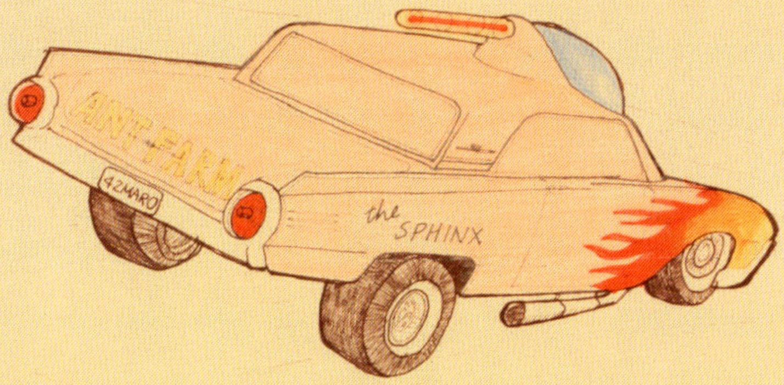

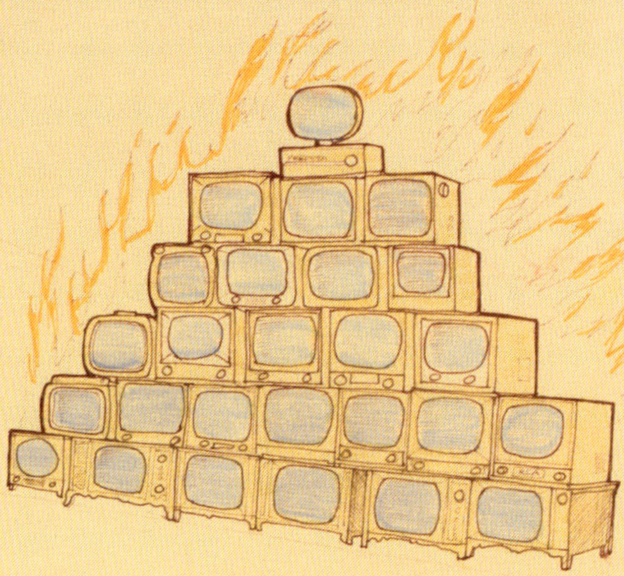

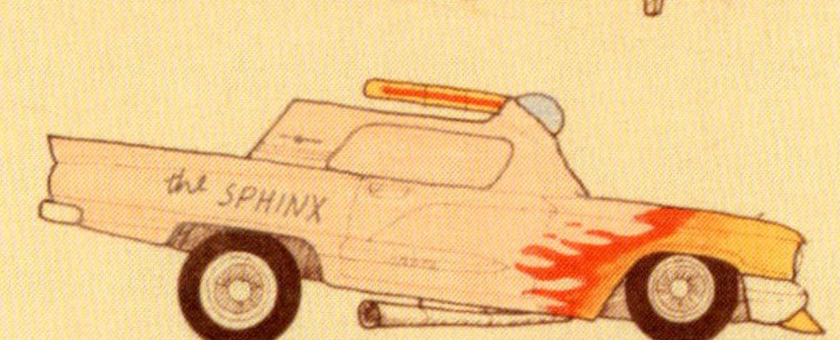

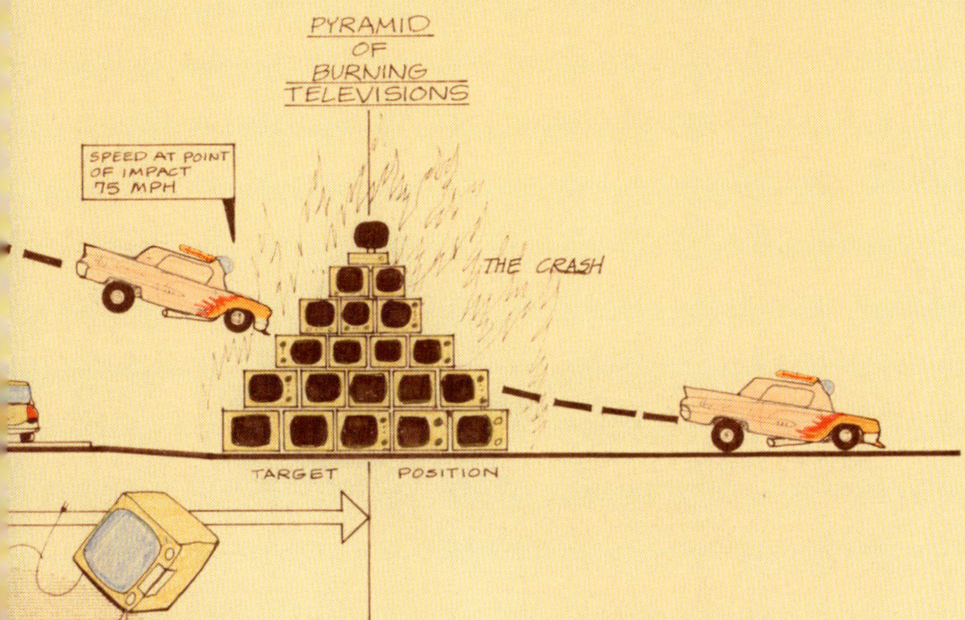

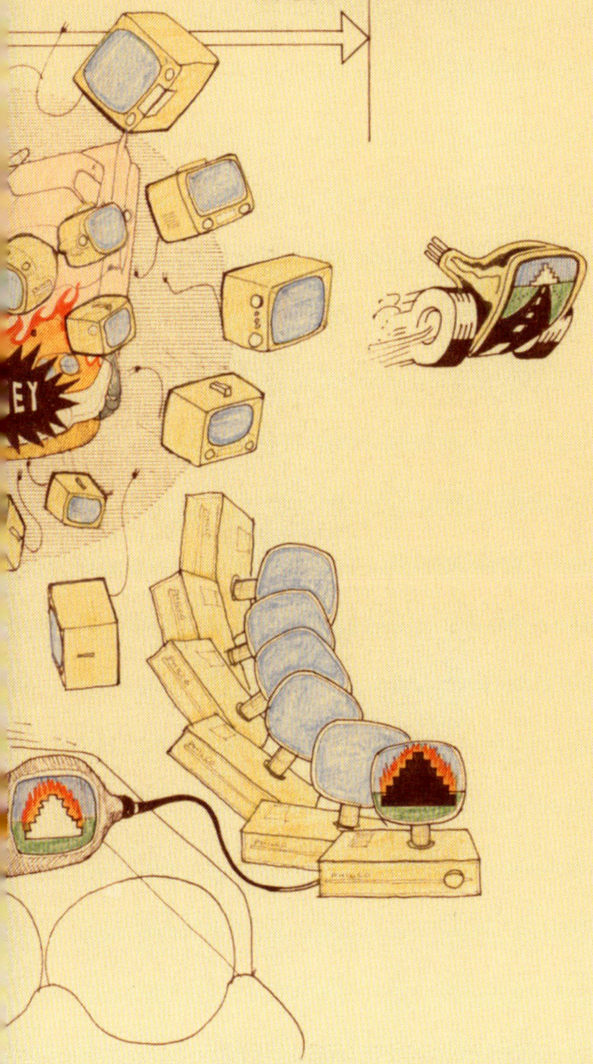

EASY MONEY

© 1974 ANT FARM

ON OCTOBER 11, 1974 THREE MEMBERS OF THE ANT FARM RIDING IN A MODIFIED 1958 FORD THUNDERBIRD WILL JUMP THE SOUTH WEST FREEWAY IN HOUSTON, TEXAS AND CRASH THRU A PYRAMID OF BURNING T.V. SETS IN AN ART WORK CALLED 'EASY MONEY'

'EASY MONEY' WILL BE PRODUCED AS A 30' VIDEO DOCUMENTARY PROGRAM BY ANT FARM.

BUDGET

1958-61 FORD THUNDERBIRD (LAUNCH VEHICLE)	500 ✳
MODIFICATIONS: SONIC SHIELD	25
FIBERGLAS WINDSHIELD COVER	250
16mm CAMERA MOUNT	50
SAFETY SEAT HARNESS	150
" FOAM CRASH PADS	50
PAINT AUTO (FLAMES & LETTERING)	150
TELEVISION PYRAMID	
PURCHASE OF TELEVISION SETS	250
TRUCK RENTAL	150 ✳
REMOVAL OF TRASH AFTER EVENT	150 ✳
DOCUMENTATION	
RENTAL 16mm CAMERAS (2)	100
MOBILE VIDEO STUDIO 2 hr	400
VIDEO TAPE, FILM & DEVELOPING	300
TUBES SONGWRITING FEE	300
VIDEO STUDIO EDITING TIME	1,200
ANT FARM CONCEPT FEE	500 ✳
ARTISTS FEE (500 EA. ARTIST)	1 500
CONSULTANTS FEE	500
TRANSPORTATION SF-HOU/TX-SF	900 ✳
LIVING EXP IN HOU/TX	200 ✳
EASY MONEY T-SHIRTS, PRESS HYPE, ETC.	300
TOTAL	7 825
less ✳ = PAID FOR BY HOUSTON C.OF.C.	2 400
⟶	5425

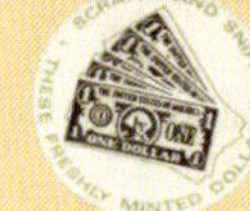

Easy Money

© 1974 ANT FARM

Box 471, San Francisco, Cal. 94101

REVISIONS			SPONSORED BY		
NO.	DATE	BY	HOUSTON CHAMBER OF COMMERCE		
1			FOR		
2			MAIN STREET '74		
3			DRAWN BY DM	SCALE	MATERIAL
4			CHK'D	DATE SEPT 1, 74	DRAWING NO.
5			TRACED	APP'D	

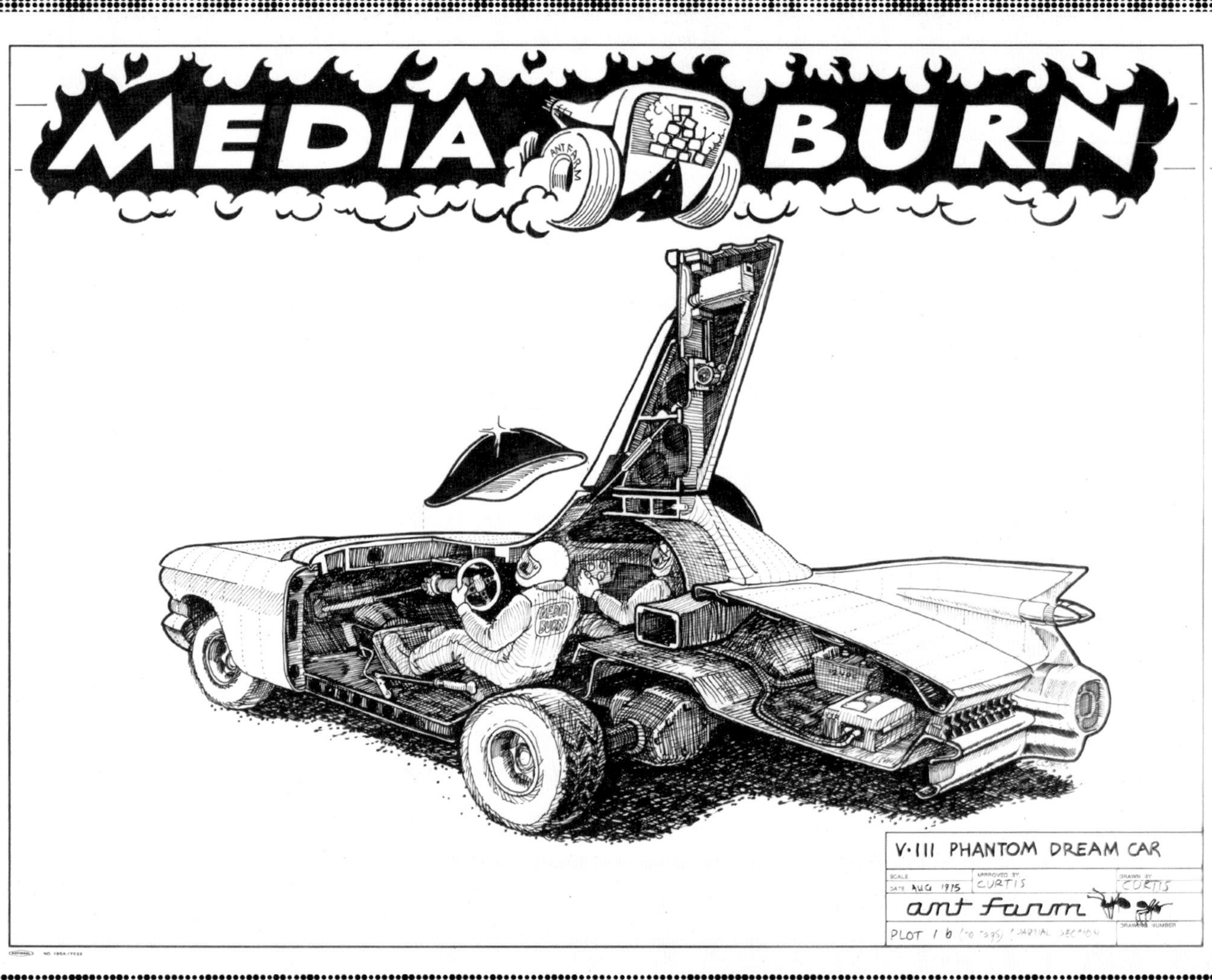

Curtis Schreier's cutaway drawing completed in the month following the July 4, 1975, performance. Note the videotape recorder in the trunk and the cabling leading to the portapak camera in the tail fin.

NAMING OPPORTUNITIES

Ant Farm didn't just get Tom Weinberg's $3,000 and his expertise as Executive Producer. They got a name. *"Media Vision"* was too blunt, though the proposed vehicle did navigate via video. *"Transformational Access: Coming and Going"* was too clinical and read more like a New Age motivational technique. *"Easy Money"* was too sarcastic yet matched Doug Michels' bilious reality show with equal lead-footedness. But *"Media Burn"*: that had punch and ambiguity.

An active member of TVTV and a Chicago-based nonfiction TV producer, Tom Weinberg had coined the term "Media Burn" in 1970 in response to the trial of the Chicago Seven.[68] He had attended the daily court sessions, often providing commentary for Pacifica Radio. Though no TV cameras were allowed in the courtroom, what impressed Weinberg was not only the way in which the trial was transformed through the media, but more importantly how the activists-turned-defendants were further turned into celebrities. "They aren't elected officials or TV game show hosts, newscasters or paid performers. They are stand-ins for our generation, for our beliefs, hopes and antiestablishment identities ... The distinctive nature of their fame as it has been generated by TV has a direct effect on who they are and how they behave, both on camera and in the courtroom and ultimately on their personalities and lives."[69] It was this transformation—from authenticity to artificiality—that Weinberg termed "Media Burn."

A by-product of media exposure, celebrity itself was prompted by an inherent desire for affirmation and fame that in extreme cases induced "acquired situational narcissism."[70] Weinberg seemed to fear a growing pandemic of everyday people under the sway of a "powerful

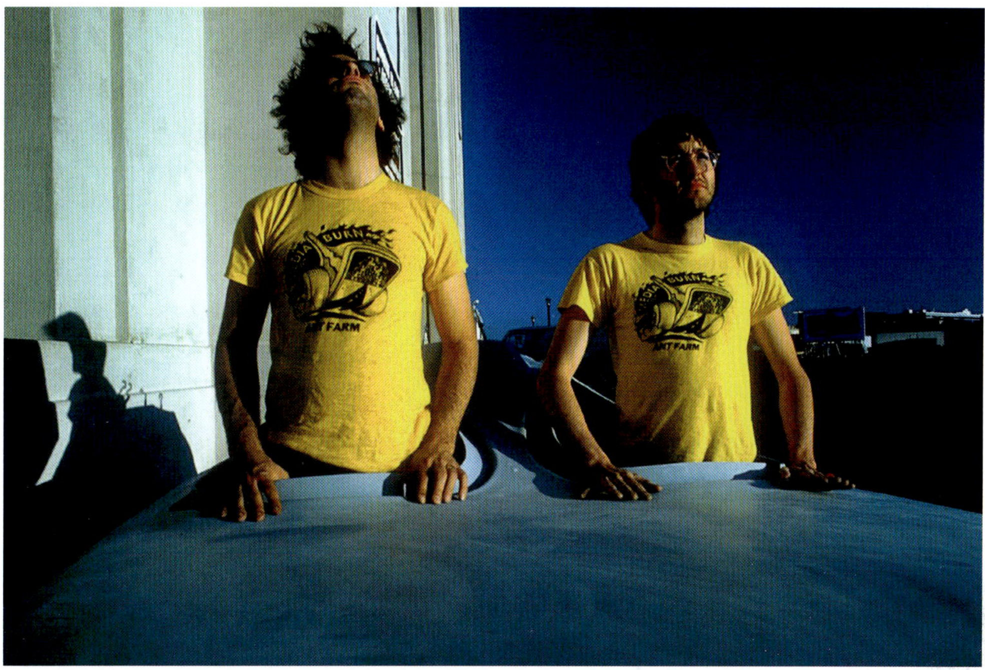

Tom "Score" Weinberg (left) and Chip Lord standing in the bubble ports of the under-construction Phantom Dream Car. Photograph by Phil Makanna. ©Phil Makanna.

self-fascination that is triggered and enhanced by appearing on-screen." His lifelong endeavors with alternative media were, at some level, an attempt to use the seductive technology without fanning the fame flame. Free of corporate prompts, alternative media would create a beneficial mirror for reflection—an antidote to celebrity culture.

The Ant Farmers were architects and artists, not psychologists. They looked for structural deficiencies not emotional debilitators. But sometimes the manifestations were similar. In an undated statement, titled "TV Addiction," handed out to the press, they wrote: "Television addiction has grown across America faster than heroin addiction. This addiction is not physical like heroin, but it is a psychological addiction that produces a compelling mindlessness and a narrowing view of reality ... Television addiction is ultimately more serious than heroin or alcohol because it goes straight to the mind to condition responses and create artificial needs." The "narrowing view of reality," aided by "superficial information transferal," was responsible for the "zombie-like complacency of Americans toward the forces in motion around them ... In the end," they wrote, "television like heroin is a burn."

Driving a customized Cadillac through a pyramid of burning TV sets would create an image so dense and indecipherable yet so intuitively familiar that it would stir us from our "zombie-like complacency." The image was waiting for its animation. All it needed was a name, and Tom Weinberg had one—*Media Burn*.

---

68   The following comments are gleaned from an article penned by Weinberg for the *Journal of Film and Video*, Spring/Summer, 2012, pp. 51-56.

69   Ibid., p. 52.

70   Cited by Weinberg in reference to a syndrome first observed by Robert B. Millman, professor of psychiatry at the Weill Cornell Medical College of Cornell University.

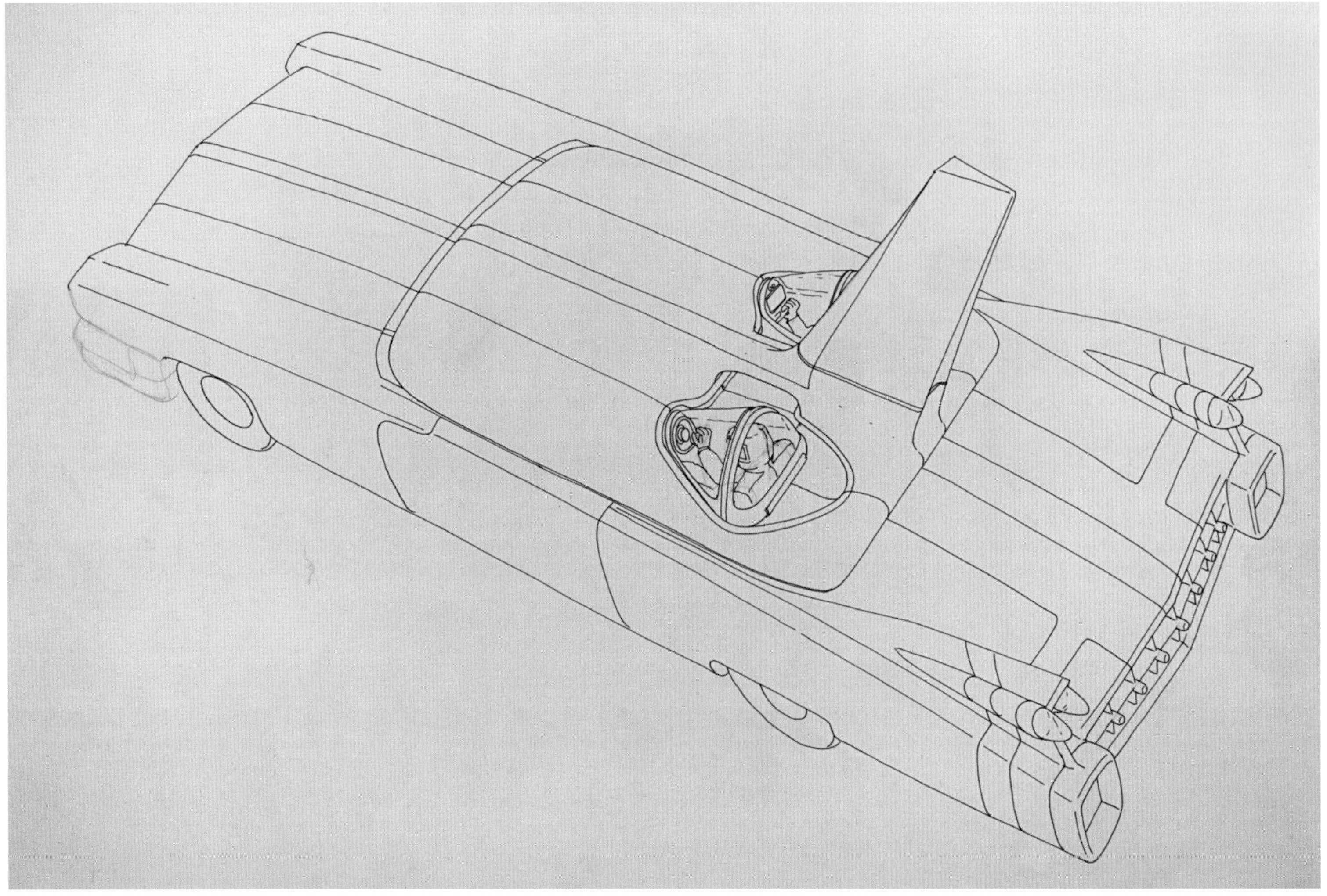

An unusual overhead rendering of the Phantom Dream Car by Curtis Schreier.

Having abandoned all hope that *Petroleum Paradise* (or any other unctuous act) would be enabled in oily Houston, Chip Lord and Doug Michels returned to Ant Farm's studio on Pier 40[71] in San Francisco, where Curtis Schreier was contemplating the customization of the 1959 Cadillac Eldorado Biarritz that they purchased, used, in the fall of 1973 from John Rewind, a member of the Bay Area rock band The Hoodoo Rhythm Devils.[72] Rewind had sold the car in part

—

71   This space, rented since June 1973, would burn in 1978, signaling the end of Ant Farm.

72   The second Hoodoo Rhythm Devils album, *The Barbecue of DeVille*, was released in late 1972. The LP cover features the tail fin of Rewind's 1959 Cadillac, photographed in Oakland. An interesting provenance for this celebrity automobile.

because the gas crisis of 1973 had sent the price of fuel wildly upward. Ant Farm used the car for luxurious personal transport and was about to have it repainted when a fender bender damaged the relatively pristine body. And so the Cadillac, license plate BIJ870, would be sacrificed to the radical alterations required to embody the Phantom Dream Car.

It's worth noting again that the Phantom Dream Car sits as the apotheosis of a custom car lineage that goes back several iterations and numerous auto manufacturers. An early concept, the impact vehicle for *Media Vision*, was a "late model sedan" painted "flat black." Its principal modification was a metal shark fin mounted on the roof as a pseudo-stabilizer. A small hole punched in the fin was echoed in the steel plate with like hole that replaced the windshield. This vehicle,

like the Phantom Dream Car, would be navigated by viewing the road on a small monitor mounted above the steering wheel. Nearby a small video camera peered out through the hole, the view tinted by a "yellow Plexiglas" sheet.

Easy Money was built around a "1958–61 Ford Thunderbird," dubbed The Sphinx. The general modifications involved a "fiberglass windshield cover," variously called a "sonic shield" and a "surveillance bubble," exterior exhaust pipes, and pronounced flames and lettering as part of the body paint. The main feature, the sonic shield, was a plastic bubble mounted above the windshield as a port for the 16mm camera affixed within the cabin. In one early drawing, a rod-like appendage dubbed a "broadcast antenna" extended behind the bubble and above the roofline. Broadcast capability would have been a spectacular attribute, allowing The Sphinx to transmit

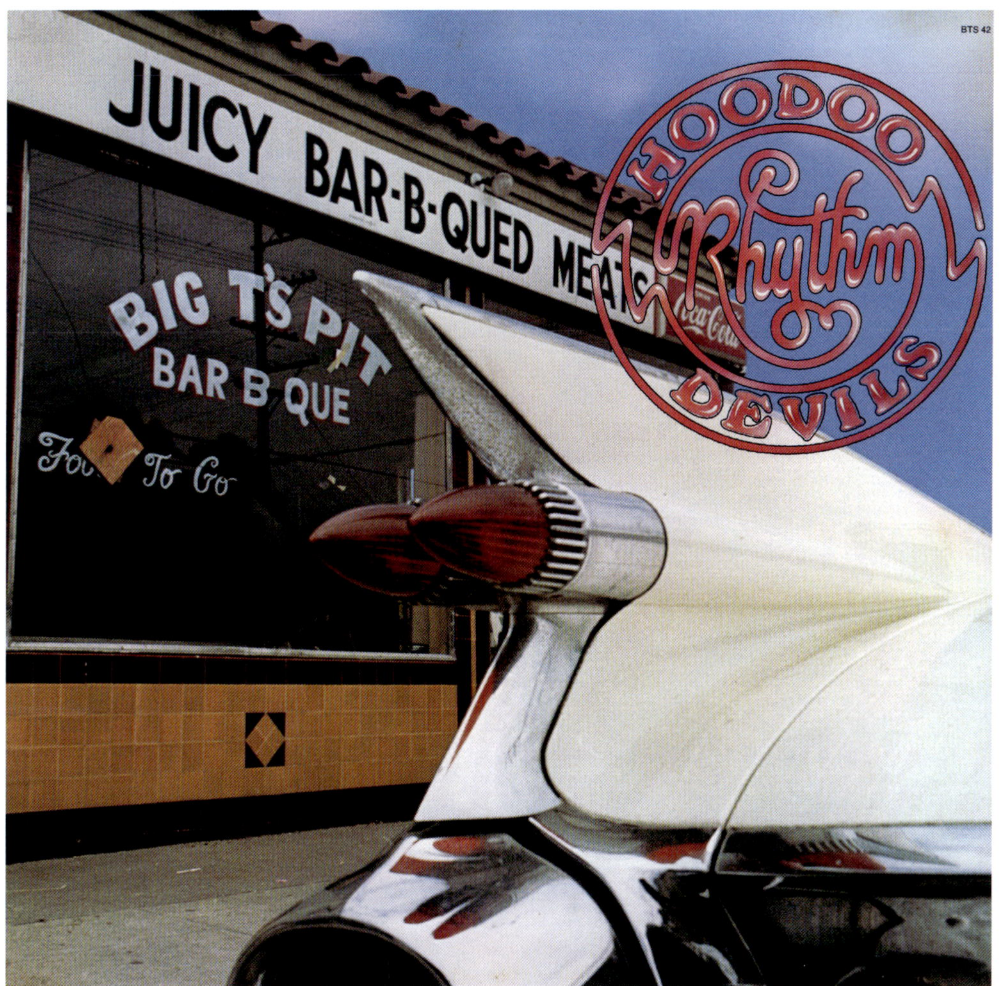

Cover of the Hoodoo Rhythm Devils' LP *The Barbecue of DeVille* (1972) with the tail fin of the Cadillac El Dorado they sold to Ant Farm.

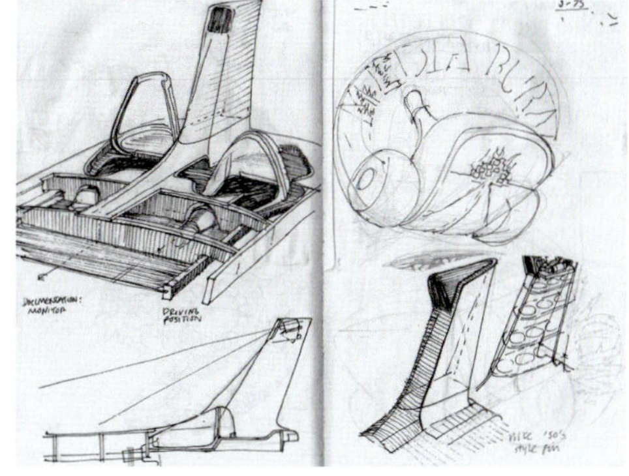

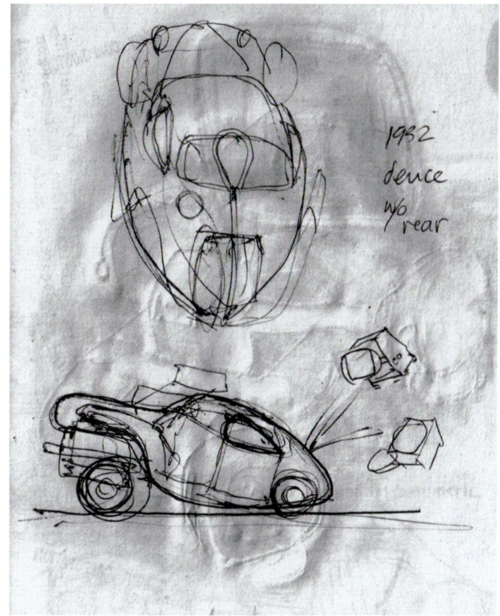

Top: Excerpts from Curtis Schreier's sketchbooks showing the logo with type treatment.

Bottom: Another discarded concept: a heavily modified 1932 Ford Deuce Coupe with the drivetrain reversed so that the car could be driven backwards. Drawing by Curtis Schreier.

Following spread: Doug Michels (rear) and Curtis Schreier working on the fiberglass cover for the extended cockpit of the Phantom Dream Car. Photograph by Ant Farm.

its own collision, perhaps its own demise, in real time. Live, participatory, and catastrophic TV marshaled in protest of monolithic media.

The principal *Easy Money* illustration, drawn by Doug Michels in early September 1974, has a subtle detail depicting the interior of The Sphinx, though this is only corroborated by a second detail taken from a triptych of undated Sphinx reworkings. The highly stylized cockpit, outfitted with three "protective bubbles" for the three potential Ant Farm occupants, also has a "surveillance gland" with two video cameras, providing the dashboard with "stereovision." This vehicle is clearly navigated through a live video feed. The actual steering mechanism, a pretzel-shaped metal or wood grip, has an image at its center, as though the steering column contained a viewing surface. In yet another undated drawing with related design elements, the steering column does in fact support a central "oscilloscope tube" upon which a mock image is registered. Here, the drivers are once removed from their path, their only orientation being technical and pictorial displays of the road ahead. The video cameras capture their own potential annihilation through a high-speed collision with television. A transcendental feedback loop? Or just death by cathode ray?

A more radical departure is partially developed as The Sphinx-2. Preliminary drawings in Schreier's sketchbook picture a "1932 Deuce," the street name for a '32 Ford Coupe, Model B. Schreier radically chopped and dropped the body, tapering the rear end to accommodate a single wheel. It appears from these simple drawings that The Sphinx-2 would be driven in reverse; TV sets are even pictured ricocheting off the former trunk.

Returning to the '59 Caddy, an unattributed drawing exists with minor mods. The soft-top roofline is lower and two options are briefly illustrated, one being a "road" position with a raised driver looking through a Plexiglas bubble and the second, denoted as "track," having a lower profile and the driver prone along the floor line. These collective designs are called "Tumbling Dice," and the Caddy is seen colliding with several "TV Dice" that look very much like television sets. On the trunk is an illustration of a winged hourglass, but instead of sand we have miniature TVs.

Indeed time was running out for a plausible design to pursue.

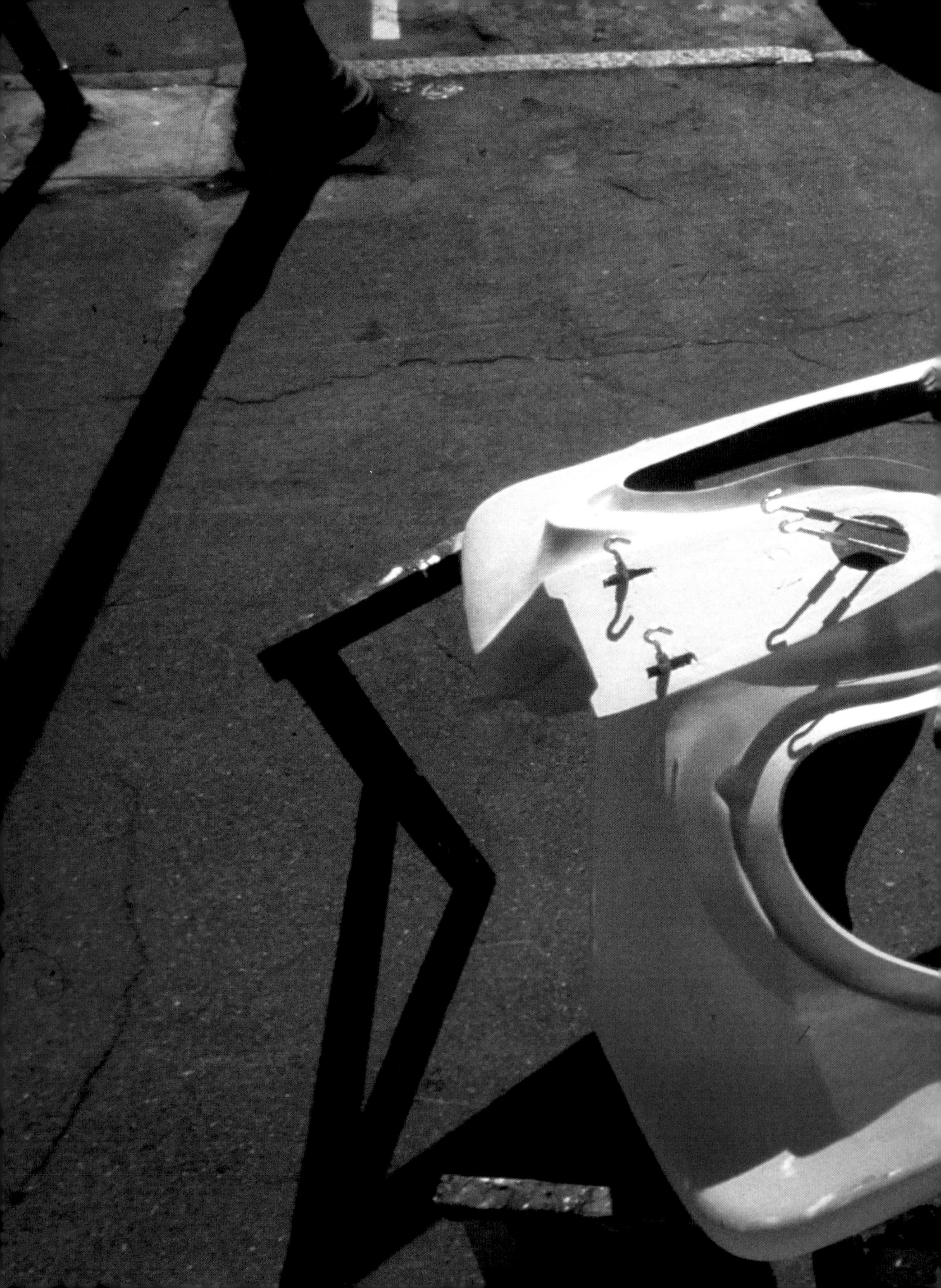

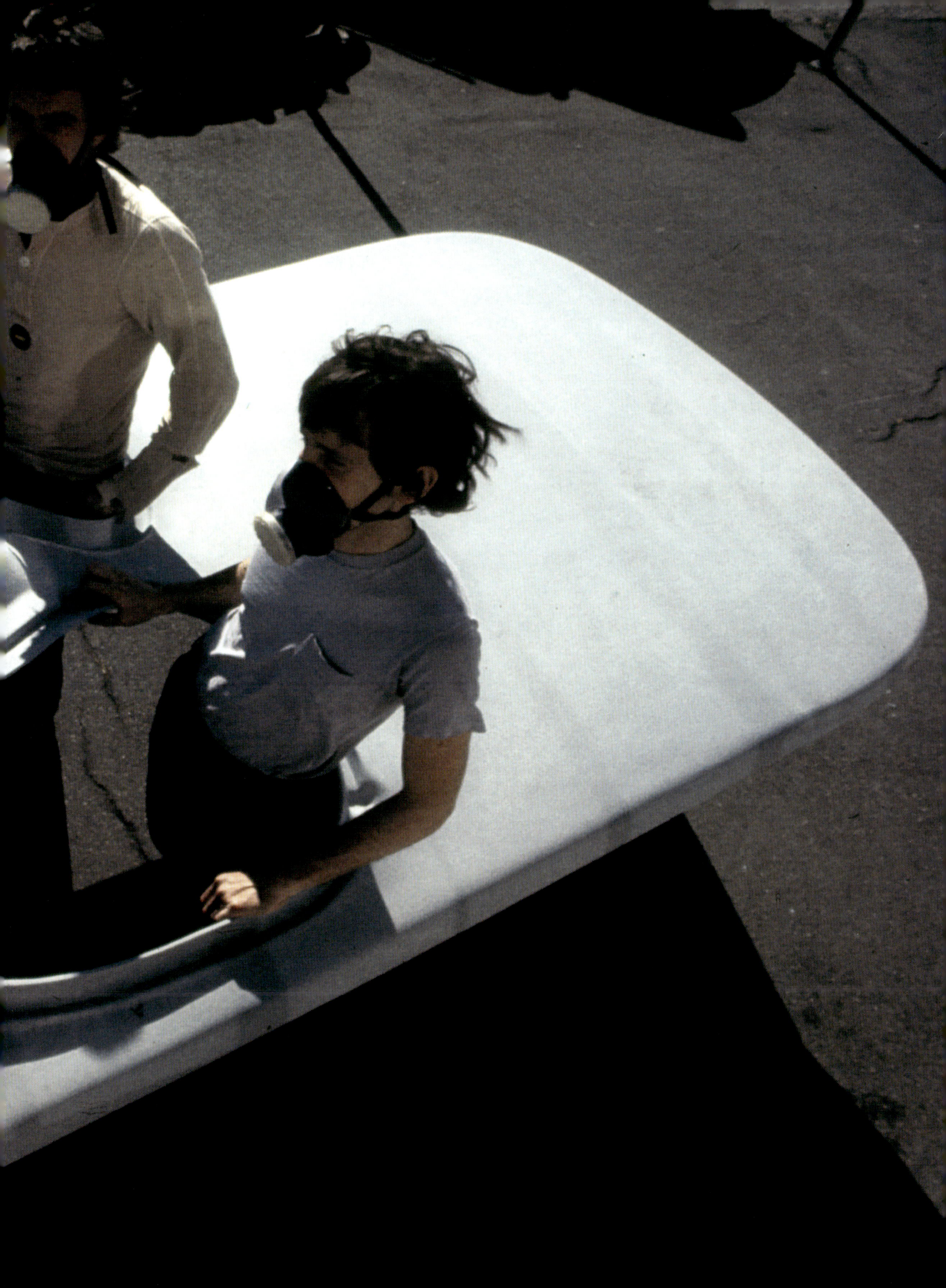

A PHANTOM DREAM COME TRUE

The car design that was emerging from the unbridled head of Curtis Schreier in late 1974 was a paean, a reference, and a metaphorical accelerant to many things mobile. Chief among them was the earlier mentioned Dream Car that had triggered the testosterone of a generation of auto admirers. The Sphinx with its embedded riddle was out and the Phantom Dream Car was in: a Phantom perhaps because the Dream Car of the fifties was just a delusory memory, or because, like the classic ghost, the Dream Car was an unsettled soul that would haunt our lives until righteously purged. Driving the Phantom Dream Car into a pyramid of burning TV sets at the ample speed of fifty-five miles per hour might be just such a purgative.

With a body length of almost nineteen feet, the 1959 Cadillac Eldorado provided an expansive sculptural plane for reinvention. Schreier's first act was to remove all vestiges of the ragtop, the windshield, and the innards of the passenger compartment. The dashboard was gutted, the seats, side panels, and steering column pulled, the gas and brake pedals removed. This grotesque bit of luxury iron would be converted from a spacious six-seater to a cockpit outfitted for just two occupants, requiring the extension of the steering column and other navigational controls about five feet to the rear. This modification would place the protective canopies at midship and visually exaggerate the front end of the Phantom Dream Car.

The cockpit insert Schreier built was a wonder of artisanal woodworking, an ironic addition to this monument to industrial metal on wheels. It had a gracefully curved rim of plywood that would accommodate the instrumentation and extended steering column and provide the base support for the towering tail fin that would rise above the trunk. The trickiest bit of design would be the protective bubbles that would sit snugly atop the cockpit cover. Schreier was no newcomer to extruded Plexiglas. The Ant Farm Media Van, built in 1971, had five Plexiglas bubbles, three spherical and two teardrop-shaped. But the fabrication of the Phantom Dream Car domes was complicated by the curved surface of the driver's compartment and by a second concern, safety.

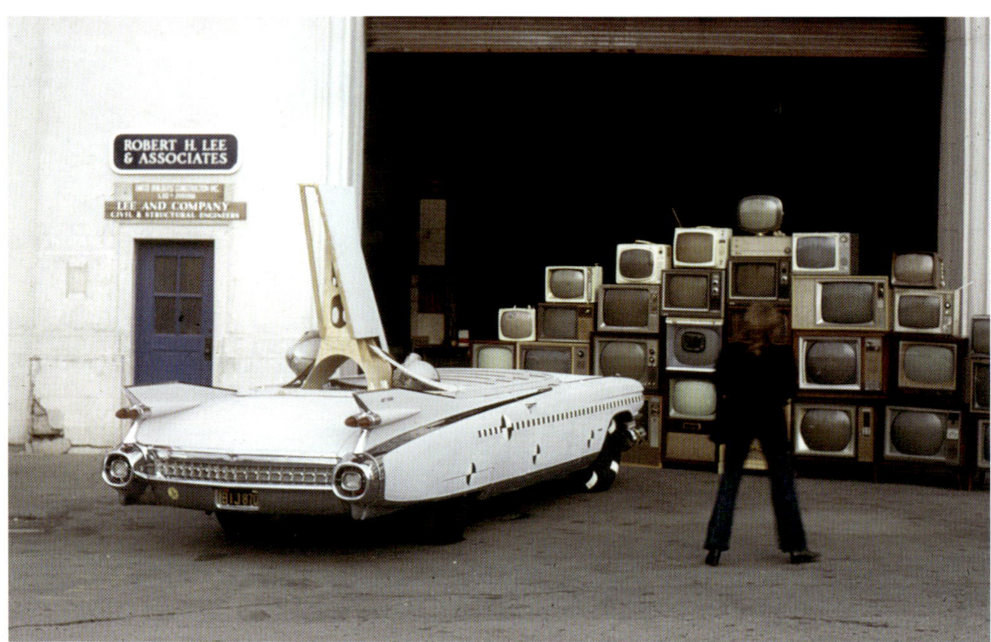

The nearly finished Phantom Dream Car in front of the Ant Farm studio. The TV sets represent about half the number gathered for the Fourth of July performance. Photograph by Ant Farm.

The Phantom Dream Car would be outfitted with two separate canopies, one of clear Plexiglas used for traditional navigation—looking directly at the road ahead—and the other a reinforced fiberglass dome, opaque and sturdy, specific to the coming collision.[73] This blackened canopy would withstand the pounding of flying television consoles. The domes would be swapped out at the performance site during the countdown. Like the Sphinx prototype, the Phantom Dream Car would be driven via video display. A camera mounted inside the outsized tail fin would give the driver the exclusive view of the burning impact zone.

Wishing to survive the performance, Schreier spent considerable time determining the implications of collision. Several drawings exist in which a fifty-five-mile-per-hour impact is diagrammed, illustrating the distribution of the television sets as they are propelled skyward. No specific math is applied—such as X weighted TV set dislodged by 5,100-pound automobile at Y speed equals Z

trajectory—nor are there calculations about the structural strength of, say, fiberglass. But estimated impact points along the Caddy's length are keenly noted. One drawing classifies the TV sets for their positioning in the pyramid: heavier sets on ground level and in the off-center positions; lightweight cases, some without their CRTs, in the dead center; and small sets for the apex of the pyramid. Early sketches often feature an unusual swivel-mounted television set[74] for the peak position. This all-seeing eye-like vintage set gave the pyramid the appearance of "The Eye of Providence," that strange Masonic symbol that appears on the one dollar bill.

Discreetly titled *Secret Location, San Francisco, CA*, yet another drawing takes the macro view, creating several zones: impact, press, and spectator. A series of concentric circles defines the central Impact Zone with an adamant "danger—fire zone" at its core. Just beyond the circle of safety is the Press Zone, though some camera positions are noted inside of danger. The Spectator Zone is placed far beyond the path of flying debris.

---

73   A plastic point: In drawings, the second, more impervious domes are listed as "fiberglass." However, during the actual event, the announcer describes them as "Lexan," a polycarbonate resin that has been used for aircraft canopies.

---

74   Somewhat like the Philco Predicta, from the late 1950s.

Ant Farm wanted to outlive this TV thrill ride. Involving a proposed jump over a four-lane freeway, *Easy Money* would have been a jump straight to the morgue with the entire art collective as corpse. *Media Burn* whittled the crew down to two, guaranteeing at least one survivor. But something else radiated from the Phantom Dream Car. Along the flank of this nineteen-foot juggernaut was a series of registration circles and a checked line running horizontally from the headlights to the rear wheel well—the same markings that can be found on crash test vehicles.

Automobile safety had long been an issue. After all, there had been a steady increase in auto casualties since Henry Bliss unwittingly supplied the first statistic for death rendered by car in 1899. During 1974, 45,196 people died in car crashes, actually a slow year for fatalities. The Dream Car had turned many a driver into a phantom. And so Ant Farm's automotive creation acknowledged both the desire for mobility, affluence, and modernity as symbolized by the industrial Dream Car and, simultaneously, the lethal undercarriage of that same dream.

The Phantom Dream Car's markings reference crash tests and, by extension, the vehicle's imminent structural failures. Drive two and a half tons of heavy metal into a stationary object, say a pyramid of TV sets, and something's got to give. But this was more than some sly allusion to the National Highway Traffic Safety Administration.

During the early design stage, Tim Taggart, editor of *Motor Trend* magazine, responded to Doug Michels' query about sources for crash films.[75] There were plenty out there, many in the hands of the auto manufacturers who for years had been testing their vehicles for impact failures. They say automobiles are built for speed, but they are really built for abrupt alterations in speed, i.e., crashes. Ant Farm's premeditated crack-up had its antecedents in an engineering pursuit as old as the vehicle itself. Segments of crash films would be incorporated into the final *Media Burn* videowork as part of a collision collage, and not only as visual evidence.[76] The Phantom Dream Car was both the dream and the nightmare. At some level,

the mad rush down the tarmac toward its intended obstruction was a poetic ritual of survival, a ritual performed cooperatively and for all of us.

But every ritual must have its sacrifice. If the Phantom Dream Car was part of a ceremonial process, who were the initiates? Who else but the crew of this exploratory dream vehicle. Though they are often referred to as artists during the July 4 performance, the navigator (Curtis Schreier) and pilot (Doug Michels) are also notably deemed the "Artist-Dummies." In the auto safety field, they would be known as full-scale anthropomorphic test devices, a.k.a. crash test dummies. Safety engineers had stopped using cadavers in 1949, but that wouldn't stop our forward-thinking artist-projectiles. They would be bent, folded, and mutilated as sacramental citizens colliding with a stubborn and monolithic media. The impact would be writ upon their bodies like data nodes of the spirit. Gray striped jumpsuits and large, bulbous crash helmets would make these dummies more plumbers than pilots.[77] But then again, everything about *Media Burn* was a dressing down.

Beyond the drastically elongated prow and the double bubbles was the final prominence: a vertical stabilizer rising some six feet in the air. Though it had its visual vector, this stabilizer was not simply for show; it gave the concealed video camera a lofty vantage. This elevated P.O.V. provided the "dummies" with a clear view of the fiery impact while a video recorder concealed in the trunk stored the images.

Clearly, the extravagant tail fin also alluded to dreams of flight, embodied by jet aircraft and their land-based kin, jet-propelled cars such as Craig Breedlove's Spirit of America.[78] Much was contained within this metaphor—escape from the confines of gravity, the triumph of technology over nature, a weightless pursuit of the material, the fantastical shedding of one's fragile skin for the fast-moving fuselage of the future. All this would be contained within the Phantom Dream Car as it warmed its 390-cubic-inch engine on the asphalt outside the Cow Palace.

With the radical rearrangement of the Cadillac Eldorado's body parts, one conventional feature was eliminated: a way in.

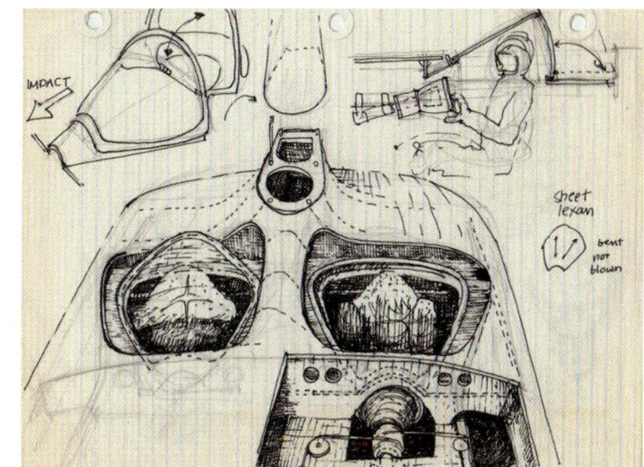

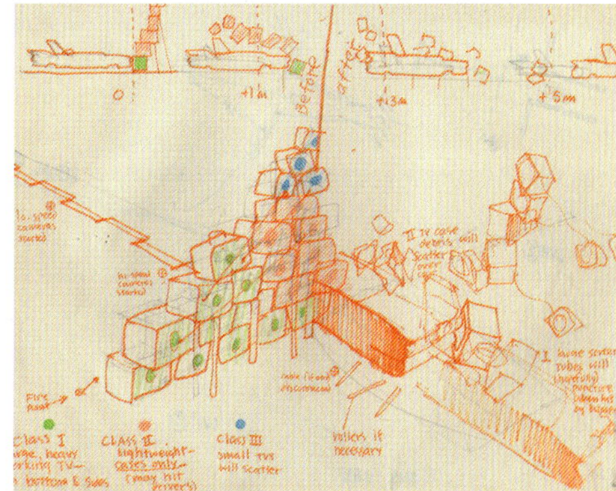

Top: Phantom Dream Car details showing the modified steering column and Lexan impact shields.

Bottom: One of several safety studies created by Curtis Schreier. This one calculates the dispersal and impact of the dislodged TV sets.

Following spread: Chip Lord standing beside the pyramid of TV sets in the San Francisco studio, June 1975. Note the refrigerator unit to the right that would be used for a time capsule, *Aerosol Arsenal*, later in the year. Photograph by Ant Farm.

The driver's side door had been damaged in a previous (unintentional) collision and was bolted shut. The passenger door was reserved for the emergency exit. To resolve the issue of ingress, a more theatrical solution was sought. Behind and below the tail fin, Schreier included a tight passageway that led from atop the trunk hood into the cockpit. One at a time, the Artist-Dummies would climb along the trunk top, crouch down, thrust their legs through the pinched portal, compress their shoulders, then slip into the cabin. It was birthing in reverse. Once the opaque domes were installed, the Ant Farmers would be in a womb without a view.

---

75   The letter is dated December 10, 1974, with apologies for the slow response. Taggart also notes that their article on *Cadillac Ranch* will appear in the February 1975 issue.

76   Doug Michels' *Easy Money* for Main Street '74 drawing lists as a visual resource, amid other footage including 16mm high-speed footage and mobile video coverage, a "government auto safety crash test film."

---

77   Tom Weinberg put the crash helmets on his credit card, then returned them on Monday after the performance.

78   Again, there is precedent for this within the classic 1950s dream cars, such as GM's Firebird series designed between 1953 and 1958: all sport a prominent central tail fin.

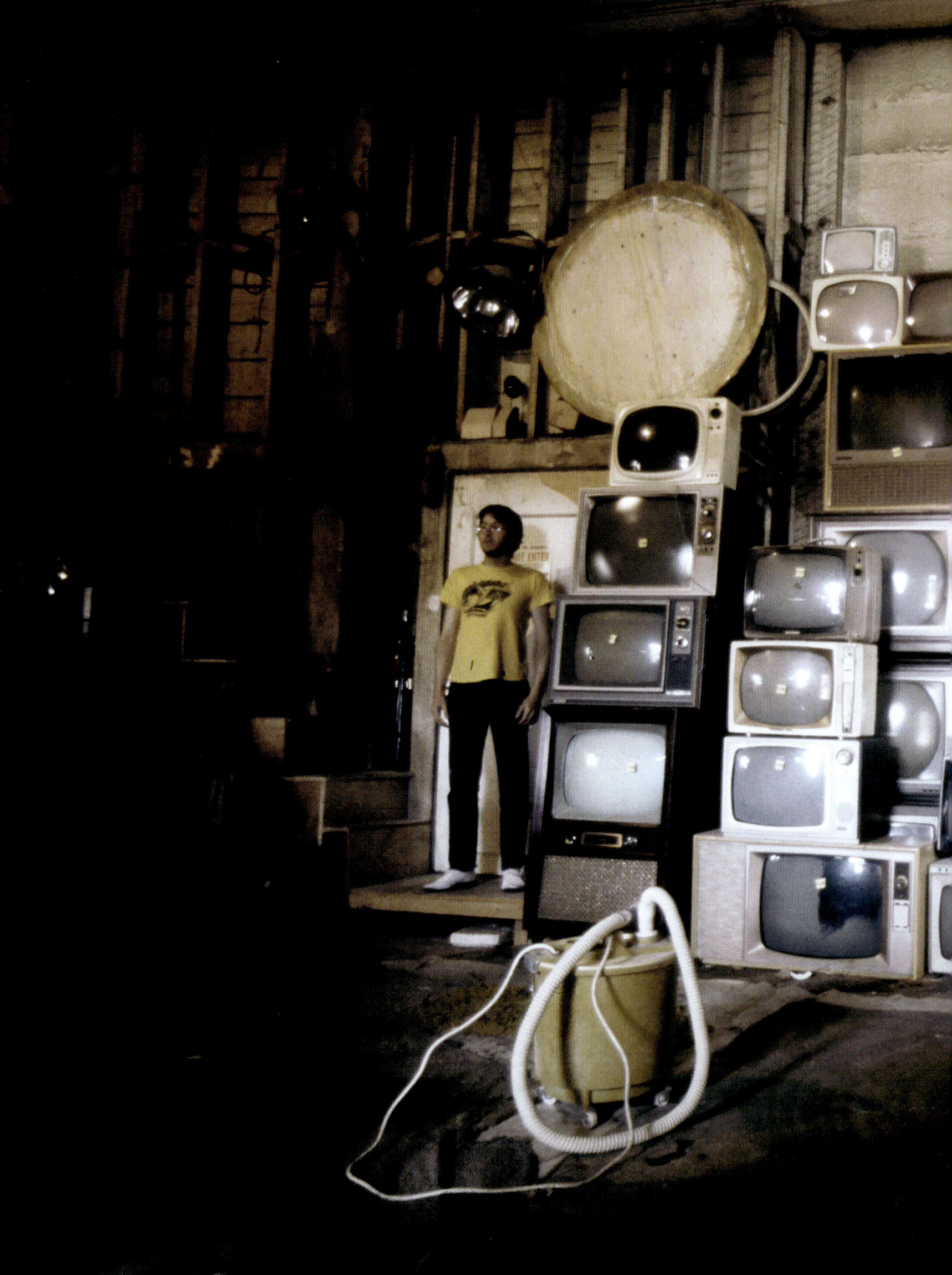

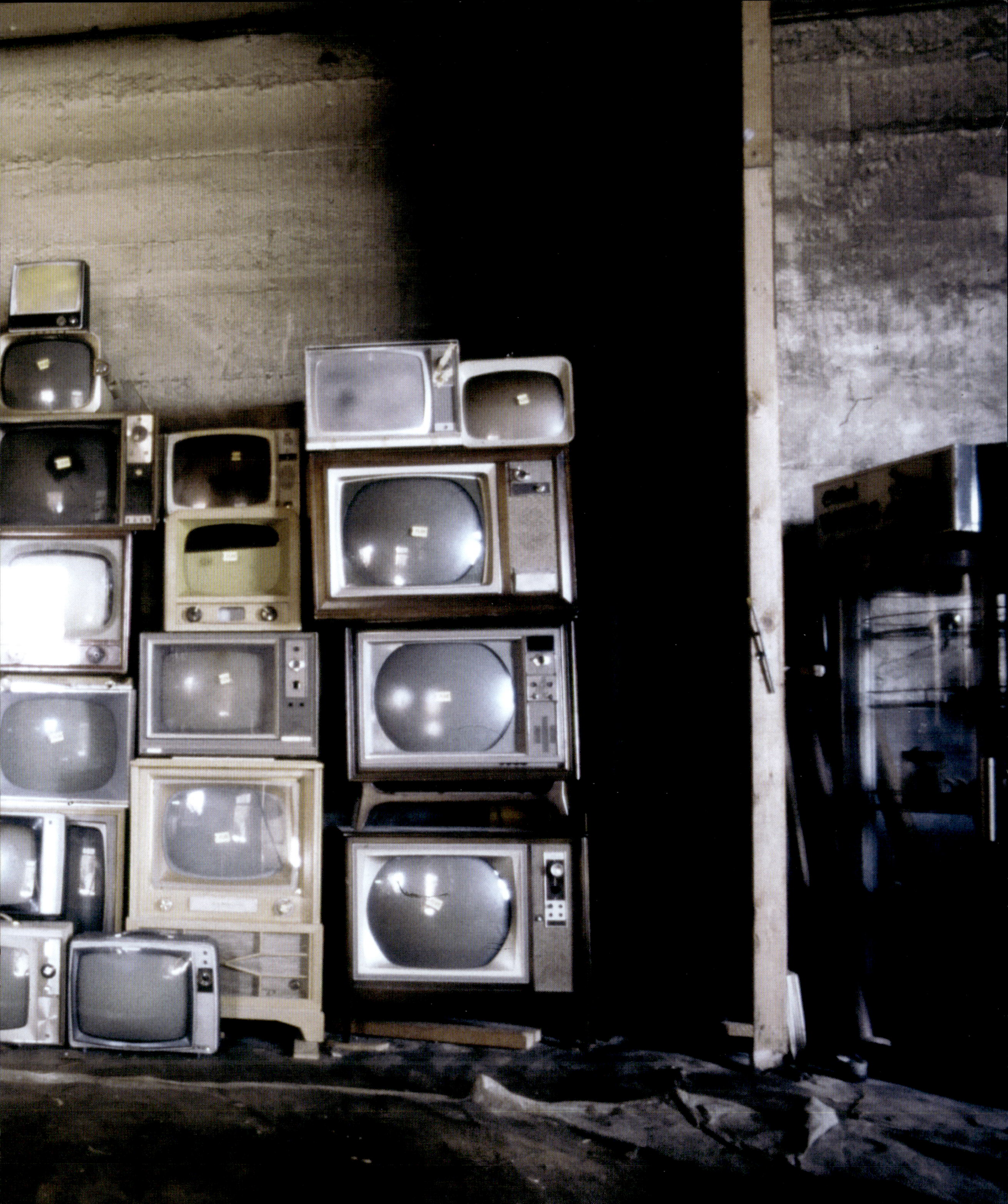

MEDIA BURN

december 16,1974

robert siegel
schroeder gallery
1367 post street
san francisco,94109

dear robert,

i am of course very sorry to hear that the
first video art gallery in california is
going under. we were looking foward to the
ant farm's exhibit at the schroeder gallery.

in preparation for the media burn exhibit we
have occured expences that we would like to have
reimbursement for.

based on your commitment to the ant farm and
signed contract of dec. 10,1974 we have
incurred the following expences.

1959 cadillac convert............$350
ant farm labor on auto modification...$250

                    total $600

we would hope to recieve a check from you
for this ammount as soon as possible.

best wishes,

doug michels
ant farm

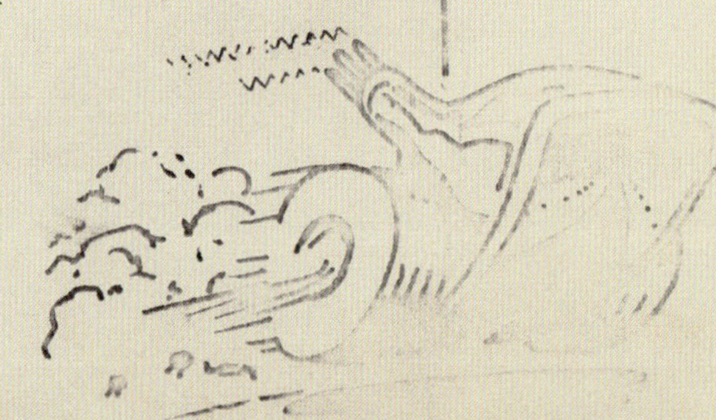

ANT CORPS
Architecture and Design
P.O. Box 471

LOOKING TOWARD INDEPENDENCE DAY

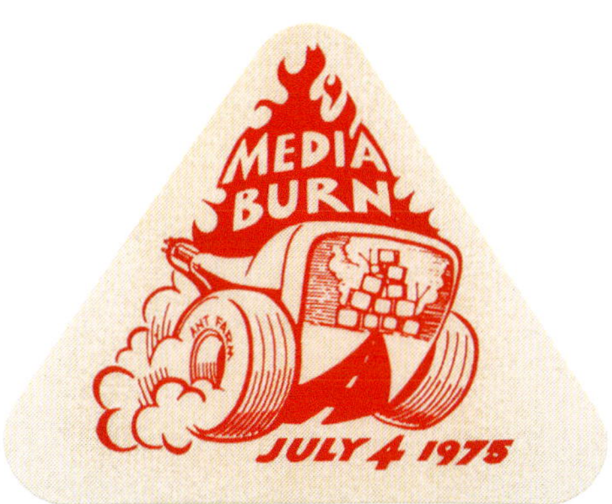

The final *Media Burn* logo seen here as a triangular decal sold at the performance.

Cancellations, suspensions, setbacks, and rearrangements: *Media Burn* had an abortive history, marked by frustrating postponements since its first inception as *Media Vision* in early 1973. The initial invitation from Main Street '74 in Houston had set in motion a series of delays and detours as project approval collapsed, funding flagged, and ambitions altered the very performance concept. The October 11 date set for Main Street '74 held through the summer but was soon pushed to "december 1974/san francisco" in a sponsorship appeal to Suzanne Foley at SFMOMA. That vague date gave way to clarity with December 25 at the Cow Palace as the stocking stuffer for Christmas Day. Later an undated Ant Farm press release involving Environmental Communications and the Schroeder Gallery[79] declared February 14 the target date. This was quickly superseded by Schroeder Gallery's announcement for the (eventually canceled) exhibition of the Phantom Dream Car on view, March 7 through April 1. The canceled exhibition was presumably a preview of the coming performance, showing off a fully modified Phantom Dream Car (which, in fact, was not completed until late June). By mid-January, Doug Michels was pitching a two-part *Media Burn* article to *Motor Trend*. Part one, focusing on the alteration of the completed Cadillac, would be available in mid-March, with part two, the event itself, available in mid-June, post-impact.

Sometime in early spring, the auspicious date of July 4 was finally selected (even though access to the Cow Palace's main parking lot was not officially granted until June 17). Independence Day rang with a higher purpose, cast fireworks skyward, and reiterated the nation's foundational story of revolution and reinvention. And it was a guaranteed slow news day when the mainstream media would be eager to forgo the obligatory VFW picnics, star-spangled pet parades, and pie-eating contests in favor of an enticing "media event."

First, however, there was an extensive to-do list, not the least being the branding of *Media Burn* itself. Ant Farm had learned much from *Cadillac Ranch* about the control and dissemination of that entrenched tribute to the tail fin. For the plain-speaking sculpture to extend its influence, Ant Farm launched a closely guarded campaign of licensed images, official postcards, and other merchandising elements. This of course earned them some revenues, but more important, they could tightly steer the message of those ten Cadillacs impaled in the Texas range.

Media Burn would undergo the same thoughtful process of deliberate image design and control. *Media Burn* was, after all, about the creation of a singular image with all other elements of the performance subordinate to that final iconic outcome. But the campaign would be launched with the final revelatory image in absentia, unbirthed as it were. The branding would be more like a beautifully crafted pedestal waiting for its prized object to be displayed. All would sit upon this fully realized base, consisting of a heavily repeated *Media Burn* logo, tersely honed press releases, T-shirts, and an eight-page souvenir booklet complete with a brief manifesto, "television addiction statistics," the Artist-President's speech on White House letterhead, a pitch about the Phantom Dream Car, and an audience feedback card.

Admittance to the Cow Palace parking lot was by invitation only. Some 400 guests were among the lucky ones and of those, the press outweighed the public, at least on paper. The mainstream media crews were almost outmatched by invited guerrilla crews, gathered from video collectives like Optic Nerve, Marin Community Video, and the California Video Resource Project, for *Media Burn* required two forms of documentation: one, recording the elements of the event itself; the other, covering the coverage. Several photographers—Phil Makanna, John Turner, Diane Andrews Hall, and Edmund Shea—had official Ant Farm status, and it was their charge to capture an encapsulating image for immediate dissemination to the wire services.[80] Diane Hall's explosive black-and-white shot of the slightly blurred Phantom Dream Car, piercing the still-standing pyramid of TV sets while flames lick the undercarriage of the car, would be selected. And by July 5, *Media Burn*, that free-floating signifier, would be forcefully propelled into the mediasphere.

But I get ahead of myself.

---

79   Both these organizations had been listed as sponsors in a budget from November 1974.

80   Co-producer Tom Weinberg outlined a specific strategy for getting prints to the Associated Press and United Press International offices in San Francisco for the immediate dispersal of the *Media Burn* image.

FROM CAR TO CARTOON

During the spring, another vehicular event was being planned. This one was the Artists' Soapbox Derby, a May 18 benefit for the San Francisco Museum of Modern Art. The fundraiser had been announced the previous year, giving Bay Area artists a bounty of time for design and construction. Seventy-nine cars were built by 104 artists. Among them was Ant Farm, represented by Chip Lord as his alter ego, "Uncle Buddie," a former used car salesman from Houston, who submitted a car, and Curtis Schreier, providing a trophy in the form of a readymade bumper yanked from the front end of a Cadillac.[81]

Uncle Buddie's entry was a wonder of metaphoric containment. Titled *7 Car Pile Up*, it was a chaotic assemblage of seven vintage pedal cars. Unrestored, they represented different miniaturized modes of transport, and once welded together, they were an almost unsteerable tangle. The emblematic pileup read like an auto safety advisory or a Pirandellian spectacle: seven cars in search of a crash site. Marketed to children for as long as there had been automobiles, pedal cars were also a medium of social indoctrination. Replicas of popular car models, made of steel and often painted with captivating colors, the scaled-down pedalers allowed kids to enact adulthood via that most coveted object. The pileup was more than marred metal on the road; it was about the inevitable collision with life itself, and it was deadly and out of control.

May 18 was judgment day, or at least a day of judging. Contestants in the Artists' Soapbox Derby gathered at McLaren Park, in the Excelsior district, where they showed off their vehicles, then raced down a lengthy, winding hill, bordered by bystanders. Schreier served as Uncle Buddie's de facto pit crew. Wearing a dark suit and a self-reflexive Uncle Buddie T-Shirt, Lord powered down the hill with

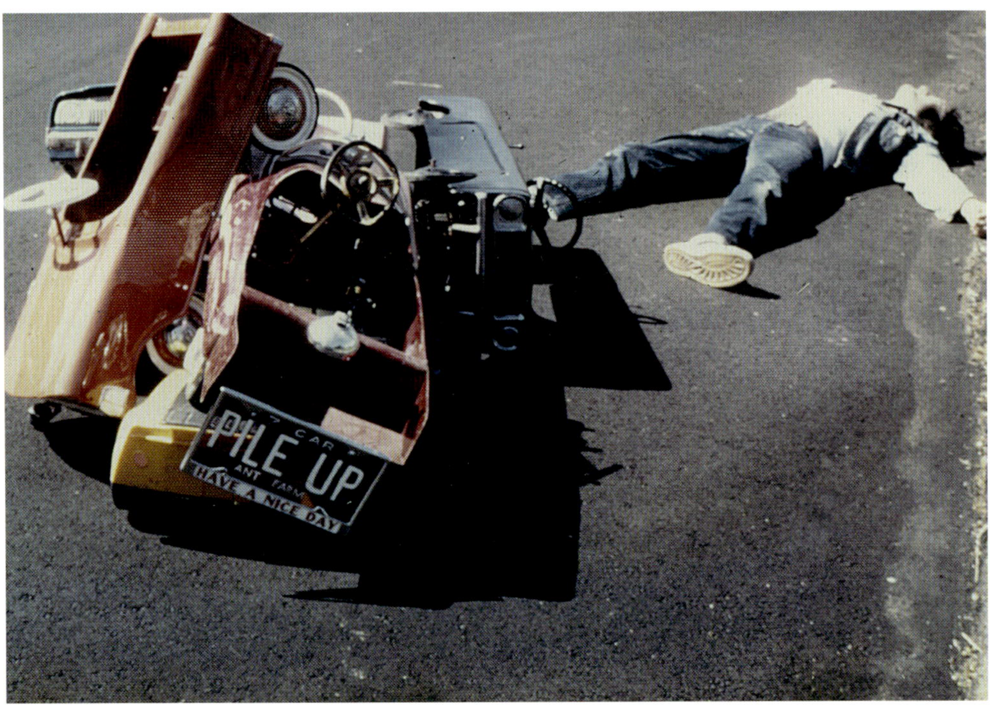

Chip Lord lying on the asphalt next to his Artists' Soapbox Derby entry, *7 Car Pile Up*. Photograph by Doug Michels.

Facing page: Chip Lord ready to pilot his Artists' Soapbox Derby entry down the hill in McLaren Park for the SFMOMA-sponsored event, June 1975. Photograph by Curtis Schreier.

a wooden lever as his only braking device. It was hell on wheels. But *7 Car Pile Up* prevailed as a transitory sculpture bent on racing to the bottom.[82]

Like *Cadillac Ranch*, *7 Car Pile Up* existed inside of an art practice that used the mythopoeic potency of the automobile as its raw material. Car culture itself could be included within this practice. An initial impulse driving this culture was the need to announce one's individuality by appropriating an industrial product and altering it, leaving one's mark on mass manufacture. Gearheads beefed up engine performance to add muscle and chopped, lowered, and painted car bodies to suit their sense of aftermarket cool. By the forties, a group of master car customizers emerged who could produce jalopies of stunning invention, technical wizardry, and peerless craft. Much-admired customizers like Ed Iskenderian, Norm Grabowski, and Blackie Gejeian produced remarkable rods while a few like George

Barris and Ed "Big Daddy" Roth became outright celebrities with audacious entries like Barris' Hirohata Mercury (1952) and Roth's Beatnik Bandit (1961). These radically ratcheted rods were objects of performative artistry that mobilized an essential American myth.[83]

Elsewhere, the automobile, its meanings, myths, and matter, captured the well-fueled imaginations of artists pursuing a practice that led to the gallery, not the racetrack. Most notably, contemporary artists like Edward Kienholz and John Chamberlain made works that relied on the motor vehicle whether whole or in scraps. Kienholz's infamous *Back Seat Dodge '38* (1964) was scandalous because of its restaging of a desperate sexual encounter. The tawdry, cramped "back seat" was intrinsic to his dark theatric, as was the bruised and truncated look of the

---

81   It should be noted that a derby car called, coincidentally, Easy Money made an appearance. It was part battering ram, part pontoon boat, part NASCAR vehicle, all sitting atop two shopping carts. Decals from auto performance product lines adorned the outer skin and, set back from the nose cone, two lengthy side cylinders were crowned with Styrofoam busts. The designer of this car remains unidentified.

82   The car was awarded a trophy for "Most Imaginative" Soapbox Derby entry.

83   Emerging during that same postwar period was a second car culture of equal artistry, the lowrider. Many of the design features of these cars, especially the intricately painted hood murals, were linked directly to Mexican American culture and aesthetics.

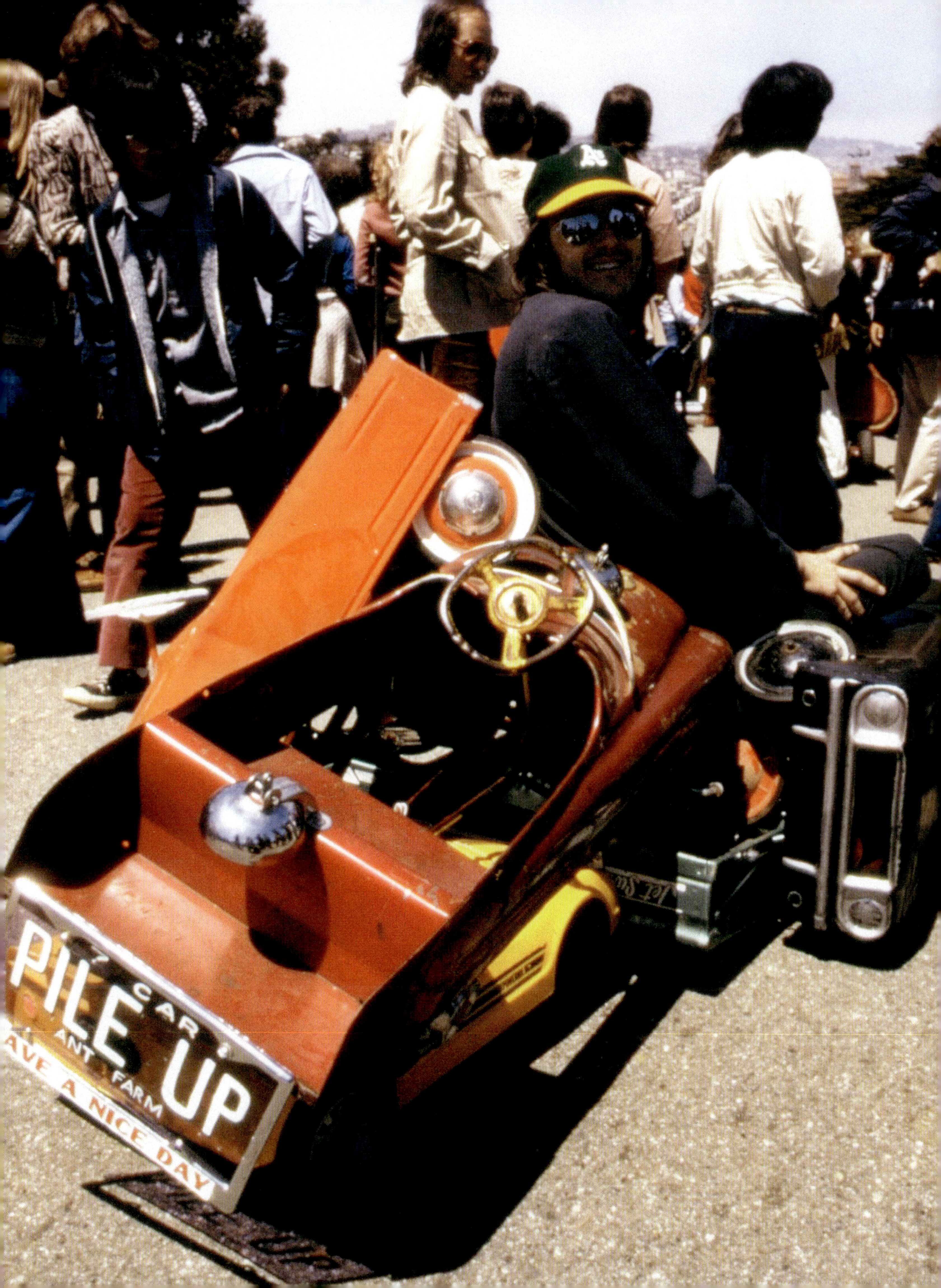
CAR
PILE UP
ANT FARM
AVE A NICE DAY

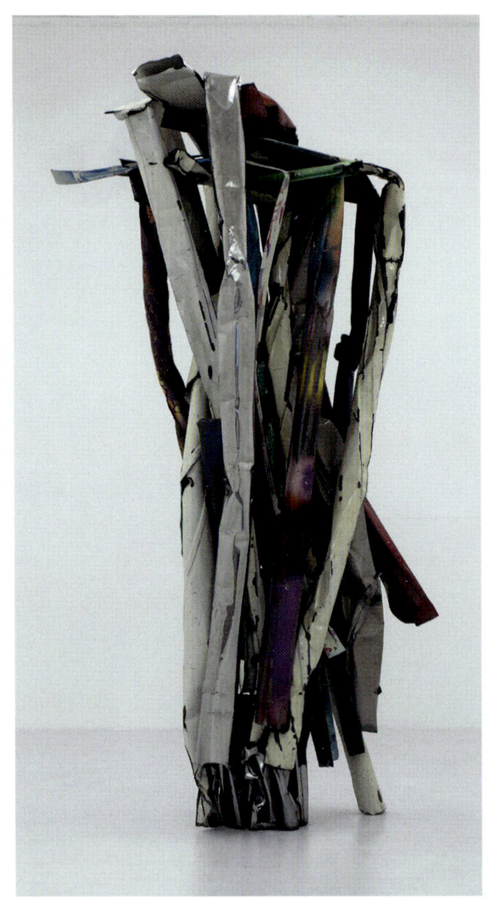

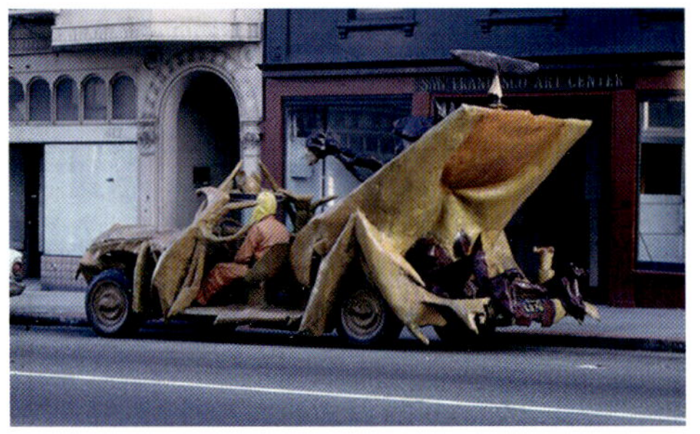

Top: *Whirled Peas* (1991), made of scrapped auto parts by John Chamberlain.

Bottom: In the mid-1960s, Fredrlc Hobbs created a mobile artform he called "parade sculpture." This is the *Trojan Horse*, an automobile chassis with stretched hide, horn-like objects, and assorted sculptural parts.

car itself. This was not a tricked-out '38 rod that would take you somewhere fast, but a junker more fit for a cul-de-sac of concupiscence. With the door flung open and the illicit couple fully exposed, the viewer became a strange voyeur in this road-to-nowhere romance.

An even more sensational use of the auto came five years later with Kienholz's *Five Car Stud* (1969–72), a nightmarish tableau that places four cars and a pickup truck in a semi-circle to illuminate (with their headlights) a group of white men having their sadistic way with a black man caught with an Anglo woman. The viewer is permitted to walk amidst this gruesome, life-size scene, experiencing in close proximity the terrifying play of racial hatred. The autos provide an edge of eerie immediacy, as though they had just arrived on the scene, their indifferent gaze lighting this tragic sight.

Where Kienholz used the automobile as a charged element in his unfolding sculptural narrative, John Chamberlain deployed Detroit detritus as a more abstract gesture. Chamberlain extended the free-form and spontaneous marks of Abstract Expressionism onto monumental assemblages, rife with jutting edges, tarnished colorations, and tottering tangles. Principally constructed from crushed or wrecked auto parts, his sculptures were grand examples of an intentional reuse that left behind the readymade associations. "My work has nothing to do with car wrecks," Chamberlain has declared. Still, it is difficult to view the voluptuous sculptures, with their bent and battered body parts, as disconnected from the screeching smash-ups that were as "accidental" as the artist's own gestures.

Chamberlain's earlier works such as *S* (1959) and *Moto* (1963) were more gravity-bound and restrained, but bold in their arrangement of salvaged materials and resident color. For several years, he retreated to geometric paintings using sprayed auto paint for his treatment. Then he abandoned the pursuit entirely, until 1972 when he resurfaced with an even more vigorous technique. This second wave of repurposed auto scrap often thrust upward like an extrusion of energy. Embodying the force of collision, these sculptures were the wreck reified, concentrated, and directed. Works like *The Hot Lady from Bristol* (1979) and *Remnant Gardens* (1986) suggest the focused liberation of impact energy, giving them a dynamic auto eroticism.[84]

With its reputation for championing the ecological, the Bay Area was still home to many an aesthetic gearhead. Having emerged from the late fifties Beat scene, Fredric Hobbs was one of them. Formerly a painter, in 1963 Hobbs introduced his new propulsive genre, "parade sculpture," precursor to the art car yet something more. By eliminating much of the car's body, Hobbs would use the remaining carriage to construct a massive assemblage of organic forms, many mimicking folk totems, thus creating a drivable sculpture. Often made from salvaged materials, there was something ritualistic, almost pagan, about this peripatetic display.[85] These eco-assemblages also freed Hobbs from the confines of the gallery, so his moveable feast gained an immediate public dimension. By the early seventies, Hobbs had redirected much of his energy toward feature filmmaking. In *Alabama's Ghost* (1973), a psychotronic oddity, the principal character, Alabama, King of the Cosmos, drives what appears to be the parade sculpture called the *Trojan Horse*. This vehicle is wrapped in a great undulating sheath of animal hide. A short film,[86] made in 1967, documents the making of the Trojan Horse, ending with Hobbs, dressed in a bright orange jumpsuit, maneuvering around San Francisco in what is undoubtedly not a street-legal car. The closing shot has the perturbed artist getting ticketed by a member of the SFPD.

If Fredric Hobbs was the feral motorhead, then Don Potts was the priestly fabricator of fantastical dragsters. Actually, just the chassis. Five years younger than Hobbs, Potts discovered early on that he had a great facility with laminated lumber. He created a number of sensual wood, leather, and fur sculptures that possessed an innate bawdiness, something that would soon vanish from his work. His masterpiece, *My First Car*, was a suite of four semi-autonomous chassis, gathered in their final configuration after six years of almost monastic concentration.[87] These

---

84   Chamberlain's return to the auto scrap medium was greatly encouraged by Stanley

---

Marsh 3. Chamberlain assembled many of his early seventies sculptures on Marsh's ranch, near Amarillo, Texas. A large work was installed outside Marsh's home when Ant Farm created *Cadillac Ranch* elsewhere on his property.

85   It would be fair to say that you can see Hobbs' progeny driving about the playa at Burning Man.

86   *Trojan Horse*, directed by Ronald Bostwick and Robert Blasdell, 1967, 27 mins.

87   This sculptural grouping was toured by the Newport Harbor Art Museum, beginning with its premiere in April 1972. Highlights of that tour

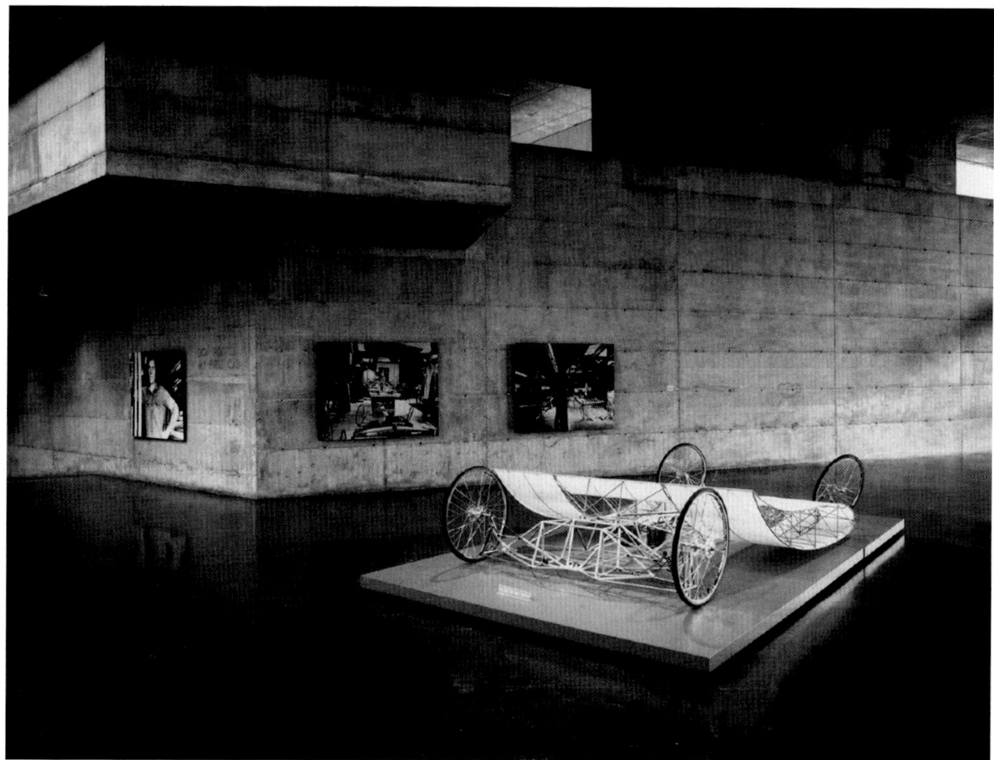

An installation image of San Francisco artist Don Potts' *My First Car* at the Berkeley Art Museum in 1972. Of the four works on display, pictured is *Fabric and Steel Body*.

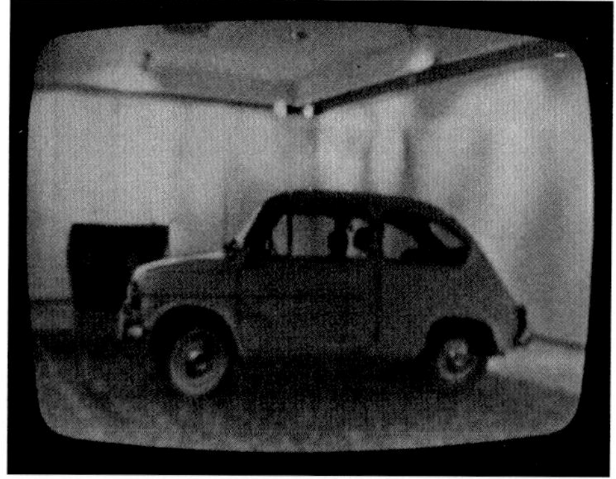

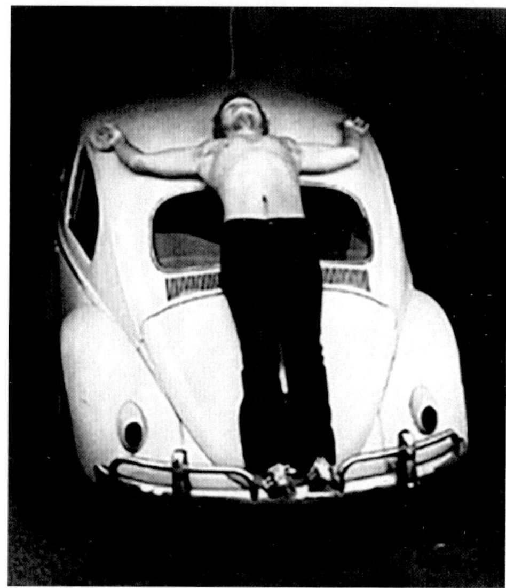

Top: An installation image of San Francisco artist Tom Marioni's *My First Car* at the de Saisset Art Museum in Santa Clara, California, March 1972.

Bottom: For the notorious performance *Trans-Fixed* (1974), Chris Burden leaned against the rear of a Volkswagen Beetle, had his hands nailed to the roof, then had the car slowly backed out of the garage. Photograph ©Chris Burden.

sculptures weren't replicas or tributes; rather they were dreams of speed, elegantly captured in material form. Exquisite craft turned every wooden strut, curved metal pipe, fiberglass foil, and aluminum manifold into its perfected aftermarket imaginary.

"Operating outside the conventions of both auto mechanics and sculpture, he [Potts] has fashioned the chassis from such diverse materials as racing bike wheels, wheelchair spokes, go-cart breaks, surplus valves from F-111 bombers, and a two-cycle aircraft engine."[88] What Potts couldn't easily turn, temper, or mold, he appropriated. In a conflation of form and function, he was able to incorporate preexisting aircraft and automotive parts into his precise visual scheme, advancing what Wayne Andersen called "the illusion of speed and power."

The initial entry in *My First Car* was *Basic Chassis*, a marvel of bent and laminated wood. An elegant skeletal framework, its perfect symmetry intimated some pent-up power, speed in suspension. The only chassis with truly implied power was the *Master Chassis*, an angular carriage with bicycle wheels and a complex strut system, bearing a McCulloch MAC-101 aircraft engine. Whether this two-stroke engine (also used for go-karts) was functional was irrelevant—its purpose was to be the centerpiece of a series of ducts, gracefully twisted pipes, and fantastical engine parts that hint at a kind of grace through motion.[89]

The final two chassis, *Stainless Body* and *Fabric and Steel Body*, were of a more gossamer nature. The intricacy of their stainless steel webbing is apparent, but their airfoils, stainless on one, diaphanous cloth on the other, almost augur weightlessness. When the means of travel is perfected the mythos of movement is null and void.[90]

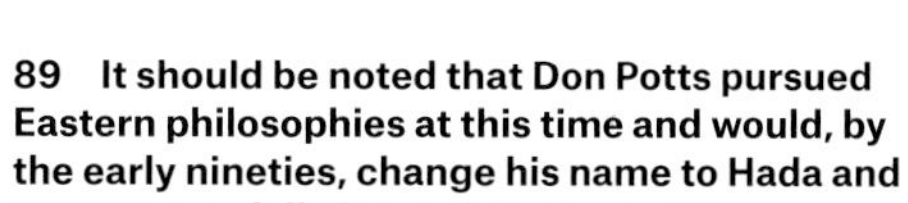

were stops at the Walker Art Center, Minneapolis; the Whitney Museum of American Art, New York; and the Museum of Contemporary Art, Chicago.

88   Wayne V. Andersen, *American Sculpture in Process: 1930–1970* (Boston: Little Brown, 1975), p. 163.

89   It should be noted that Don Potts pursued Eastern philosophies at this time and would, by the early nineties, change his name to Hada and emerge as a full-time spiritual practitioner.

90   In a strange turn of events, Potts, seeking to destroy his earthbound ego, took the three metal chassis to a San Francisco scrap yard and had them crushed on November 6, 1987. He titled this deed *The Last Performance of the Late Don Potts*.

Potts' *My First Car* hadn't even hit the road when Tom Marioni, the great art insurrectionist, put his "spoof"[91] in gear. Marioni's *My First Car* was a subversive exhibition, staged at the de Saisset Museum at Santa Clara University, in March 1972.[92] Given a $500 budget and an opening date by the museum's curator, Lydia Modi-Vitale, Marioni spent $350 on an early sixties Fiat 500 D and the remaining $150 on promotional items like a postcard and lettering on the car announcing the show. Opening night, March 3, found him driving the fifty-two-inch-wide Fiat up the broad front steps of the de Saisset, through the double doors, and onto the gallery's waiting nineteenth-century carpet.[93] Champagne glass in hand, Marioni spent the evening in the car, talking with art patrons while a video camera recorded the event.

At some significant level, Marioni's *My First Car* is about the object itself. Where Don Potts spent a half a dozen years perfecting his sculptural chassis, Marioni drove his preassembled sculpture off the lot, readymade, and used at that. To many artists of the burgeoning Conceptual movement, the object was a fetishized, overvalued affair, meant as little more than an exchange commodity for the marketplace. This mass-produced art object was antithetical to the aims of the market. It was the product of displaced creativity and its attendant labor. And rare it would be if an assembly-line car, even a sweet city car like the Fiat 500, appreciated in value.

It was Marioni's intention as an Italian Catholic artist, working beside an Italian Catholic curator and for a Jesuit institution, that classic patronage be called into play. "I believe," he explained to critic Thomas Albright, "during the Renaissance the church supported the artist … I thought the church should support an artist now, and I needed a car."[94] Sometimes the best of intentions call forth the best of resentments. By the following day, the university's president had canceled the show. Tom Marioni had wanted to give the car to the de Saisset, but instead he hung a U-turn in the gallery and headed home. Six months later, the 500cc engine blew up.

Marioni wasn't the only artist who "needed a car." And he wasn't the only artist who saw the car as a vehicle of spiritual transport. For a performance called *Trans-Fixed*, Chris Burden[95] mounted the rear fender of a Volkswagen Beetle, splayed his body out, face up, in a cruciform, and had his palms nailed to the roof. The Bug was partially backed out of the garage it was stored in,[96] the engine revved at high rpm for exactly two minutes, then the car retreated back inside. A garage as Golgotha on April 23, 1974.

Josh Baer, curator of a 2004 Burden exhibition at Zwirner and Wirth Gallery in New York, wrote, "The Volkswagen was chosen because it was the car of the 'people' and Burden wanted his crucifixion to liberate not just himself but everyone."[97] But the car of the "people" was literal, in this case, not colloquial. Desiring an auto accessible to all German citizens, Adolf Hitler promoted the Volkswagen, the people's car. Perhaps this makes it more appropriate, as the burden of mass production was the people's cross to bear.[98] Further, as Burden himself

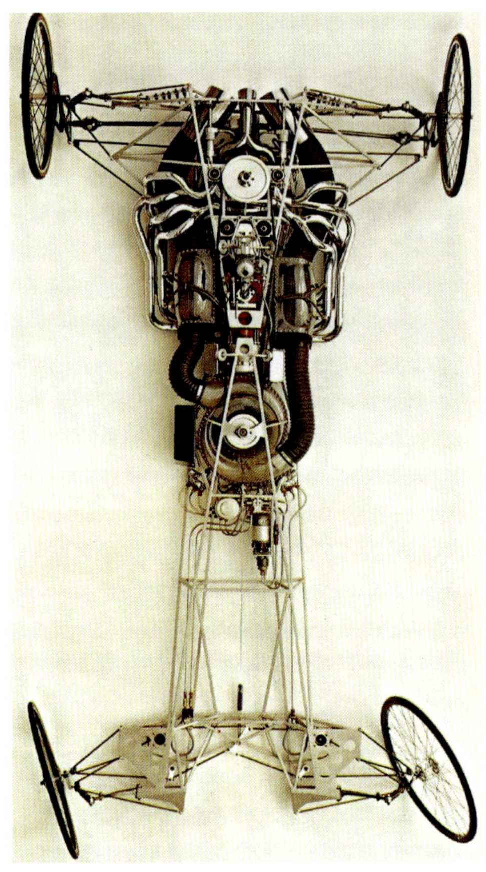

Don Potts' *Master Chassis* (1972), the most complex of the four sculptures known as *My First Car*. Photograph by Penny Dhaemers.

Facing page: A Supergraphics billboard in Doug Michels' apartment, circa 1967. Photograph by John T. Hill.

noted, the redlining engine was "screaming for me."[99]

Here, Burden's own, very real pain was ironically both masked and amplified by the car's roaring exhaust. His body melded with the body of the Volkswagen in a double bind of martyrdom.[100]

---

91   Quoted from an interview with Hilla Futterman in *Art & Artists*, August 1973.

92   Many sources, including Carl Loeffler and Darlene Tong's *Performance Anthology*, 1980, and Thomas Albright's *Art in the San Francisco Bay Area*, 1985, list Marioni's show as February 1972. Lindsey Kouvaris, curator at the de Saisset, confirmed it opened and closed on March 3, 1972.

93   Marioni insists he spread paper on this rug, thus doing it no harm, a major contention of the gallery administrators.

94   Quoted from Thomas Albright's *Art in the San Francisco Bay Area, 1945–1980: An Illustrated History* (University of California Press, 1985).

95   Burden was once described as "The Evel Knievel of Art" by critic Ellen Brown of the *Cincinnati Enquirer*, December 14, 1974.

96   The garage was on Speedway Avenue, a block from the ocean, in Venice, California.

97   Exhibition announcement, www.zwirner-andwirth.com/exhibitions/2004/0904Burden/press.html.

98   June 13, 1998, *New York Times*: "Volkswagen Faces Suit Over Jewish Slave Labor."

99   Artist's statement, www.zwirnerandwirth.com/exhibitions/2004/0904Burden/transfixed.html.

100   Burden was engaged in two other important car-related works. The first was the *B-Car* (1975), a lightweight four-wheeled vehicle that would travel 100 miles per hour and achieve 100 mpg. He built the prototype. The second project involved a 16,000-pound freight truck named Big Job. *Big Wrench* (1980) is a videowork about Burden's troubled relationship to his truck.

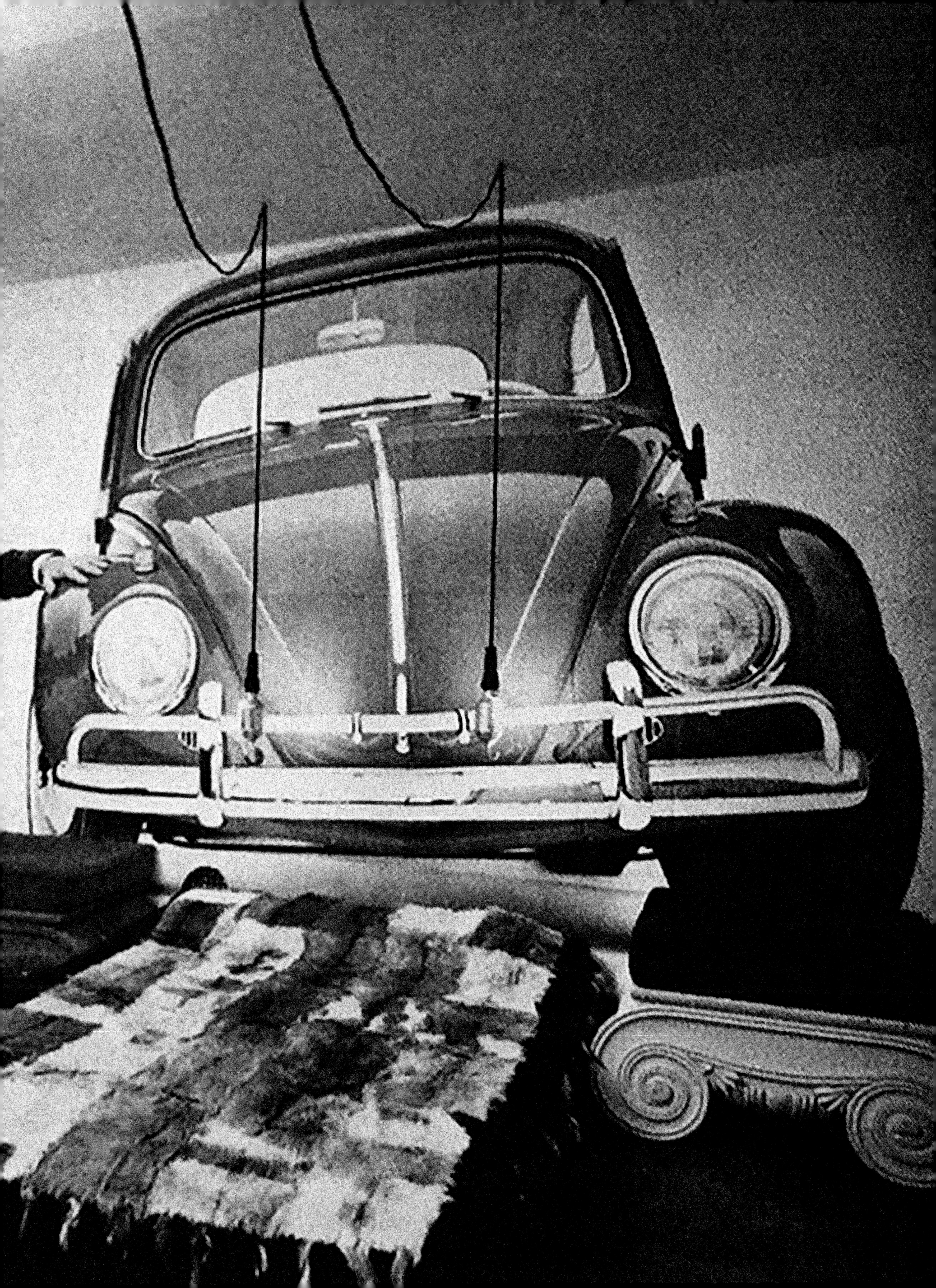

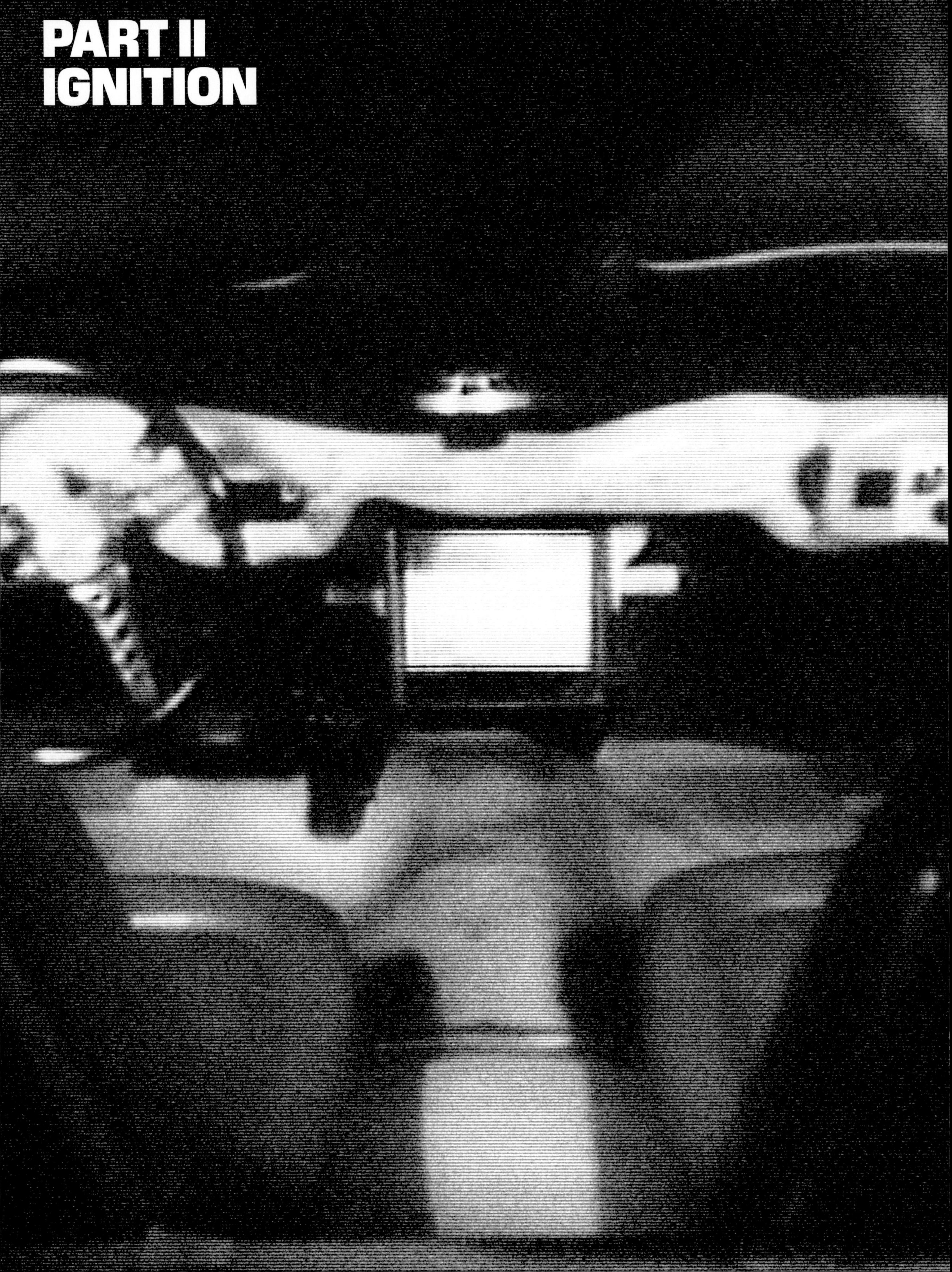
PART II
IGNITION

IN THE COMPANY OF TRUTH

Selecting the Fourth of July as detonation day opened up dramatic new possibilities for *Media Burn*. Previously, there was "just that spectacle: Boom!"[101] But Independence Day would be nothing without "the tradition of a politician speaking at a Fourth of July celebration,"[102] coaxing the question: "Who might this rousing speaker be?"

Ant Farm had several allies, aligned spirits who could be called upon to bail out unwieldy collective projects. TVTV was certainly one, as was Optic Nerve. T. R. Uthco, or Truth Company, was another. Composed of three artists—Doug Hall, Jody Procter, and Diane Andrews Hall—and a fourth occasional member, John Hillding, T. R. Uthco was founded in 1970 after its members moved to San Francisco following graduate studies at the Rinehart School of Sculpture of The Maryland Institute. Some of T. R. Uthco's earliest interventions involved parodic restagings of performance art that they dubbed "Great Moments." According to a January 4, 1975, issue of *Artweek*, "nearly every major performance artist from Acconci to Wegman receives a tasty conceptual pie in his or her face before the last Great Moment has passed."

In the fall of 1974, Hall and Procter began developing a new performance character, the presidential personality. Procter would write blustery speeches that Hall would deliver with all the overblown gestures of a pompous politician.[103] The generic Artist-President soon solidified in a figure identifiable as John F. Kennedy. Hall was quite familiar with JFK's executive comportment, having unleashed impressions of him since his college days at Harvard. The impersonation came complete with the famed Boston accent.

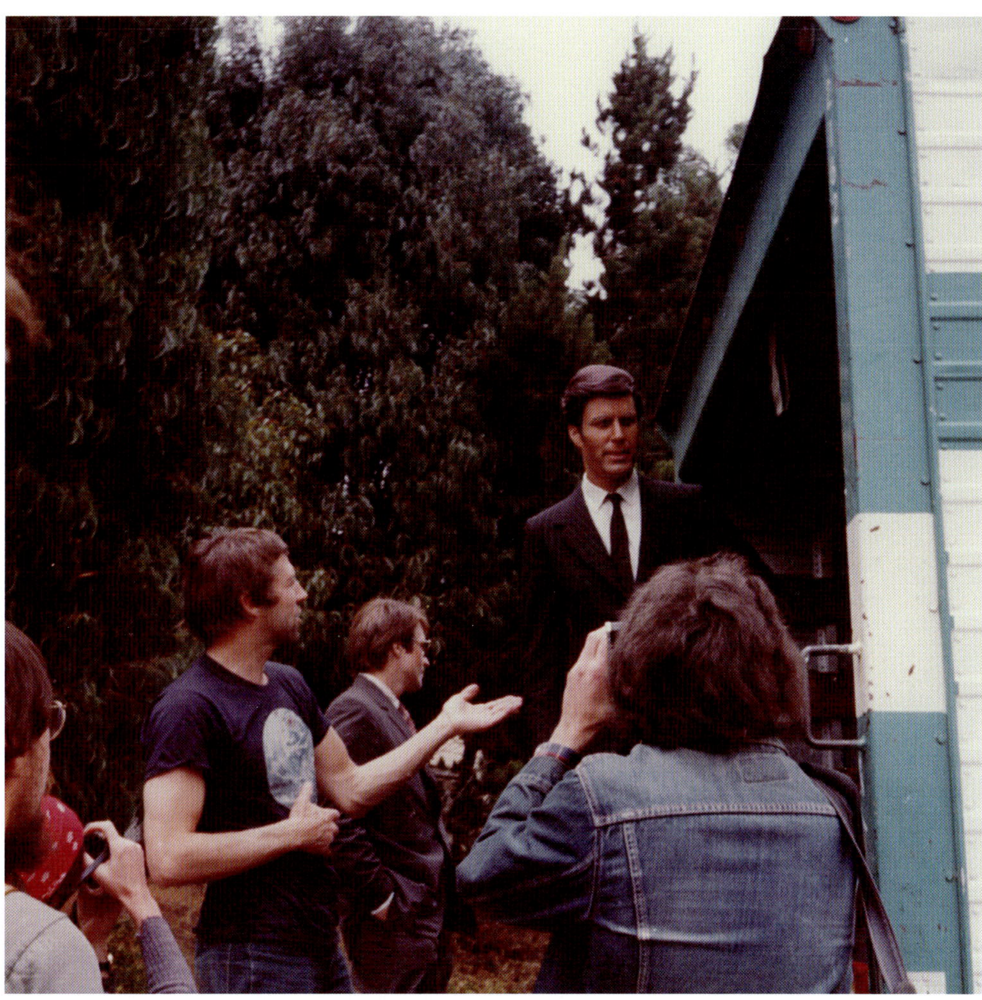

Doug Hall as the Artist-President emerging from the logistics truck, parked "backstage" at the Cow Palace. Doug Michels is to the left, wearing the Earth Day T-shirt. Photograph by Ant Farm.

Add the wizardry of a makeup artist and Hall could do an uncanny Kennedy.

Obviously, John F. Kennedy was no neutral figure; he was beloved, mourned, and idealized—the stuff of a generation's trauma. Twelve years after his assassination, Kennedy remained an open sore on the skin of American democracy. To do a send-up of JFK was rash to some, vulgar to others, but usefully jarring and pointedly iconoclastic when performed with thoughtfully barbed intention.[104]

The presence of Doug Hall as the Artist-President at *Media Burn* would elevate the proceedings, adding much-needed complexity to the whirlwind of errant signifiers: the Phantom Dream Car, towed along by the myth of upward (or at least linear) mobility; the Artist-Dummies, sacrificial pilots on a one-way trip to mediated oblivion; and the blazing pyramid of television sets, one of the seven wonders of modern manipulation.

Ascending the stairs of the bandstand, the Artist-President would issue his edifying address, establishing a tone and purpose, while focusing the gathered crowd's attention on the image to be created here. "And so my fellow Americans, let me say this finally about *Media Burn* ..."

---

101   Chip Lord, interview by Constance Lewallen, July 19, 2002. Chip Lord, Doug Michels, and Curtis Schreier were present.

102   Ibid.

103   This fascination with the gestures of power would continue. In the early 1980s, Hall would create three works—*The Speech* (1982), *This Is the Truth* (1983), and *These Are the Rules* (1983)—that stage and critique the semiotics of televisual power.

104   There is an incomplete note from Jody Procter in which he says, "Things that could be done to make it in more bad taste: 1) Have Jack wear a blood-soaked head bandage. 2) Stage a phony assassination while he is speaking. Etc etc."

THE SPEECH

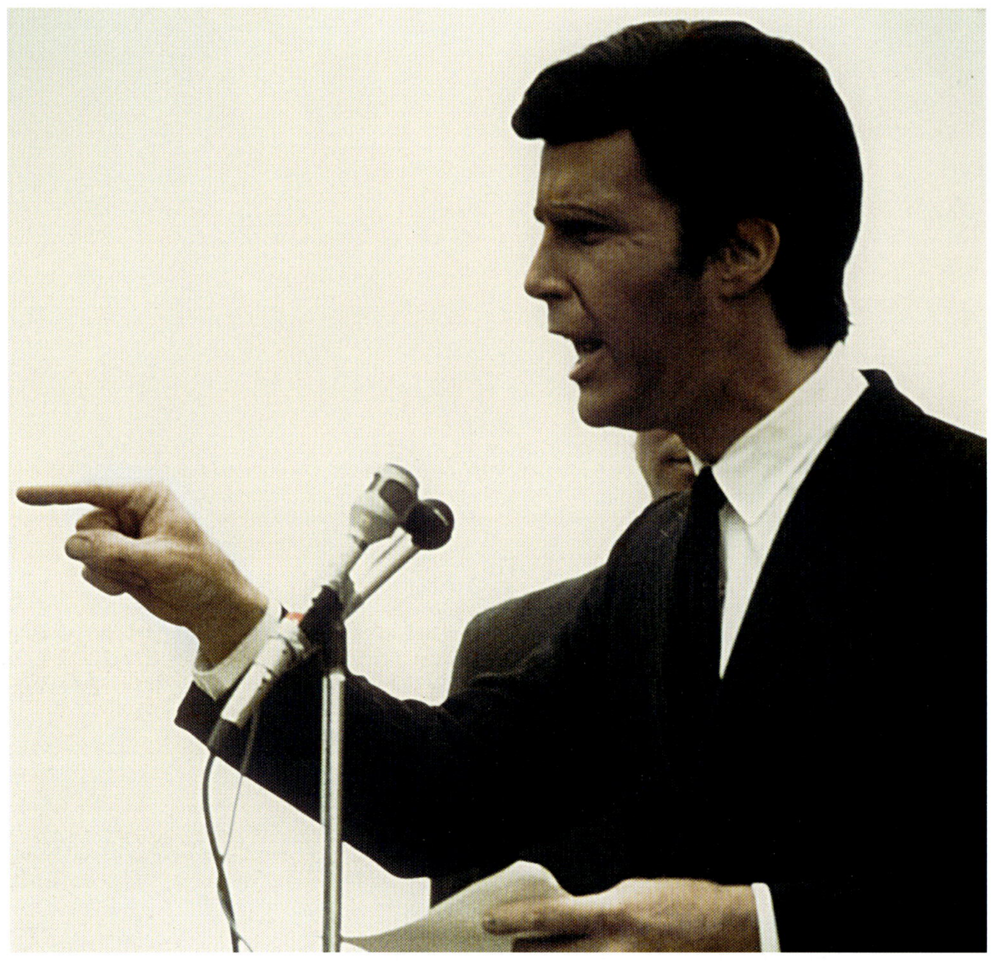

Doug Hall as the Artist-President addresses the July 4 crowd from the bandstand. Photograph by Diane Andrews Hall.

Depending on where you look, there are lots of words, most penned by Chip Lord with revisionist advice from Doug Hall and Jody Procter, as well as from external sources that were quietly tapped. There is the speech by the Artist-President before an aghast but amused audience, and the longer, more pointed version printed in the $1 souvenir booklet. There is a "first draft" lacking the tone that would soon surface and a satiric speech that would have significantly altered the reception of the event, which was (wisely) rejected.[105] There even survives, on a sheet of paper, the speech's closing lines repeated thrice with minor variations, trying to establish not just the meaning but the cadence of

the Artist-President's finale. As found in the souvenir booklet, the speech appears as a two-page spread, brazenly printed on blue White House stationery with a Presidential Seal and John F. Kennedy's signature. The impersonation begins here, donning the legitimacy and force of an official document and, better yet, making the wild surmise that if in fact the president were here to deliver a Fourth of July crowd-pleaser, this is what he would have authored. There is something almost presidential about the valiant verbiage, for these are the actual words of someone who was almost president, George S. McGovern, a standing U.S. Senator from South Dakota. The first half-dozen paragraphs in the Artist-President oration are either verbatim borrowings or close imitations of McGovern's essay, "State of the Union," published in the March 13, 1975, issue of *Rolling Stone*. A

stalwart antiwar activist, McGovern had run against Richard Nixon in 1972. His grassroots campaign failed to gather the necessary votes and his vice-presidential running mate, Thomas Eagleton, plunged the ticket into scandal when it was made known he had been treated for depression.

Defeated or not, Senator McGovern still held unexpectedly progressive views, even more necessary to voice now that the country was burdened with the Gerald Ford presidency. To counter Ford's January 15, 1975, State of the Union address, *Rolling Stone* brought McGovern on board as their respondent. "In this issue," they declared, "George McGovern assumes the role he rejected in 1972 as the principal spokesperson of the Democratic party by writing a State of the Union message considerably different than the one deliver[ed] by President Ford in January." The operative phrase here is "assumes the role." With artistic fervor, Doug Hall as the Artist-President was also assuming the role. What could be more fitting, literally, than to lift the very words of a fellow impersonator?

McGovern's State of the Union is a clear-eyed, left-leaning critique of a country burdened by an unworthy war,[106] an inflationary economy, maldistribution of wealth, aggravated energy dependence, and, ultimately, the unshakeable sway of what he termed "economic royalists."[107] He begins, as does the Artist-President, with the disquieting line, "The American spirit is uncertain." This is a great destabilizing statement, and when uttered by Doug Hall it would swiftly deflate the windbaggery of Independence Day zeal. The Ant Farm speechwriters obediently follow McGovern's ensuing words,

---

105   Penned by Jody Procter, the satiric speech was "in bad taste but not in super bad taste," as he notes in an aside on the manuscript.

---

106   The fall of Saigon would occur in the next month.

107   In 1936, Franklin D. Roosevelt delivered his "A Rendezvous with Destiny" speech in Philadelphia. He coined the phrase "economic royalists" to describe a class of privileged citizens whose dynasties were "built upon concentration of control over material things. Through new uses of corporations, banks and securities, new machinery of industry and agriculture, of labor and capital—all undreamed of by the Fathers—the whole structure of modern life was impressed into this royal service."

The State of the Union by George S. McGovern

The American spirit is uncertain. First there was an unworthy, unended war. Then there was Watergate. Now there is economic collapse. And from these things has come not only the dangerous condition of our country, but a pervasive doubt about our capacity to correct it.

I believe we can find solutions in our origins.

Our nation comes from a revolution against political tyranny. Now we must finish that revolution by replacing the structure of economic privilege and by repudiating the tyranny of the warmakers.

What has happened to us is not a random visitation of fate. It is the result of forces which have assumed control of the American structure—economic royalists as oppressive as the Crown 200 years ago. These forces are militarism, monopoly and the maldistribution of wealth.

Militarism still depletes our economy because it still dominates our foreign policy.

The horror of Vietnam continues, now with surrogate bullies firing American bullets and dropping American bombs. American troops are gone; the color of the bodies has changed, but the bodies still fall to save the face of the militarists who wanted this war, who fought it with our sons and who lost it. The militarists are still lavishing arms and money on the generals in Saigon who will not keep the peace agreement because they want more war to keep their own power.

Lately we have been shocked by revelations about the CIA and domestic spying. But these are not isolated evils any more than Vietnam has been simply a tactical mistake. CIA spying symbolizes our strategy for the rest of the world turned inward — a bad barrel spoiling the apples.

In fact it is entirely reasonable to suppose that Watergate itself was just a logical extension of dirty tricks abroad—all "in the national interest."

But the still dirtier trick is the one we play on ourselves and others by giving first call on our wealth to the militarists who measure our position in the world solely by the size of the arms establishment we can rattle to impress friends or foes; to the militarists who do not believe that foreign policy exists to serve the country and instead believe that the country exists to serve the global ambitions of the elite.

The domination of militarists is the only way to explain what has happened, for example, in the Strategic Arms Limitation Talks.

Scientists have estimated that, if they were properly targeted, the bombs and missiles of either the United States or the Soviet Union could destroy all human life on the planet 50 times over. Our own stockpile is now equal to roughly 615,000 Hiroshimas and is still mounting.

It requires no extraordinary common sense to suggest that we reverse this arms race. Instead SALT has become another excuse to build more weapons we do not need, but which the Pentagon and its Kremlin counterpart want anyway. Now we multiply missiles and warheads not merely to "maintain superiority" or to be a "first-rate power" but, ironically, to serve as "bargaining chips" in arms-control negotiations.

Yet in the end we never bargain away anything we already have. The "bargaining chips" join the permanent arms establishment and arms control becomes another way of saying arms competition.

This happens because the ground rules are set in the Pentagon. Never mind what we can negotiate with the Russians; what can we negotiate with the Joint Chiefs of Staff? Not much, apparently, for the arms agreement announced recently at Vladivostok actually calls for a dramatic increase in nuclear arms.

The same view shapes our conventional commitments. Not counting naval manpower at sea, we have 400,000 American troops stationed around the globe with half of them in Europe. Most of them could come home without endangering our security. But our policy is not confined to security; it reaches toward empire. American forces stay in Europe as "bargaining chips." An American division remains in South Korea so the dictatorship there will have a "bargaining chip" if it ever decides to negotiate with the North. In Vietnam, we inflicted such incurred terrible losses long after it was clear that the war was lost so that Secretary Kissinger would have a "bargaining chip" for the return of our prisoners — which we could have secured years before simply by withdrawing our forces.

This year the Pentagon will demand over $100 billion to perpetuate this insanity. The generals will claim three-fifths of all the money Congress can spend just to underwrite past and present wars and to maintain a far-flung military machine for the future.

Of course the United States is not alone. Worldwide military spending now totals more than $250 billion each year—more than the combined Gross National Product of Africa, the Middle East and South Asia. The Institute for World Order estimates that from 1960 through 1972 the nations of the world have spent $2400 billion—$2.4 trillion —on arms.

But we unquestionably lead the way among developed nations and we set the example for the rest. The United States accounts for more than a third of all arms spending in the world. We were the first country to develop and the only country to use nuclear arms and strategy. In every phase of the arms race we have been running practice laps and then daring other aspirants to catch up. We propagate an ethic of militarism which has no decent relevance to the problems the world has or the solutions the world needs.

We have the option, if we choose it, to turn toward peace instead and to take others with us.

That choice is now a matter of necessity as well as morality. For we have learned, if very late, that the militarism which brings repression to millions abroad also brings chaos to our own economy. The arms industry is parasitic. It consumes our resources, but returns nothing that can be bought or sold or used to add to the national wealth. Economic breakdown was an inevitable result of maintaining an all-out war economy for 35 years.

It is time to say no to the militarists. We must refuse to be persuaded that the process of negotiation is more important than their purpose. We must repudiate the "bargaining chip" absurdity and reduce a bloated arms budget. We must reject a $20 billion B-1 bomber and the host of other useless refinements in overkill.

A rational assessment of any external threat and a realistic understanding of the costs, the futility and the danger of arms will take away tens of billions of dollars from the Pentagon. And it will wipe away the stain of a militarism which supplies the means for torture in Chile, fuels dictatorship and forces human misery in Vietnam, Korea, the Philippines and elsewhere.

The second force disrupting our national economy is monopoly—the concentration of corporate enterprise which makes us a people without power in our own marketplace.

Just 200 massive corporations now control nearly two-thirds of America's manufacturing assets. And mass means power.

It means not only economic power to control the market but political power to guarantee a privileged position. It means lavish advertising budgets to brainwash the consumer in favor of senseless differentiations. It means influencing and often dominating the government regulatory agencies which are supposed to protect the consumer. It means enterprise that need not be concerned with sound business principles and quality products because there is no threat of competition and, in any case, the government will always save the day with a regulatory ruling, a new tax loophole or a Lockheed loan.

Most of all the concentration of industrial wealth means free enterprise rules· cannot work. Economic remedies based on those rules are predestined to fail.

We have heard that we suffer skyrocketing inflation in a faltering economy simply because food and petroleum have been in short supply. It has hardly been mentioned that those commodities are controlled by two of the most concentrated industries.

The nature of the oil industry has been exposed in a short and painful time. Just seven multinational companies control 80% of the world's supply of petroleum. They control it from the well to the gas pump and at every stage in between. The consumer's sacrifice has been big oil's opportunity to extort more government favors and secure an even tighter grip on the market. And now the shared petroleum monopoly is striving to become an energy monopoly by buying up coal companies and leases on Western coal reserves.

In the food industry the six largest grain dealers handle 90% of all wheat; one soup company, Campbells, sells 90% of all soup; four large processors control 90% of all breakfast food; in each of more than 200 major metropolitan areas four large grocery chains control more than half of the retail sales.

What is the effect on prices and profits? Even that is hard to learn because business refuses to tell. Continental Baking, for example, is owned by ITT which does not report the profits of its subsidiaries separately. Safeway, a large food manufacturer as well as a retailer, publishes only companywide figures. Nearly all conglomerates practice a similar concealment.

But we can measure the dollar impact from field to table. Last August, when ranchers were receiving 27% less for their cattle than a year earlier, retail meat prices were nearly 12% higher. While the wheat earnings of farmers went down 5%, bread prices shot up 35%.

The consumer's money is disappearing somewhere. We must find out why that happens and where it goes. This year the Senate Committee on Nutrition and Human Needs will search out the truth through a comprehensive investigation of the food industry.

Giantism, not only in food and oil but across the economy, is a major underlying cause of inflation. One stand defines a shared monopoly as four or fewer firms controlling 50% or more of a market—and one Federal Trade Commission report has concluded that if the market share of those firms could be cut to 40% or less, prices would fall by at least 25%.

Against these estimates it is foolish to expect that any fiscal or monetary policy will work, whether the adversary is inflation or recession or both. This is a post-Keynesian economy. A monopolistic structure can bleed off every stimulus and pass on every restraint. It will stifle each answer we try.

It will welcome especially the answers which have so far prevailed—the "trickle down" tax cuts, price hikes and deregulations which swell profits without ever sharing a portion with the people.

If entrenched power defeats economic management now, it also disrupts intelligent economic priorities for the future.

No one was ever born, for example, with a taste for huge gas-guzzling automobiles. That is one of so many

CAPITOL CHATTER

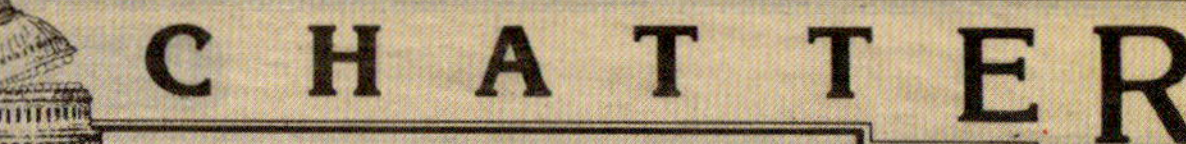

On the very same day that President Ford requested an additional $522 million in aid for Southeast Asia and Secretary Kissinger said he didn't want the appropriation to "reopen" the Vietnam debate, there was a special Congressional preview in Washington D.C. of *Hearts and Minds*, the bitter antiwar documentary on Vietnam.

The guest list included 83 congressmen and senators [**Gary Hart** (D-Colorado), **Quentin Burdick** (D-North Dakota), **Les Aspin** (D-Wisconsin), **Don Fraser** (D-Minnesota), **Bob Kastenmeier** (D-Wisconsin)], assorted celebrities [**Candice Bergen** and **Mike Nichols**] and reporters [**Sy Hersh**, **Carl Bernstein** and **Eric Sevareid**].

When the credits rolled at the end of the film, no one moved from their seats. Producer Bert Schneider said it was the same as any other showing of the film. "People are lost inside themselves when it's over," he said. "It's very encouraging. It tells me that congressmen are people. Sometimes we forget that and sometimes I don't believe it, but tonight they are human."

"I'm sure President Ford hasn't heard about the film," Father **Robert Drinan** (D-Massachusetts) said sarcastically as he left. "I'm beginning to think that the administration puts this request [for more aid] in very unacceptable terms, knowing that it'll be refused by the Congress, knowing that Vietnam eventually will be reunited, knowing that Saigon will fall. Then the administration will try to blame this on the Democratic Congress . . . I suppose it will come to McCarthyism. It's conceivable, but I hope I'm wrong."

Senator **Jacob Javits** (R-New York) was clearly flustered by the film. He refused to comment, then added that, as a member of the Senate Foreign Relations Committee, he would have to consider the president's request. "I've seen these things before," he said of the film, "But it's still very impressive."

Daniel Ellsberg walked out of the theater so distraught he couldn't talk to anyone. He had seen himself, on film, break into tears and choke back sobs as he recalled meeting with Robert Kennedy the day he was shot in Los Angeles.

Max Baucus, a freshman Democrat from Montana, said the film would play in Missoula (or Peoria). "I think the film would be very effective in Montana. It carried its message very well. It just strengthened my own views."

Boston School Committee member **John J. Kerrigan**, after being splattered with paint by protesting students at Boston State College: "They were just a couple of kids with low mentality—most likely journalism majors." . . . A favorite guessing game in Washington these days is how much CBS News paid **Gordon Liddy** for that interview with **Mike Wallace** on *60 Minutes*. CBS News won't say anything officially, but estimates range from $15,000 to $30,000.

One of the best stories to emerge (rather belatedly) from the Democratic midterm convention in Kansas City concerns **Hubert Humphrey**: It seems that after **George McGovern** gave his rousing and very well received speech, Humphrey charged the podium and demanded that he be allowed to speak too. Party chairman **Bob Strauss** attempted to calm Hubert down, explaining that there wasn't time and that the convention had to get on with the business of ratifying the new party charter. But Humphrey rattled on, causing one nearby delegate to suggest, "Someone should drive a stake through that man's heart." Unable to gain access to the podium, Humphrey immediately called a press conference which, according to our sources, "went on for two hours, until the last high school newspaper reporter got tired and left."

The State of the Union

created demands. Yet the auto industry holds hostage the workers who could make smaller cars. For ransom the auto manufacturers expect to have environmental safeguards relaxed and taxes for the wealthy reduced, so they can continue to sell big cars.

Some Americans are cold this winter and we will all suffer in the future because there is too little fuel to run all the Cadillacs and heat all the homes at the same time.

Now a helpless government is supposed to say to the American people: "You can drive your cars—and you can breathe nitrogen instead of air; you can accept more emphysema, more lung disease, more despoilation of the commons; you can threaten your children's future to comfort yourselves. That is the only choice we dare to offer."

The arms industry exerts a similar control. Aerospace corporations hold their workers hostage for higher arms budgets and a permanent arms race. It is too complicated to retool and convert to peacetime pursuits, too hard to meet the demand for the necessities of life — for housing, health or mass transit.

Despite the Sherman Act, the Clayton Act and regulatory laws, government has not been a contestant on behalf of the public, but a servant of monopoly power. In that role government only worsens our economic plight.

So instead of leaving antitrust laws to languish in the hands of a lax administration, the new Congress must strengthen them and demand their enforcement.

If there are places where free enterprise cannot be made to work government has an obligation to intervene on behalf of the public with long-term economic controls—not only on prices and wages, but on profits and interest rates as well.

The Nixon administration gave controls a bad name. But the fault was not in government itself; it was in the incompetence and corruption of the men in the White House. The last and worst effect of Watergate will be if we henceforth measure the capacity of our system by the culpability of Nixon.

We must move to democratize our economy so the buyer will not always have to beware of shoddy products, swollen prices and stolen resources.

And government has much to do as an agent of effective economic planning.

The monopolists denounce a "planned economy" as heresy. But what they really oppose is not planning—for the most part our economy is already shaped by a handful of officials. Raw materials are used or abused, prices are set and profits are maintained not by the operation of free market forces, but by the bureaucrats of the corporate structure. What the monopolists object to is any measure of planning for the public good instead of private profits. What they say is that we are restricting free enterprise; what they mean is that they want unrestricted power to manipulate an unfree enterprise system.

Through direct public participation in the management of major corporations or through federal chartering or through other measures, we must direct private economic plans according to the public interest. We have intervened before to protect monopoly and to preserve kinds of enterprise that have outlived their time; now we must intervene to save our economy and to convert wasteful or harmful enterprise to essential work for the nation.

The third flaw in our economic structure is the maldistribution of national income.

The statistics are as simple as they are shameful: For the last 20 years, despite heralded social programs, poverty wars and the rest, the relative distribution of America's national wealth has stayed essentially the same. The most prosperous fifth of the population receives more than 40% of all money income. The poorest fifth barely exists on a tenth as much.

There must be a reasonable incentive for individual initiative—but that is no reason for insensitivity to human deprivation. Perhaps no society in the world can be truly classless—but that is no excuse for a class-dominated economy in America.

Millions of Americans need and want jobs which are not there. Past leadership has played a cruel trick on them. It has scorned them as "loafers" and worse. At the same time it has called full employment a "myth," and has contrived to drive unemployment to the highest level in a generation. Government has forced the indignity of joblessness, then compounded the pain with derision.

We must replace this economics of exploitation with an economics of equity. Our policy must be a prosperity fairly achieved and fairly distributed.

That means first that the burdens of today's crisis and its immediate solutions must be fairly shared. We must conserve energy. But we must do it through an equitable system of rationing, not through devices to raise prices so the wealthy can buy all they want while the poor cannot afford what they need. We must stimulate the economy. But we must do it through public investment and the reduction of regressive payroll taxes, not through a new feast of tax rebates and loopholes for the rich. We must preserve today's jobs and create millions more. But we must do it by converting the economy to meet urgent national needs, not by across-the-board investment credits that subsidize the wrong endeavors and subvert the redirection of enterprise.

For more than a decade tax reform has been a campaign rallying cry, sometimes even a title on legislation, but never a reality of economic life. Now we must make it real, not only to demonstrate our political freedom from big money, but to pay the cost of critical public work.

With the revenue from tax reform and the savings from military cuts we can invest in shelter for people who cannot find it at their price or any price; we can invest directly in new sources of energy to break the monopoly of oil; we can invest in food production and a fair food delivery system to nourish ourselves and nations in famine at reasonable cost; we can underwrite mass transit for both people and goods, to break our dependence on the automobile; we can at last end our shameful trailing position in international health comparisons and establish a national health insurance system to take the dollar sign off human survival.

It is folly to talk of massive permanent tax cuts with those tasks before us. And it is folly to suffer mass unemployment. With a decent public agenda, we will require only an occasional resort to temporary public service employment to guarantee a job for every American who is able to work.

And for little more than it costs now to maintain a bureaucratic welfare maze, we can act through the tax structure to guarantee a fair minimum income to those who cannot work and a supplemental income for those whose work barely sustains them between the higher reaches of poverty and the lower edges of a decent life. As the food stamp program does now for just one human necessity, we must erase for all necessities the divisive line between the oppressed who have jobs and the oppressed who do not.

Just as the morality of an Asian war challenged America's conscience in the Sixties, so the distribution of our resources and the fairness of our economy will be the test of our character in the Seventies. We cannot serve both the people and the exploiters. We must fight for the people, to give them back their economy.

The Constitution charges the president to report on the state of the Union. In his message to the Congress, President Ford conceded the obvious: "The state of the Union is not good." But he also called for policies which will make it worse. At every point where the president had a choice, he picked a policy that will help the rich and hurt the rest of us. Nowhere did he discuss the underlying causes of crisis.

Our time has been stained by the bloodiest wars and the darkest genocide. Yet we are confronted still by stark questions of human and national existence.

We dare not respond with conventional rhetoric, with empty measures, with paper promises signifying nothing but a thirst for political power. For the people know better. They seek leadership that will shake and reshape things as they are, for they know we cannot go on the way we have been.

There is a great wave cresting across America. It first stirred and then mounted during the protest against racism and war; it has been swelled by a revulsion against the corruption of our values and a revolt against the exploitation of our economy.

The economic royalists will fight to turn it aside. For it threatens to sweep over the status quo and sweep down the walls which guard the citadels of economic privilege.

But for us this is not a threat; it is an opportunity. For if we ride and reinforce the wave of change, then before it is spent, we will restore the ideals of this land and lift the quality of life among ourselves and for our brothers and sisters around the world.

a short list of the bad that has befallen us: "political scandal,"[108] "economic turmoil," and "a pervasive doubt about our ability to correct it." Then a finely phrased corrective: "I believe we can find solutions in our origins." Here, the breadth of history and the Founding Fathers are invoked: "Our nation comes from a revolution against political tyranny. Now we must finish that revolution by replacing the structure of economic privilege and by repudiating the tyranny of the warmakers and the moneymakers."

Then another pithy phrase that rings in the ear: "What has happened to us is not a random visitation of fate." For emphasis Ant Farm swaps out words, substituting "What has gone wrong with America is …" This verbal maneuver leaves behind the individual for a body, a body politic now ailing. "It is the result of forces which have assumed control of the American structure—economic royalists as oppressive as the Crown 200 years ago. These forces are militarism, monopoly and the maldistribution of wealth."

But now Ant Farm begins asserting their new direction by nixing the "maldistribution of wealth" in favor of "and the mass media." With several thousand more words in his State of the Union address, McGovern had time to broach a plethora of ills, from domestic spying by the CIA to trickle-down tax cuts, from the SALT treaty to antitrust laws, from the corporate food chain to rising unemployment. Anxious to engage their eager audience, Ant Farm would bring the mass media front and center from the podium while staying closer to the Senator in the souvenir booklet: "Militarism depletes our economy because it still dominates our foreign policy … The arms industry consumes our resources but returns nothing to the national wealth. But foremost, our expanding militarism is morally wrong. AND I SAY IT IS TIME TO SAY NO TO THE MILITARISTS!"

This should be an award-winning compression algorithm. Ant Farm retains the spirit of McGovern's antimilitary rant, but the rhetorical distance between their opening line ("Militarism depletes") and their rousing finale ("NO TO THE MILITARISTS!") is an additional 750 argumentative words. Ant Farm then continues: "The second force disrupting our country is Monopoly. Today just 200 corporations control nearly two-thirds of America's manufacturing assets. Not only

economic control of markets, but political control to guarantee themselves a privileged position. These monopolies often dominate government regulatory agencies which are supposed to protect the citizen. And this too is morally wrong. NOW I SAY IT IS TIME TO END MONOPOLY BY BUSINESS RULERS!"

The above argument also heavily truncates McGovern's grand unraveling of the injustices levied by the "economic royalists." By broaching the two previous perils, militarism and monopoly, Ant Farm is able to broaden the context of *Media Burn*. Though the main target is mass media, they gain scope from this collateral critique of other systemic ills. A more sweeping statement also lends weightier credibility to the final, unforgettable statement.

After abbreviating the speech thus far, the Artist-President resumes. He is now ready to reveal his real intent, to lambast the mass media.

> Television because of its technology and the way it must be used can only produce autocratic political forms, hierarchies, and hopeless alienation. Mass media monopolies control people by their control of information. In our vast society, it is virtually impossible to escape the influence of commercial advertising.[109]

> And who can deny that we are a nation addicted to television and the constant flow of media? And not a few of us are frustrated by this addiction.[110]

> Now I ask you, my fellow Americans, haven't you ever wanted to put your foot through your television screen?[111]

This was not a rhetorical question asked by our Artist-President. If, as was said in the souvenir booklet, "99.9% of all homes in the USA with electricity have TV sets,"

this assured that many (if not all) members of the audience, presumably standing on two feet at that very moment, had at least one foot they wanted to propel toward their TV screen. The commonality being TV ownership, the shared political orientation being infuriation, this was, in effect, an appeal to mobilize the audience's frustration with the Tube.

Jerry Mander's influential book, *Four Arguments for the Elimination of Television*, would not be released until 1977, but its influence rode upon a preexisting cultural sentiment.[112] "Kill Your Television" was already a favored slogan; FCC Chairman Newton N. Minow had long ago declared television to be a "vast wasteland"; the TV-Turnoff Week had been launched in 1974; grassroots movements would rally around such books as Raymond Williams' *Television: Technology and Cultural Form*;[113] and anti-television groups like White Dot would gain followings decades after *Media Burn*.

In the coming videotape version of the performance, Doug Michels, wearing his Artist-Dummy jumpsuit, would reinforce this notion, stating in an impromptu interview: "If everyone in America would burn just one TV set …"

---

108   "Political scandal" here is a direct substitute for McGovern's inclusion of Watergate.

109   In the souvenir booklet, this text would follow "commercial advertising": "be it billboards on our highways, ad messages on the airwaves, or ad layout in our magazines and newspapers."

110   The souvenir booklet contains a two-page spread with "Television Addiction Statistics." This spread has a condensed version of a general statement handed out to the press that compares television addiction to heroin. A graphic used in the eventual videotape displays a series of statistics such as "26% of each hour is advertising" and "There are 60.5 million TV sets in American homes."

111   Following this rousing question would be the souvenir booklet text: "I SAY IT IS TIME TO LOOSEN THE GRIP OF MASS MEDIA ON THE FLOW OF INFORMATION AND IMAGES!"

112   The August 3, 1975, issue of Francis Ford Coppola's *City* magazine published a truncated version of Mander's not-yet published book, summarized here as "The Case for the Elimination of Television," starting on pages 24-25, then continuing in the back of the issue. Spread across the double-truck of pages 26–27 is a visualization of Mander's statement embodied by the grand collision from *Media Burn* as taken by Diane Hall. A very bold typeface announces "MEDIA BURN" in a vertical column and "AN EVENT BY THE ANT FARM" burned into the image itself. This issue came off the press less than one month after the July 4 performance.

113   Like Jerry Mander, Raymond Williams resided in the San Francisco area while preparing his very influential study of a communications technology that "could control our whole social process … But they are also the tools of what would be … a short and successful counter-revolution, in which, under cover of talk about choice and competition, a few para-national corporations … could reach farther into our lives." (New York: Schocken Books, 1974), p. 151.

THE SPEECH PART TWO

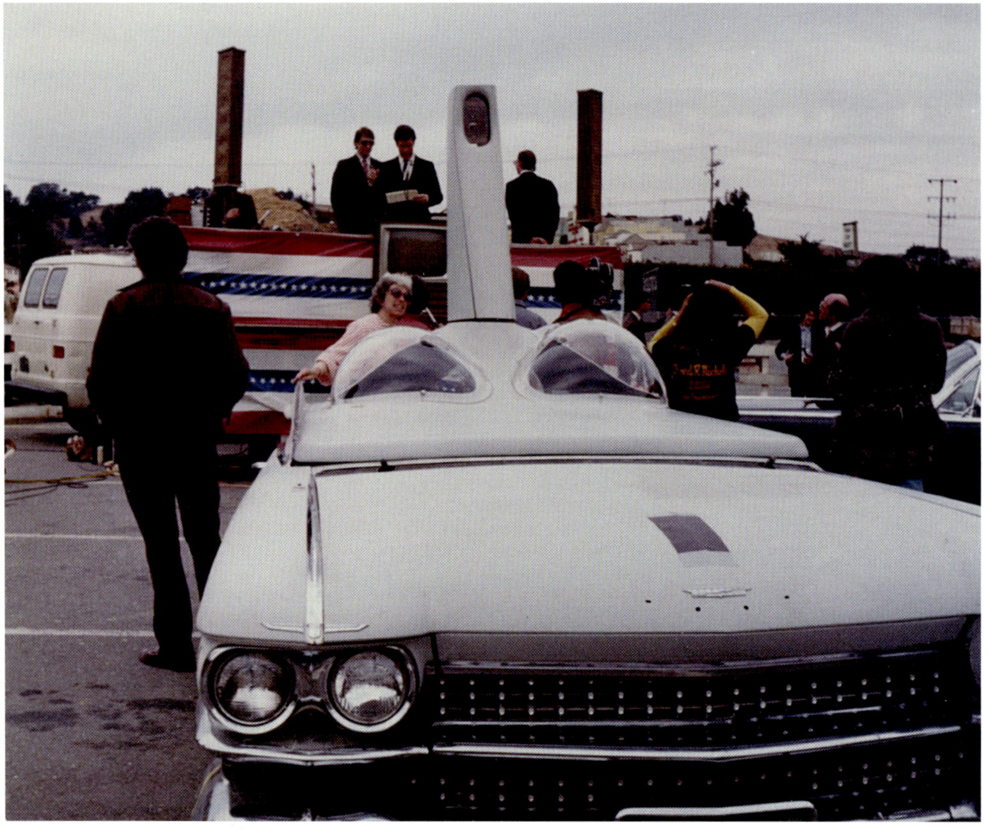

View of the bandstand from the front end of the Phantom Dream Car. Doug Hall as the Artist-President is reading his notes. Photograph by Ant Farm.

"Now I ask you, my fellow Americans, haven't you ever wanted to put your foot through your television screen?" Not just a question, but a question issued in the unique Boston tempos of a dead president. On the bandstand between strips of patriotic bunting, a television console was mounted where the presidential seal might hang. Yet this affixed screen was as dead as the president himself—the Commander-in-Chief of the Televisual, expired. With the ideological underpinnings in place, the Artist-President could shift his attention to the imminent spectacle, the Artist-Dummies and their date with destiny. "Today there stand before us two media matadors, brave young men from Ant Farm who are about to go forth into the unknown."

But I must stop here and correct a mis-attribution. In the souvenir booklet, this section of the speech begins with an elaboration, explaining the "media matador" reference: "As Robert Blake wrote about matadors: 'Bullfight critics row on row

crowd the enormous Plaza de Toros, but only one is there who knows, and he is the one who fights the bull.'"

There is attribution for the poem, titled "Bullfight Poem," translated from Spanish by Robert Graves, famed poet and classicist. Graves was fluent in Spanish, having lived in Majorca for decades, and in his masterwork *The White Goddess* (1948), he writes about the origins of the cult of bulls that migrated from Rome to Spain. It is also known who wrote the original poem: the famous bullfighter Domingo Ortega, who was an active matador throughout the thirties and forties.

This poem has a peculiar history of mistaken identities, and Ant Farm joins this fine tradition. In an April 11, 1971, letter to the editor of the *Washington Post*, Congressman F. Edward Hebert wrote, "President Kennedy was fond of quoting some lines from the Spanish poet Garcia Lorca," and followed with the Ortega poem. Kennedy, in fact, did quote the poem during an October 16, 1962,

meeting with the National Foreign Policy Conference for Editors and Radio-TV Public Affairs Broadcasters.[114] Reciting from memory, Kennedy misquoted the poem itself: Bullfight critics row on row / Fill the enormous Plaza de Toros / But only one is there who knows / And he is the one who fights the bull.[115]

How Kennedy came to know this poem is explained in yet another letter to the editor, this time to *Life* magazine on August 6, 1965. "Can Mr. Schlesinger give us the name and author of a favorite poem of John Kennedy that referred to the matadors and the bulls?" the writer asks. After the verse in question is presented, Arthur Schlesinger Jr. replies: "The author is Bullfighter Domingo Ortega who, at the time of the Bay of Pigs disaster, sent a signed photograph to Kennedy with these lines inscribed as a gesture of sympathy and encouragement at what he felt was a difficult moment for the President."

The Bay of Pigs took place in April 1961; Kennedy's off-the-cuff use of the poem was delivered during the Cuban Missile Crisis in October 1962. This simple bit of doggerel explains much about the horns of a dilemma. It is only the man in the arena, facing the bull, who can truly understand the implications of the cape and the consequences of the sword. And it is only by standing upon that bloodied circle of soil that you can suitably respond to the stunning fury of the moment. By quoting that poem during a time of crisis, Kennedy was overtly requesting some sympathy for the man in the ring, himself.

A dozen years later and the "Bullfight Poem" would once again be thrown about by Kennedy, this time in impersonation. And the "two media matadors, brave young men from Ant Farm" would stand not in the Plaza de Toros but in the Cow Palace parking lot facing a very bullish mass media.

---

114   White House Staff Files of Pierre Salinger, box 134, John F. Kennedy Presidential Library.

115   The Graves translation is as follows: Bullfight critics ranked in rows / Crowd the enormous Plaza full / But only one is there who knows / And he's the man who fights the bull.

FIRST DRAFT

President John F. Kennedy   **The White House**

Washington D.C. 20505

```
       SPEECH OF PRESIDENT  JOHN F. KENNEDY
                      FOR
                MEDIA    BURN
       RELEASE:   JULY $4L1975
```

Ladies + Gentlemen, distinguished guests,

My fellow Americans, on this Independence day 1975, the

American spirit is uncertain. We have seen an unworthy,

unended war, We have seen Watergate, now we are seeing

~~near~~ economic *turmoil.* ~~collapse.~~ From these ~~things~~ has come not

only the dangerous condition of our country, but a pervasive

doubt about our ability to correct it.

I believe we can find solutions in our origins.

Our nation grew from a revolution against political tyranny.
Our fore fathers ~~~~ *threw out a distance, unresponsive ruler.*
Now we must finish that revolution by replacing the structure

of economic privilege and by repudiating the tyranny of

the warmakers, *and the image makers.*

What has *gone wrong* ~~happened to us~~ is not a random visitation of fate.

It is the result of forces which have assumed control of the

American system- economic royalists as oppressive as the

Crown 200 years ago. These forces are militarism, monopoly,

and the *MASS MEDIA.* ~~maldistribution of wealth.~~

Militarism depletes our economy because it still dominates

our foreign policy. The arms industry is parasitic, It consumes

our resources but returns nothing ~~to all~~ to the national

wealth. And I say it is time to say no to the militarists. *!!*

Applause

But let us continue: "And let me say this: these artists are pioneers, they are pioneers just as surely as were Lewis and Clark when they explored uncharted territory. They are pioneers as surely as [were] Armstrong and Aldrin when they set foot on the moon."[116]

This pithy passage relies on a rhetorical device that might be called "the build-up." It heightens the stakes and through comparison elevates the forthcoming deed. The Artist-Dummies are not simply accelerating across a few hundred yards of pavement to culminate in a well-engineered collision; they are now partners in a long-standing continuum of courageous exploration and risk-taking. They stand side by side with the men who opened up the Northwest Territories and stepped upon the surface of the moon. But the Artist-Dummies also distinguish themselves from these explorers of geologic surfaces—they were going dimensional, into conceptual territory little known, and they would do this by propelling a political gesture with great force toward its implacable, reified subject. The remembered result would be a single image very much like Neil Armstrong's boot imprint on the lunar surface—but here, it's a boot on the face of mass media. "They do this not from self-interest, but intuitively as an act of patriotism. They do this not for themselves, alone, but for all Americans. And I believe they are by this act reiterating a most cherished and deeply felt belief: that the greatest statements about this great country of ours are heart-felt by individuals and never pre-arranged by committee."

The contemporary cliché is that all artistic practice is intrinsically generous, a gift to the community, an aesthetic insight altruistically shared, a glimpse of the future kindly revealed. But here the daring deeds of the Artist-Dummies rise to the plane of patriotism like rushing headlong into the fixed bayonets at Gettysburg: "not for themselves, alone, but for all Americans." Then to confirm one of Kennedy's most

THE WORLD MAY NEVER UNDERSTAND WHAT WAS DONE HERE,
BUT IT SHALL NOT FORGET THE IMAGE CREATED HERE.

WHAT WAS DONE HERE TODAY MAY NEVER BE UNDERSTOOD,
BUT THE IMAGE CREATED HERE TODAY MAY NEVER BE FORGOTTEN

THE WORLD MAY NEVER UNDERSTAND WHAT WAS DONE HERE TODAY,
BUT THE IMAGE CREATED SHALL NEVER BE FORGOTTEN

The final sentences of the Artist-President's speech revised for rhythm and meaning. Note similarity to several lines from Abraham Lincoln's Gettysburg Address: "The world will little note, nor long remember what we say here, but it can never forget what they did here."

Pages 59–70: The official "souvenir booklet," which sold for $1 at the performance.

appealing notions, the reiteration of a "cherished and deeply felt belief." Recall that in his 1961 Inaugural Address, the President proclaimed, "Ask not what your country can do for you, ask what you can do for your country." Yes, the Artist President is now on solid ground, jettisoning the loathsome "committee" for the bighearted gift of individual derring-do. Right about now, the crowd should be shoulder to shoulder, teary eyed before the imminent act of patriotism. "And so, my fellow Americans, let me say this finally about MEDIA BURN: THE WORLD MAY NEVER UNDERSTAND WHAT WAS DONE HERE TODAY, BUT THE IMAGE CREATED HERE ... SHALL NEVER BE FORGOTTEN!"[117]

Here, the Artist-President has gone from proclamation to prophecy. Not the "world" per se and not the assembled crowd with its predisposed sympathies, but the mass media would never quite understand what was done here, as Ant Farm would soon demonstrate. The response would be mocking and annoyed, disbelieving and belittling, condescending and disingenuous.[118] For the gathered choir, though, the "understanding" caveat was more like a spoiler alert for Conceptual art. The meaning would not be found in the action, but in the image of that action. And that image would be unforgettable.

---

116 "Were" does not appear in the spoken version.

117 Months after writing this section, I was brought to my senses by a Jeff Kelley essay titled "The Passage through Space Into Image," written in 2004. In this fanciful article, Kelley makes mention of a line from Lincoln's "Gettysburg Address" clearly echoed in cadence and verbiage in the Artist-President's speech: "The world will little note, nor long remember what we say here, but it can never forget what they did here." Lincoln, of course, was referencing the great sacrifice of lives made on the field before him. What he says in memoriam is of little consequence, but the bravery shall persist always. Likewise, the *Media Burn* performance in that expanse of asphalt shall fall from memory, but the image of that performance shall endure.

118 Just one of many examples: an on-air exchange from KTVU-TV News, "Oh, what's it all mean? Well, presumably the message is for the media. Get it?"

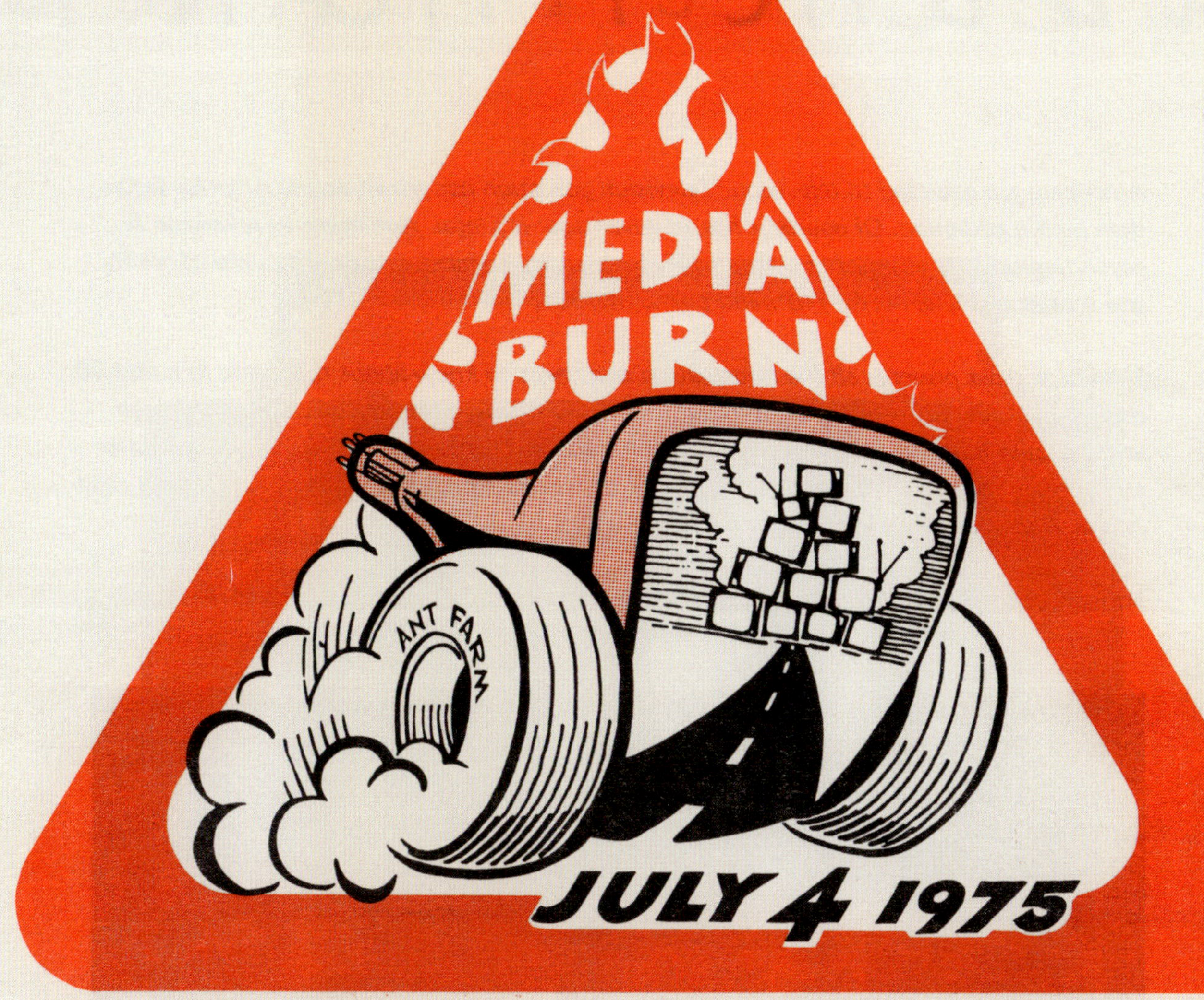

COW PALACE
SAN FRANCISCO

ANT FARM

souvenir booklet:

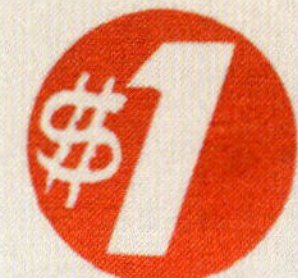

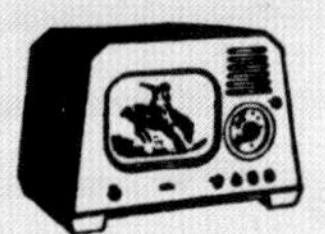

T E L E
A D D I C T I O N !

Americans are addicted to television. Television addiction has grown across America faster than heroin addiction. Of course it has an advantage: it's legal. Addiction to television is psychological, not physical like drug addiction, but it produces a narrowing view of reality and creates artificial needs. The mind police of 1984.

Television news presents all the information one needs to know about the world in a tidy 30 minute package. Eight of the 30 minutes is devoted to ads, currently oil company 'image ads', because television exists to sell advertising space. This superficial information transferral is presented as 'all the news of the day'. Zombie-like Americans reach out to change channels as Walter Cronkite says, "And that's the way it is . . ."

At least once in your life, haven't you wanted to kick the shit out of your television set?

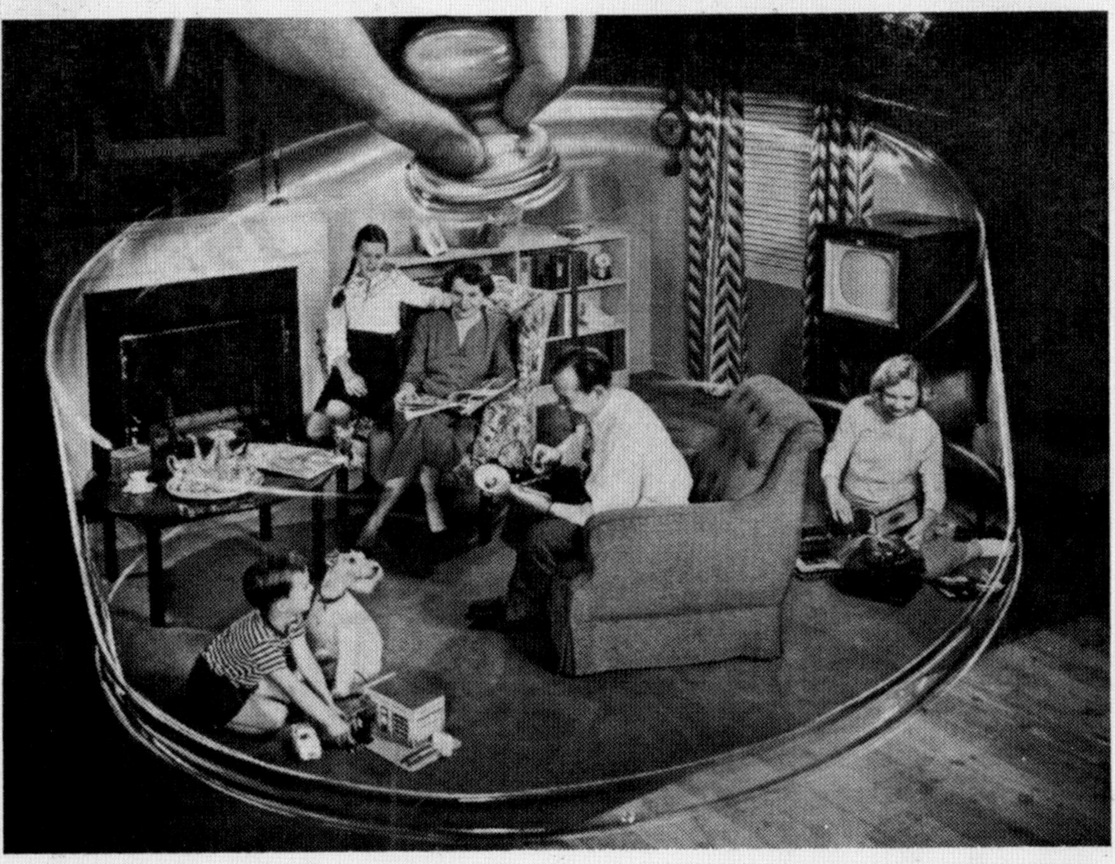

VISION STATISTICS

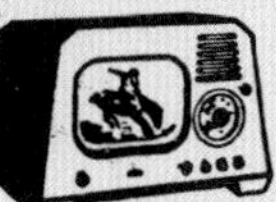

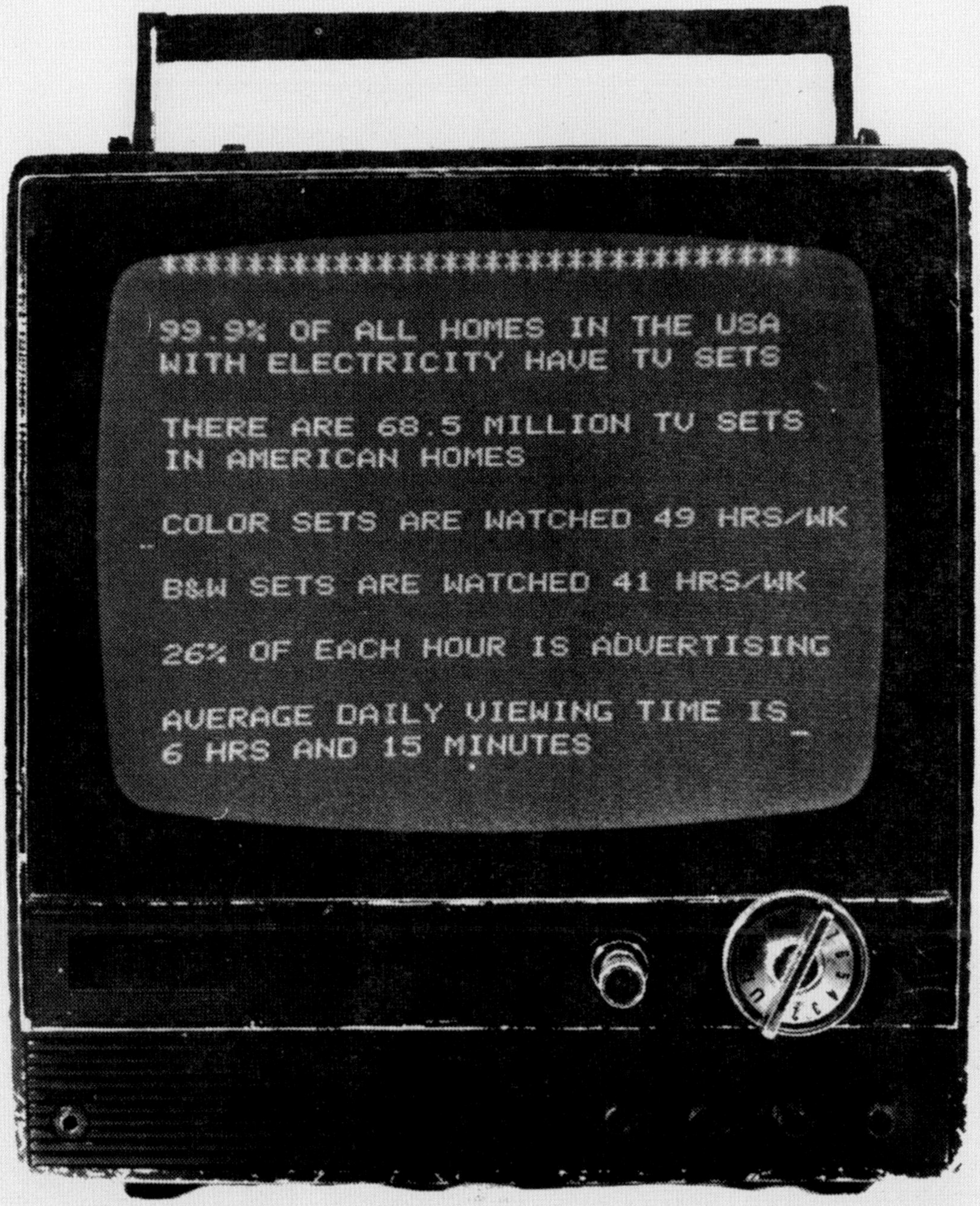

AUTO
ABSOLUTION

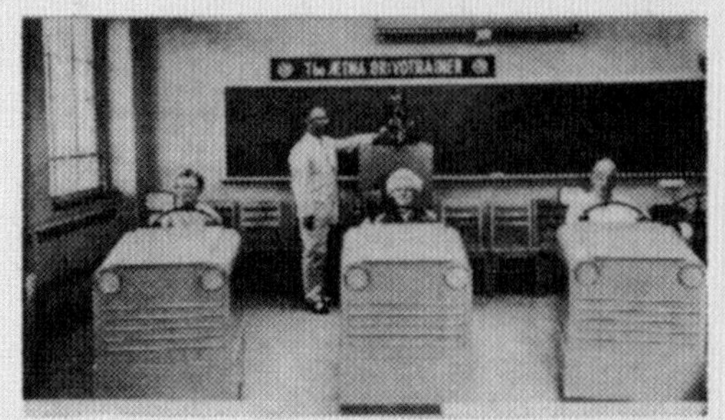

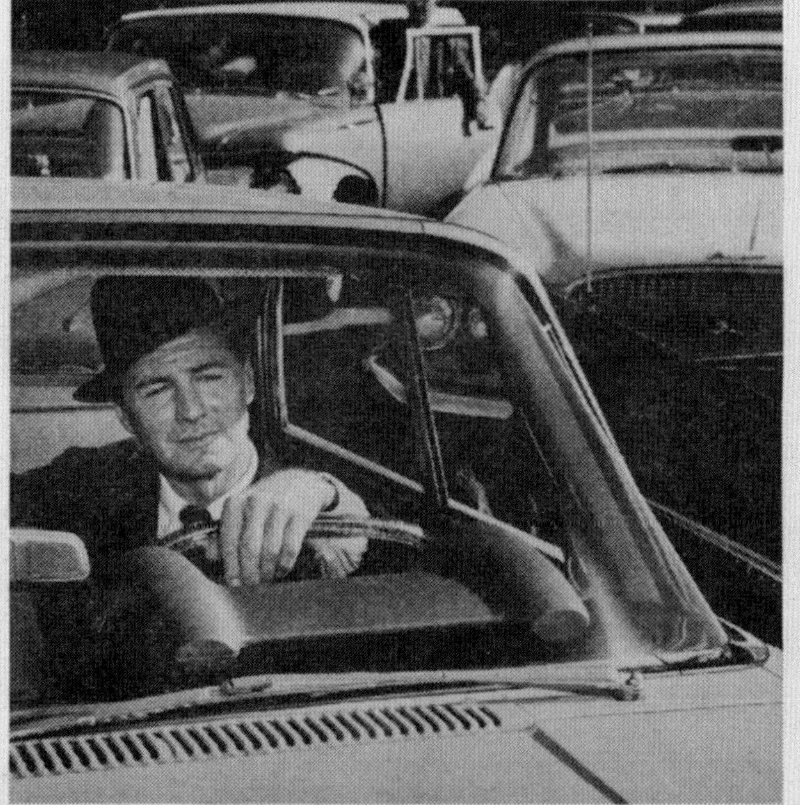

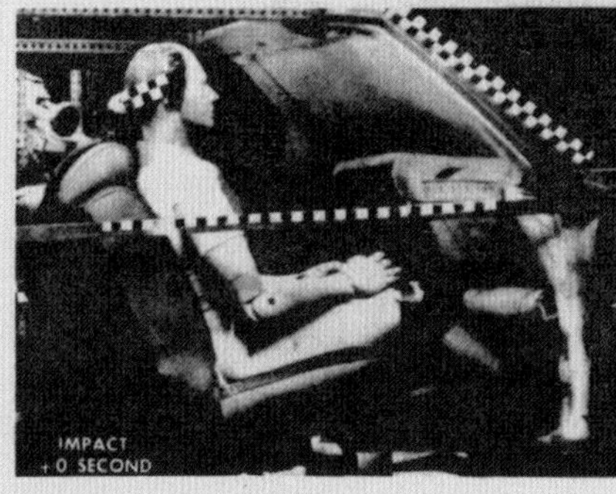

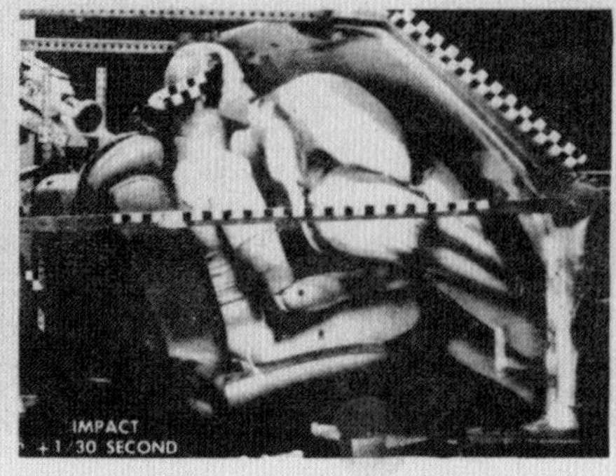

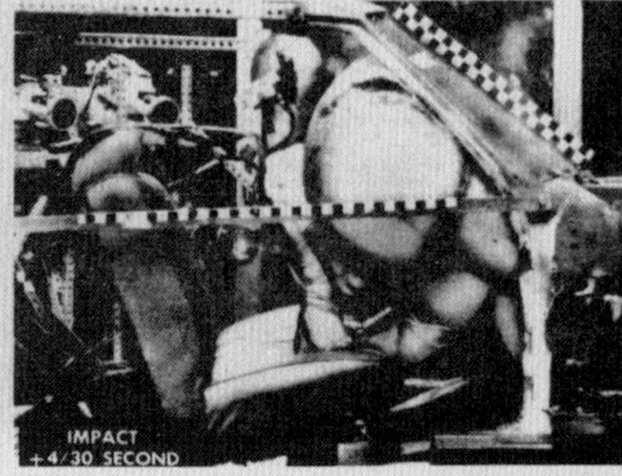

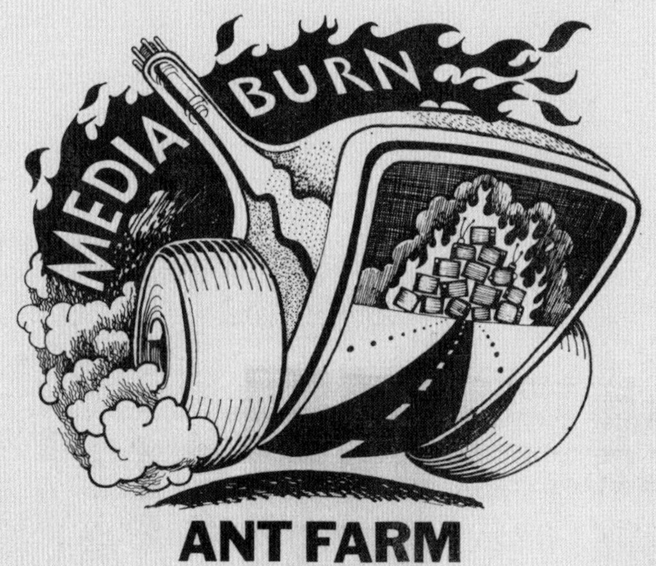

There was born in America during World War II a generation of children who were to be introduced to the new invention, television, at a formative age. This generation, different from those older whose view of reality was catalyized before television and those younger who never knew a reality without the tube, is the 'television generation'. They grew up as the medium itself was growing up. Media Burn is a statement from representatives of the 'television generation'.

At 2:50 today the phantom dream car (pictured on the next page) will start its engine to begin an historic trip. It will shoot across the Cow Palace parking lot into the just-ignited stack of 50 television sets. At the moment of impact Admirals, RCA's, G.E.'s, Sylvanias, Zeniths, and Hoffmans will fly apart in a cathartic explosion. The car will shoot on through to the other side and, God willing, the two dummies will step out unhurt, free at last from the addiction of television.

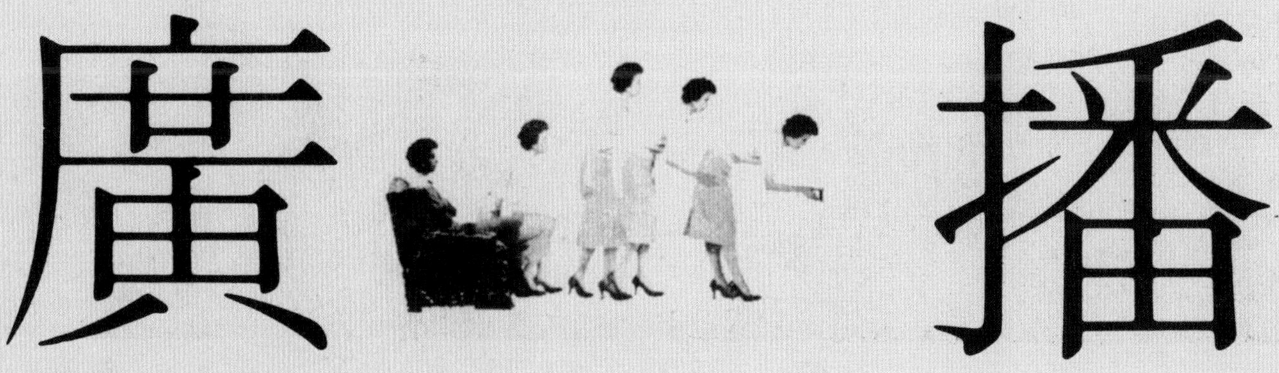

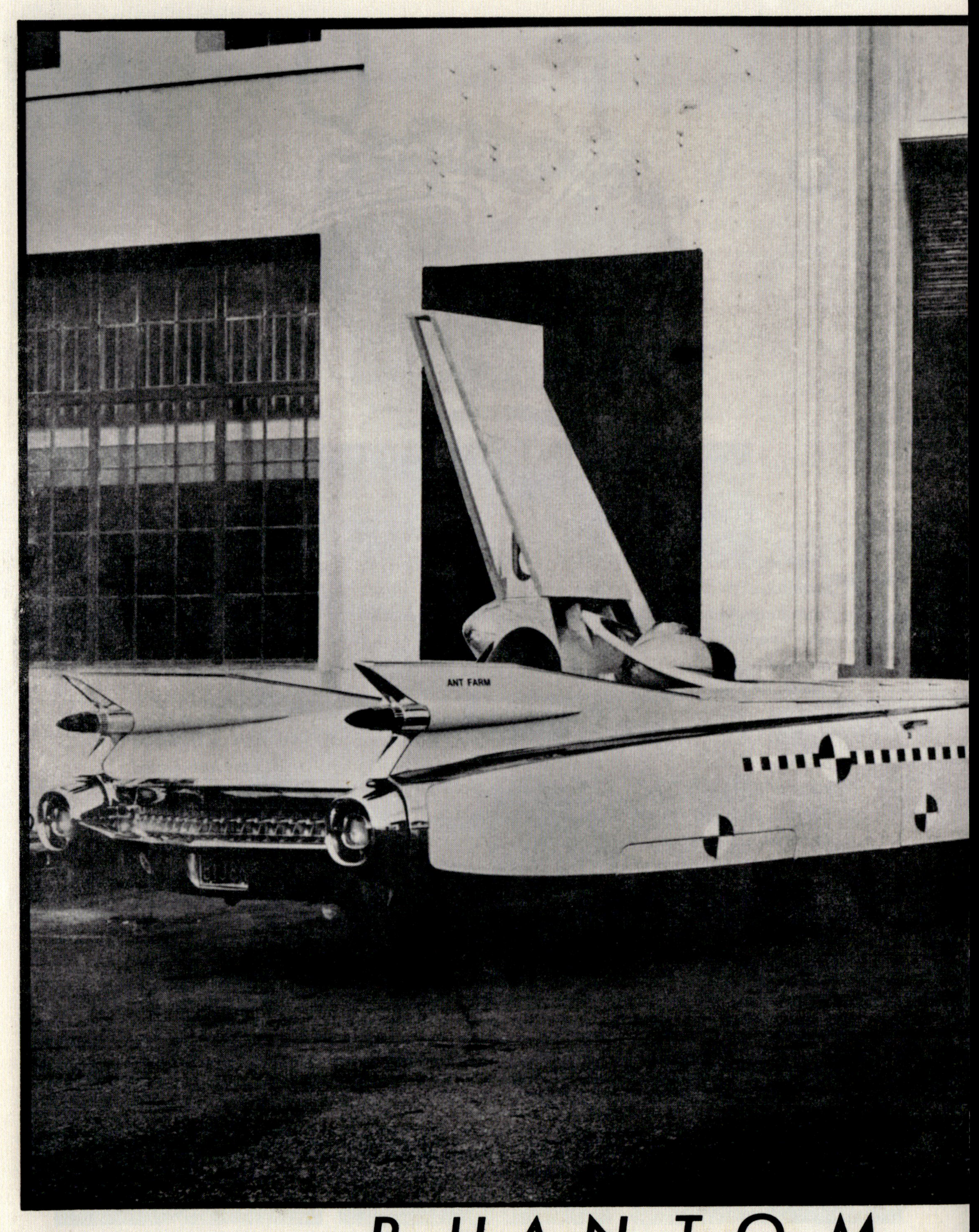

PHANTOM

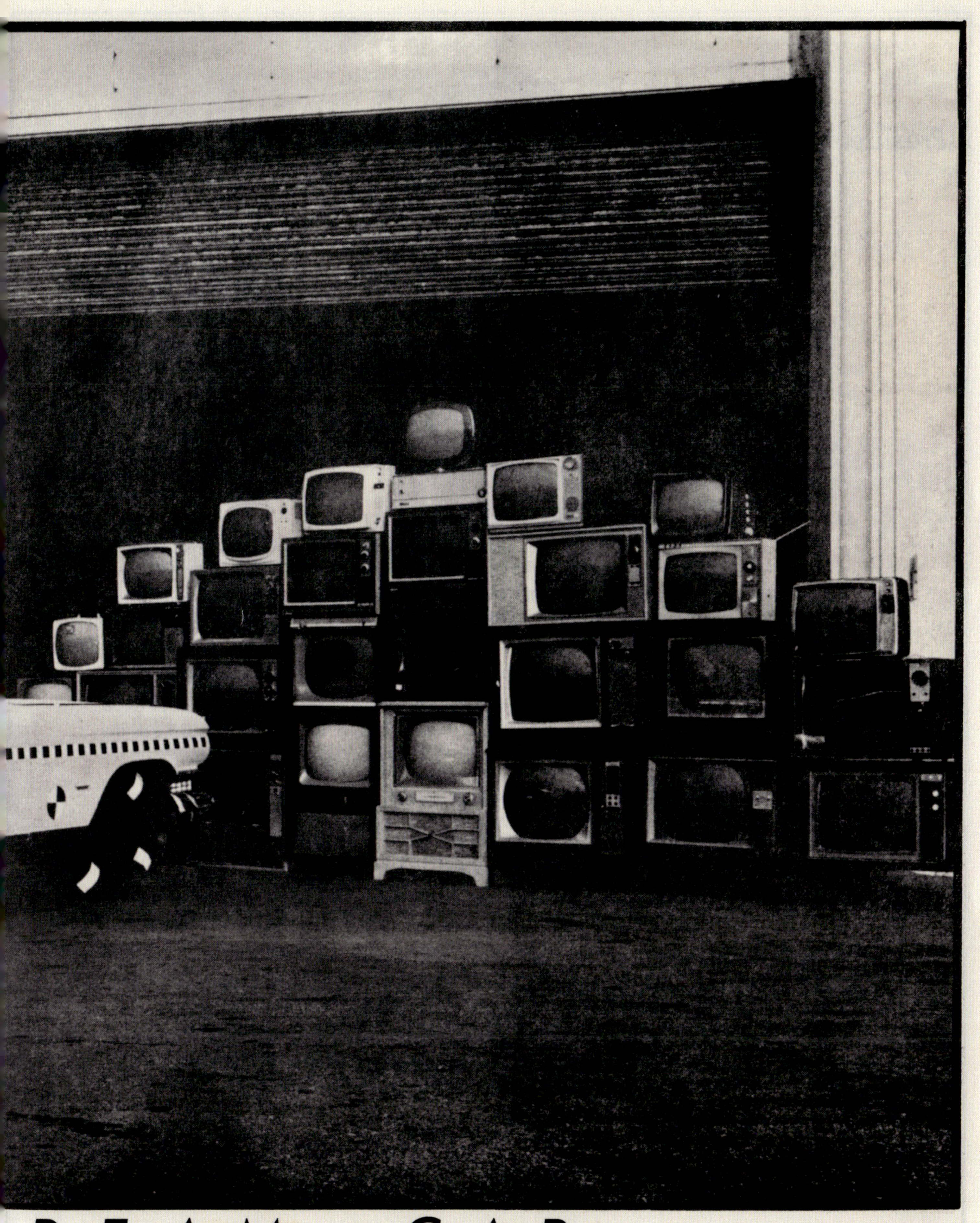

REAM CAR

President John F. Kennedy      **The White House**

Distinguished guests, members of the press, my fellow Americans: On this Independence Day 1975 the American Spirit is uncertain. We have seen, in this decade, an unworthy war. We have seen political scandal. Now we are seeing economic turmoil. From these has come not only the dangerous condition of our country, but a pervasive doubt of our ability to correct it.

I believe we can find solutions in our origins!

Our nation grew from a revolution against political tyranny. Our forefathers threw out a distant alien government. Now we must finish that revolution by replacing the structure of economic privilege and by throwing out the alien tyranny of the warmakers and the money makers.

What has gone wrong with America is not a random visitation of fate. It is the result of forces which have assumed control of the American system: Economic royalists as oppressive as the Crown 200 years ago. These forces are: Militarism, Monopoly, and the Mass Media!

Militarism depletes our economy because it still dominates our foreign policy. The arms industry consumes our resources but returns nothing to the national wealth. But foremost, our expanding militarism is morally wrong. AND I SAY IT IS TIME TO SAY NO TO THE MILITARISTS!

The second force disrupting our country is Monopoly. Today just 200 corporations control nearly two-thirds of America's manufacturing assets. Not only economic control of markets, but political control to guarantee themselves a priviledged position. These monopolies often dominate government regulatory agencies which are supposed to protect the citizen. And this too is morally wrong. NOW I SAY IT IS TIME TO END MONOPOLY BY BUSINESS RULERS!

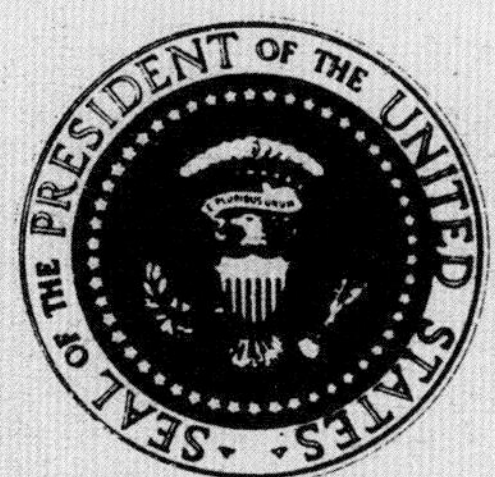

The third force disrupting our lives is the Mass Media, and it is this issue that I want to address this Independence day. Television because of it's technology and the way it must be used can only produce autocratic political forms, hierarchies, and hopeless alienation. Mass media monopolies control people by their control of information. In our vast society it is virtually impossible to escape the influence of commercial advertising, be it billboards on our highways, ad messages on the airwaves, or ad layouts in our magazines and newspapers. And who can deny that we are a nation addicted to television and the constant flow of media. And not a few of us are frustrated by this addiction. Now I ask you, my fellow Americans, haven't you ever wanted to put your foot through your television screen?

I SAY IT IS TIME TO LOOSEN THE GRIP OF MASS MEDIA ON THE FLOW OF INFORMATION AND IMAGES!

As Robert Blake wrote about matadors: "Bullfight critics row on row crowd the enormous Plaza de Toros, but only one is there who knows, and he is the one who fights the bull." Today there stand before us two media matadors, brave young men from Ant Farm who are about to go forth into the unknown. And let me say this: These artists are pioneers. They are pioneers as surely as were Lewis and Clark when they explored uncharted territory; as surely as were Armstrong and Aldrin when they set foot on the moon. They do this not from self interest but intuitively as an act of patriotism. They do this not for themselves alone, but for all Americans. And I believe they are by this act reiterating a most cherished and deeply felt belief: That the greatest statements about this great country of ours are heart-felt by individuals and never prearranged by committee.

And so my fellow Americans, let me say this finally about MEDIA BURN:
THE WORLD MAY NEVER UNDERSTAND WHAT WAS DONE HERE TODAY, BUT
THE IMAGE CREATED HERE . . . SHALL NEVER BE FORGOTTEN!!

Speech of President John F. Kennedy
delivered at MEDIA BURN, July 4, 1975

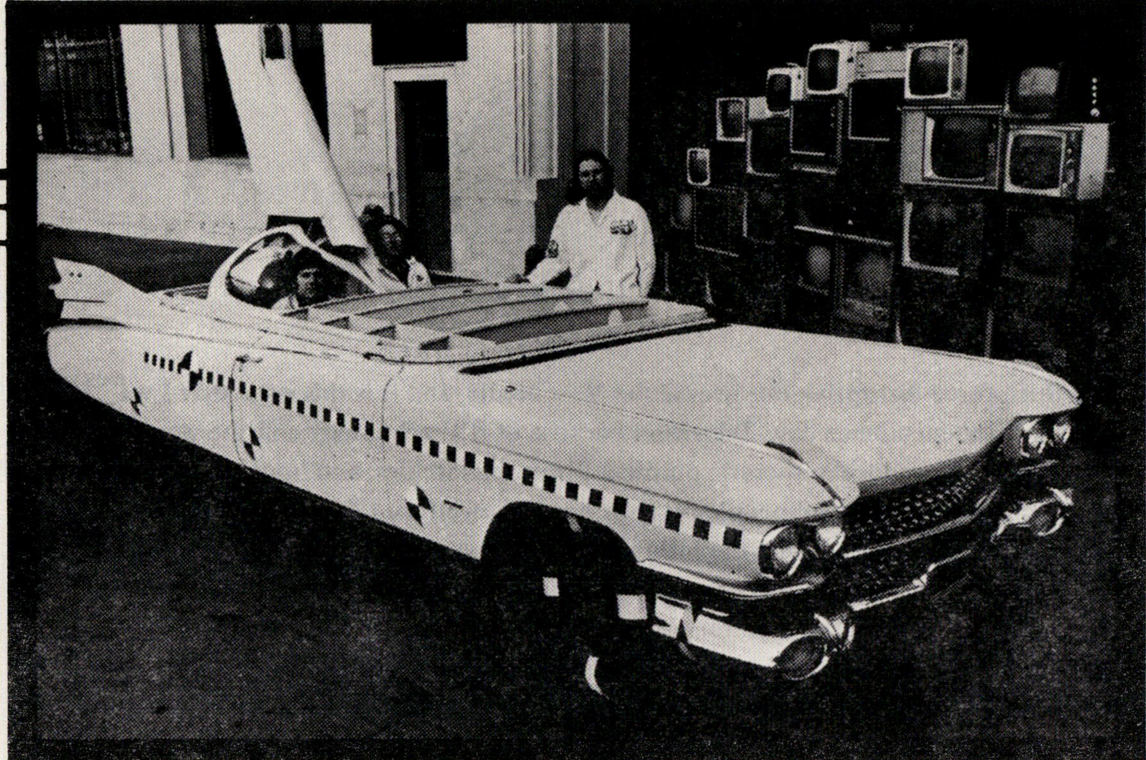

ANT FARM: (l. to r.) Curtis Schreier, Chip Lord, Doug Michels.   photo: Diane Hall

The Phantom Dreamcar is a modified 1959 Cadillac Biarritz. The Ant Farm customizing job has consumed over 1,200 man hours and several thousand dollars. The main feature of the Phantom Dreamcar is the dual-cockpit fiberglass impact shield that affords maximum security and safety to the two man crew and technical equipment. Other technological innovations include Video-Vision (an on-board image seeking guidance system), a navigation computer, and electronic digital instrumentation. All systems have been designed with a 55 m.p.h. impact rating.

MEDIA BURN has been conceived, promoted, and today executed by Ant Farm (Curtis Schreier, Uncle Buddie, Doug Michels, and Chip Lord). "We're not like traditional artists who have a product to sell," says Uncle Buddie, "We're more like an art agency that promotes ideas that have no commercial potential but which we think are important vehicles of cultural introspection."

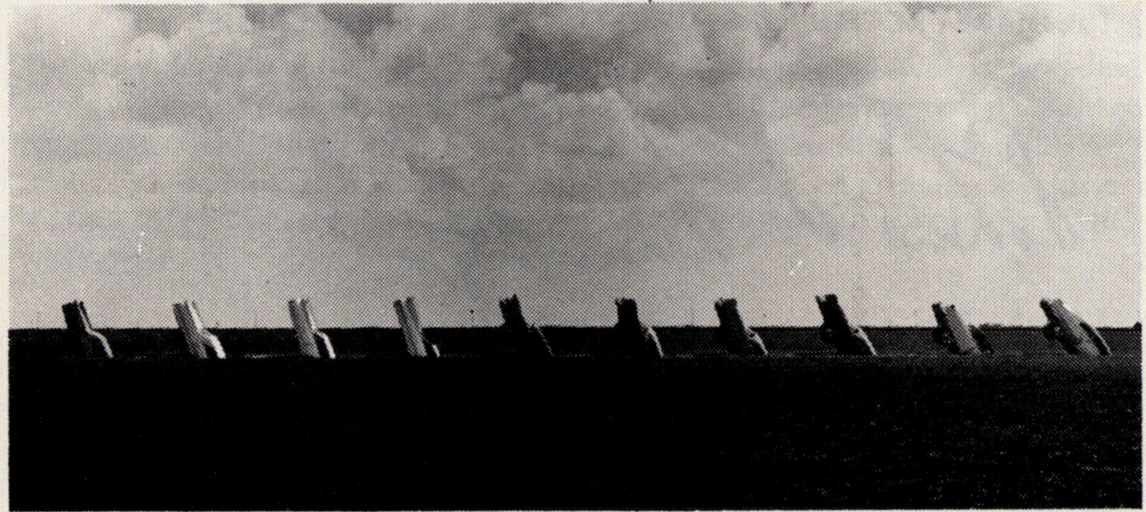

Ant Farm's Cadillac Ranch four miles west of Amarillo Texas on Route 66.

F E E D B A C K

I _did_ / _did not_ attend MEDIA BURN.

I thought the event on the whole _______________________________________

It did relieve my frustration with television   true ☐   false ☐

I am not frustrated by television, I like it in fact.

In the future I would like to see ANT FARM ______________________________

____

____

Other comments.

signed: _______________________________ (optional)

ACKNOWLEDGEMENTS:

Tom Score Weinberg, Chicago
Spiritual, Promotional

Thanks to:

Electronic Arts Intermix Inc., New York

The Cow Palace   Doug Hall
Kim Kacere   Jody Proctor
Phil Garner   Diane Hall

Video Production, thanks to:

Craig Schiller & the CALIFORNIA Video Resources Project
Optic Nerve   Marin Community Video
Howard Wise   Dana Atchley & Ace Spade Co.
T. L. Morey & Video Sales Inc., Houston
William Farley

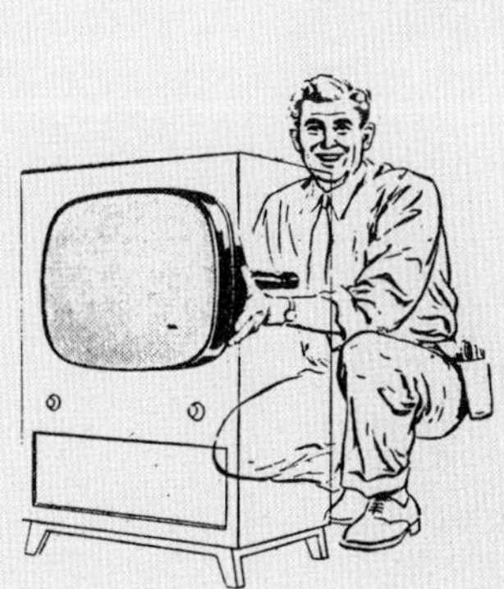
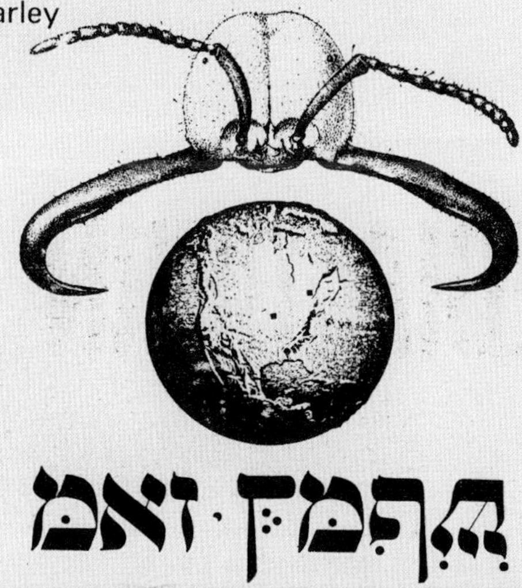
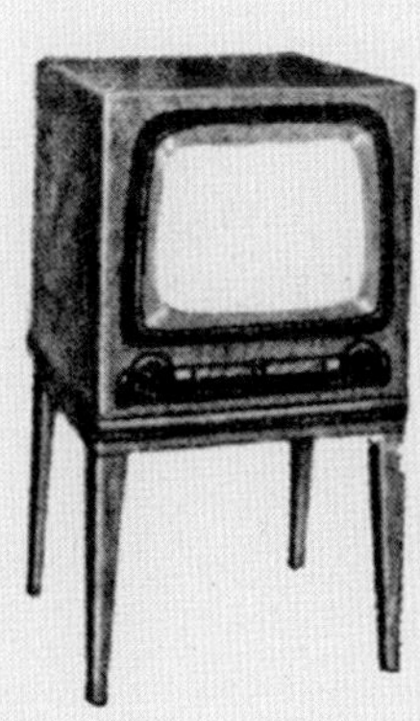

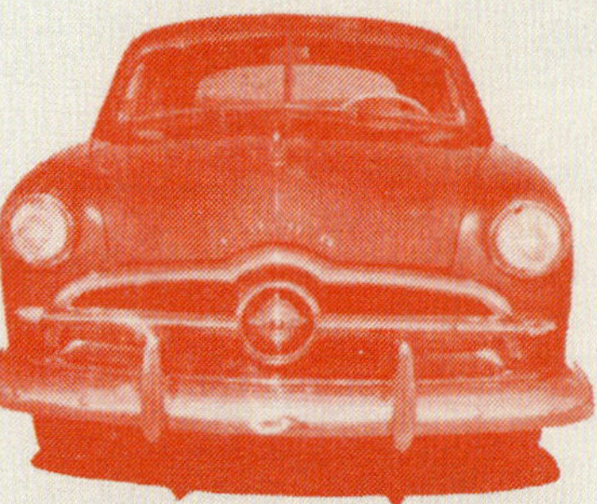

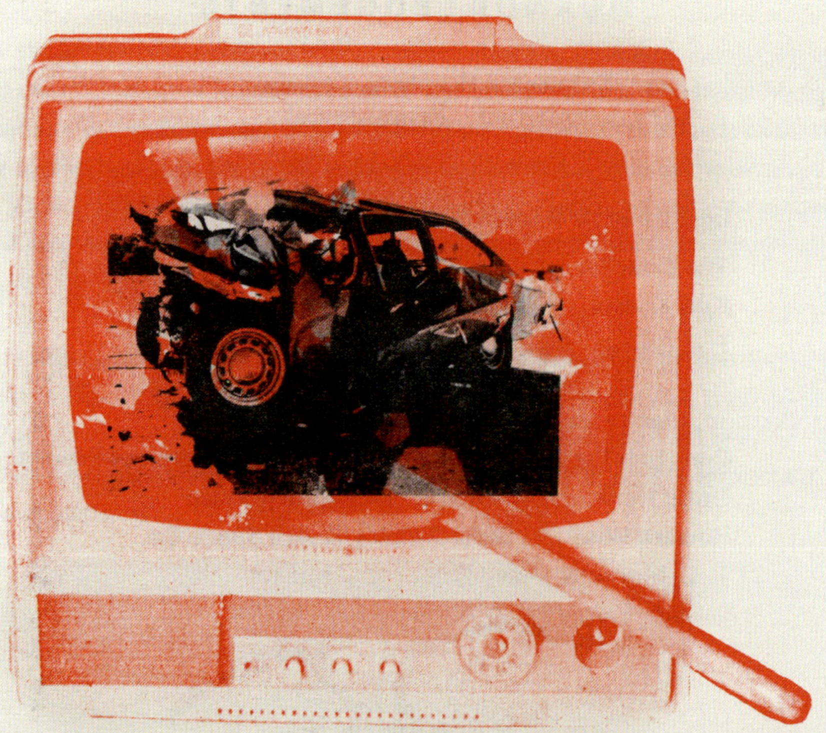

MEDIA BURN

© 1975 by ANT FARM

ART POLITICS

THE SS-100-X

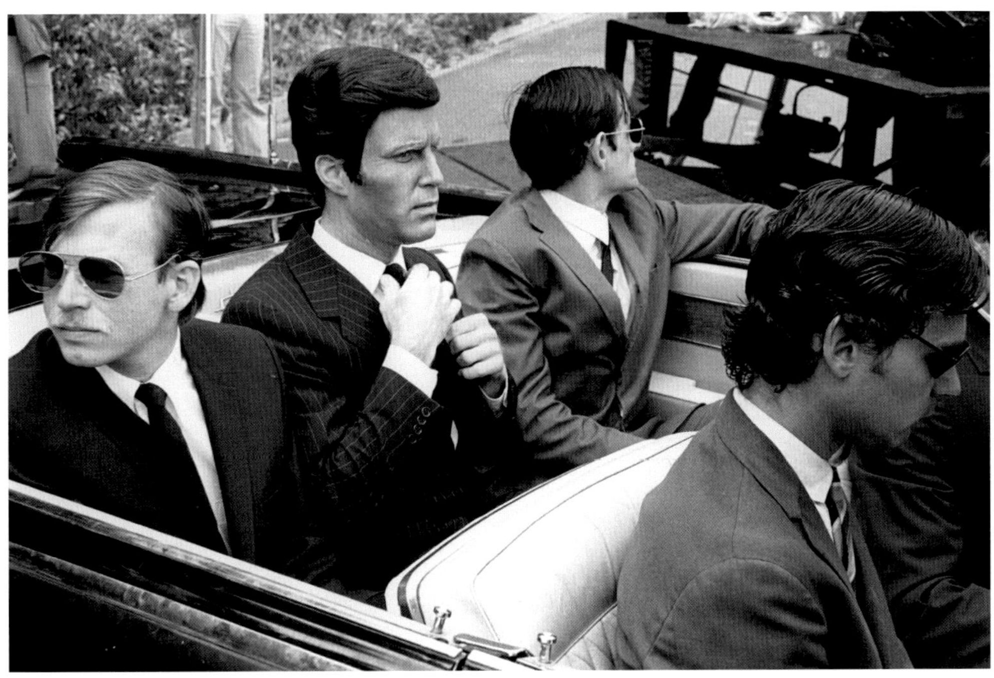

The purposeful artificiality of the Artist-President is evident here in Doug Hall's excessive make-up and perfectly coiffed hair. Photograph by Diane Andrews Hall.

When President Kennedy was assassinated, in November 1963, he was being driven in a Lincoln Continental, code-named SS-100-X by the Secret Service. It was a midnight blue 1961 convertible (model 74A), and worth about $200,000.[119] In spring 1975 you could still get your hands on a reasonably priced, mint condition convertible with the necessary "suicide doors," rear-hinged doors that allowed easy exit from the back seat.

Though the completion of *Media Burn* was still months off, Ant Farm, with collaborators T. R. Uthco, were already planning their next project, *The Eternal Frame*. Shot in Dallas' Dealey Plaza on August 10, 1975, *The Eternal Frame* was a restaging of the Kennedy assassination with Doug Hall in the Artist-President role and Doug Michels as Jacqueline Kennedy. Naturally, the reenactment, guided by the Zapruder footage, would require a Lincoln Continental, preferably a 1961.

"We bought it as the first commitment to *The Eternal Frame*," Chip Lord recalled.[120] It would also add a touch of authenticity to *Media Burn*, in which the Artist-President was delivered to the stage in the executive limo, surrounded by a handful of dead-serious Secret Service operatives. The four dark-suited agents scanned the suspicious crowd through metal-framed sunglasses. T. R. Uthco mainstay Jody Procter was to have been an agent, accompanied by two members of The Cryptic Corporation,[121] Homer Flynn and Hardy Fox, and Graeme Whifler, a local filmmaker, but he was elsewhere. In his stead Dan Calderwood, a local artist, donned the dark attire. Once Doug Hall was safely positioned at the podium, Flynn and Whifler took on crowd control, keeping the media at bay. No incidents were reported.

The following month, Jody Procter accompanied the Lincoln as it was towed to Dallas via Amarillo, and there he would don the dark suit, playing, ultimately, a Secret Service agent who failed to protect the President. A certain elegance of symmetry was in evidence here, as Doug Hall explained: "It was decided that the Artist-President, after delivering the keynote address at *Media Burn*, would travel to Dallas, TX where he would be assassinated."[122] The alpha and omega of the impersonation.

But this finality did not deter Procter. In September 1975—after both *Media Burn* and *The Eternal Frame*—he realized a highly risky performance, *Social Experiment: Avant Garde Security*, in which he infiltrated the security network for President Gerald Ford's visit to San Francisco. Dressed as a police officer with the name tag "Dingus," Procter stood guard and aided in crowd control, sometimes literally standing shoulder to shoulder with the SFPD. Later that day, Sarah Jane Moore would fire a single shot from a .38 revolver, almost hitting the President. So much for security, avant-garde or traditional.

The 1961 Lincoln Continental used in *The Eternal Frame* would also survive, though not well. To this day, it resides in a metal barn on the property of the late Stanley Marsh 3.

---

119   The SS-100-X is on view at the Henry Ford Museum in Dearborn, Michigan.

120   Email to the author, April 1, 2015.

121   The Cryptic Corporation is the corporate cover for The Residents, a San Francisco–based avant-garde rock band, known as well for a series of pioneering multimedia projects. Their debut album, *Meet the Residents*, came out in 1974.

122   From a conversation with Hall in early 2015.

BULLISH ABOUT THE COW PALACE

On June 17, Ant Farm finalized their contract with the Cow Palace. For the tidy sum of "$100 payable in advance," they would have the use of the main parking lot for "the purpose of a conceptual art event called 'Media Burn.' This event will consist of the filming of an automobile driving through a stack of burning television sets." Smartly, the Cow Palace included the stipulation that they would be "in no way responsible for the consequences of this event"—real or conceptual.

On a parking lot capable of housing 4,000 cars, just one, the Phantom Dream Car, would stand ready as the asphalt baked in the afternoon sun. Four hours—noon to 4 p.m.—was the allotted window for the *Media Burn* preparation and realization. As announced in the press releases and invitations, the festivities would begin at 2:30 p.m. If you had arrived at noon, you would have seen the frantic activity common to any fair, carnival, or impromptu amusement. The area was cordoned off by portable traffic barriers, an admissions desk was positioned, bandstand scaffolding erected, a souvenir stand with booklets, T-shirts, and postcards assembled;[123] red, white, and blue bunting was hung here and there, a public address system was plugged in and ready, a panel truck loaded with used televisions sat idle, the towed Phantom Dream Car set before the podium then concealed with additional bunting. And all around, the swarm of arriving volunteers and media crews.

A five-page "production script"[124] accounted for everything from the noon rehearsal to Bill Ding's first announcement as Master of Ceremonies that "the

---

123   The souvenir stand was assembled in the back of Curtis Schreier's VW Crew Cab Transporter.

124   Bill Ding is performed by John Hillding, an occasional member of T. R. Uthco. The character itself can be traced back to at least *Dirty Dishes* (1971) in which Ding's wedding is staged using as a prop an actual "Bill Ding Balancing Clown" made by Strombeck Manufacturing. It should also be noted that in 1967, famed architect Robert Venturi designed a structure in New Brunswick, N.J. called "Bill-Ding-Board National Football Hall of Fame." Venturi's declaration that buildings would be subsumed by media, i.e., become Bill-Ding-Boards, was quite notorious.

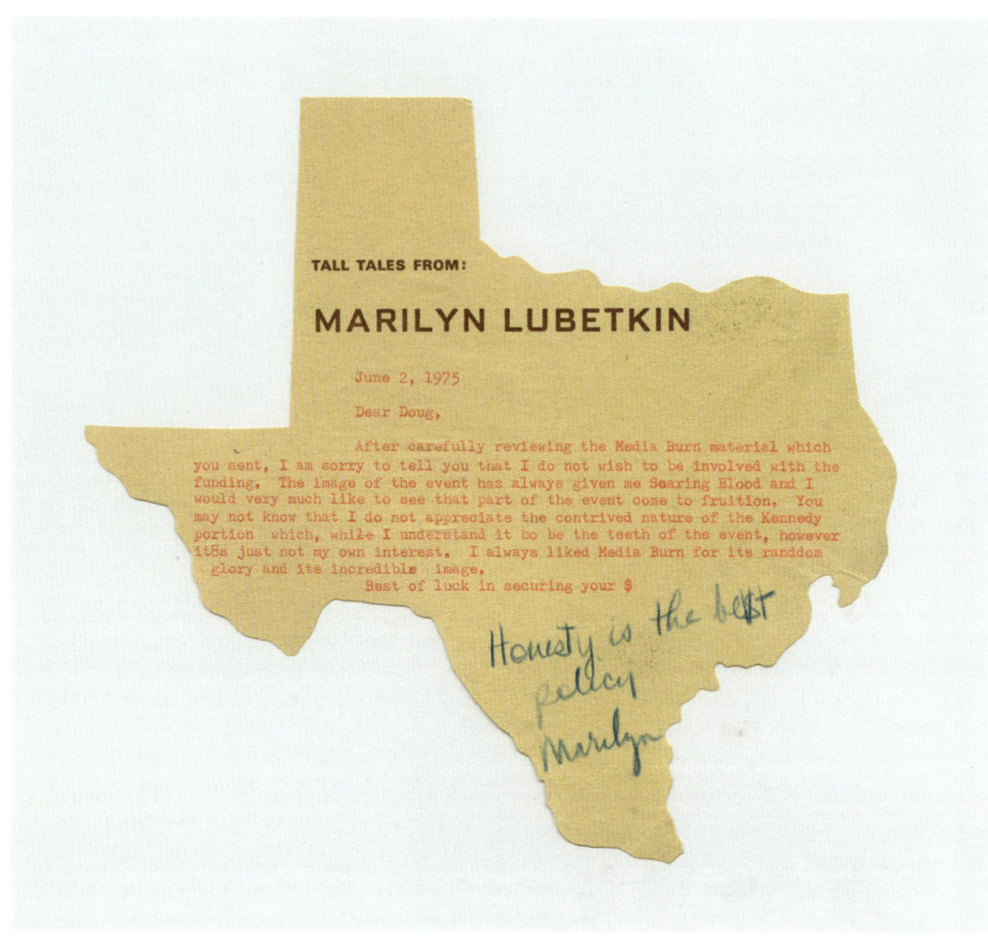

Objections to the concept of *Media Burn*, expressed by Marilyn Lubetkin on fanciful note paper. Ms. Lubetkin was a longtime supporter of Ant Farm and owner of House of the Century, completed two years prior to this missive.

Following spread: The Phantom Dream Car being readied for its grand performance. Here, the behind-the-scenes battery charging. Photograph by Ant Farm.

event that is about to take place may not be appropriate for young children." At 2:10 p.m., Ding would announce that there remained "twenty minutes until the Burn," then another announcement ten minutes later. As we neared the actual "official program," the countdown would grow more discrete in increments of time, building tension.

Media Burn, the event, was physically divided into three zones: Most distant from the impact was the invited public, kept at bay by wood traffic barriers. The staging area containing the bandstand, Phantom Dream Car, and cast and crew was off-limits to the general crowd but open to official press who displayed their custom-designed press passes. Finally there was the impact zone surrounding the pyramid of television sets, approachable only by select camera crews and still photographers. This zone was approximately 150 feet in diameter. The runway, oriented generally westward, about 250 feet long leading directly to the pyramid, was also cleared of observers. Beyond the pyramid was a second cleared area, an unbroken expanse of parking lot leading to a tree line. This was the space needed for deceleration. In one drawing, titled *Secret Location*, the deceleration is aided by a deployed parachute, but this showy technique was never enabled.

COW PALACE

June 17, 1975

Mr. Douglas Michaels
Ant Farm
Box 471
San Francisco, CA 94101

LETTER OF AGREEMENT

The COW PALACE agrees to rent to the Ant Farm the main parking
lot on July 4, 1975, for the purpose of a conceptual art event
called "Media Burn". This event will consist of the filming
of an automobile driving through a stack of burning television
sets.

The COW PALACE is in no way responsible for the consequences
of this event. It will not be open to the public. Due caution
with regard to security, Fire Department clearance will be exer-
cised by the Ant Farm.

Rental for this event -- from Noon until 4:00 P.M. -- will be
$100 payable in advance. Cleanup (estimated at $50), security
and any other labor requested will be payable in advance.

Shirley Sawyer
Rentals Director

SS:jl

Accepted by _______________________
            for Ant Farm

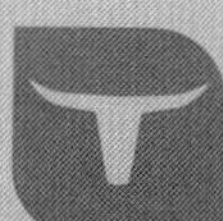

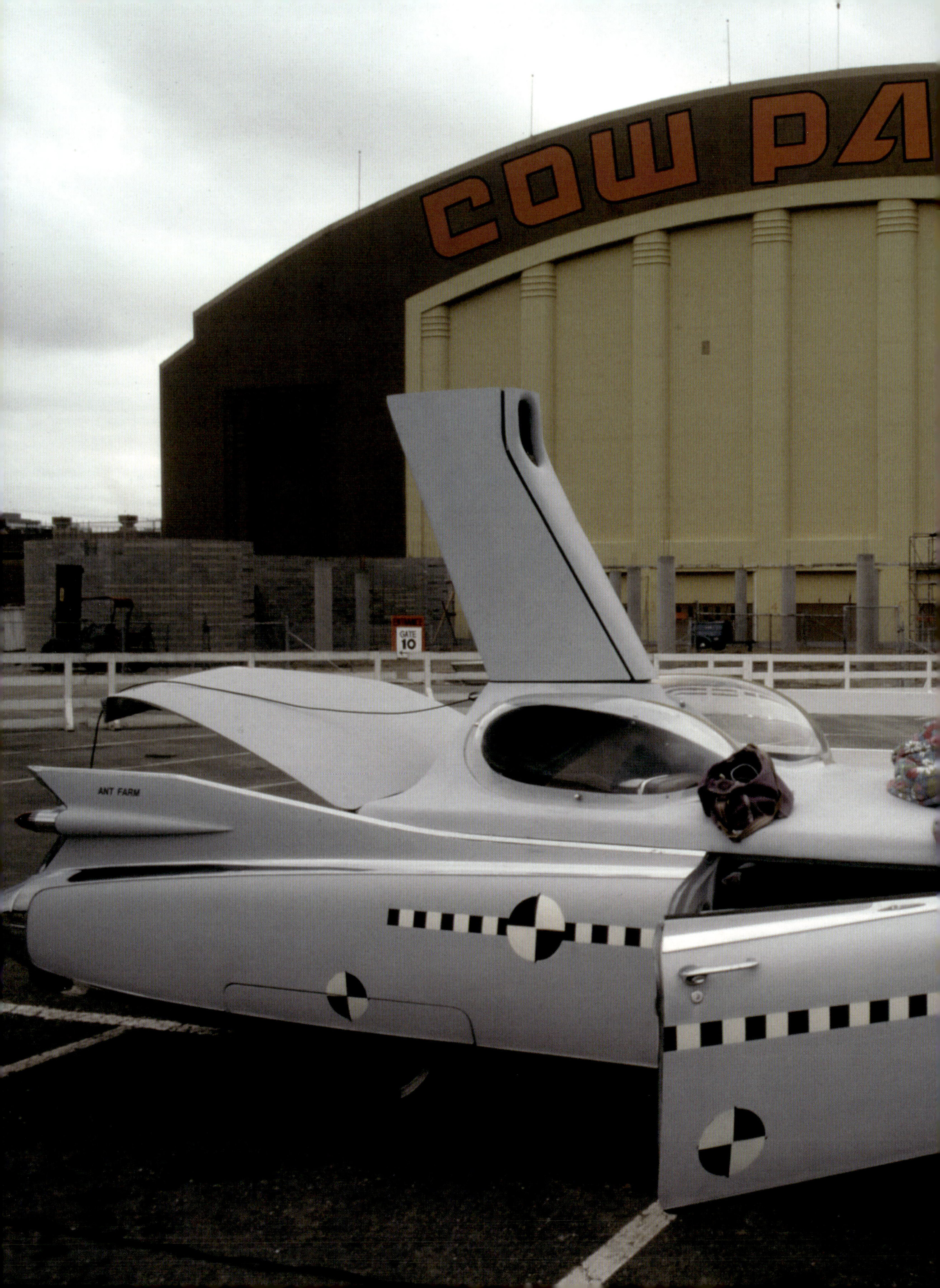

COW PA
GATE
10
ANT FARM

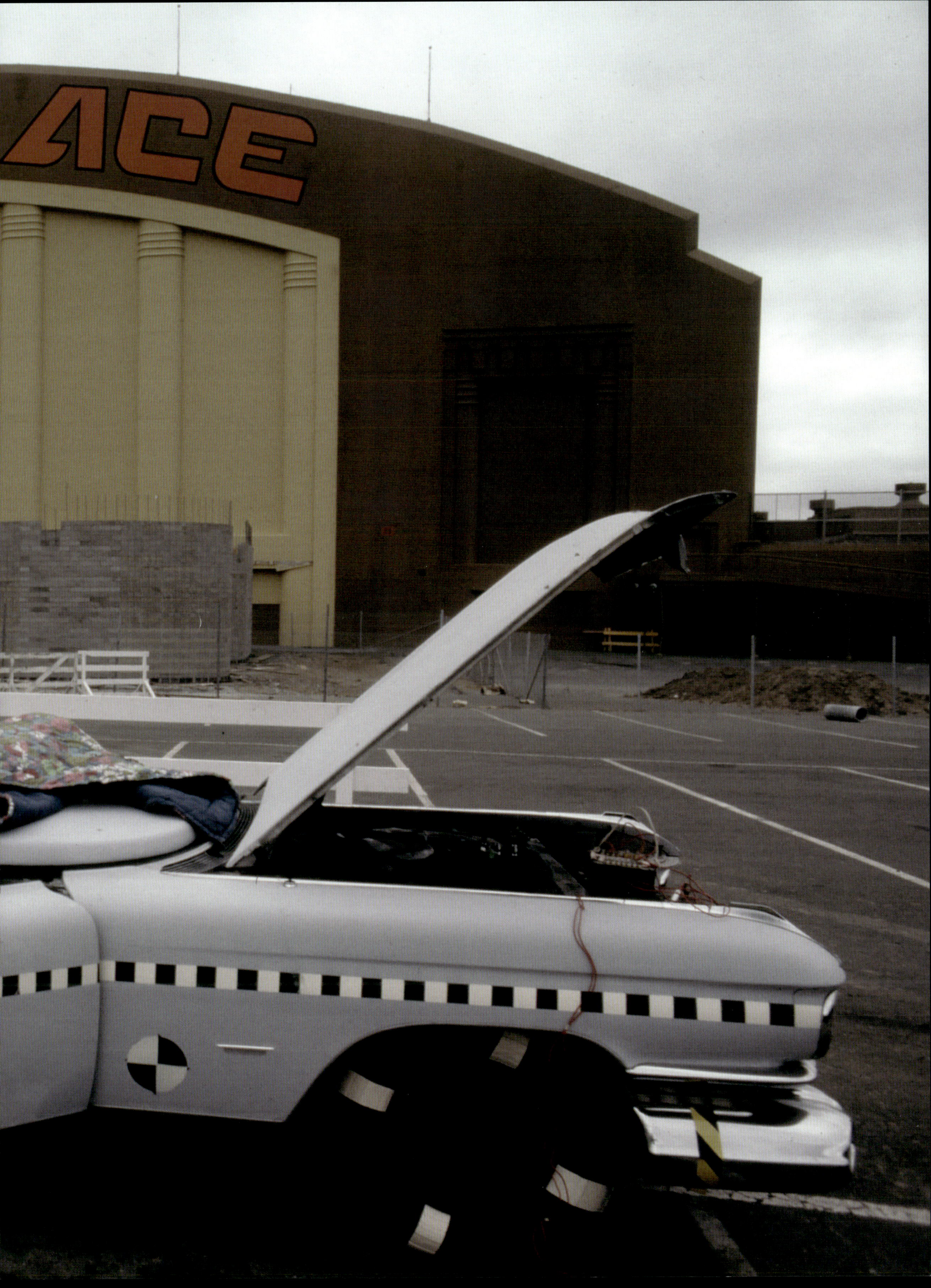
ACE

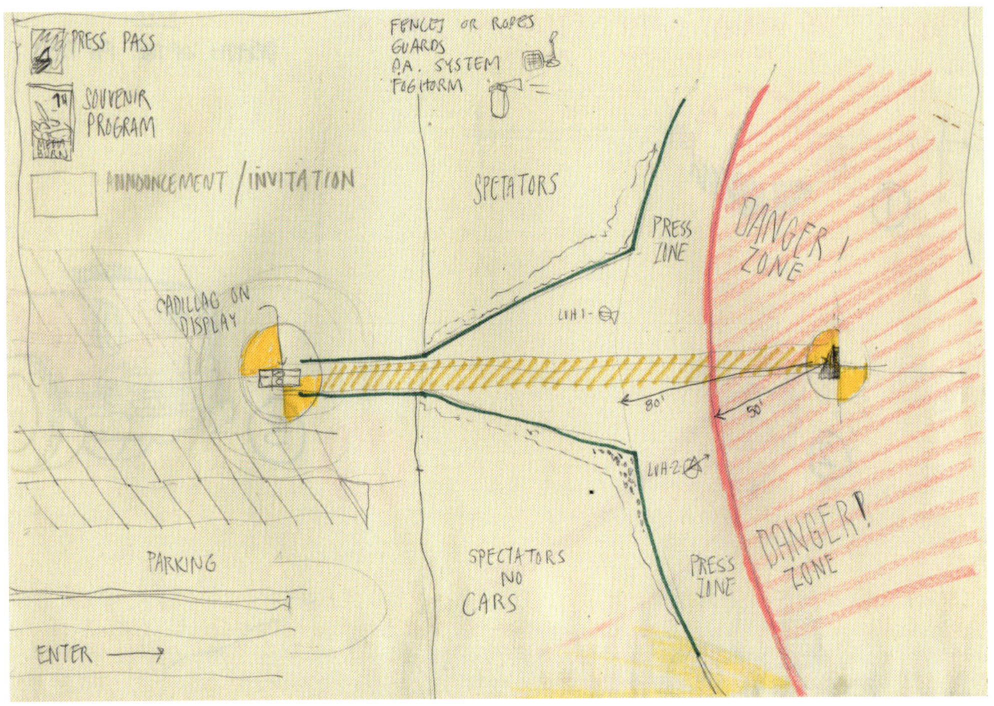

Numerous drawings were rendered to illustrate the physical arrangement of the performance. Here, the "Danger Zone" radiates outward from the impact site, creating a fifty-foot buffer. Drawing by Chip Lord.

At precisely 2:30 p.m., the "official program begins" with Bill Ding's greeting, leading to an ironic disclaimer: "The views expressed here today are solely those of the artists." The Artist-President himself will soon contradict this notion when he asks, "Haven't you ever wanted to put your foot through your television screen?" A shared view if ever there was one. By 2:35, the Phantom Dream Car is revealed, and Ding describes in detail the laborious preparation of the 1959 Cadillac Eldorado Biarritz, "transformed by over 1,500 hours of handcrafted labor by the artists of Ant Farm." Safety features are lauded. The ricocheting PA system informs us that "the two dummies will drive by closed circuit television. There's a camera mounted in the vertical tail fin and protected by a Lexan shield. They view a monitor mounted between their bucket seats." And then the opportunity of a lifetime: "The Phantom Dream Car will be for sale after *Media Burn*." (With no takers, the Dream Car was towed home, the worse for wear.)[125]

While all this talk of "digital count-downs" and "fiberglass canopies" transpires, off in the prep area the black Lincoln Continental has begun its slow drive to the bandstand. "And now, ladies and gentlemen," Bill Ding gently intones, "I would like to introduce an important guest who will be delivering the July 4th Independence Day speech." The executive limo halts behind the stand and its passengers disembark, leaving Doug Hall as the Artist-President, in all his face pan-caked glory, the last to leave. Surrounded by his Secret Service agents, the Artist-President ascends the steps to the micro-phone and, with a hasty "Thank you very much," proceeds with the speech. The time is now about 2:38.

Alternately satiric, confusing, brazen, literary, and poetic, but always propheti-cally pointed, the Artist-President's four-minute-and-thirty-four-second speech ends with the indelible "But the image created here ... shall never be forgotten!"

Then a polite "Thank you very much, ladies and gentlemen," and he is whisked away by his waiting security detail.

As the Artist-President departs, we can see a blue van nearing the stage. It is now 2:45. Bill Ding blurts: "And now here come the artists." The Artist-Dummies—Doug Michels as Driver, Curtis Schreier as Navigator—exit the van and immediately mount the back of the Phantom Dream Car, standing finally beside the enormous central tail fin. A recording of the national anthem rings out.

Less than two minutes later, the anthem ebbs, and the Artist-Dummies slip lubriciously through the entry port of the Phantom Dream Car and into the interior. They start the engine and the Dream Car pulls forward, repositioning its trajectory. At approximately 2:50, Mr. Ding declaims: "Now the artists will go through their final countdown." While the launch crew swaps out the plastic bubbles, the Artist-Dummies check the readiness of their instruments, their operations synced with a digital countdown declin-ing from three minutes.[126] Meanwhile on the asphalt, the camera crew from Optic Nerve records the preparations;[127] farther down, on the perimeter of the impact zone, two additional camera crews, from Marin Community Video and California Video Resource Project, are getting in posi-tion. Nearby, the still photographers vie for vantage.

---

125   After three and a half years of garage stor-age and no buyers, David Ross, then a curator at the Berkeley Art Museum, agreed to house the car in his garage in Oakland. On February 19, 1979, he signed an agreement to take over stewardship of "one art work, the Phantom Dream Car."

126   Prior to the entry of the audience to the Cow Palace parking lot, the Artist-Dummies tried a dry run. They discovered a disjunction between their ability to steer and the road ahead as pic-tured on the small monitor. Some guides would be necessary to keep them on track. Hazard cones would set the parameters of the "lane" between the car's start position and the TV sets, but another solution, guaranteeing success, was needed. The ever-resourceful Starr Sutherland found a nearby construction site, stole a truck-load of 2 × 4 framing studs, quickly painted them white, and laid them out across the asphalt lot. The Artist-Dummies were able to steer along this raised white line for a dead-center collision. This story told to me by Sutherland in February 2019.

127   The passenger door is partially open now, allowing Optic Nerve to shoot inside the cramped cockpit and document the readiness checklist. A fixed camera also inside the cockpit would record the actual impact.

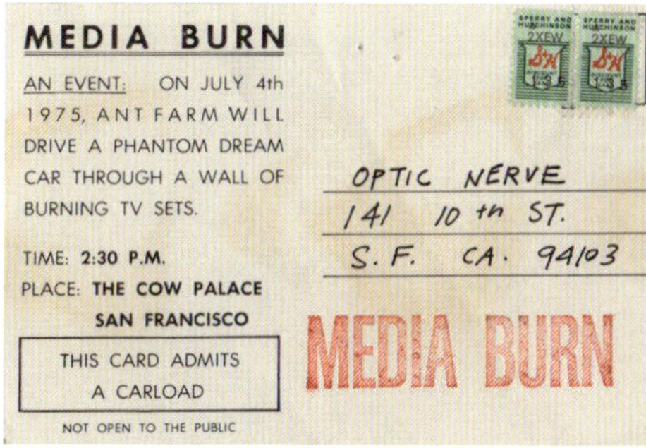

MEDIA BURN

AN EVENT: ON JULY 4th 1975, ANT FARM WILL DRIVE A PHANTOM DREAM CAR THROUGH A WALL OF BURNING TV SETS.

TIME: 2:30 P.M.

PLACE: THE COW PALACE
SAN FRANCISCO

THIS CARD ADMITS
A CARLOAD

NOT OPEN TO THE PUBLIC

OPTIC NERVE
141 10th ST.
S.F. CA. 94103

MEDIA BURN

The official *Media Burn* invitation, addressed to the video collective Optic Nerve. The S&H Green Stamps indicate it was hand-delivered.

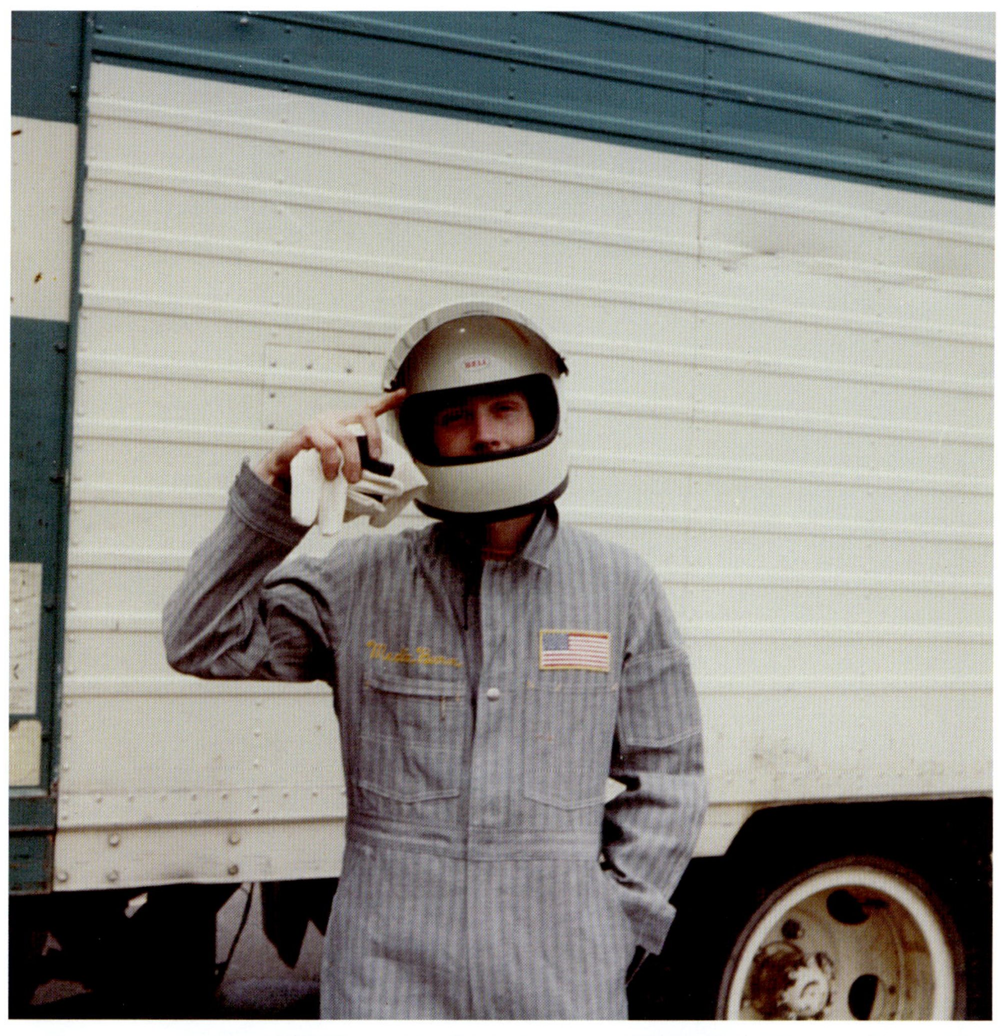

Left top: The Artist-Dummy, in this case Curtis Schreier, salutes the imaginary crowd. Photograph by Ant Farm.

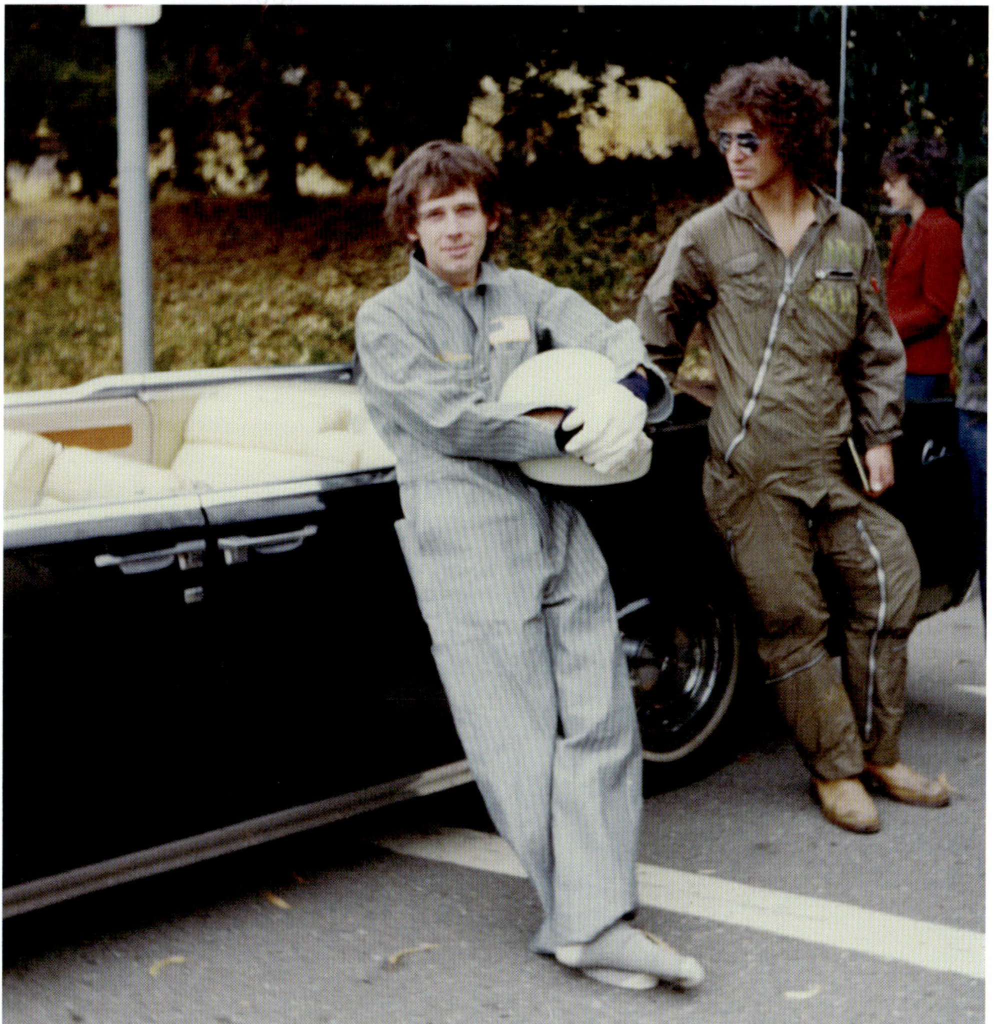

Left bottom: Looking unexpectedly relaxed, Curtis Schreier, Artist-Dummy, waits in shoeless repose. Photograph by Ant Farm.

Just minutes from impact, Ding again: "All spectators must observe the barriers for their own safety. Repeat, do not cross the white barriers."

Three p.m.: Uncle Buddie (Chip Lord) enters the danger zone and douses the stacked television sets with kerosene. He ignites the flammables and departs. A fire rages on the bottommost consoles.

With T minus fifteen seconds remaining, the Artist-Dummies are given the go-ahead. The Phantom Dream Car slowly accelerates along its prescribed path. The television sets, though not an inferno, burn briskly. Speeding along at fifty-five miles per hour, the Phantom Dream Car makes contact with the wall of flaming media.[128] The Artist-Dummies will later report that they felt the impact and then caught a strong waft of kerosene residue. The time is 3:05.

The Phantom Dream Car decelerates and comes to rest some 100 feet from the tree line. The Lincoln Continental is waiting nearby as the blue van rushes to assist the Artist-Dummies, who miraculously emerge from the slightly mangled vehicle, enter the limo, and are sped toward the gathered spectators for their victory lap.

Elapsed time: approximately thirty-five minutes.

---

128   The factory claim is that the 1959 Cadillac Biarritz will go from zero to sixty mph in 10.7 seconds, the run time for a perfectly tuned, expertly driven Cadillac. The actual timed run lasted nineteen seconds. The true speed is uncertain, though the goal was fifty-five miles per hour.

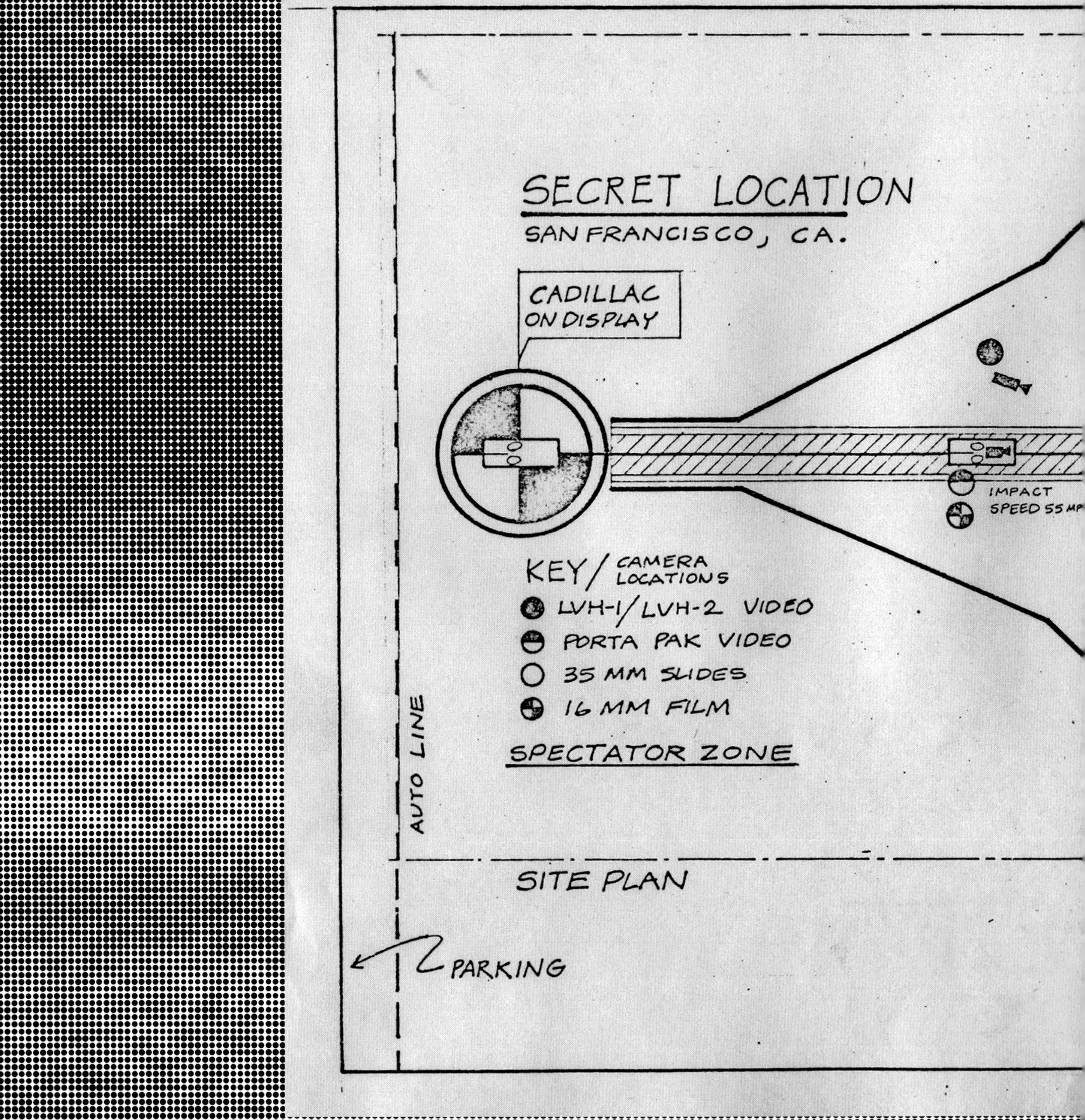

One of several drawings describing the physical configuration of *Media Burn* on the Cow Palace parking lot. In this early "secret" drawing, the Phantom Dream Car was to have a deceleration parachute, a feature that was ultimately never installed. Drawn by Doug Michels.

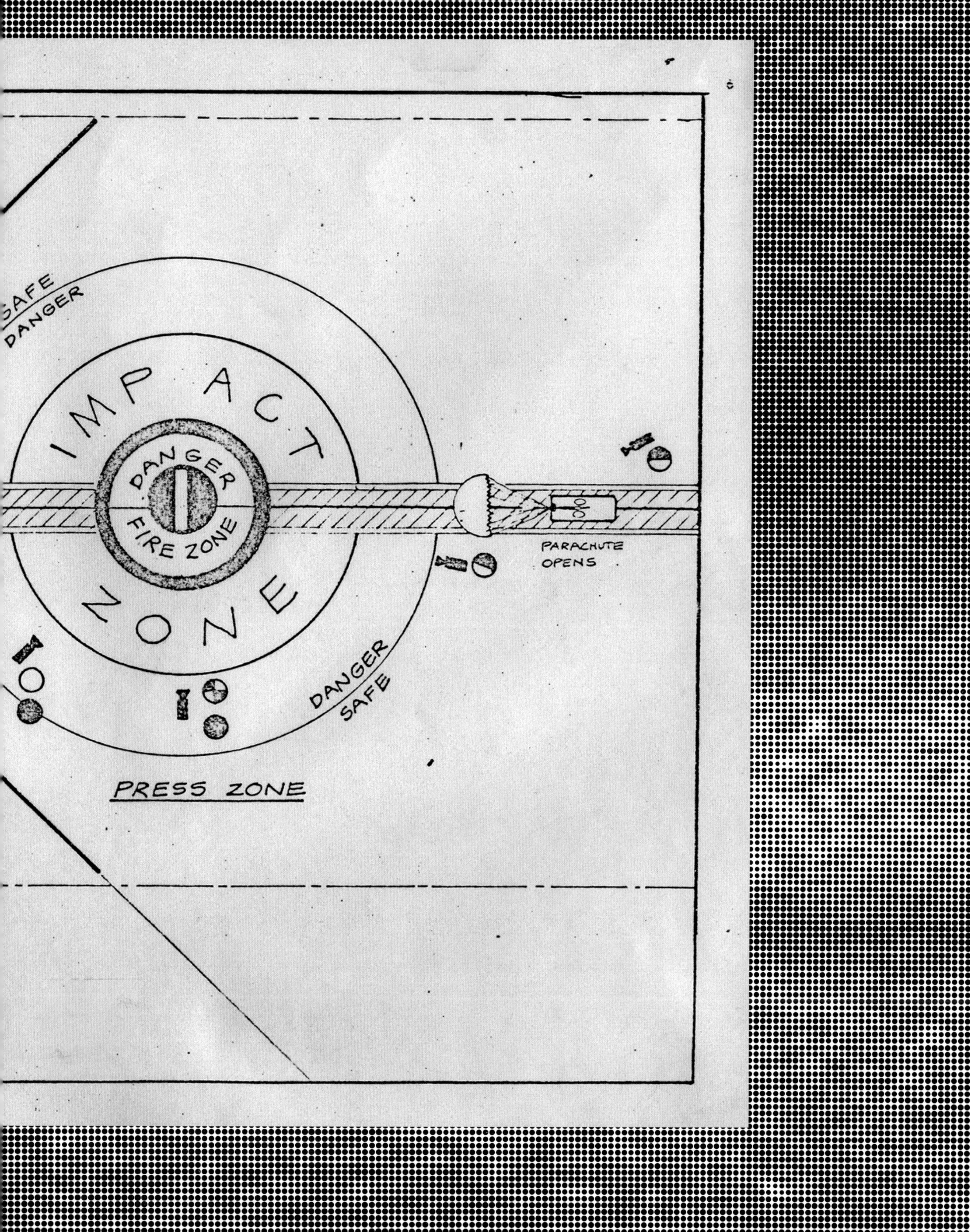

SAFE
DANGER
IMPACT
DANGER
FIRE ZONE
ZONE
DANGER
SAFE
PARACHUTE
OPENS
PRESS ZONE

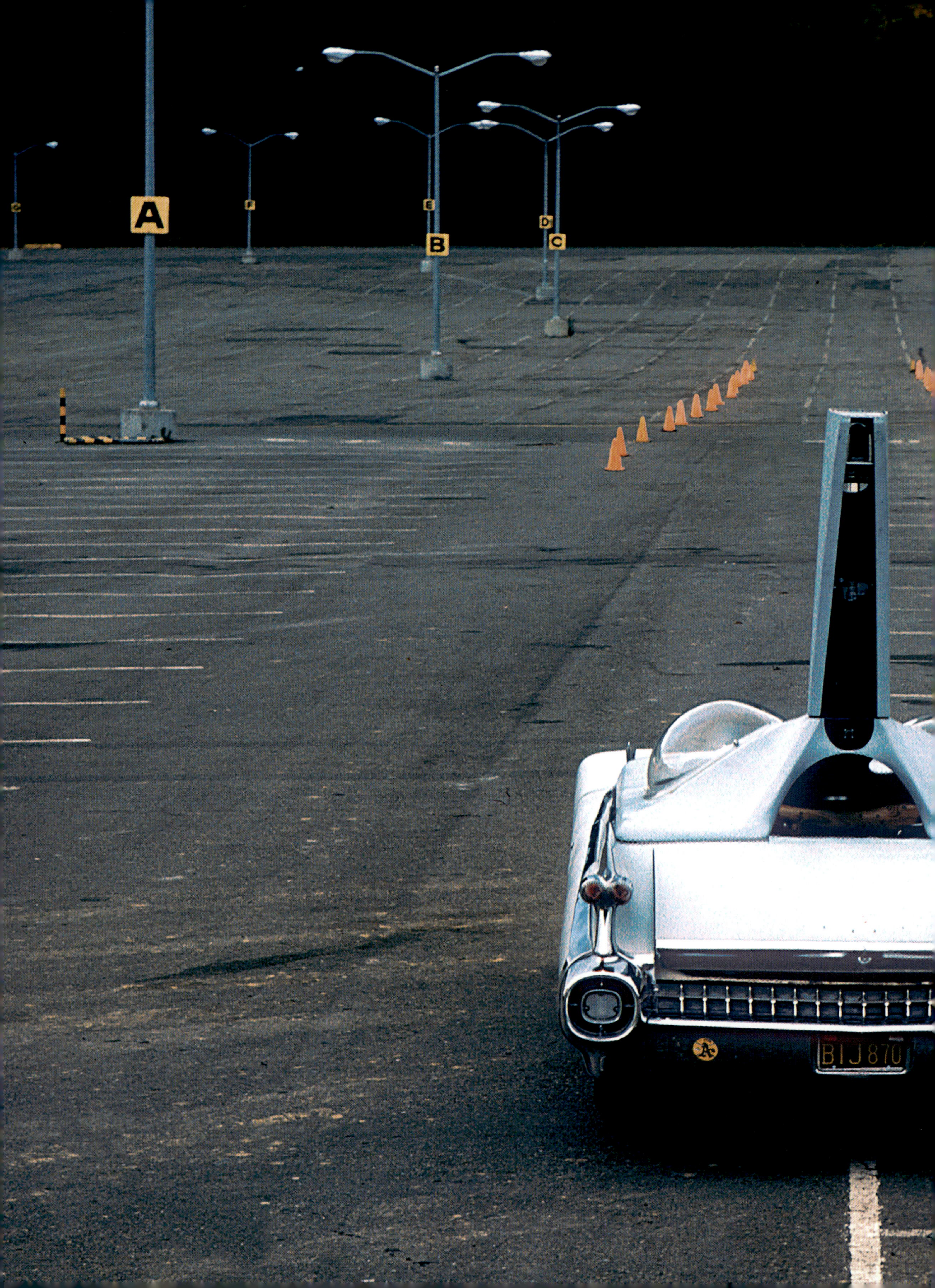
A
B
C
D
E
BIJ 870

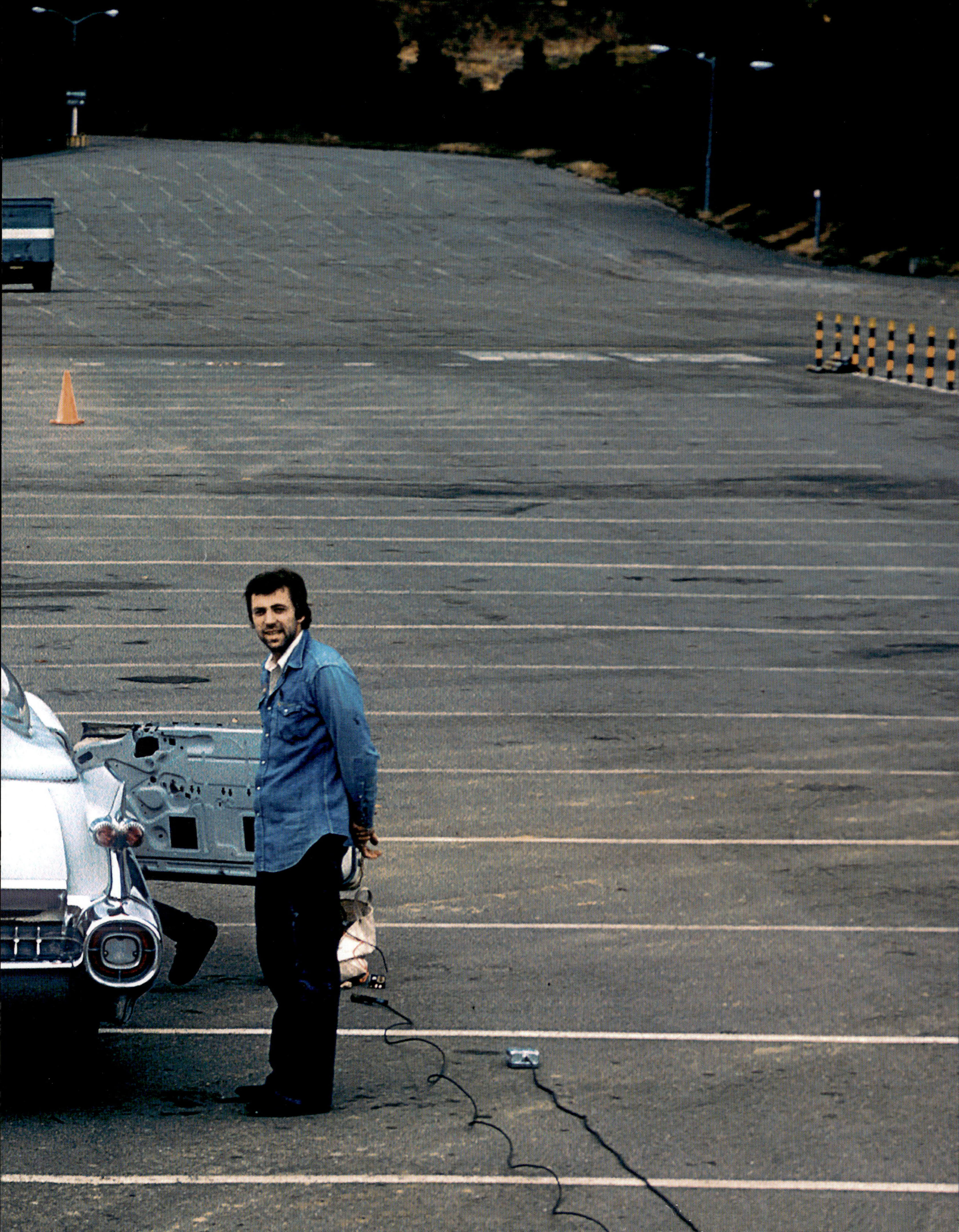

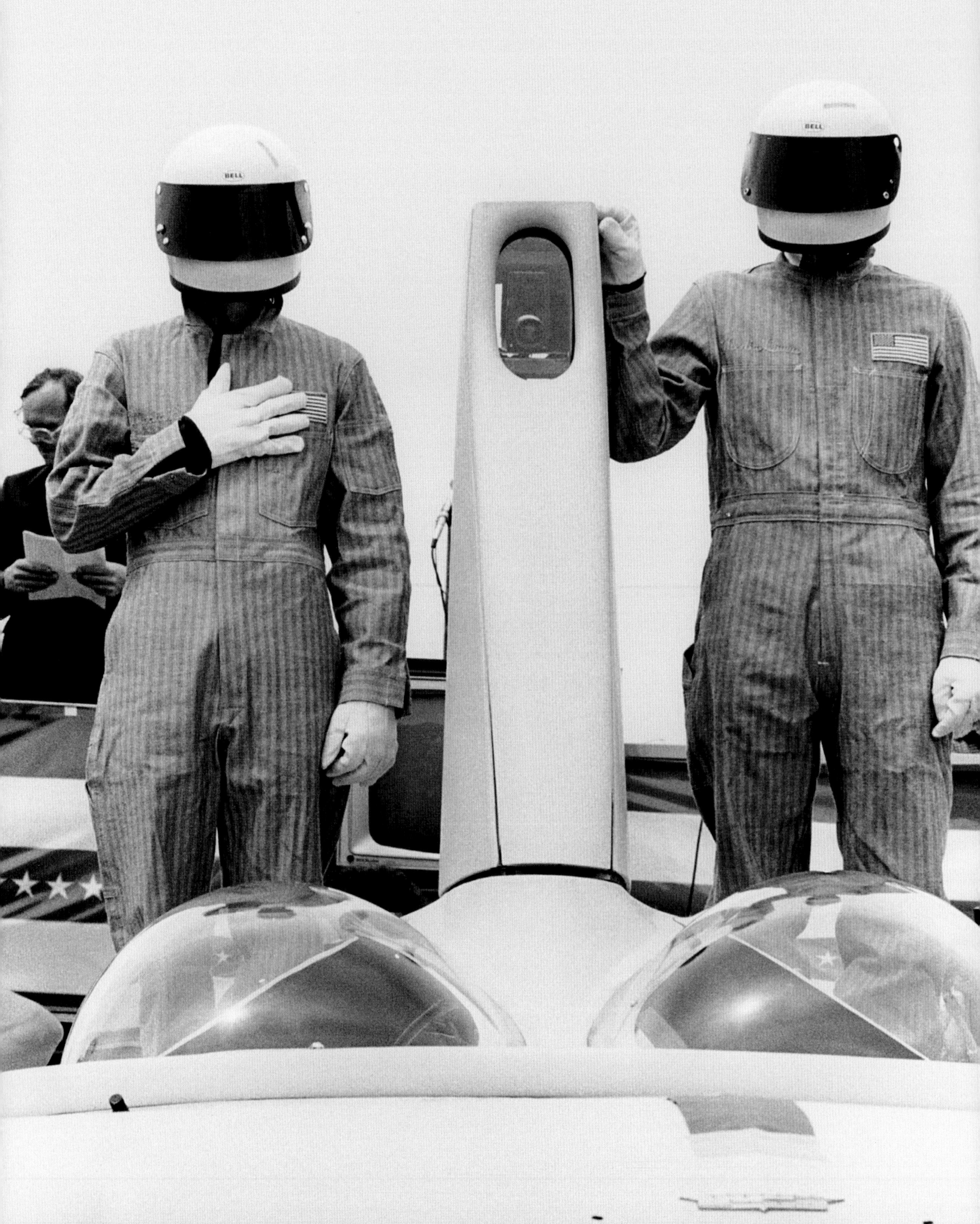

FLYING BLIND, A MISHAP

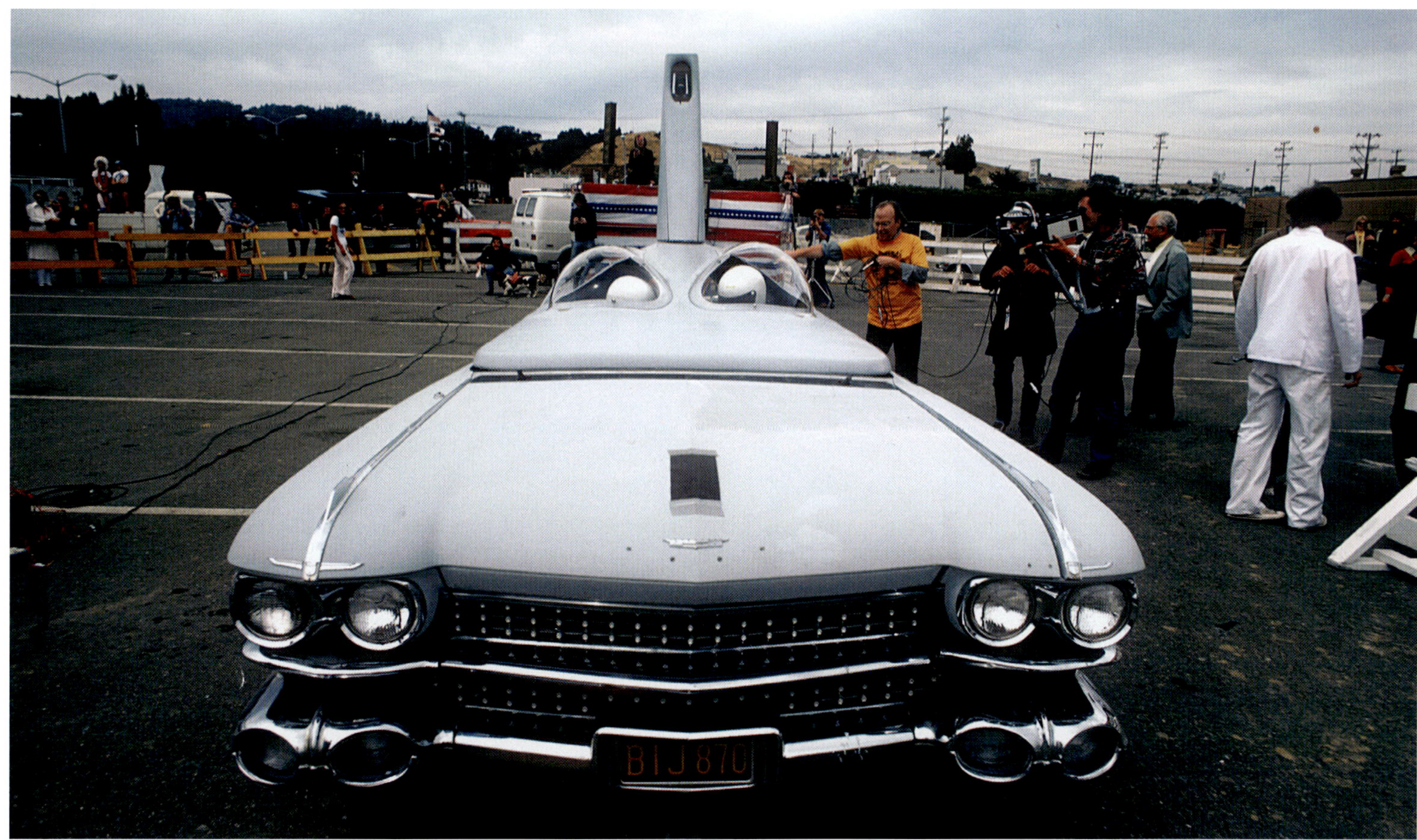

Previous spread: Soon to reemerge as an Artist-Dummy, Doug Michels early in the setup for *Media Burn*. Photograph by Phil Makanna. ©Phil Makanna.

Facing page: After the speeches, the Artist-Dummies come to attention for the "Star Spangled Banner." Photograph by Diane Andrews Hall.

Above: The video crew from Optic Nerve records the Phantom Dream Car just moments before the fated acceleration. Pictured are Jim Mayer, Jules Backus, and John Rogers. Photograph by Phil Makanna. ©Phil Makanna.

If you were to closely observe that moment when the Artist-Dummies reemerge from the entry port, you would observe something amiss. The "media matadors" are unscathed, but not so the Phantom Dream Car, which is now sans tail fin. Though the nose of the speeding vehicle initially cleared the way, enough of the burning TV sets remained airborne to shear off the tail. The monumental tail fin was left behind in the debris, to be gathered up later.

Beyond Curtis Schreier's minor miscalculation of force versus fittings, something else was awry as the car emerged from the flaming pyramid. Along with the prominent vertical stabilizer, the Phantom Dream Car was now missing its video camera—the Artist-Dummies were flying blind. The monitors had gone dead upon impact and, coincidentally, the dashboard-mounted compass had flown off. All navigation was reduced to panicky instinct. Doug Michels maintained his course, hoping to brake adequately before the bordering tree line. Fortunately, the Phantom Dream Car came to a catastrophe-free stop and the Artist-Dummies were left unharmed,[129] though bigger dummies, perhaps, in retrospect.

There was always an operative metaphor here, best summarized by Doug Michels' statement: "We were using TV to destroy TV." This would be a strain of media lethal enough to kill the host itself. At the macro level, a self-critical media event[130] would be staged for traditional media combines, then reappropriated as a source of representation for future explication. But, like a hall of mirrors, this media event was self-absorbed—it was about the media, not a client or other account. The media would be coaxed to this pseudo-event only to witness its own symbolic immolation. This was evident in the spectacle of TV sets ablaze. But what of the micro metaphors?

The Phantom Dream Car was designed specifically to be navigated via a live video feed of the road ahead. This was no incidental detail, but long planned. The prototype drawing of *Media Vision* (1973), *Media*

---

129   In a March 12, 2015, email, Schreier described how—at the last moment—he decided not to twist the locking ring on the video camera's very husky cable, but rather to just push it firmly in. When the tail fin was severed, the "unlocked" cable was able to detach from the TV monitor it was attached to instead of exerting great force on it, thus pulling the monitor wildly through the cockpit.

---

130   Like Daniel J. Boorstin's "pseudo-event," the event is staged solely for the consumption of media outlets. See Boorstin 1962.

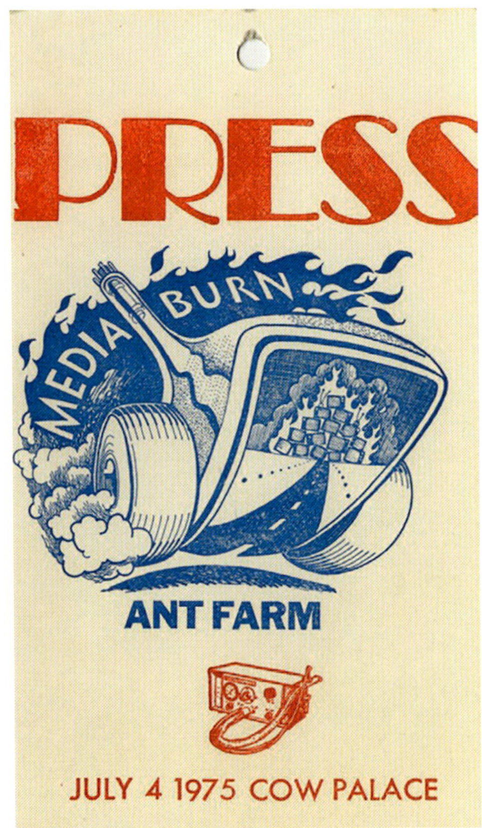

The official press pass, designed and letterpress printed by Curtis Schreier.

Facing page: Ceil Gruessing, a volunteer, in charge of the merchandising ventures for Ant Farm. Photograph by Diane Andrews Hall.

Burn's direct antecedent, goes one step farther. The *Media Vision* vehicle would not only have a dashboard-mounted camera and monitor, but it would see itself coming. A "video surveillance" camera would view the onrushing car from above and behind the "fire wall" and then feed that image to "all TV receivers."[131]

The *Media Burn* logo as displayed throughout the event—on T-shirts, the souvenir booklet, press passes, and elsewhere—reiterates this feedback circuit. The illustration is of an exaggerated cathode-ray tube with wide racing tires and a plume of black flames engulfing the background. On the screen of the CRT is presumably the road before us, a wide center-line leading to a stack of burning TV sets. This tube is the technology stripped bare, exposed, returning with a vengeance to destroy its more traditional form.

The logo image evokes the inescapable nature of the spectacle as theorized by Guy Debord. All relationships are enclosed by images and always refer back to them as a transaction. There is no limit, no edge, to this spectacle because our access to reality is really access to a mediated

131　The cost of forty-plus operating television sets was probably prohibitive and thus abandoned as a concept.

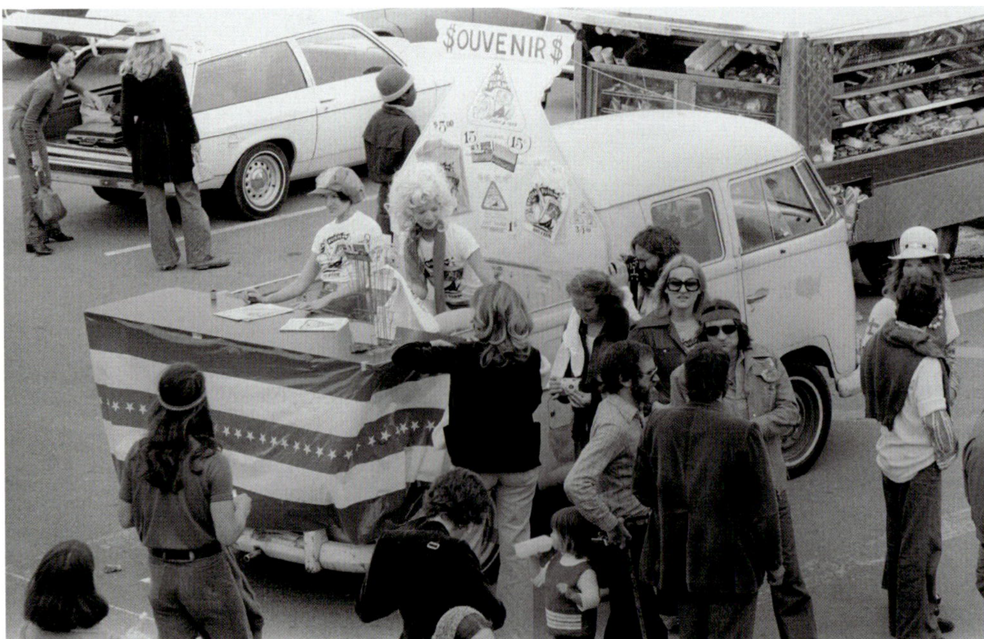

Top: Curtis Schreier's 1963 Volkswagen pickup used as the souvenir stand. Photograph by Kim Ecclesine.

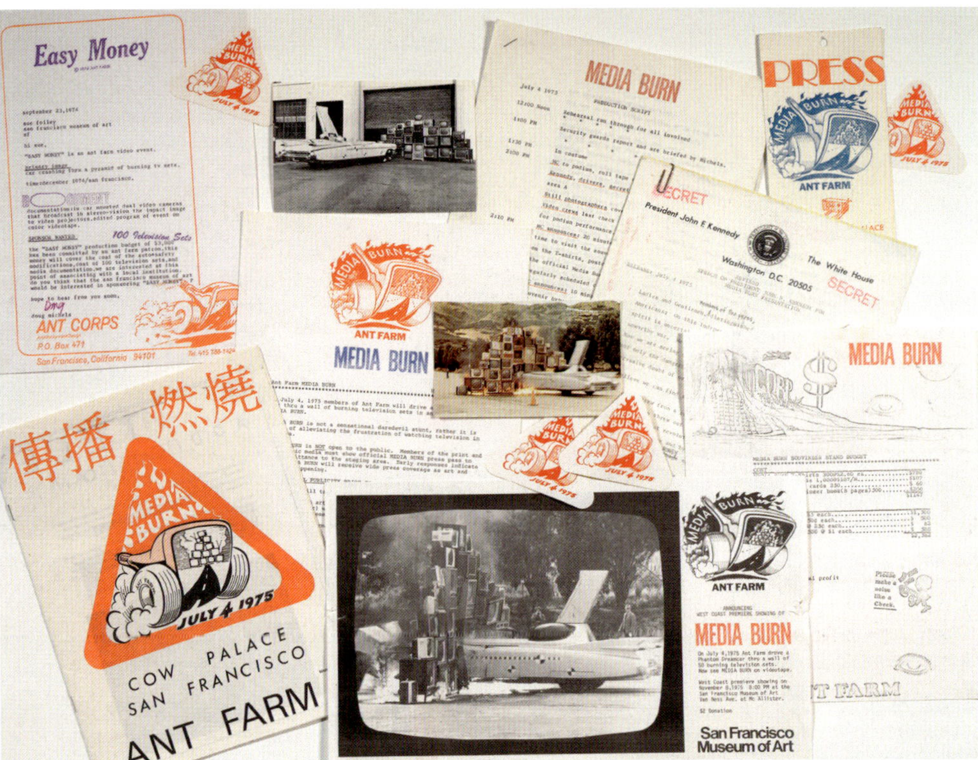

Bottom: A display of the branded materials prepared for *Media Burn*. This includes press releases, stencils, the performance schedule, postcards, and photographs by Diane Andrews Hall and Ant Farm. BAMPFA collage for 2004 retrospective exhibition.

Following spread: The Phantom Dream Car under wraps, replete with patriotic bunting. Photograph by Edmund Shea.

social construct. In this spectacular realm, we would, of course, navigate using the steering mechanism called "images." So the Artist-Dummies in attempting to "destroy TV" must resort to TV as their guide. This at once acknowledged the imprisoning ubiquity of media and suggested a first, if token, gesture toward eventual liberation—from putting your foot through your television screen to putting a nineteen-foot vehicle through that very same screen. But what happens when the monitor goes dead?

The static, the white dot, then nothing. This occurs at the moment of impact when mass media has suffered a temporary blow and the vehicle loses its tether to the technology. In that instant, the Artist-Dummies become existential travelers venturing through the void. They have for that moment been freed of the impediments of the spectacle, of media, seeing now nothing and perhaps everything. It is a giddy state, a free fall through zero signal, when only an innate sense of direction can get one home safely.

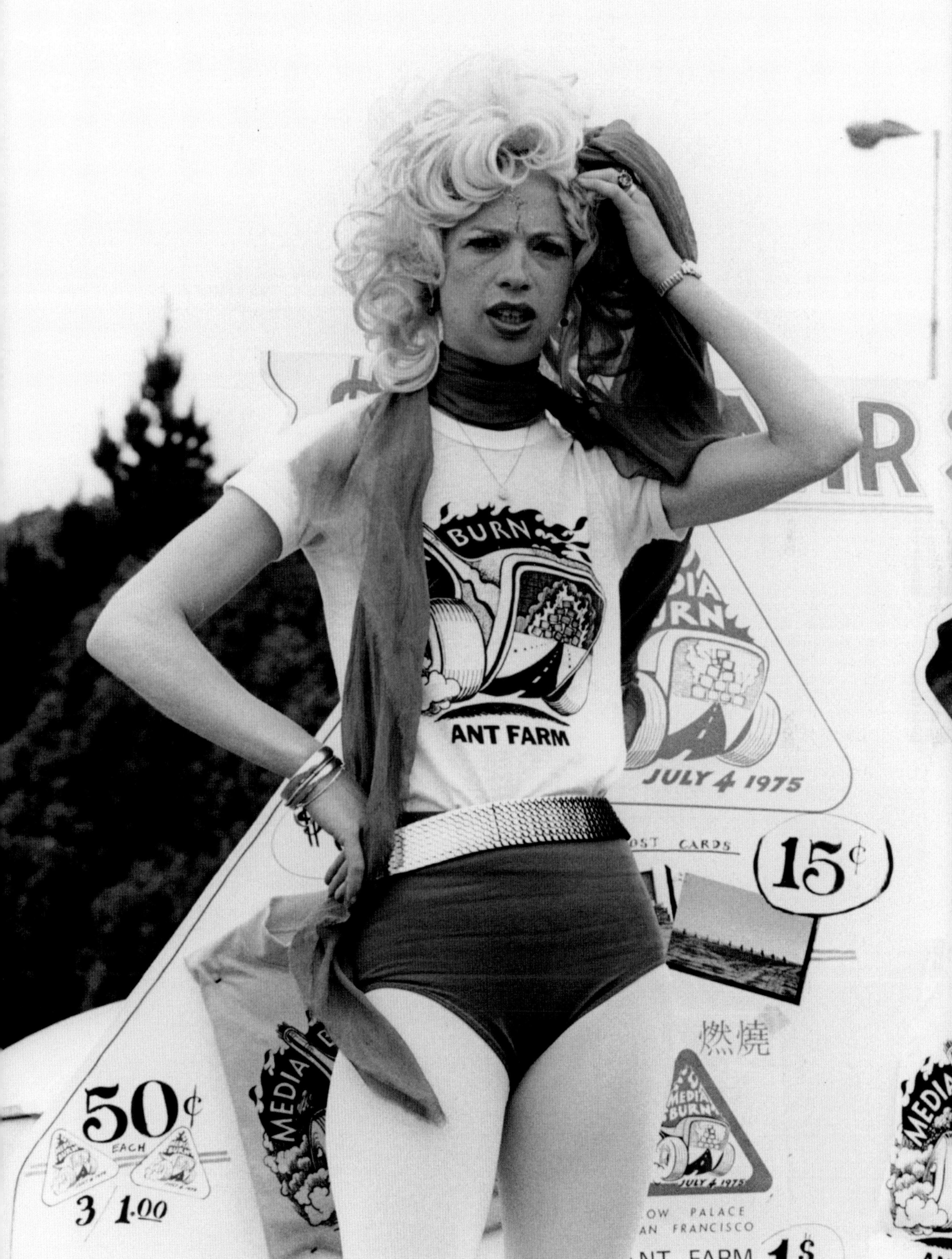

BURN
ANT FARM
JULY 4 1975
MEDIA BURN
JULY 4 1975
15¢
POST CARDS
50¢
EACH
3 / 1.00
燃燒
MEDIA BURN
OW PALACE
AN FRANCISCO
ANT FARM   1$

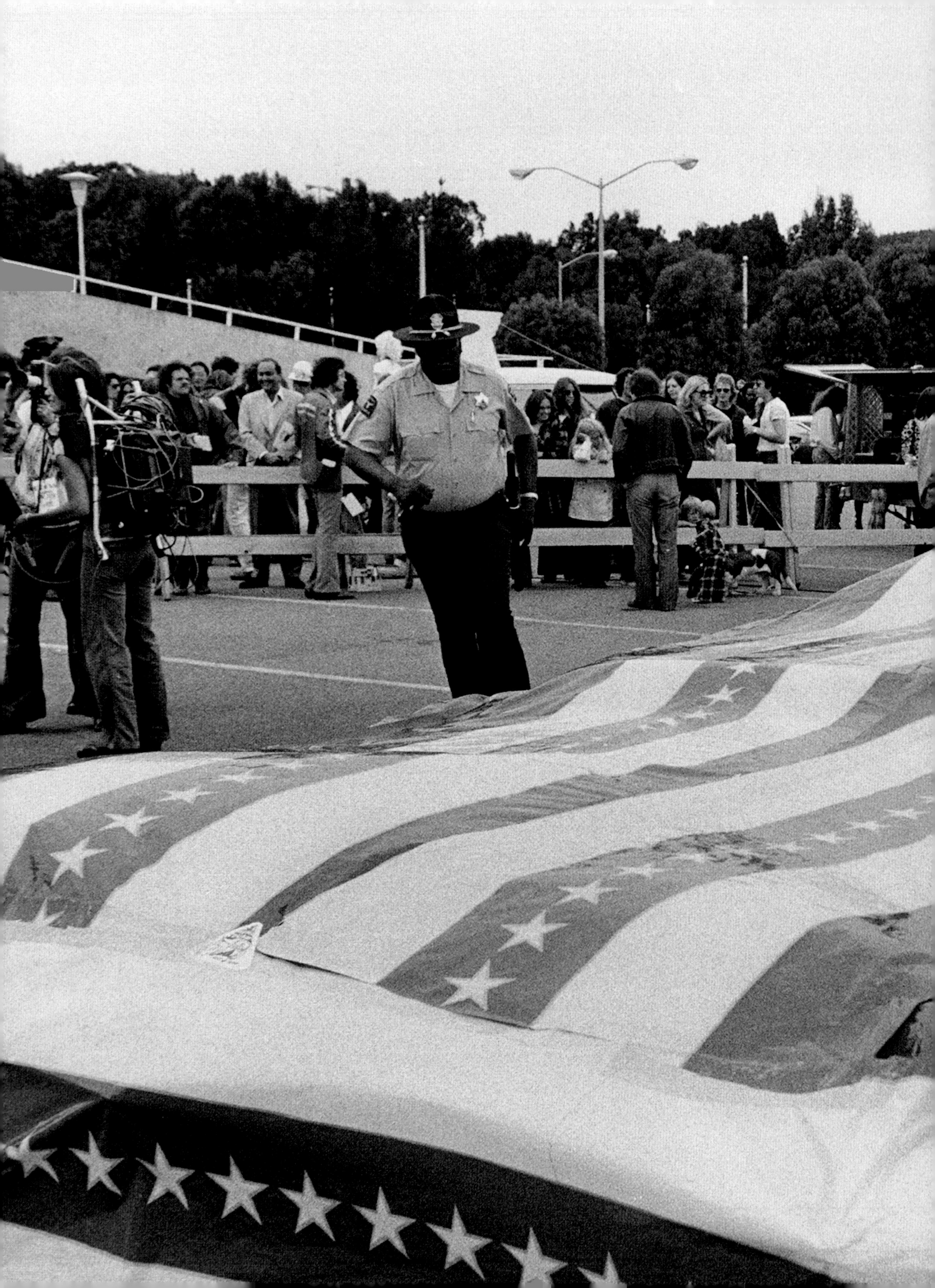

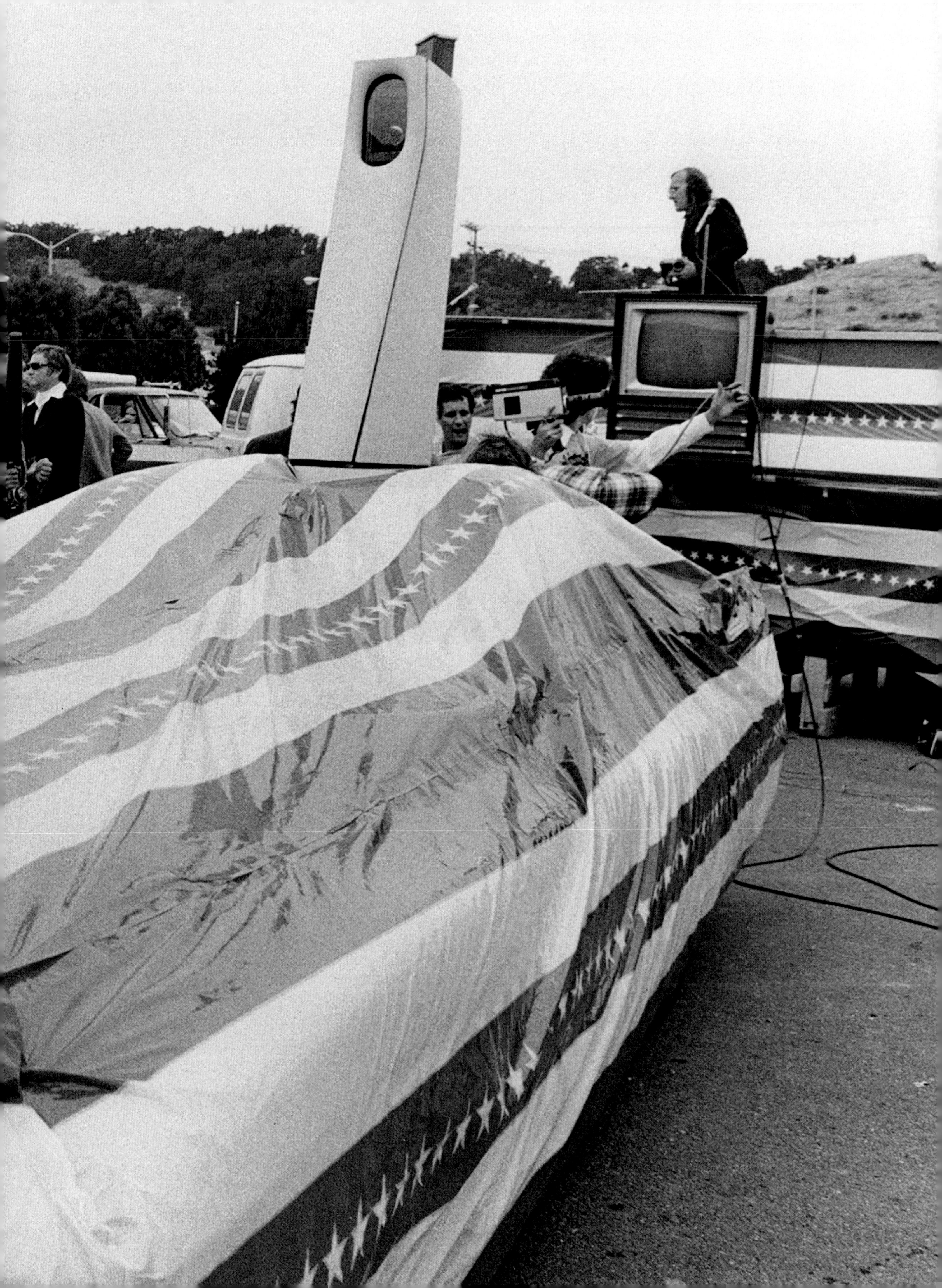

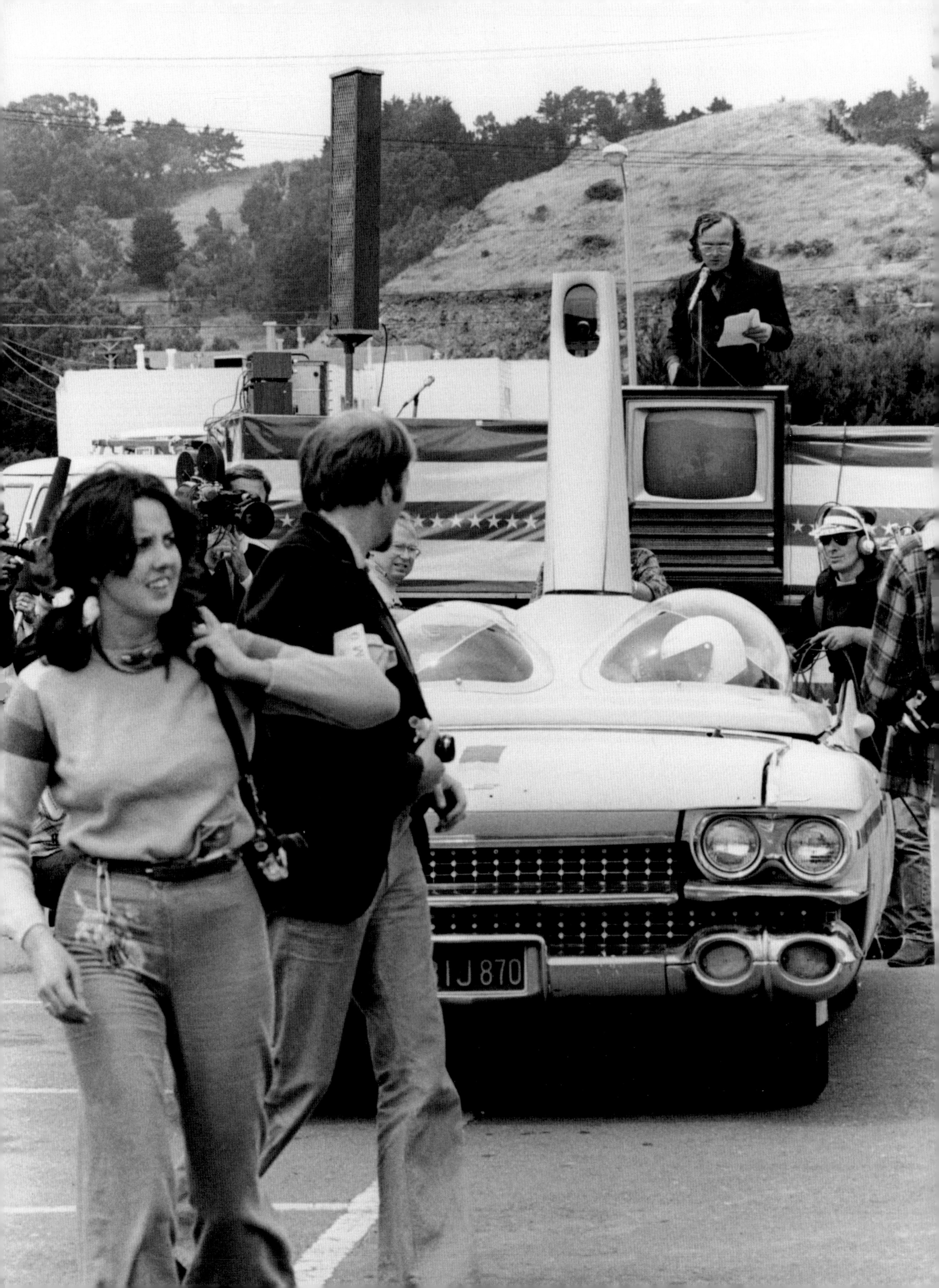

IJ 870

TWO'S COMPANY, THREE'S...

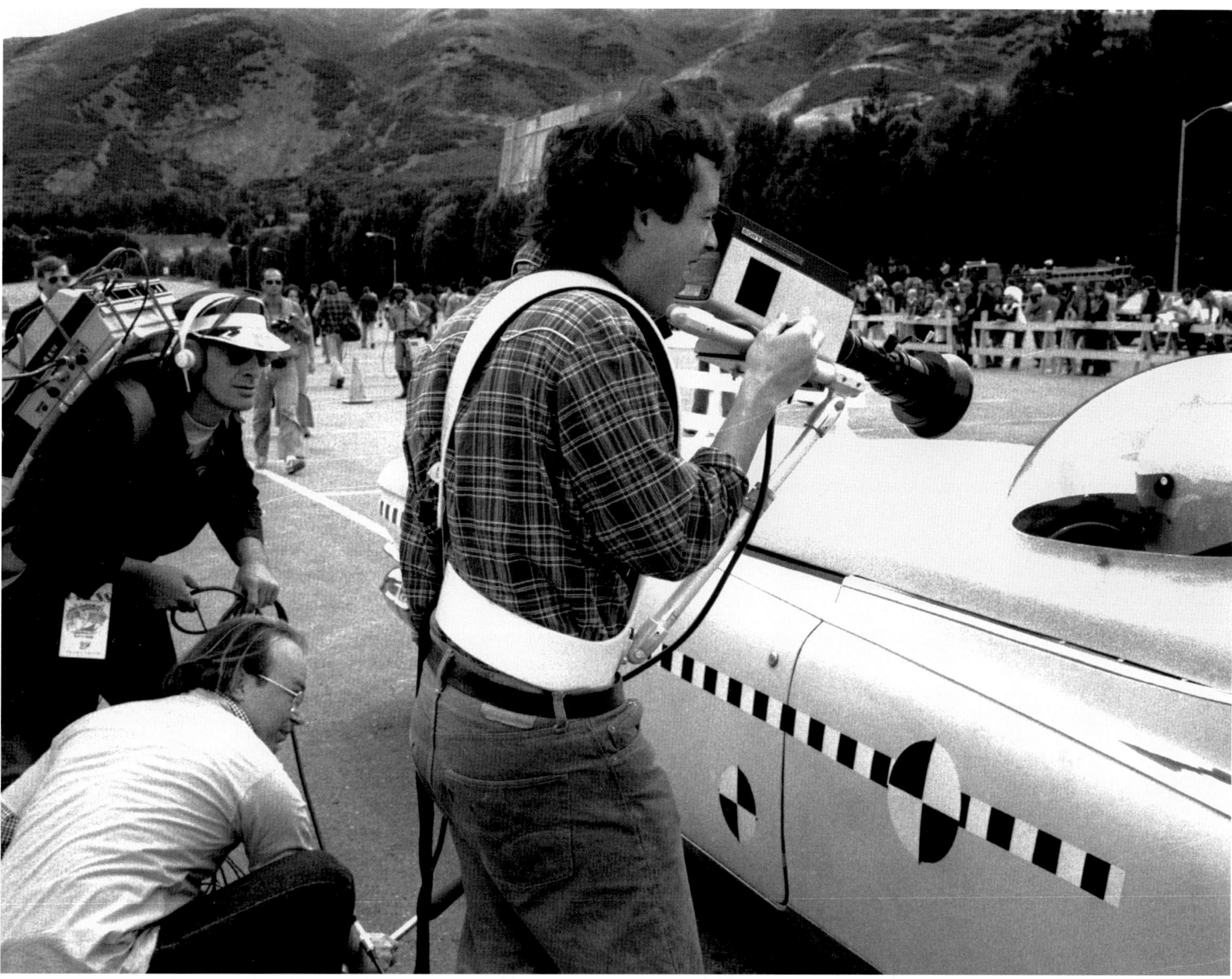

Just minutes before the fated collision, Optic Nerve members Jules Backus, Jim Mayer, and John Rogers capture the helmeted head of Doug Michels through the Lexan bubble. Photograph by Lynn Adler.

Facing page: Master of Ceremonies Bill Ding (John Hillding of T. R. Uthco) at the microphone, reading the countdown. Photograph by Diane Andrews Hall.

Following spread: Security guards at the pyramid of TV sets. Photograph by Diane Andrews Hall.

Though I would never call the Artist-President a liar, I must. In his heroic speech, the Artist-President quite explicitly says that we are about to witness "two media matadors, brave young men from Ant Farm … go forth into the unknown." The jumpsuited Artist-Dummies squeeze into the Phantom Dream Car, put the pedal to the metal, and speed off toward the "unknown." Ah, but what of "matador" number three? Lying supine between the "brave young men" was Burt Arnowitz,[132] the behelmeted cameraman, shooting the body-twisting acceleration and eventual media penetration of the Phantom Dream

———

132   Burt Arnowitz was not technically a member of Ant Farm, so therefore only two members commanded the cockpit. Part of the original Marin Community Video group, Arnowitz would go on to co-invent "Evening Magazine" at San Francisco's KPIX.

Car. It is Arnowitz's hand-held Portapak that captures the installation of the reinforced canopies, the anxiety-producing countdown, and the jarring impact, all in an upward gaze. It was also Arnowitz who was lightly showered with the burning TV debris that had unexpectedly entered through fractures in the fiberglass skin of the elongated hood.

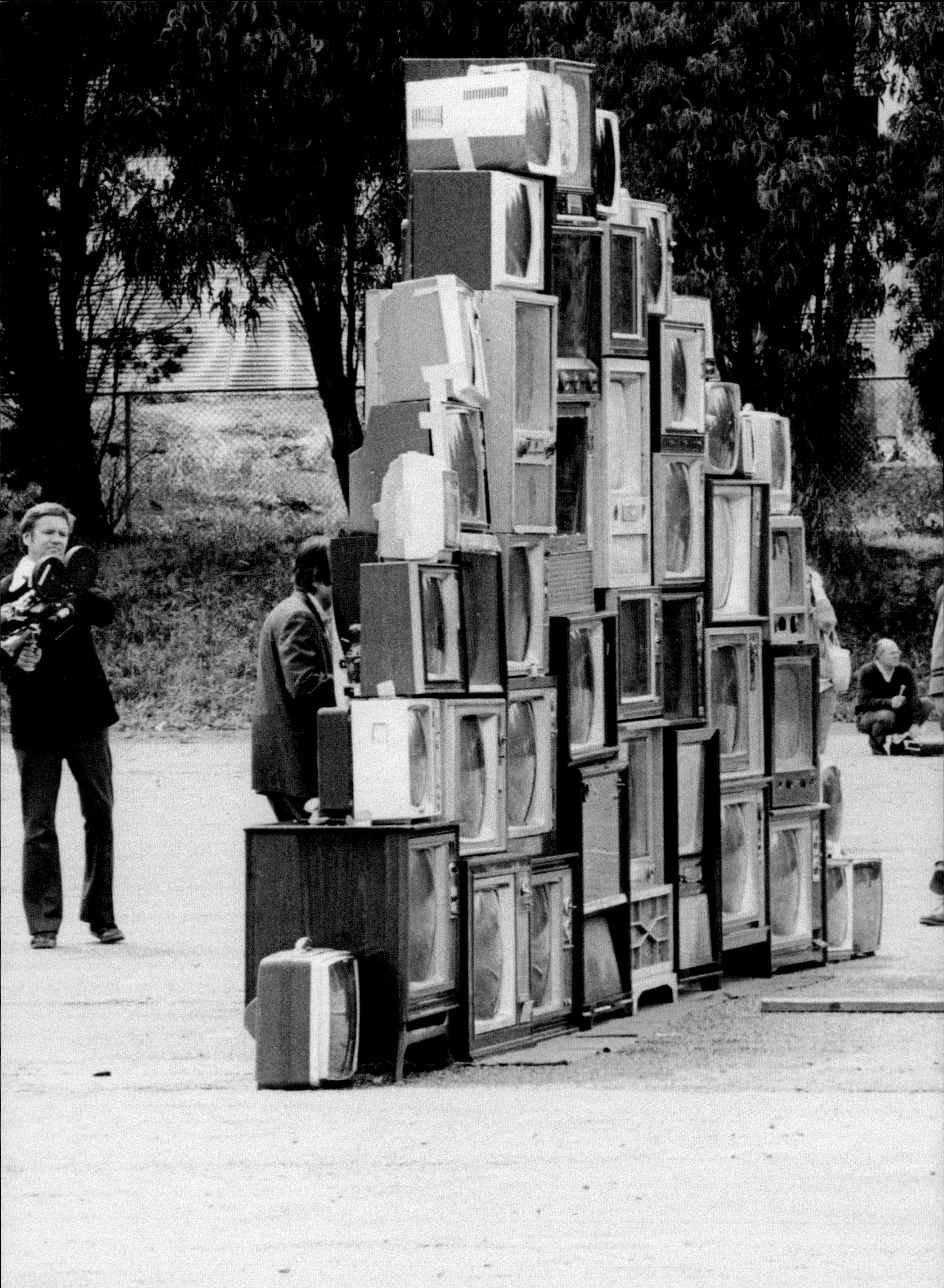

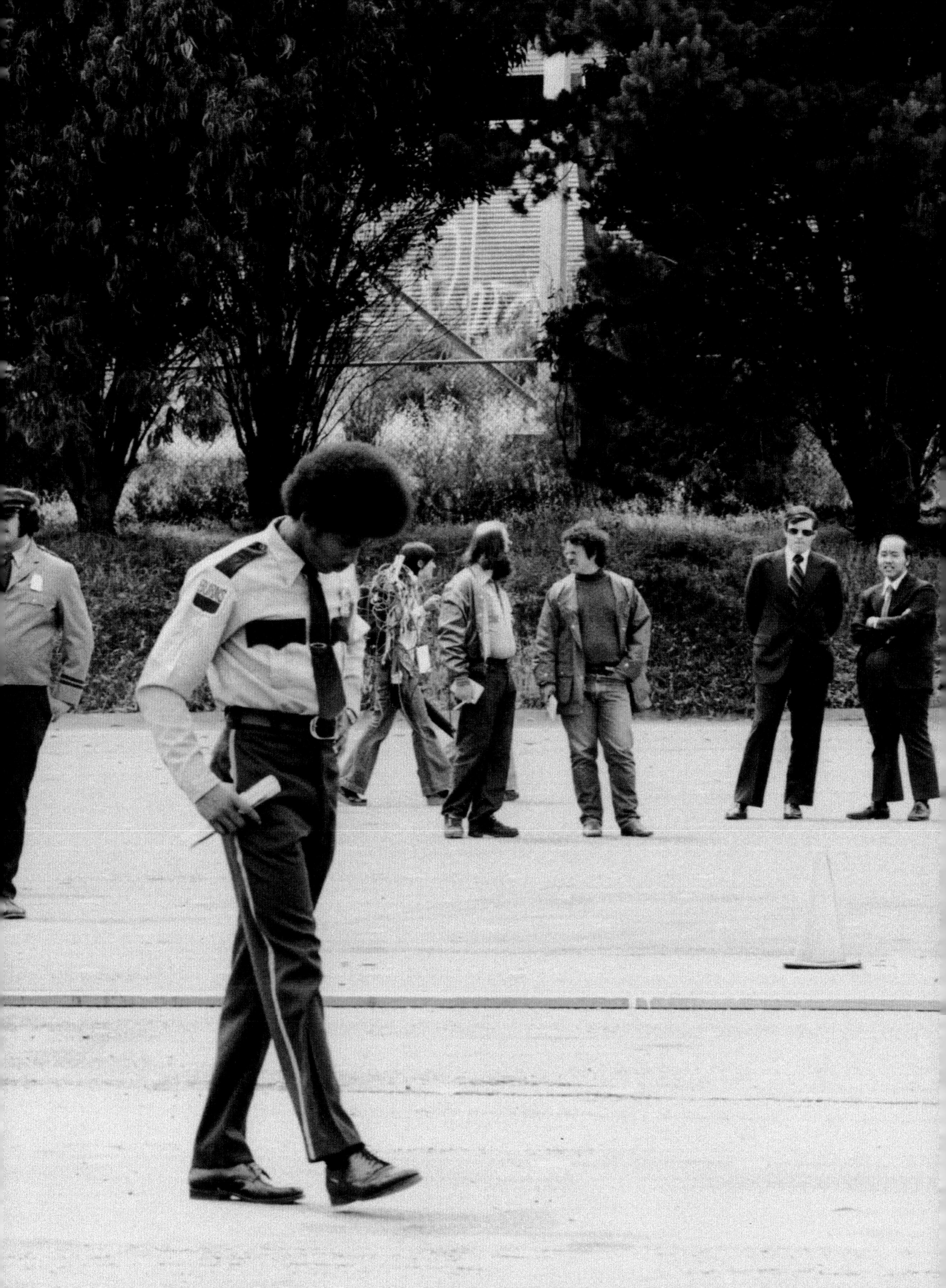

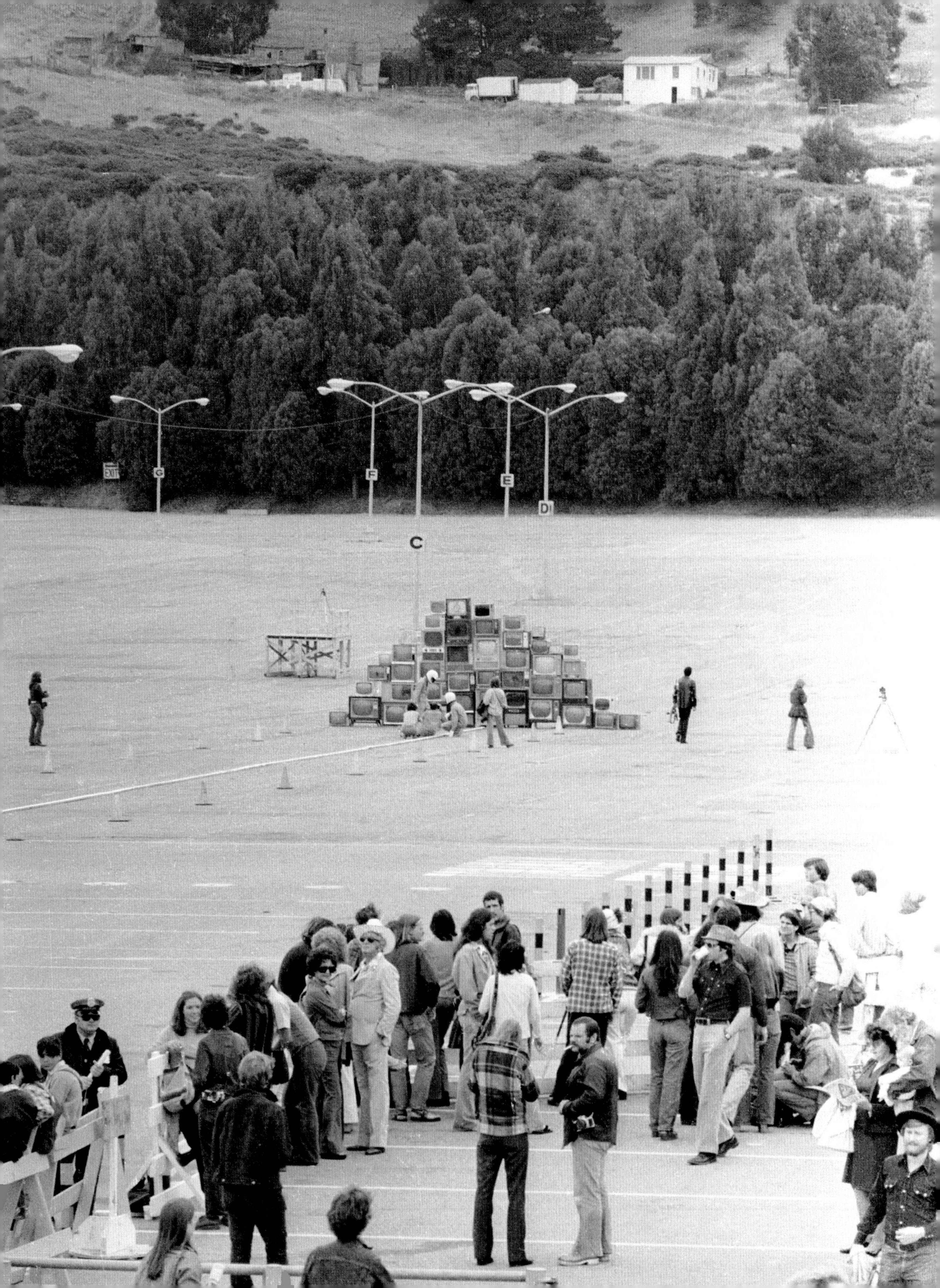

G
F
E
D
C
EXIT

THE PSEUDO-EVENT

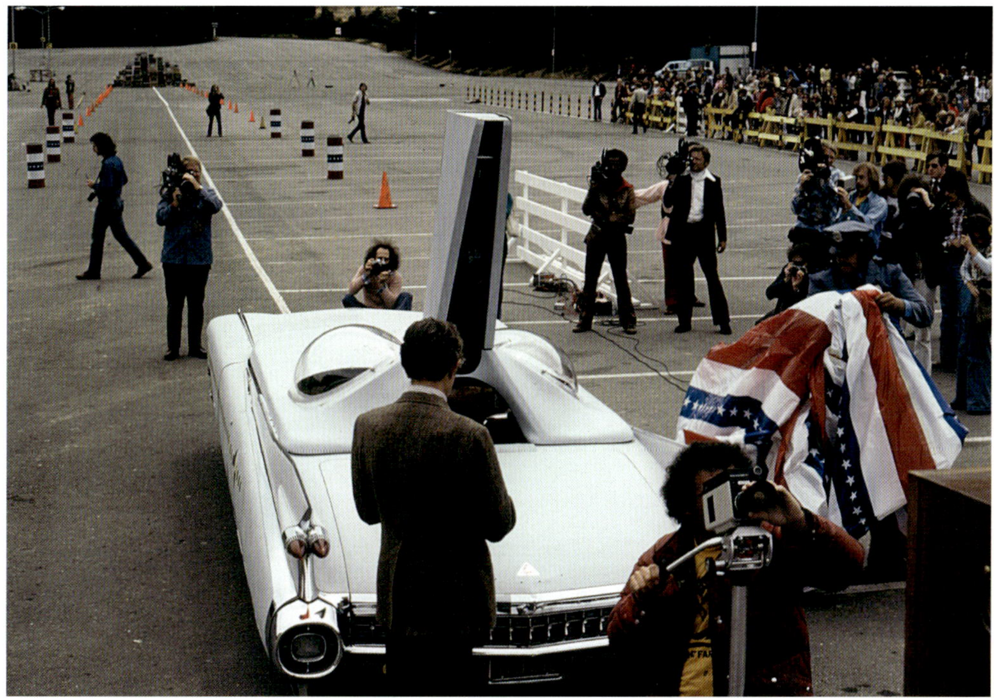

The Phantom Dream Car is revealed as a security guard removes the patriotic bunting. Photograph by Phil Makanna. ©Phil Makanna.

Facing page: The crowd throngs as the Artist-Dummies confer beside the pyramid of TV sets. Note the safety barricade. Photograph by Kim Ecclesine.

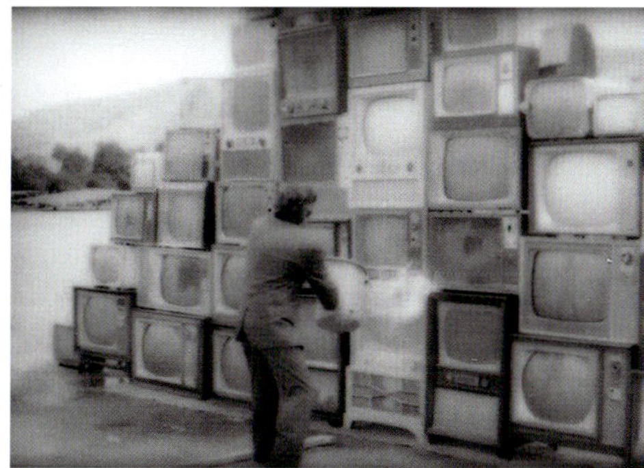

Frame enlargement from a rare contact sheet by Edmund Shea showing Chip Lord as Uncle Buddie dowsing the TV sets with kerosene. Photograph by Edmund Shea.

Following spread: This is the consummation of the image production of *Media Burn*. John F. Turner's collision shot captures the TV sets in crisp focus while the Phantom Dream Car is a blur of speed. This image was used for all the postcards. Photograph by John F. Turner.

The final gesture was yet to be put in place. If the culmination of *Media Burn* was the previously decreed "image created here," then where was it? A strategy had been formulated to deliver the encapsulating image to the wire services. Both United Press International (UPI) and Associated Press (AP) had offices on Market Street in the Fox Plaza Building. This would offer unlimited possibilities for dissemination— far beyond the local coverage the event was all but guaranteed.[133]

Chip Lord and Diane Hall rushed to Edmund Shea's darkroom, developed Diane's black-and-white film, and selected a single image to print (see p. 97). It showed the Phantom Dream Car partially penetrating the pyramid of TV sets, flames crawling along the asphalt, and a handful of TV consoles propelled forward from the initial impact. The Phantom Dream Car was intact and its forward thrust formidable. If you were to look closely, you could see another photographer, camera raised, shooting an equal but opposite shot. The circuit was complete. TV was killing TV and media was mirroring media.

By five that evening, the singular image of *Media Burn* had been placed at the wire services and its diffusion would now be self-perpetuating. The image would break free of its initial ownership as it went viral, abetted by the release of additional shots from the other on-site photographers.[134] Ant Farm itself would participate in the unbridled replication by issuing postcards and other visual paraphernalia as they had already done with *Cadillac Ranch*. That irreducible *Media Burn* image would knock about in the overarching mediasphere like an antigen, provoking—if only faintly at the cellular level—an antidotal response. No giant step for mankind, but certainly a conceptual leap toward liberation.

Ant Farm seemed to be operating in a theoretical terrain somewhere between Daniel J. Boorstin's "pseudo-event" and the developing ideas of Jean Baudrillard, whose seminal *Simulacra and Simulation* would be published in 1981. Preceding Baudrillard by two decades, Boorstin's notion was that media events found their value only in their circulation. The original event was of no consequence. It was the intended reproduction that served a purpose and at some level obliterated the original. The pseudo-event was an opportunity (like a photo op), not a historical moment. It was more a symptom of commercial necessity than a state of subsumed reality. In today's idiom, the pseudo-event would be the matter behind the meme.

By the time Baudrillard trained his attention on this phenomenon it had grown at least in severity if not in outright ascendancy to a higher level of mediation, a third order of simulation. He replaced Boorstin's "pseudo" with an advanced replica, a simulacrum, or a copy of something that in the extreme had no original. Like Debord, Baudrillard hinted at a socially constructed mediasphere in which the lives of individuals are penetrated by rootless images with no purpose other than to stand in for a prescribed reality. The environment becomes a seamless and nonorganic sensorium

---

133   It should be noted that all *Media Burn* press releases requested a news embargo until the day of the event.

134   Years later, Diane Hall would finally give Ant Farm her *Media Burn* negatives because she had grown tired of printing on-demand stills. From an email dated April 10, 2015.

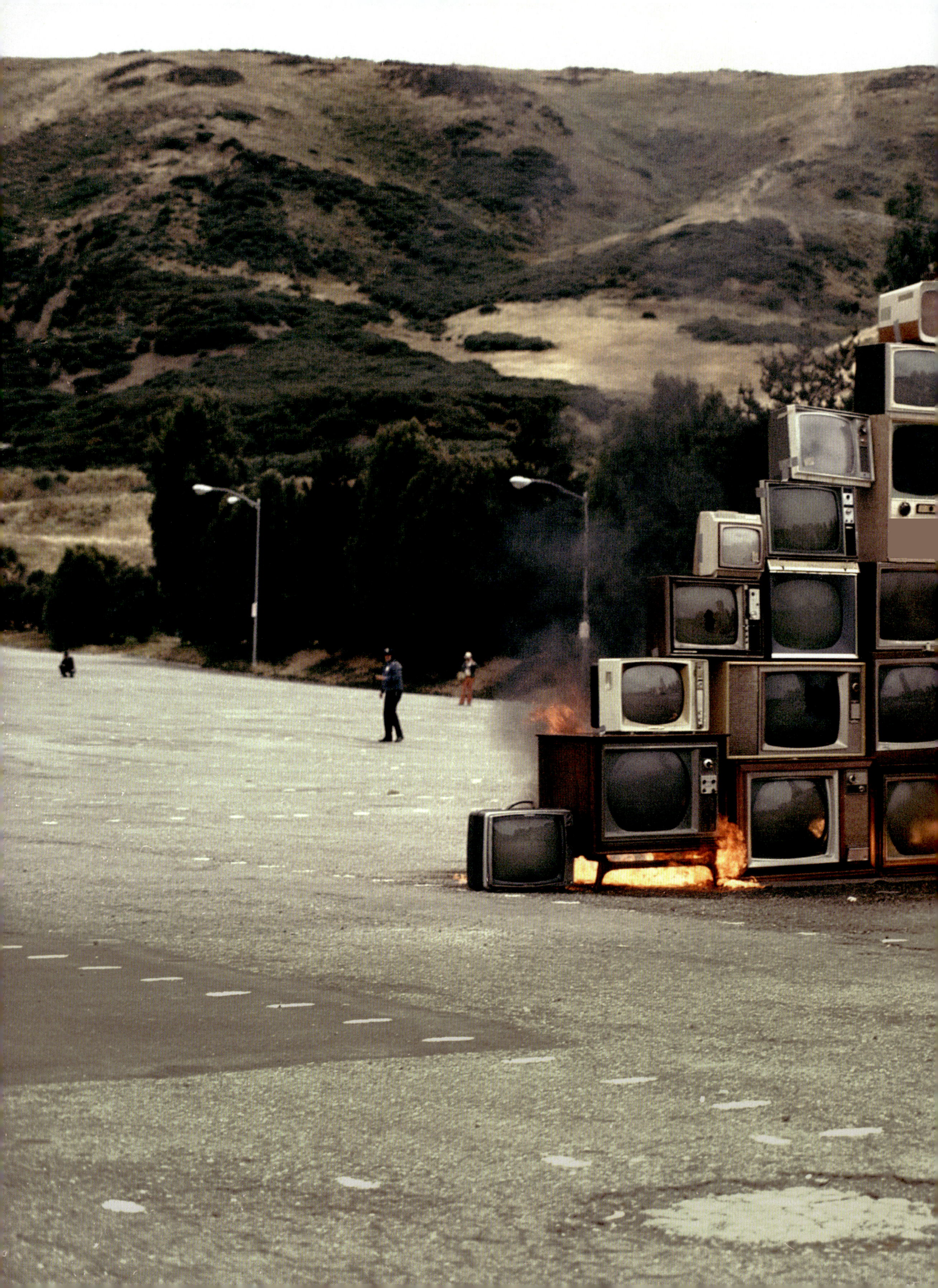

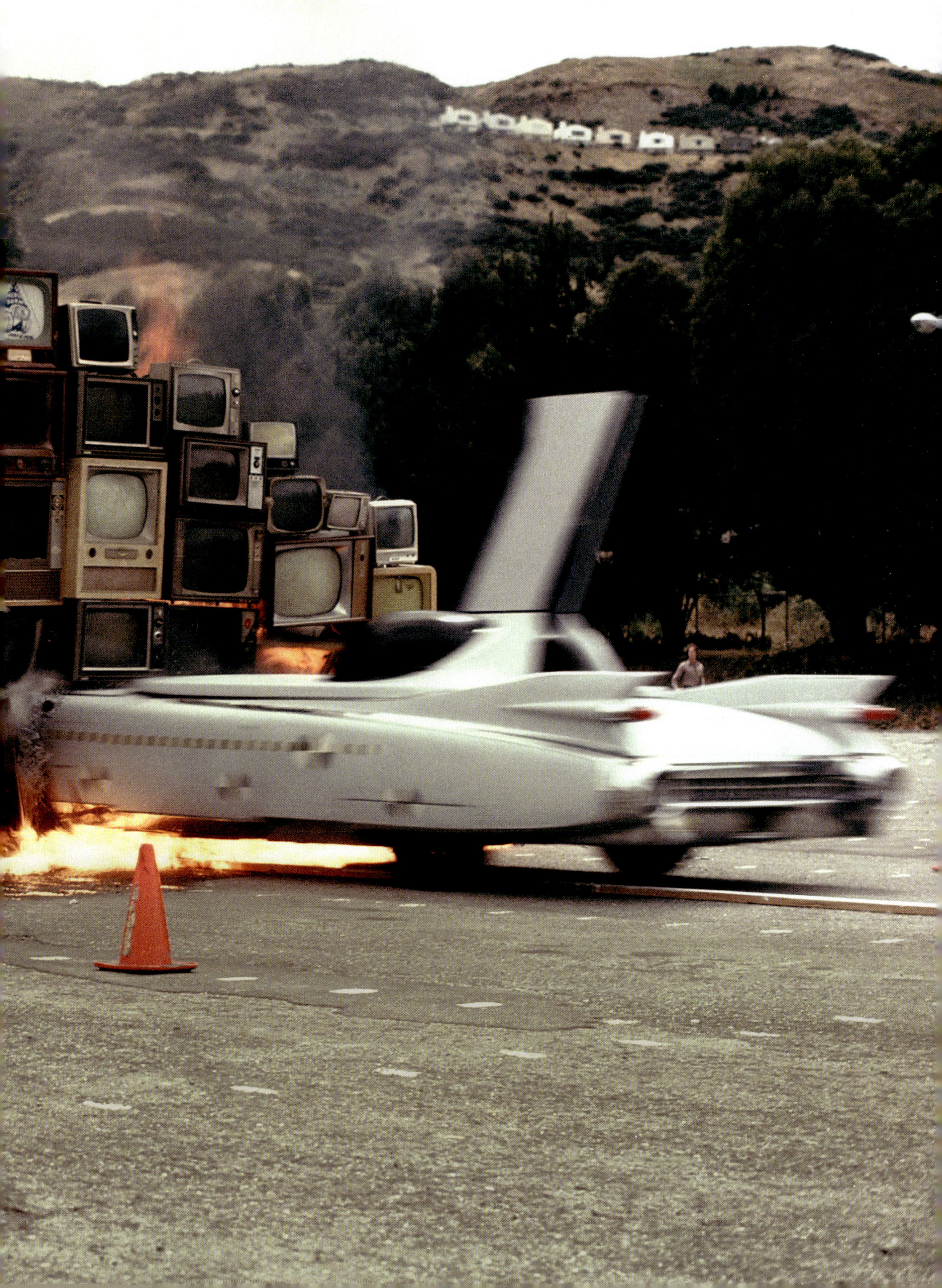

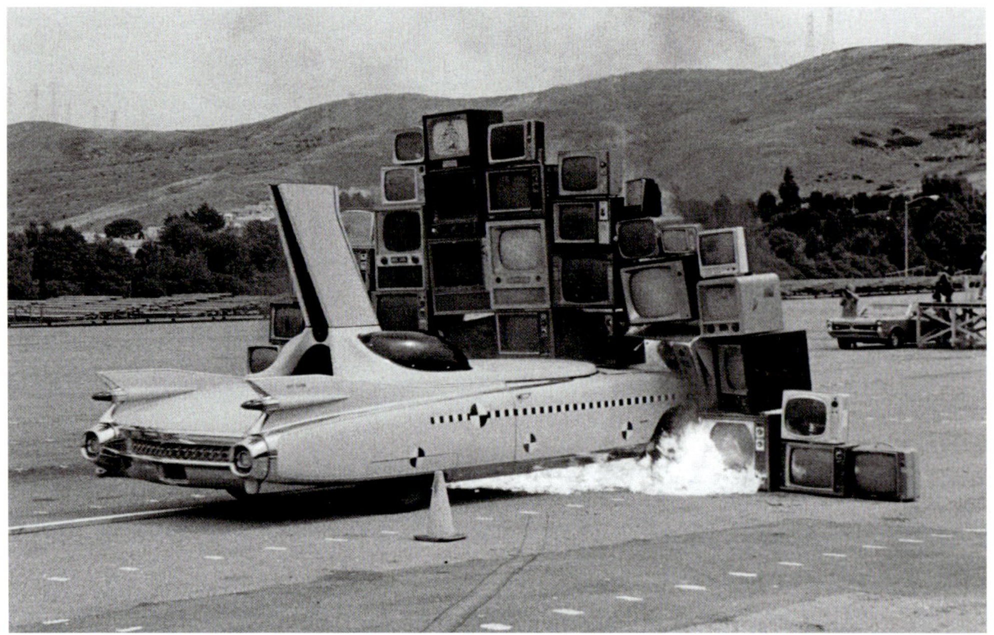

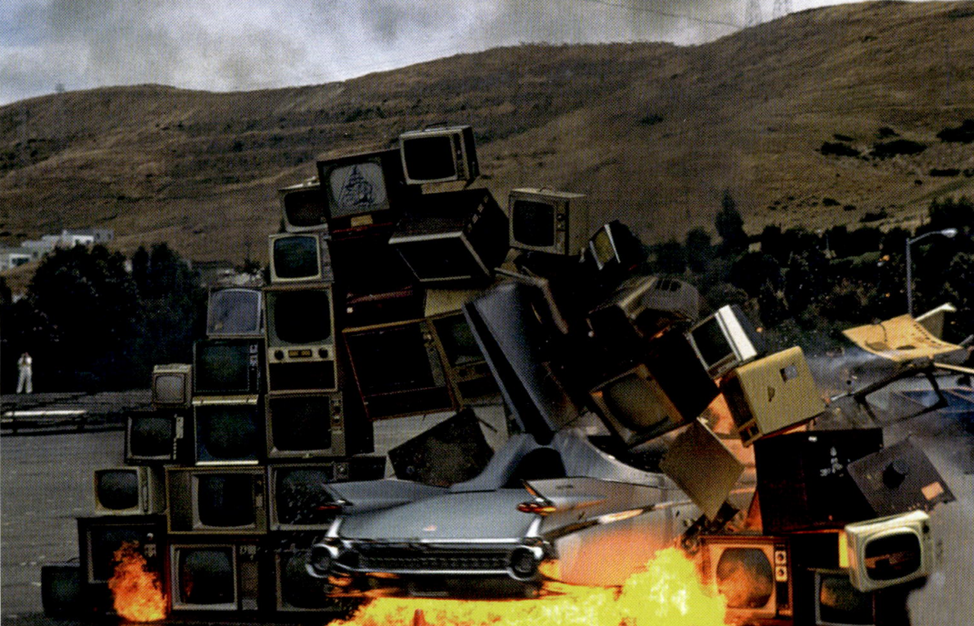

Top: The collision, looking south. Photograph by Edmund Shea.

Bottom: Like John F. Turner, Phil Makanna photographed the collision in color, enhancing the kerosene-fueled flames. ©Phil Makanna.

of pure ideology. In its final triumph, "the territory no longer precedes the map, nor survives it."[135]

Between the poles of the pseudo-event and the simulacra stands *Media Burn*,[136] at least the image thereof. If it is to survive as an inoculation, fortifying us against the media, then it has to be recuperated from the meaningless circulation of the mediadrome. This rescue mission would come in the form of the videowork known also as *Media Burn*. Where in retrospect the videowork accompanying *Cadillac Ranch* was more a promotional making-of noted for its whimsy, the *Media Burn* videowork was an extension of the event, sustaining the "image created" while advancing its own critical explication. *Media Burn* would exist in a context determined by Ant Farm, deepening its conceptual underpinnings and prolonging its longevity.

The stage was set long before, Ant Farm having arranged for three of their own designated camera crews (including a high-speed 16mm camera for the slow-motion) and four still photographers roaming the Cow Palace site. Add to this amateur photographers lining the staging area and the media's own representatives, on-air reporters from the local TV affiliates, and an equal group of print journalists with their accompanying photographers: it would be an orgy of image-capture, much of it accessible to the artists after the fact.

After July 4, all the official source footage was collected, along with TV coverage that was, for the most part, recorded off-air. Ant Farm assembled a rough cut in Lanesville, New York, using the Videofreex facilities, then the final cut was mastered on two-inch quad tape at the Synapse Video Center, housed at Syracuse University. Synapse was a center designed to support independent and experimental videowork, but to serve the needs of the campus it had also created a broadcast-quality postproduction studio. The *Media Burn* tape combined original ½-inch video, 16mm footage transferred through a film chain, and footage lifted from news coverage. Completed on September 24, 1975, the master tape was twenty-five minutes, forty-eight seconds in length.[137] Chip Lord was the principal editor, with advice and assistance from Skip Blumberg,[138] Doug Michels, and Tom Weinberg.

The videotape begins at the beginning with the *Media Burn* logo zooming forward.[139] We are then presented with a bank of TV monitors with different images playing out. From the visual cacophony emerges the anchor from KGO-TV's Action News in the studio: "The Fourth of July is notorious for heavy traffic fatalities ... This Fourth is starting out no differently. So far, there have been 120 traffic deaths and 30 drownings since the start of the holiday ..." We are deep into it, the lethal but mundane observance of Independence Day, the rote patriotism, and the desperate filler to puff up a slow news day. Some sparklers fill the screen and the news announcer adds: "So let's

135   "Simulacra and Simulations," from *Jean Baudrillard, Selected Writings*, ed. Mark Poster (Stanford, CA: Stanford University Press, 1988), p. 166.

136   It could be said that Ant Farm's next important project, *The Eternal Frame* (1975), would close the distance between the performed event and its video representation. The reenactment of the Kennedy assassination was not an announced "media event" but more a guerrilla intervention. In fact, it wasn't a reenactment of the assassination at all, but a dramatization of the Zapruder footage, the image of the assassination.

137   Ant Farm often re-edits their works, not just as rethinkings but as a way to revive interest in the works themselves, i.e., the newer, sharper version. *Media Burn* exists in a 2003 version that is 23:02 minutes long. It is not just shorter but has some sequences in new positions within the tape. The above comments refer to the original cut.

138   Skip Blumberg regularly worked on projects with TVTV and Ant Farm. He would be an important member of the collective group that created *The Eternal Frame*. Being a member of Videofreex, he was probably the most familiar with their editing capabilities.

139   This is almost an adumbration of the coming pyramid of some forty TV sets.

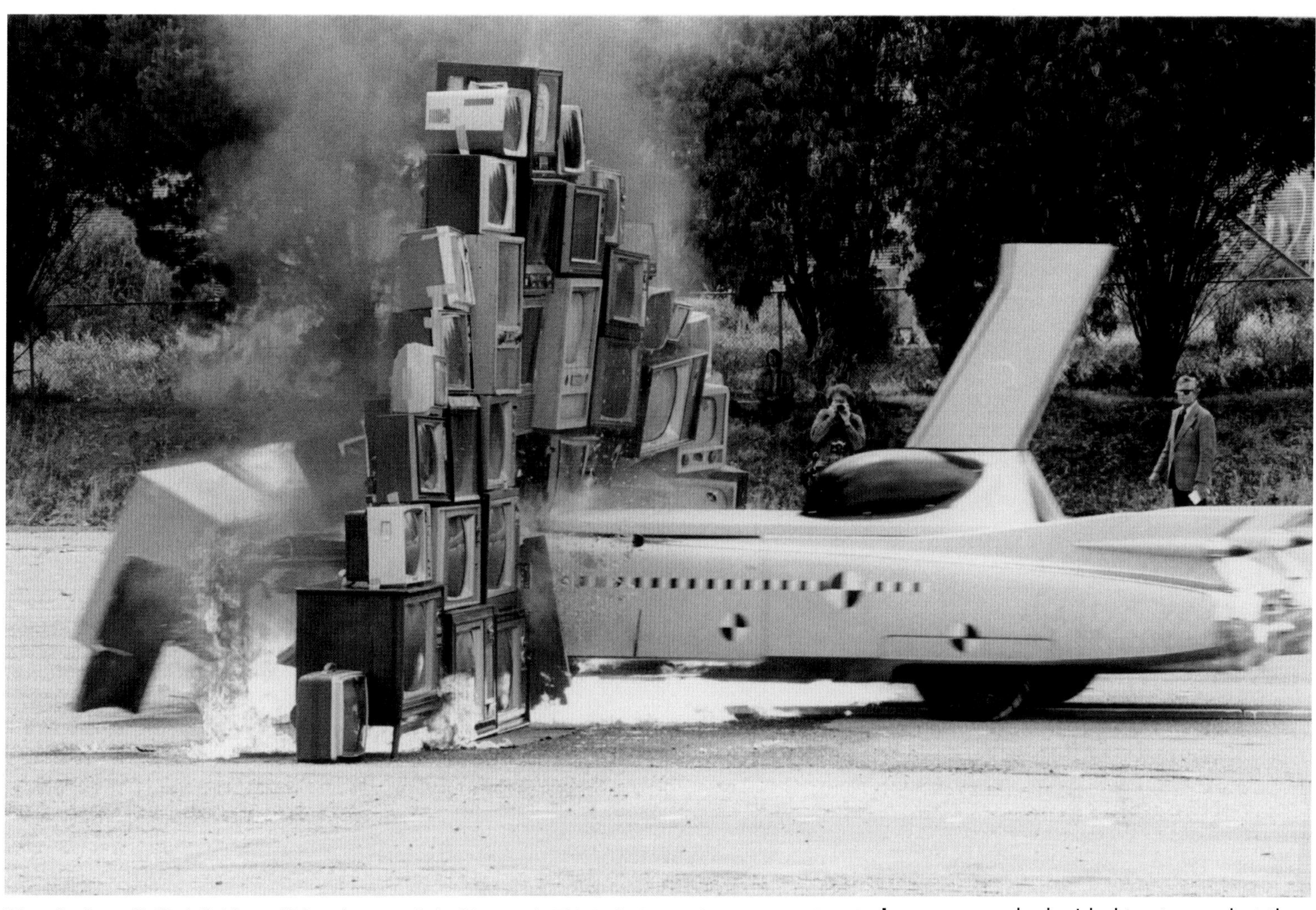

Diane Andrews Hall's definitive collision photograph, looking north. This is the image that was reproduced and distributed to the local press and wire services within hours of *Media Burn*'s climax. Photograph by Diane Andrews Hall.

Following spread: An unusual color photograph of the collision, captured from the rear of the TV pyramid. This appeared in the July 5 edition of the *San Francisco Chronicle*. Photograph by Gary Fons.

show you how the Fourth of July was celebrated around the Bay Area. Whoopee!"

A commercial interrupts: "They go beyond cold statistics and provide keen and touching insights into the TV Generation. TV Guide." Yes, Ant Farm will provide us with "cold statistics" about television use and, yes, they will provide "keen and touching insights" as they assume the mantel of their nemesis *TV Guide*. Or better: Ant Farm will be our Virgil leading us through the televisual gates of hell.

Media Burn, the tape, begins with almost four and a half minutes of media coverage. It is through this montage of clips in which the local news affiliates react to the event that Ant Farm can produce evidence of the Artist-President's claim that television can "only produce autocratic political forms, hierarchies, and hopeless alienation." If the media has one advantage it is the ability to have the last word. Here, they define what they believe *Media Burn* is, then debunk it through glib commentary, and finally discount it through an intellectual shrug of the shoulders. Huh?

Van Amburg, a prominent news anchorman for San Francisco's KGO-TV, gives the lead-in: "A media event is something that happens only because somebody made it happen, only because somebody figured the television news cameras would show up to watch it happen, whatever it is. That's a media event. It used to be called a publicity stunt."

The point is not so much what Amburg says as his tone of skepticism and loftiness. The phrase "media event" is all his. Never does Ant Farm in any of their press releases call it more than "an event." In fact, they almost negate its frivolous publicity cachet in favor of purpose: "*Media Burn* is not a sensational daredevil stunt, rather it is a way of alleviating the frustration of watching television in America."[140] From the autocratic heights of this ABC affiliate comes the demeaning label "media event," but they must fly higher (or stoop lower) by then saying, "Well, today

---

140   From an undated press release that has a *Media Burn* rubber stamp and the logo.

some people decided to stage what they call the ultimate media event. Now right away everybody perks up. The ultimate? Hmmm. That's interesting." In fact, the only mention of the word "ultimate" is found in Van Amburg's teleprompter.

And now speaking not just for himself, but for all reporters: "They told us it was a media event and they invited us down. And so with knowledge of forethought and not alone, but knowing it was going to be a good one, David Louie showed up."

Louie, a field reporter for Channel 7, starts by accentuating the positive: "It had nothing to do with the Fourth of July. Maybe that's why every camera in town showed up ... every film and electronic camera within twenty miles showed up, not a single aspect of this media event would be overlooked." Then the first inkling: "Even though the artists were knocking television, they were using it to make their point." As if this were verboten territory, a point to be made, Louie veers off: "No media event is complete without a central figure, a VIP to give credibility to the event. The media-conscious sponsors resurrected John F. Kennedy for the keynote speech." Yet not a word about that speech, before he continues to report on the surface of things: "Two daredevil drivers, in the tradition of Evel Knievel, settled into the crash car and took off." Channel 7

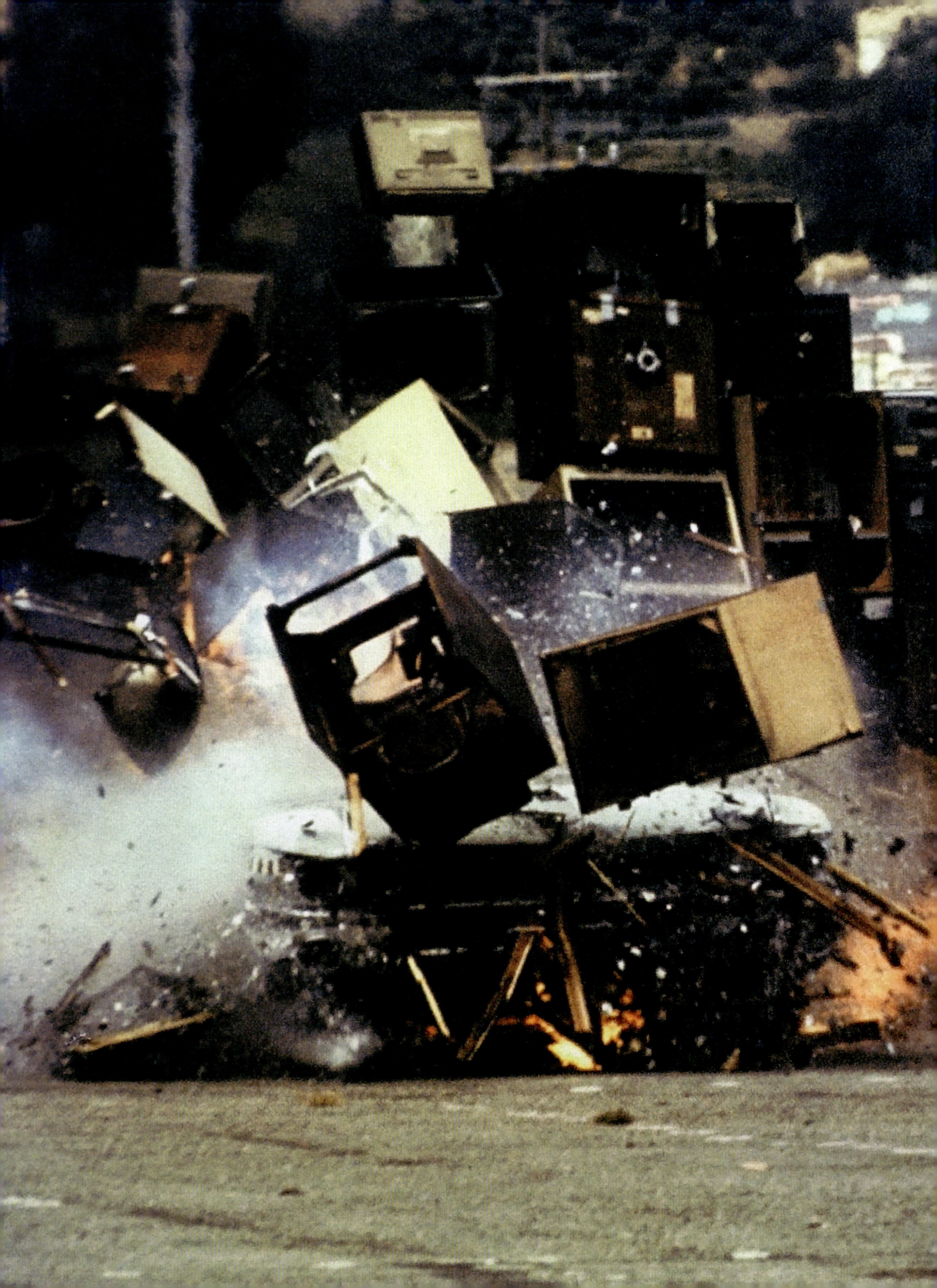

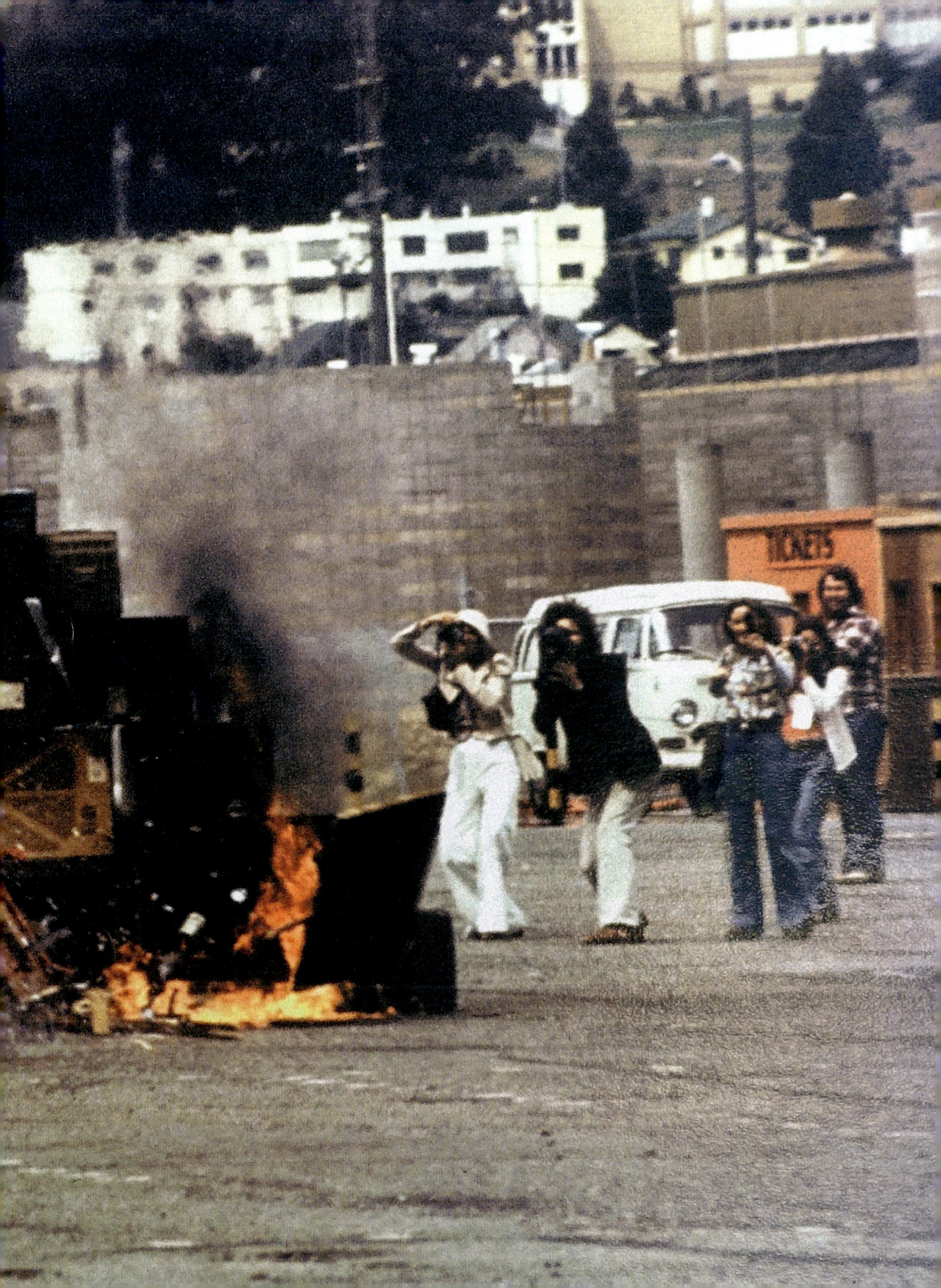
TICKETS

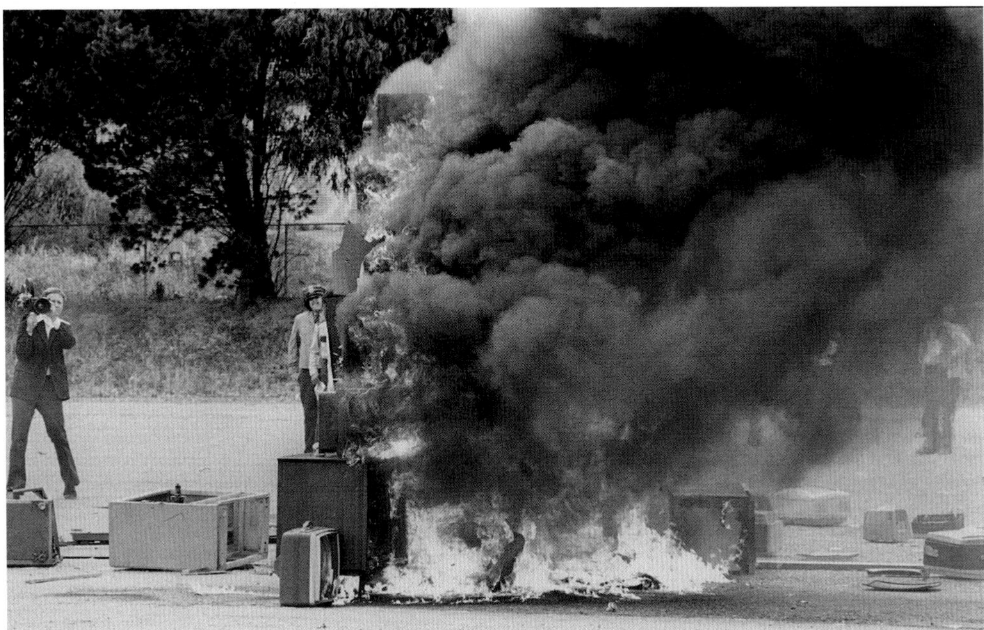

After the Phantom Dream Car muscled by, the TV sets continued to burn on the asphalt. Photograph by Diane Andrews Hall.

then shows the crash itself, but in an act of self-censorship Ant Farm imposes a black triangle (a pyramid?) on the screen, obscuring the actual impact. The money shot must not be disclosed until later.

Louie's coverage concludes with a long-overdue attribution: "The organization, by the way, that sponsored this event is Ant Farm. What other organization could make a mountain out of a molehill?" And then to divert from this nonsensical joke, the final plunge: "It may not have been good art in some people's minds but at least it was good entertainment."

The Artist-President had declared: "Mass media monopolies control people by their control of information." But this control comes in numerous forms, a prominent one being distraction. By trivializing intentions, by debasing outcomes, history unfolding could be downgraded to a category of entertainment.[141] This same media treatment could be applied to occurrences outside the norm where odd behaviors had to be curbed and abrasive ideas disparaged through derisive humor. In this way, the media could retain its homeostatic superiority while continuing its mandate as diversion. KPIX-TV, for example, reported the following, on-site: "If smashing a '59 Cadillac into a wall of old television sets is art, then the world may rest tonight with a new masterpiece. If it is culture, then perhaps we are all in a degree of difficulty not previously experienced in this society." But, in studio, the following sentiment was broadcast: "Now that is weird. You gotta say that that is pretty weird … But also the car going into the television sets and the imitation of … I think it's over our heads."[142]

> KTVU-TV, on-site:
> "Oh, what's it all mean? Well, presumably the message is for the media. Get it?"

> KTVU-TV, in-studio:
> "I don't think I want to get it. Do you?"

With the mainstream media's self-immolation now out of the way, Ant Farm goes about the business of reconstructing the actual "media event." This acts as a compression schema, condensing the available images down to those details of recuperative importance. A short montage of the Optic Nerve crew traversing the Cow Palace site, agents of the Secret Service milling about, and Uncle Buddie pouring kerosene into a red metal can begins to collate fragments of the greater event. With emcee Bill Ding's first announcement, we move away from the distanced abstraction of the TV coverage to asphalt-level encounters. The souvenir stand is in full swing; the scantily clad salesgirls are hawking souvenir booklets and T-shirts. An anonymous bystander gleefully gesticulates, "There's money in media burning," as he purchases a program.

Nearby, the Optic Nerve crew stops to interview a young woman devouring a hot dog. Off-camera, Jim Mayer asks: "What motivated you to come here to *Media Burn* today?" The anonymous subject replies, "I've always watched a lot of TV and I knew there were going to be programs for a dollar." Mayer: "What are your expectations?" Subject: "I'm hoping that there are no deaths. No fatalities. No fires burning through the asbestos suits. I'm hoping that it really kicks off the old Bicentennial." Mayer: "Do you think this is just another example of violence on television?" Subject: "Actually, I don't. I have a very kind of theoretical view of this. I see it as highlighting the themes of violence and action on television. It might even make a better television event than a real event." Was the anonymous subject a plant? Her hot dog chomping nonchalance disguises the thoughtfulness of her comments. She's not there for the "sensational daredevil stunt" that Ant Farm has disavowed; rather she's attuned to the inherent critique of the simulated violence. Ant Farm's publicity wing couldn't have penned a better summary.

After several more shots showing off the hustle and bustle of the event, Optic Nerve settles on another anonymous subject, this time a man with a quiet sincerity: "If you're going to take a Cadillac and you're going to have it go through a bunch of TVs, then I think it's real important that the people get real close to the TVs, otherwise it's like watching a football game. It's not art anymore. It's only art if you're right there." This is an appeal for engagement and risk versus the more cocooned spectatorship of television watching. In this case, art brings you into proximity with life itself, perhaps a salve for the "hopeless alienation" of spectatorial passivity. Again, Ant Farm is situating *Media Burn* in a theoretical context reinforced by seemingly spontaneous observations—unmediated and unmitigated.

In the tape's only close encounter with the Artist-Dummies, an off-camera interviewer approaches first Curtis Schreier, then Doug Michels, both in their gray jumpsuits.

> Interviewer: "Are you worried about your chances for survival?"
>
> Artist-Dummy 1: "I'm more worried for America's chances for survival than my own personal chances for survival."
>
> Interviewer: "A very heroic statement. Do you have any last words you'd like to say?"
>
> Artist-Dummy 1: "No, only first ones. We're signing on, we're not signing off."
>
> Artist-Dummy 2: "First the TVs go, then the freeways, then the factories."

---

141   In his classic tome, *Four Arguments for the Elimination of Television*, Jerry Mander lists the "inherent biases" of the medium, including "superficiality is easier than depth."

142   Aired on July 4, 1975, on KPIX-TV, a CBS affiliate in San Francisco.

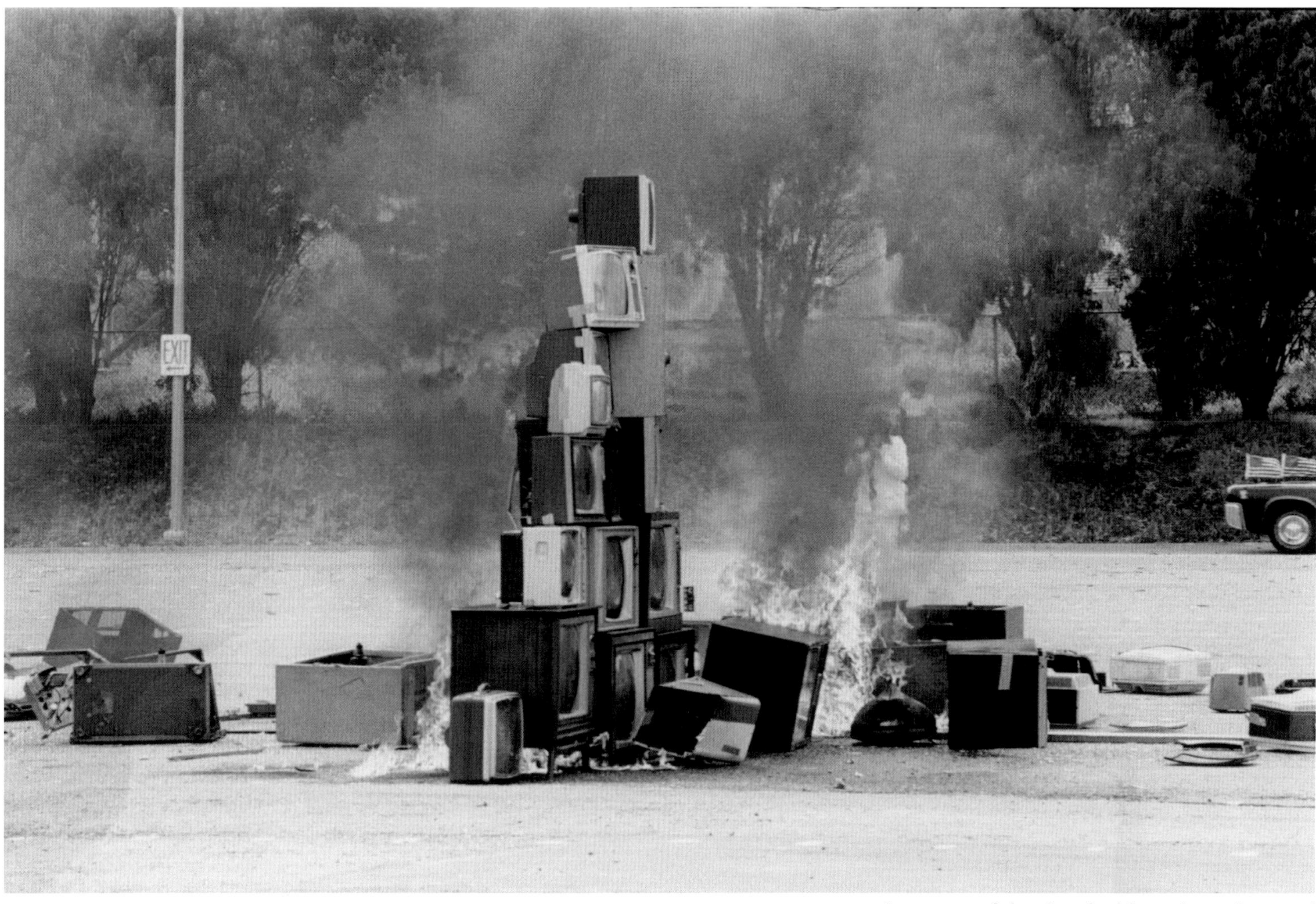

The dispersal of the burning TV sets soon after the collision. Photograph by Diane Andrews Hall.

Following Spread: The Artist-President (Doug Hall) and the two Artist-Dummies (Doug Michels and Curtis Schreier) prepare for their victory lap. Also pictured are Secret Service agents Dan Calderwood (on the right) and Homer Flynn (on the left). Photograph by Edmund Shea.

Interviewer: "When do skyscrapers come in?"

Artist-Dummy 2: "Soon, very soon. Then the McDonalds. Yeah, all of them. This is just the beginning."

Interviewer: "Can you feel the tension?"

Artist-Dummy 2: "It's all around. I believe this is going to relieve a lot of it ... If everyone in America would burn just one TV set ..."

If the coming appearance by the Artist-President presents us with a polished, calculated, and theatrical skein of ideas informing *Media Burn*, these off-the-cuff comments from the Artist-Dummies provide a more bratty, politically inflected take—feisty ideas powering a rash act. Schreier's "We're signing on, we're not signing off" defines this performance as an opening salvo.[143] Speaking more

concretely, Michels' notion that "first the TVs go, then the freeways, then the factories" implies that Ant Farm will require an entire fleet of Phantom Dream Cars for their ongoing destruction derby.

Just prior to the unveiling of the Phantom Dream Car, we get a commercial interruption, a Dodge jingle played through the PA system: "How did Dodge Colt put so much in such a little car?"[144] A pure jest as the antithesis of the "little car" is revealed from beneath the Independence Day bunting. A self-contained documentary about the Phantom Dream Car follows, with Bill Ding narrating the details of its construction. Images independent of the event are used to illustrate: a test drive of the car speeding across the Cow Palace lot, a still image of the car's interior with a moving image superimposed over the

screen of the tiny dashboard monitor, and several details from a cutaway drawing of the Phantom Dream Car drawn by Schreier sometime in August, post *Burn*. Ding's narrative is thus embellished while adhering to its proper chronological placement.

A simple segue in the *Media Burn* script brings us to the arrival of the Artist-President.[145] Within the montage, we are shown the arriving Lincoln limo before the announcement is made, directing us more swiftly to the "important guest." A medium shot of the limo passing by gives us a privileged preview of the JFK lookalike. Then a replacement shot from a second source widens the view to disclose the security entourage walking beside the executive limo.

In other words, we have now entered the realm of cinema. Ant Farm deploys the routine techniques of editing and composition to guide the viewer's point of view. Every cut is a deliberation, a delivery, then a directive. There is a visual argument at play, building a persuasive case. Linear and expository, the videowork finally reduces a piece of the real into a purposeful replica.

---

143   "Now that the entire commercial environment has been poured into my computer, I'm

getting more and more ready for another *Media Burn* ... of major proportions." Curtis Schreier, interview, MOCAtv, October 12, 2012.

144   This snappy jingle was used for the 1975 Dodge Colt advertising campaign on air and in print.

145   "And now ladies and gentlemen, I would like to introduce my important guest, who will deliver the July 4th Independence Day speech."

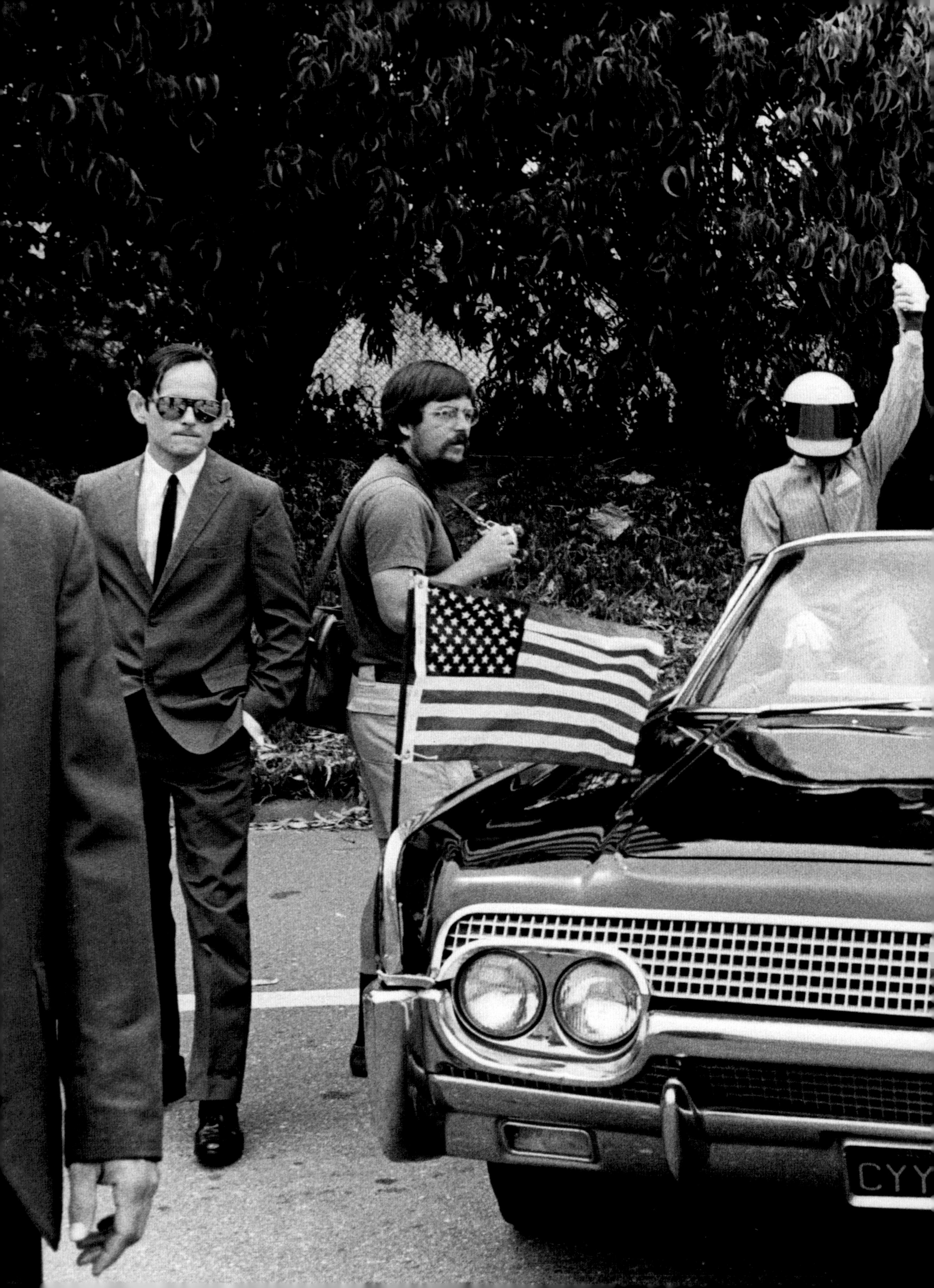

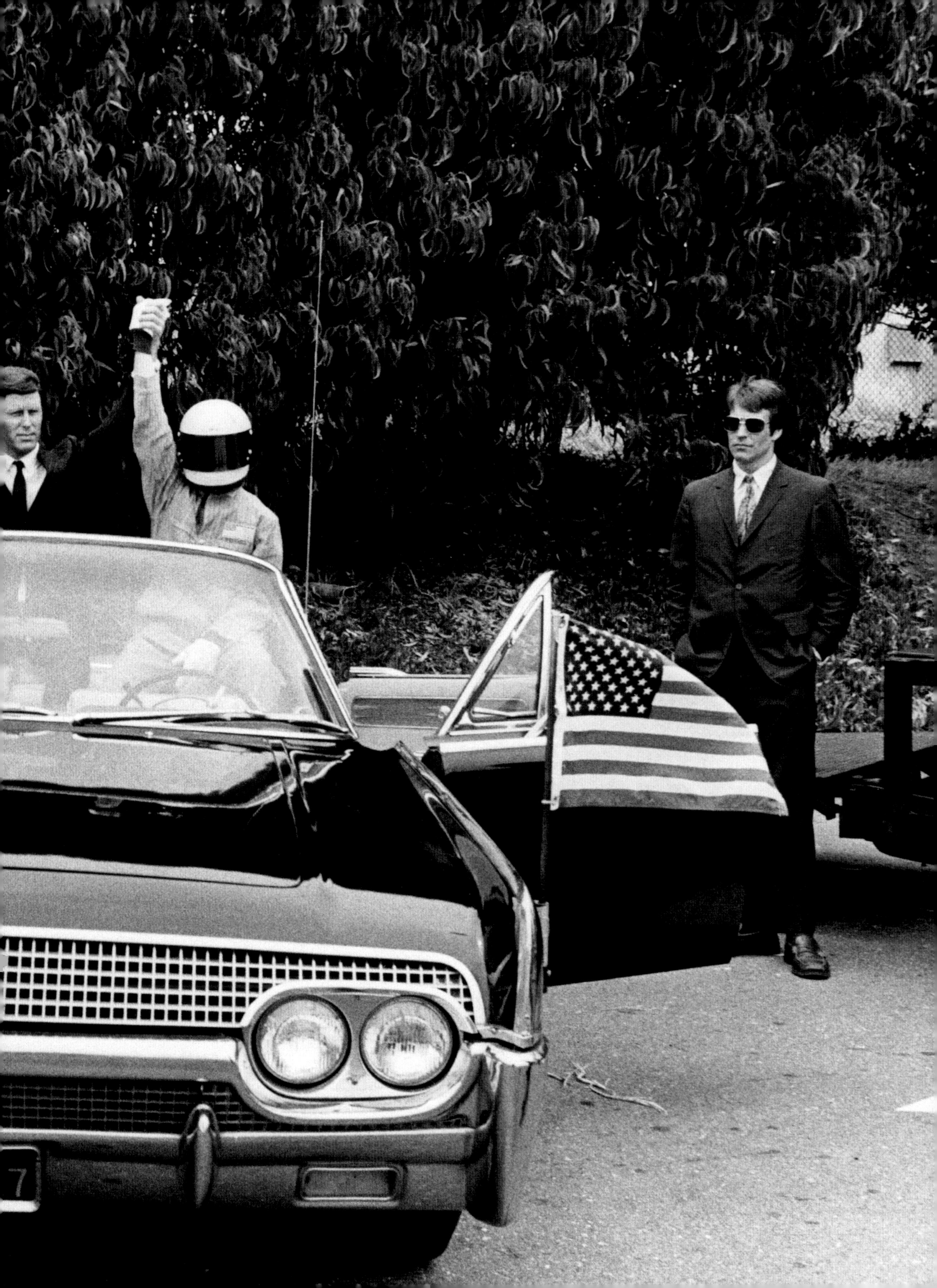

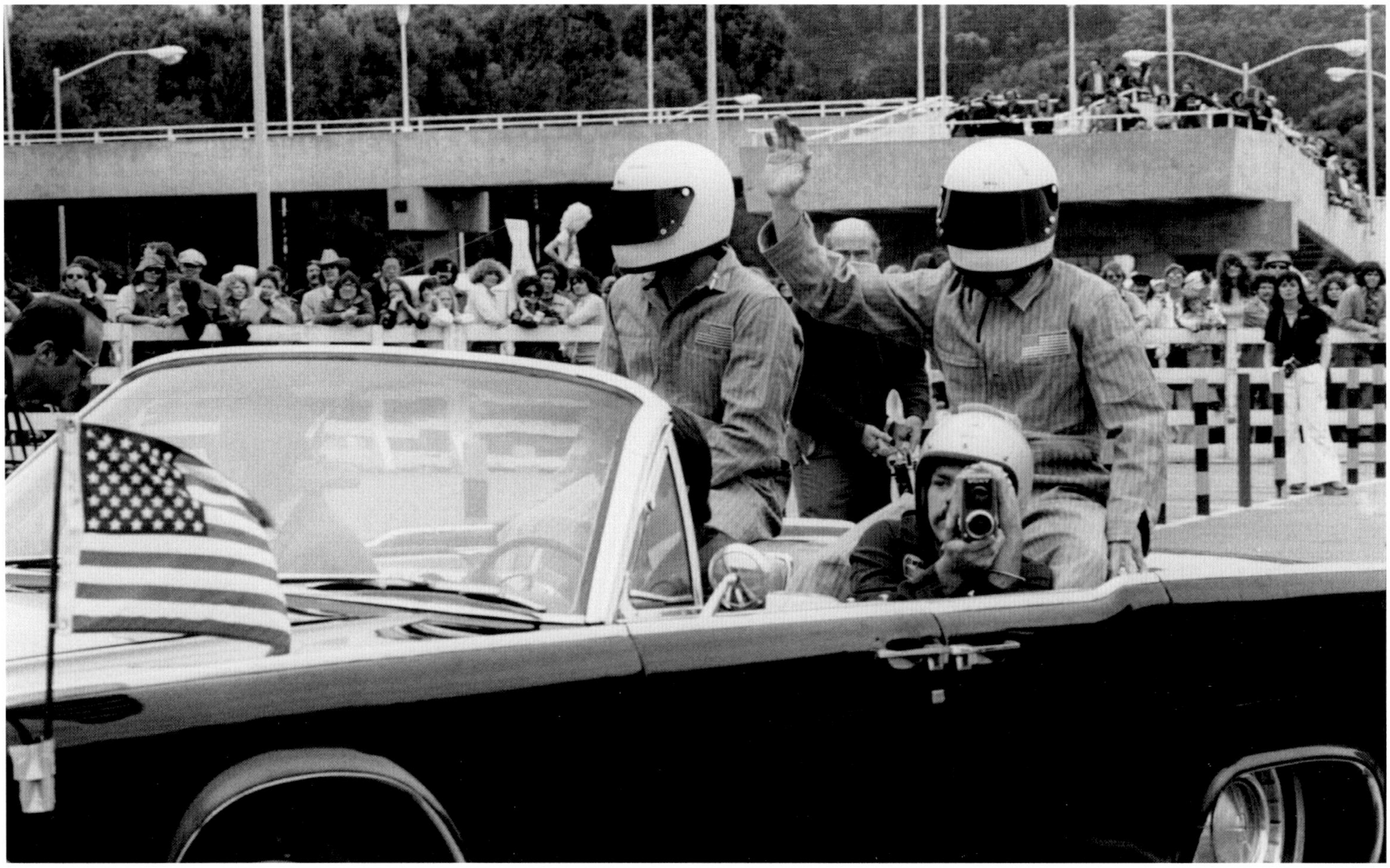

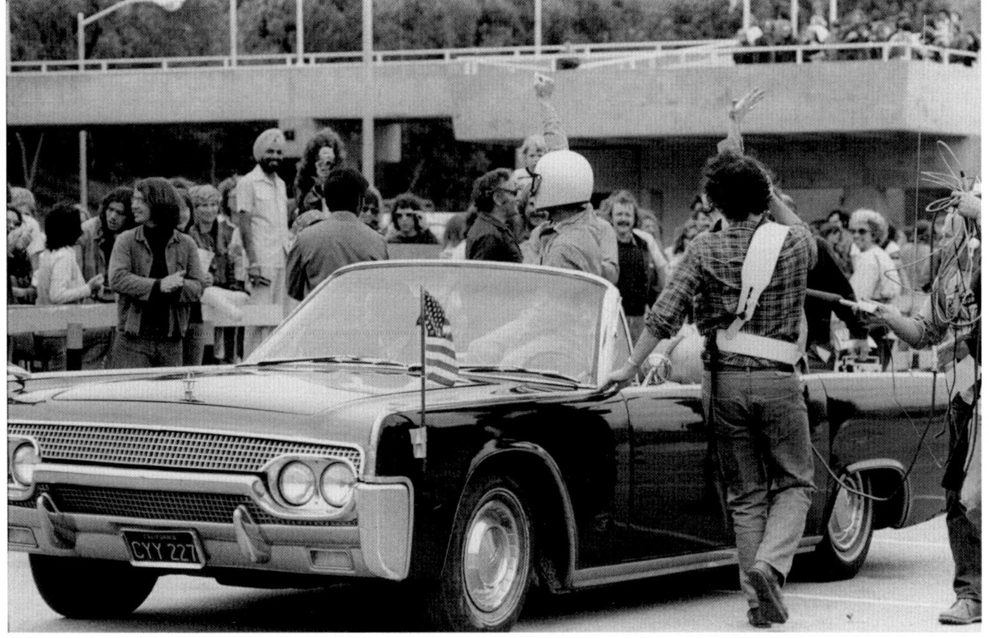

Top: In the midst of their victory lap, the Artist-Dummies greet the assembled crowd. A crouched Burt Arnowitz shoots the scene with a camera of his own. Photograph by Diane Andrews Hall.

Bottom: The media converges on the Lincoln convertible carrying the victorious Artist-Dummies. Photograph by Diane Andrews Hall.

A simple truth: *Media Burn*, the videowork, is not *Media Burn*, the performance. Where the videowork required the performance for its very existence, the performance was sui generis, autonomous yet evanescent, both suffused by time and snuffed by it. The performance was as fleeting as the accelerating vehicle, as sense-laden as the acrid aroma of kerosene, as uncertain as the gathered crowd standing shoulder-to-shoulder along the white wooden barriers. In the aftermath, there would be a moraine of media left behind: images, either moving or still, made by amateur and professional alike. And not even the entire heap equaling the event—just abraded remnants, a tumble of fragments. The imperfect reconstruction had an objective: to preserve, proliferate, and propose an end … to the meaning.

With the arrival of the Artist-President, we also realize the overwhelming presence of the media. Except for a close shot of Doug Hall on the podium, the frame is constantly intruded upon by ENG operatives and roving photographers vying for position.[146] The press area before the grandstand swarms with card-carrying communicators documenting the "ultimate media event."[147] If Ant Farm's performance is a photo opportunity, the opportunists are everywhere to be found.

The Artist-President's departure signals the Artist-Dummies' arrival. The media matadors having taken their position atop the Phantom Dream Car's trunk, the national anthem commences, accompanied by an appropriated network sign-off sequence of flags waving above a fleet of aircraft carriers. This FCC-mandated custom of introducing late-night off-air time with jingoistic montages always seemed like an odd association, as though the commercial

---

146   ENG is the acronym for Electronic News Gathering that was beginning to replace reportage on 16mm film.

147   In one shot, the reporter from KRON-TV can be seen wearing his official *Media Burn* press pass.

use of bandwidth was implicitly patriotic. Perhaps the embedded meaning was that the broadcaster would patrol its licensed airwave spectrum with the vehemence of an armada—we will be back and in force. Ant Farm's placement of this montage was probably more innocent, mocking the alleged public-spirited conceit of the broadcaster.[148]

As the Artist-Dummies slip through the entry port of the vehicle, the final process of preparation begins. They settle in—one of them utters a fond "Hi, sweetheart" to the encompassing cockpit—and at this point, a dramatic trope is kicked into motion: the countdown. To heighten the tension, an actual countdown clock is superimposed over the visual montage. Primitive LCD digits are keyed in slow declension as the two-man crew prepares. The first numbers displayed are "03:04." The go-ahead is given at nineteen seconds, the final numbers, "00:00," coincident with the collision. Here we have another instance in which *Media Burn*, the videowork, breaks with the advancing performance. The prep period took considerably more time and is heavily compressed through editing to mimic the thrilling liftoff convention.[149] The exacting zero-hour impact never really happened.

Now we arrive at the ecstatic collision of a two-and-a-half-ton projectile encountering forty-four blazing television sets.[150] Like any rapturous culmination, it is best when prolonged. Acceleration along the Cow Palace lot takes nineteen seconds; the penetration of the wall, two at best. Depicting the crash from several angles, along with the concussive sounds, the momentous wreck plays on for almost a minute and a half of tape time. The slow-motion shot, itself thirty seconds long, suspends the calamity in a silent pause where each television set becomes a toppling mass of media. Here, *Media Burn* blossoms in a lethal pullulation.

The rest is anticlimax: the obligatory victory lap atop the Lincoln limo; a glimpse of the Artist-President, now out of makeup, as though the guise were no longer necessary; bystanders amid the ruins gleefully tossing charred TV sets. Over this penultimate image, two text pages appear:

------

148 This also ironically reinforces Curtis Schreier's pronouncement, "We're not signing off, we're signing on."

149 This is verified in an email by Curtis Schreier dated April 13, 2015.

150 The uppermost television has a *Media Burn* logo covering the screen. The apex of the pyramid, it is about eleven and a half feet above the ground, standing atop four large console TVs.

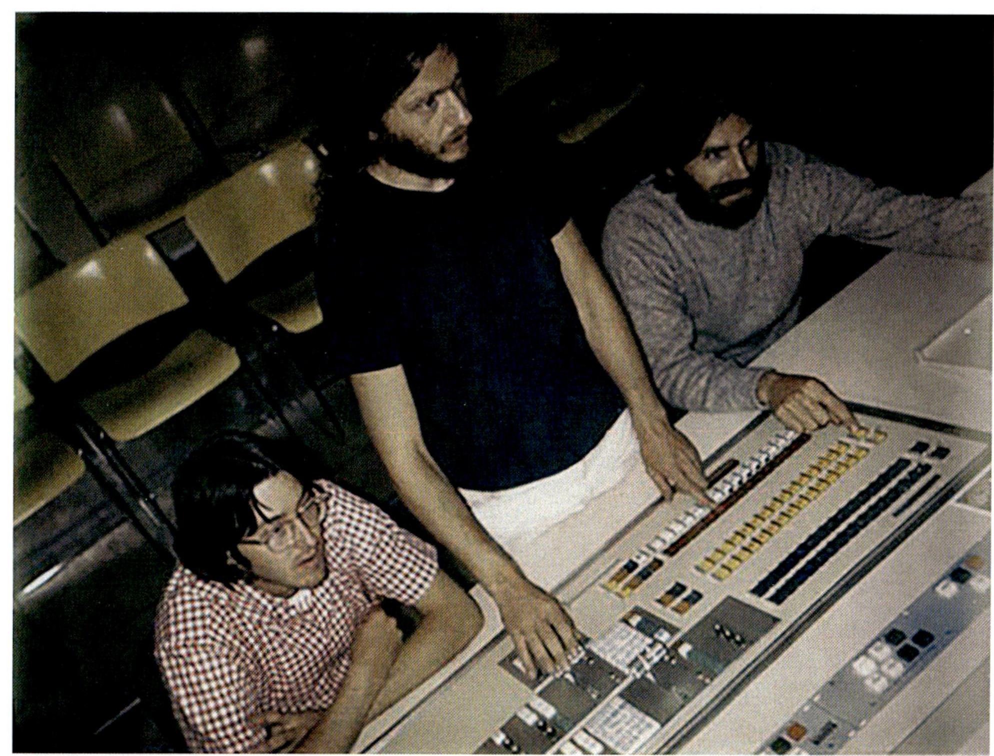

Chip Lord, Skip Blumberg (standing), and unidentified third person complete the edit of *Media Burn*, the videowork, at the Synapse Video Center, housed at Syracuse University. Photograph by Doug Michels.

99.9% OF ALL HOMES IN USA WITH
ELECTRICITY HAVE TV SETS
THERE ARE 68.5 MILLION TV SETS IN
AMERICAN HOMES
COLOR SETS ARE WATCHED 49 HRS/WK
B&W SETS ARE WATCHED 49 HRS/WK
26% OF EACH HOUR IS ADVERTISING
AVERAGE DAILY VIEWING TIME IS 6 HRS.
15 MINS.

This same quantitative data is presented in the souvenir booklet, displayed as "Television Addiction Statistics." No source is listed, and the baldness of the facts seems to counter the poetic, openended gesture they follow. It is as if, for a moment, *Media Burn* has taken on the trappings of yet another format, the educational film. In this domain of pedagogical intent and instructive exchange, the facts are commonplace. They are blunt, didactic, and meant as a caution. As in a traffic safety film, you do not want to be implicated by the gathered statistics.

While the credits are rolling, we get one final image, a high-speed compression of the wall of TV sets standing intact, soon ignited, tumbled by impact, then doused to extinguish the blaze. The heat exhaustion of an epic *Burn*.

MEDIA BURN VIDEO STILLS

Ant Farm, *Media Burn*, 1975.
Video (color, sound), 23:02 minutes.

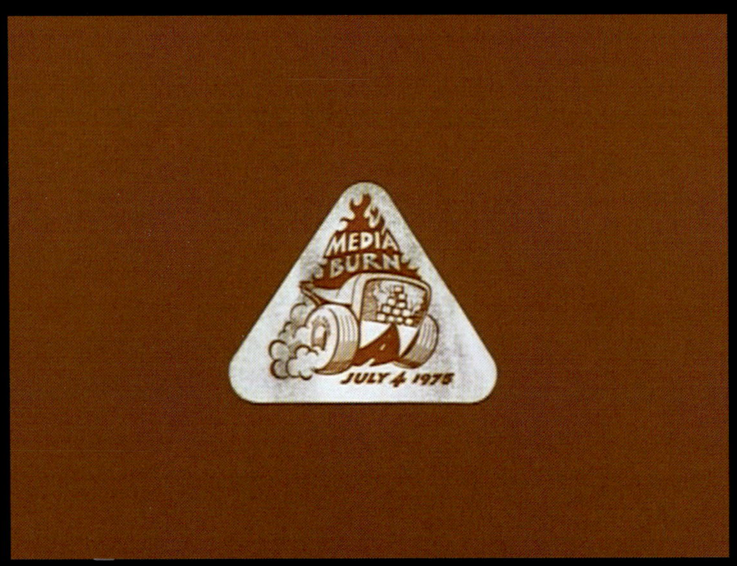

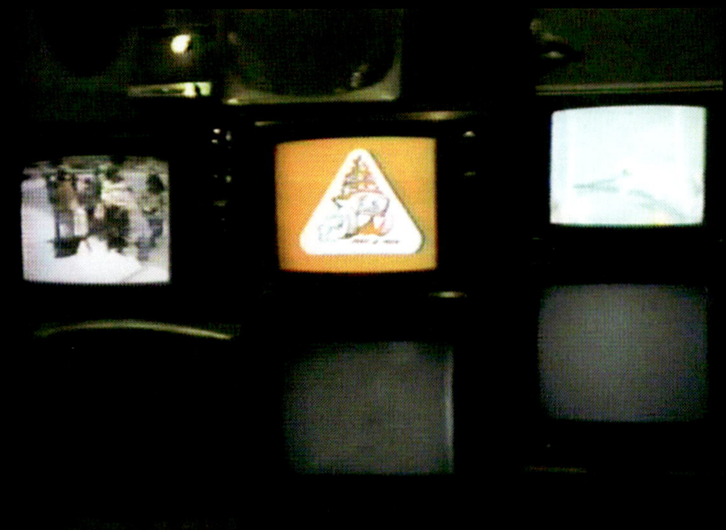

"THIS FOURTH IS STARTING OUT NO DIFFERENTLY."

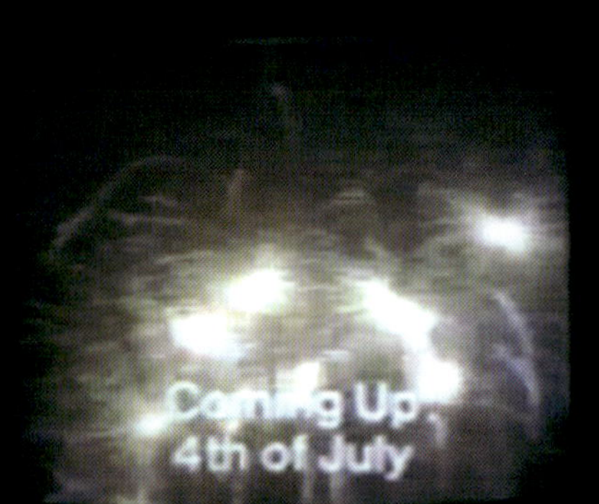

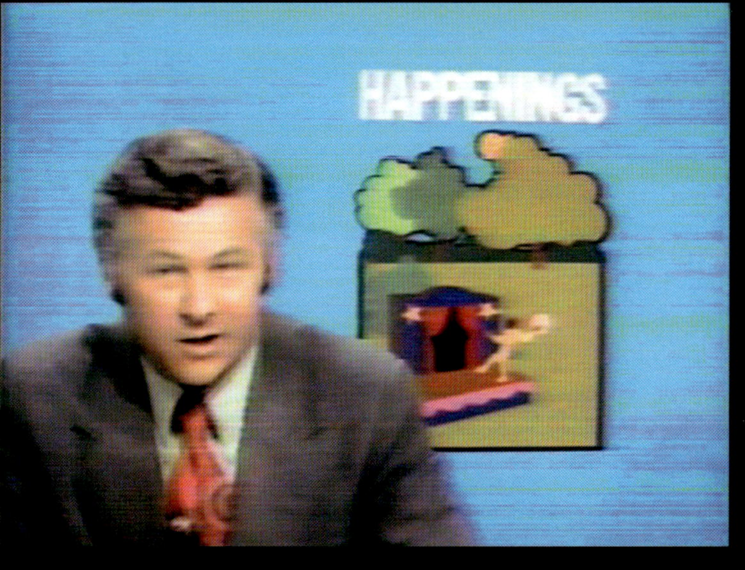

"A MEDIA EVENT IS SOMETHING THAT HAPPENS ONLY BECAUSE SOMEBODY MADE IT HAPPEN."

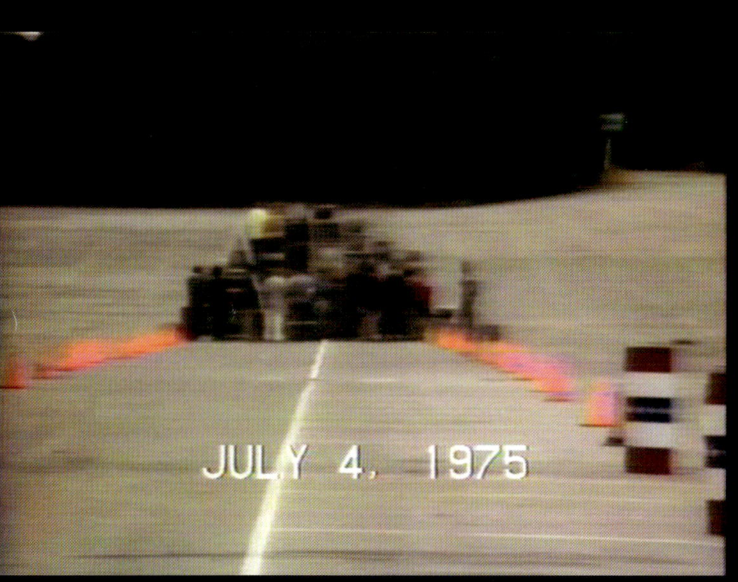

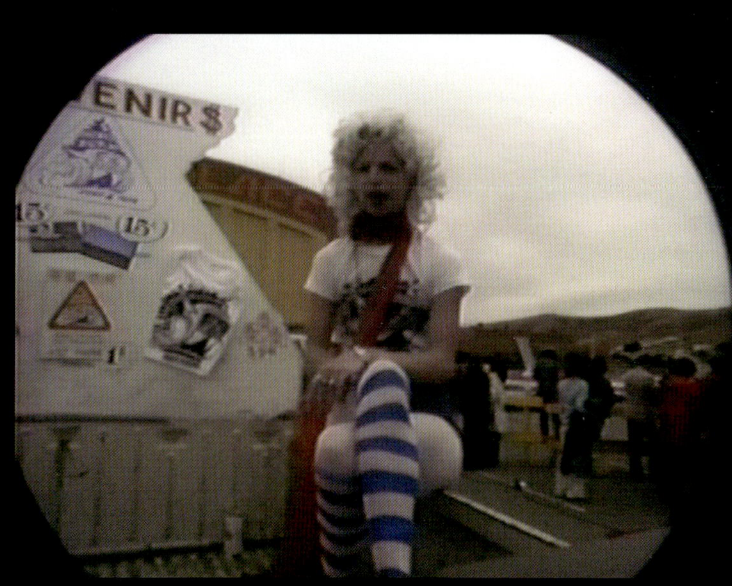

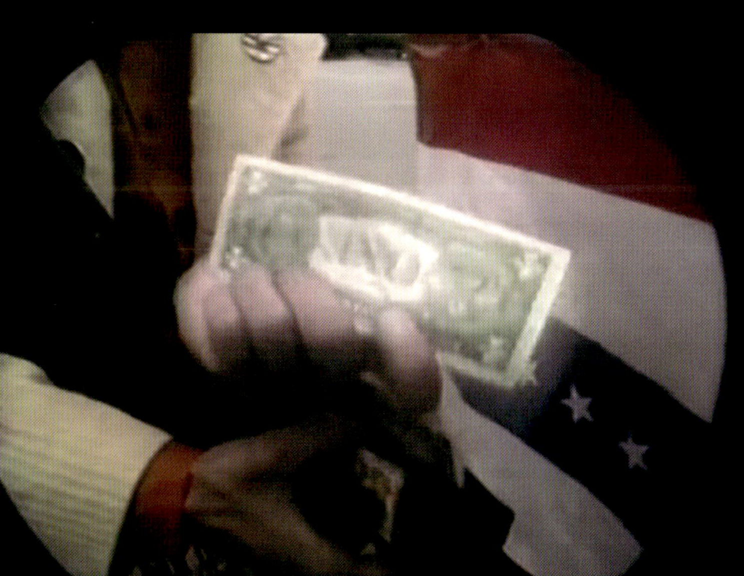

"THERE'S MONEY IN MEDIA BURNING!"

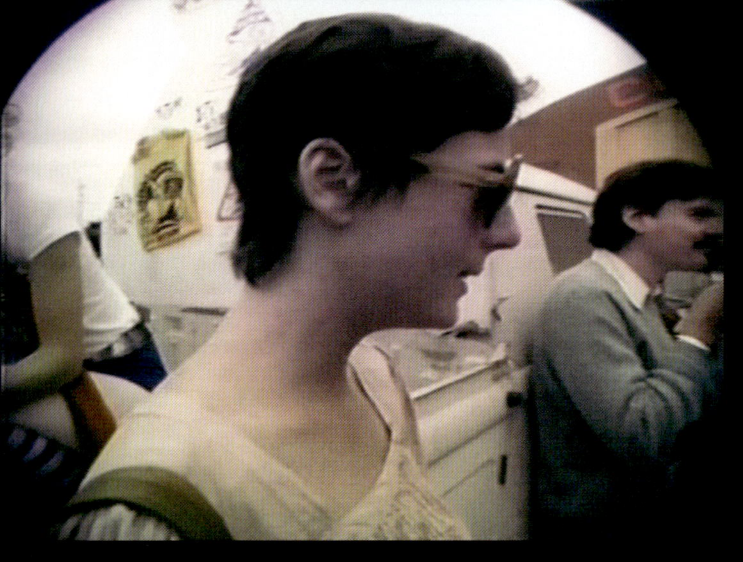
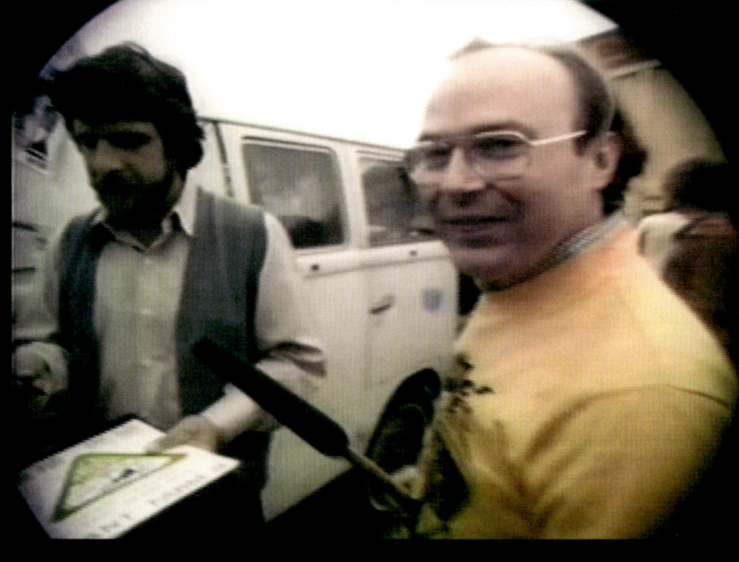
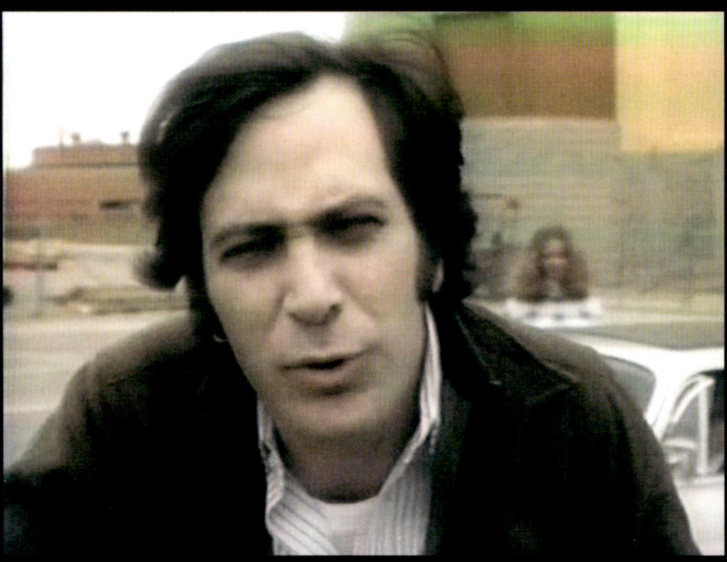

"IT'S ONLY ART
IF YOU'RE RIGHT
THERE."

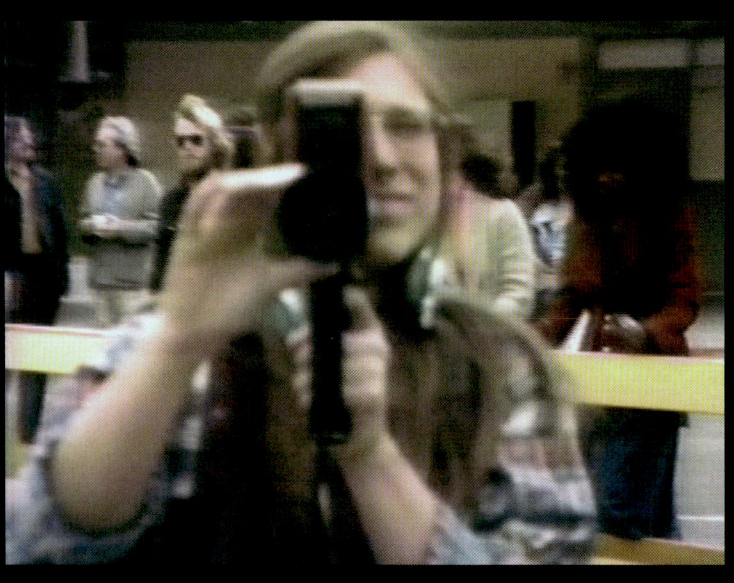
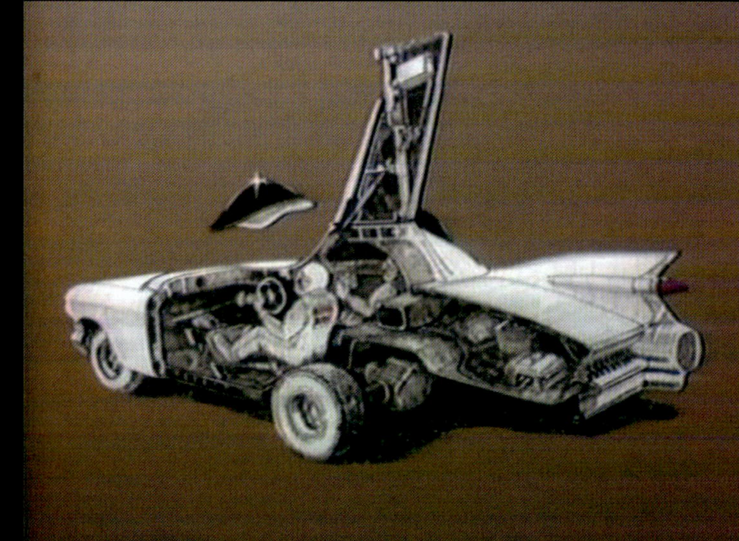

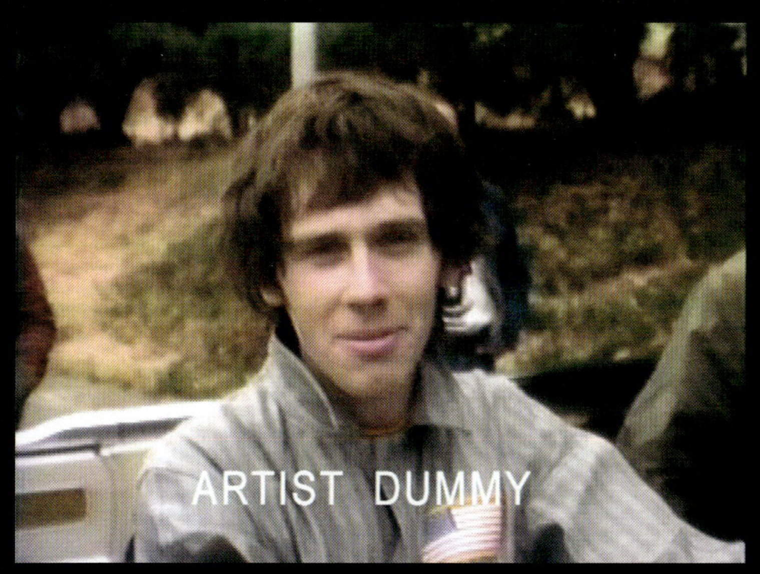

"IF EVERYONE IN AMERICA WOULD BURN JUST ONE TV SET…"

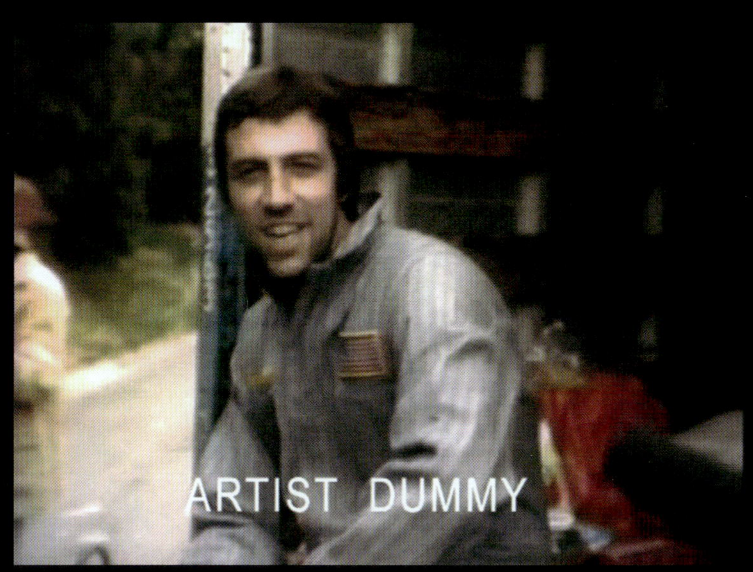

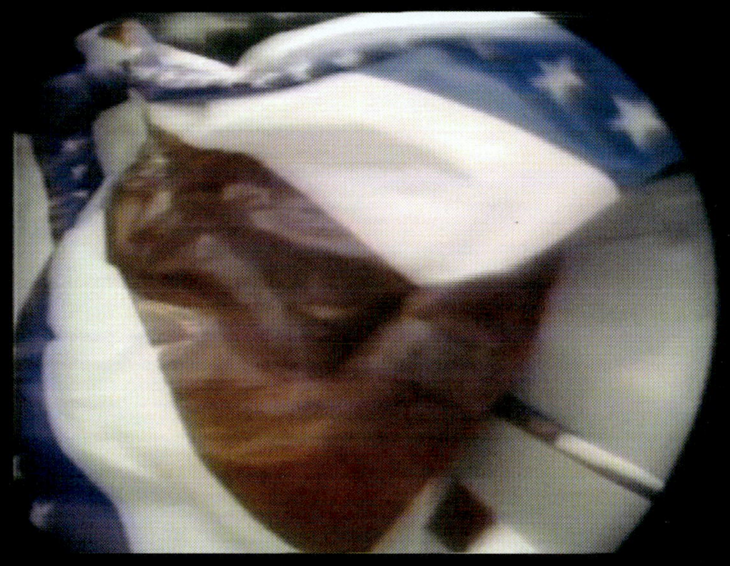

"THE TWO DUMMIES WILL DRIVE BY CLOSED CIRCUIT TELEVISION."

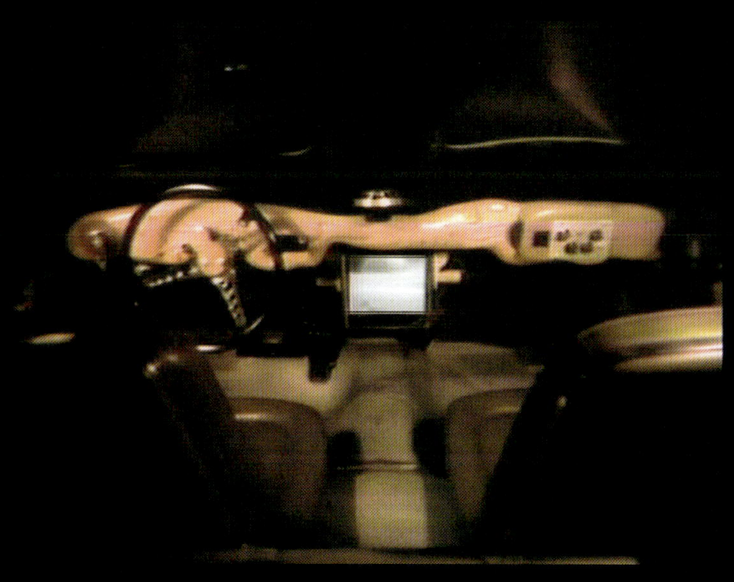

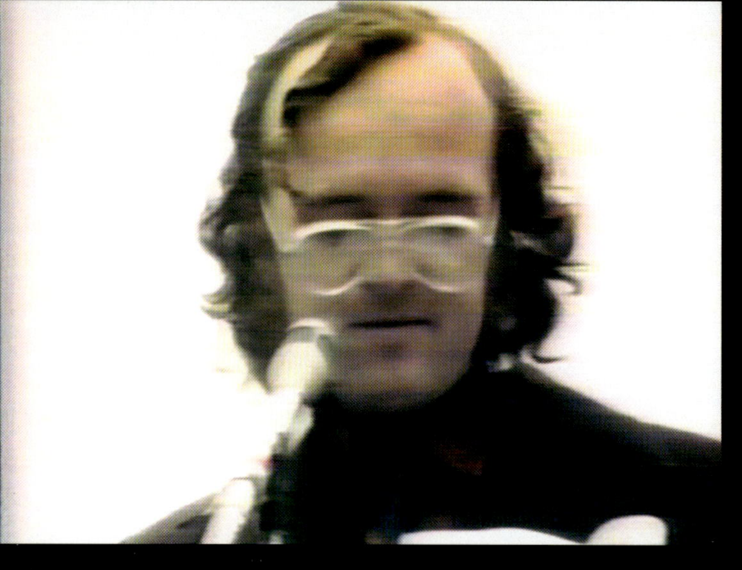

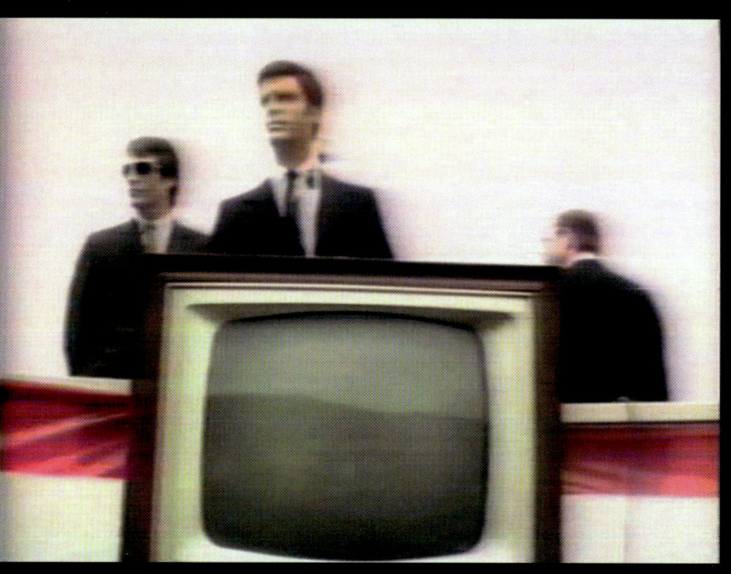

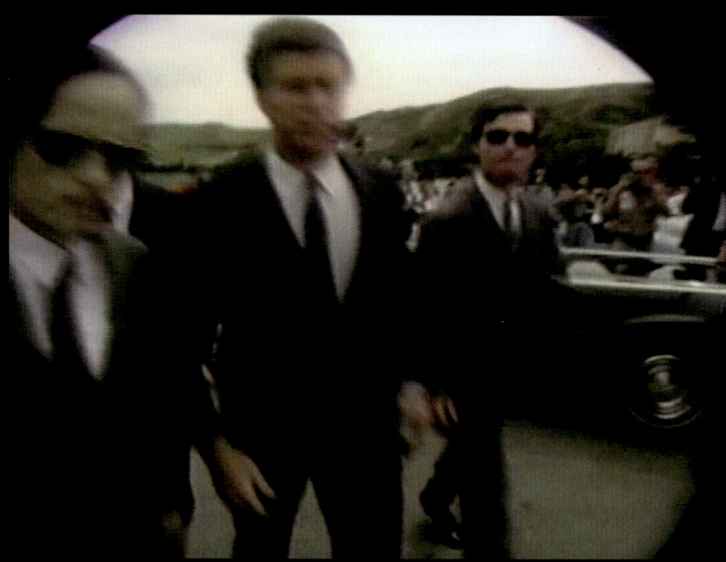
"ON THIS
INDEPENDENCE
DAY, 1975, THE
AMERICAN SPIRIT
IS UNCERTAIN."

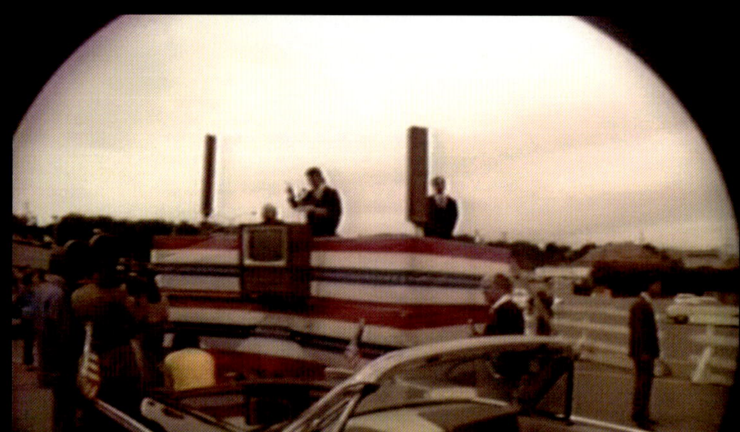
"MASS MEDIA
MONOPOLIES
CONTROL PEOPLE BY
THEIR CONTROL
OF INFORMATION."

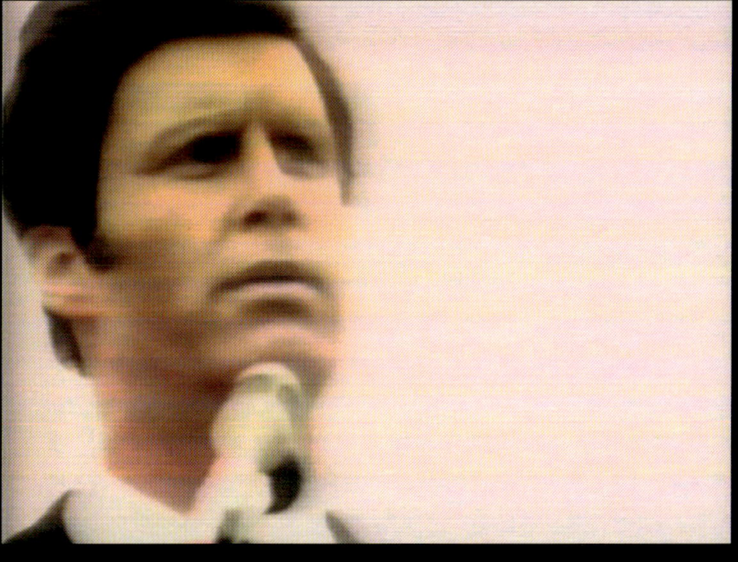

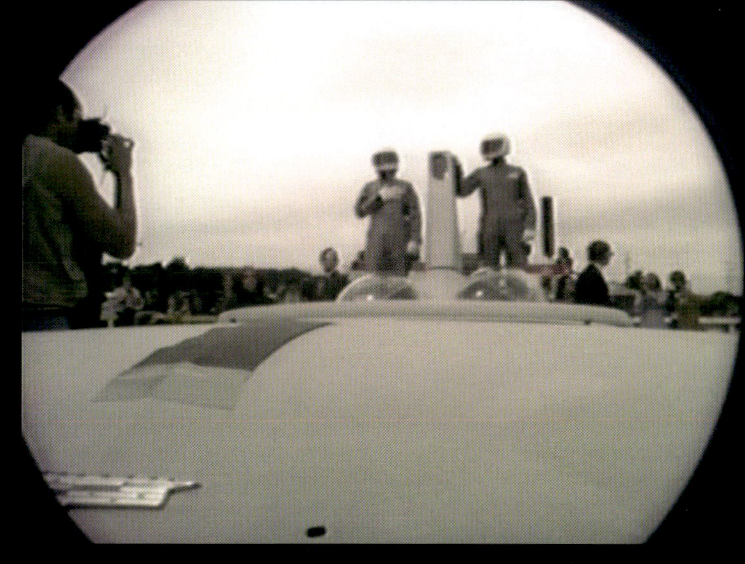

"WE'RE SIGNING
ON, WE'RE NOT
SIGNING OFF."

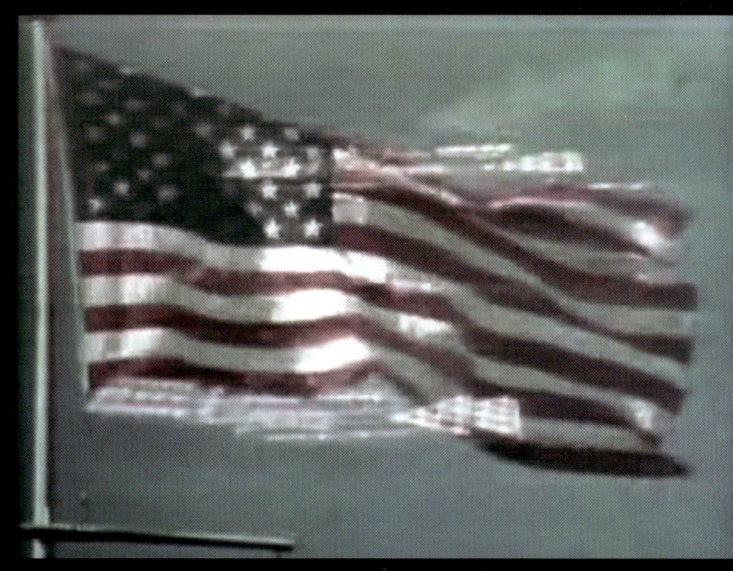

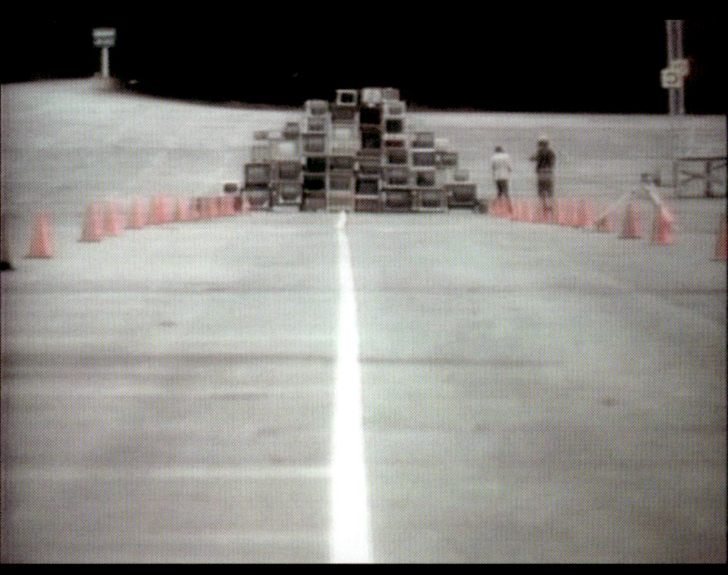

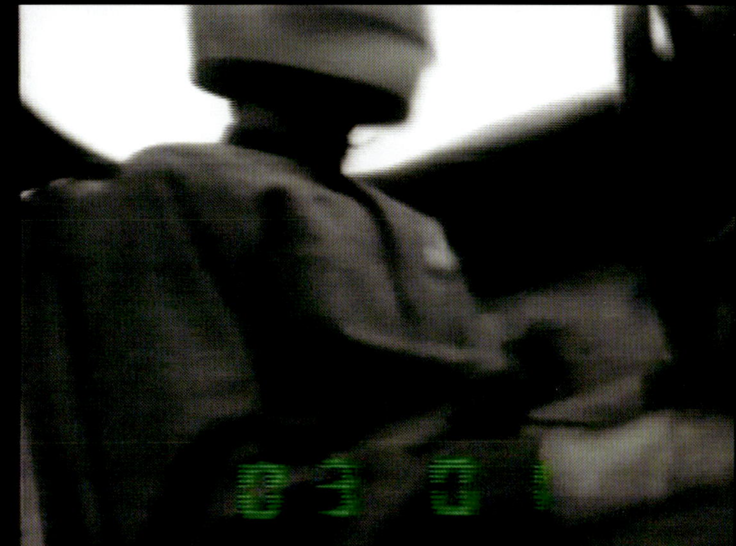

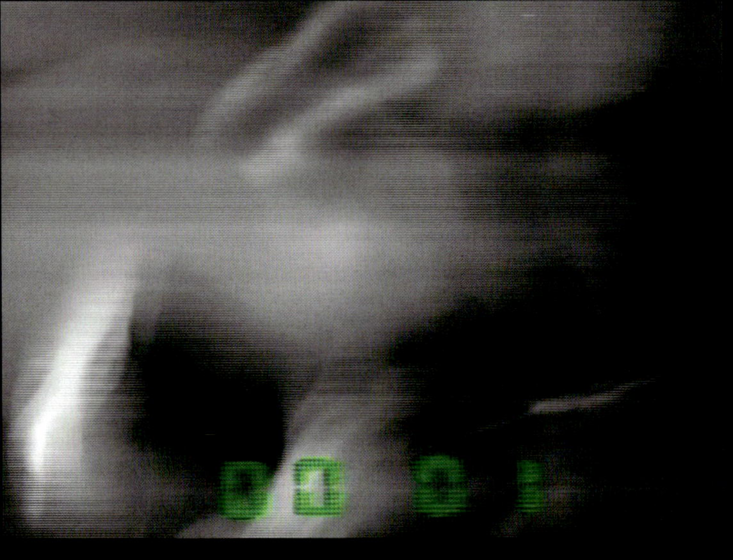

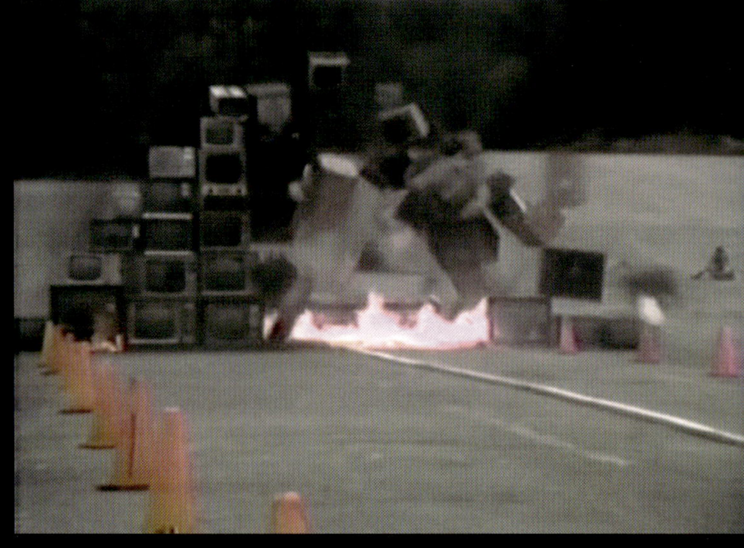

"IF SMASHING A '59 CADILLAC INTO A WALL OF TELEVISIONS IS ART, THEN THE WORLD MAY REST EASY WITH A NEW MASTERPIECE."

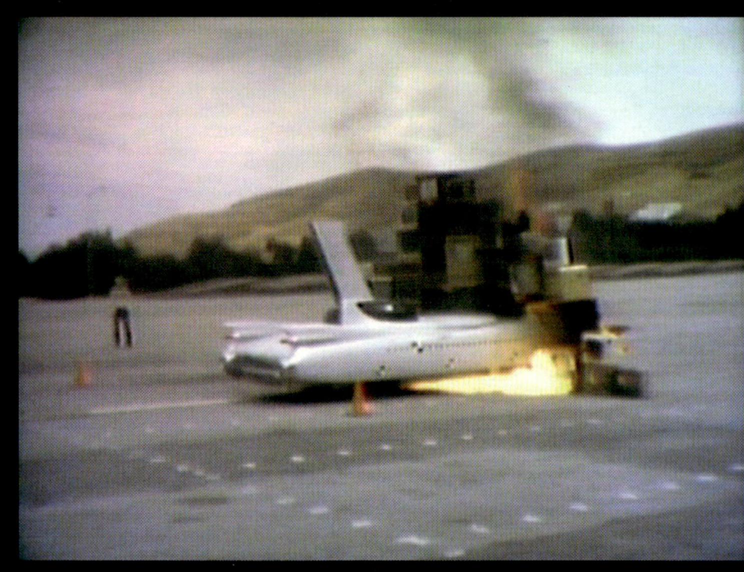

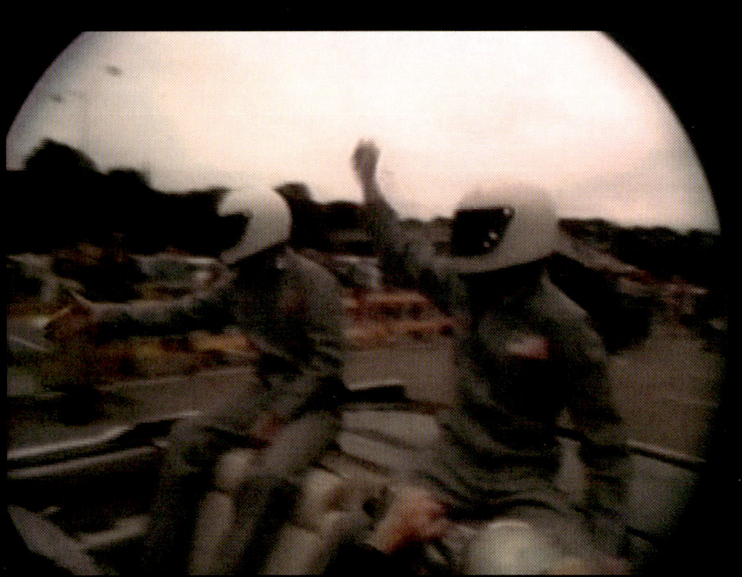

"THE WORLD MAY NEVER UNDERSTAND WHAT WAS DONE HERE TODAY BUT THE IMAGE CREATED HERE SHALL NEVER BE FORGOTTEN."

"NOW THAT IS WEIRD. YOU GOTTA SAY THAT THAT IS PRETTY WEIRD."

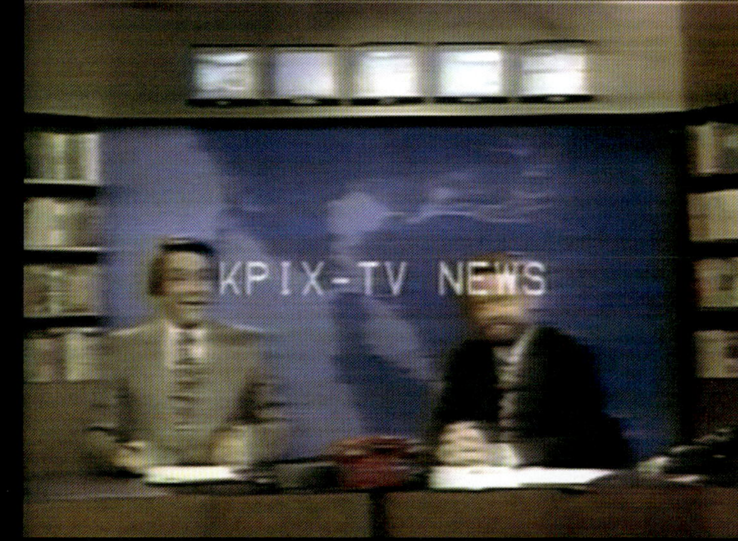

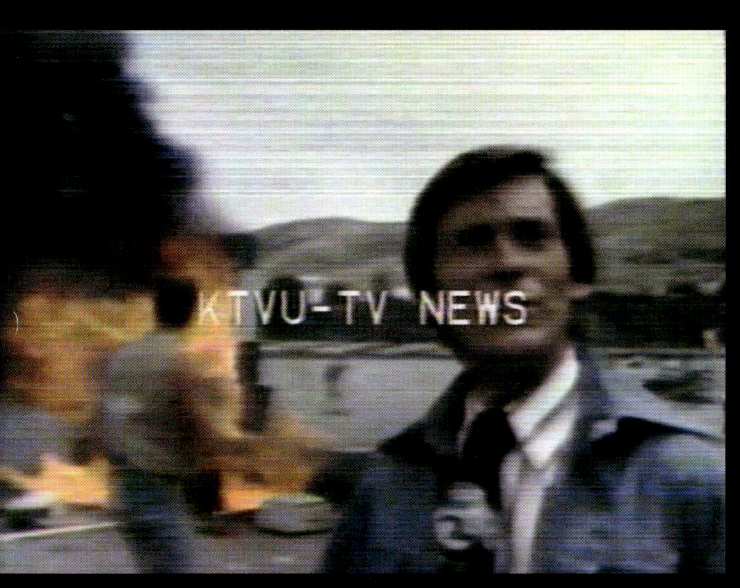

"WELL, PRESUMABLY THE MESSAGE IS FOR THE MEDIA. GET IT?"

99.9% OFF ALL HOMES IN USA WITH ELECTRICITY HAVE TV SETS

THERE ARE 68.5 MILLION TV SETS IN AMERICAN HOMES

COLOR SETS ARE WATCHED 49 HRS/WK

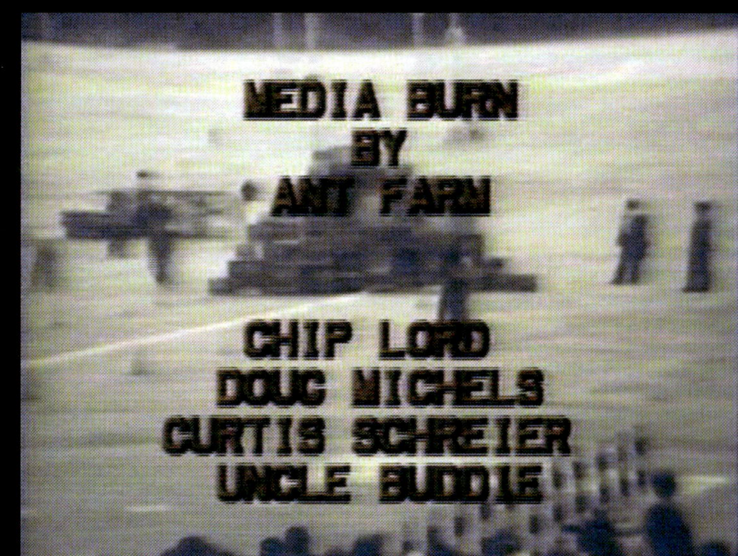

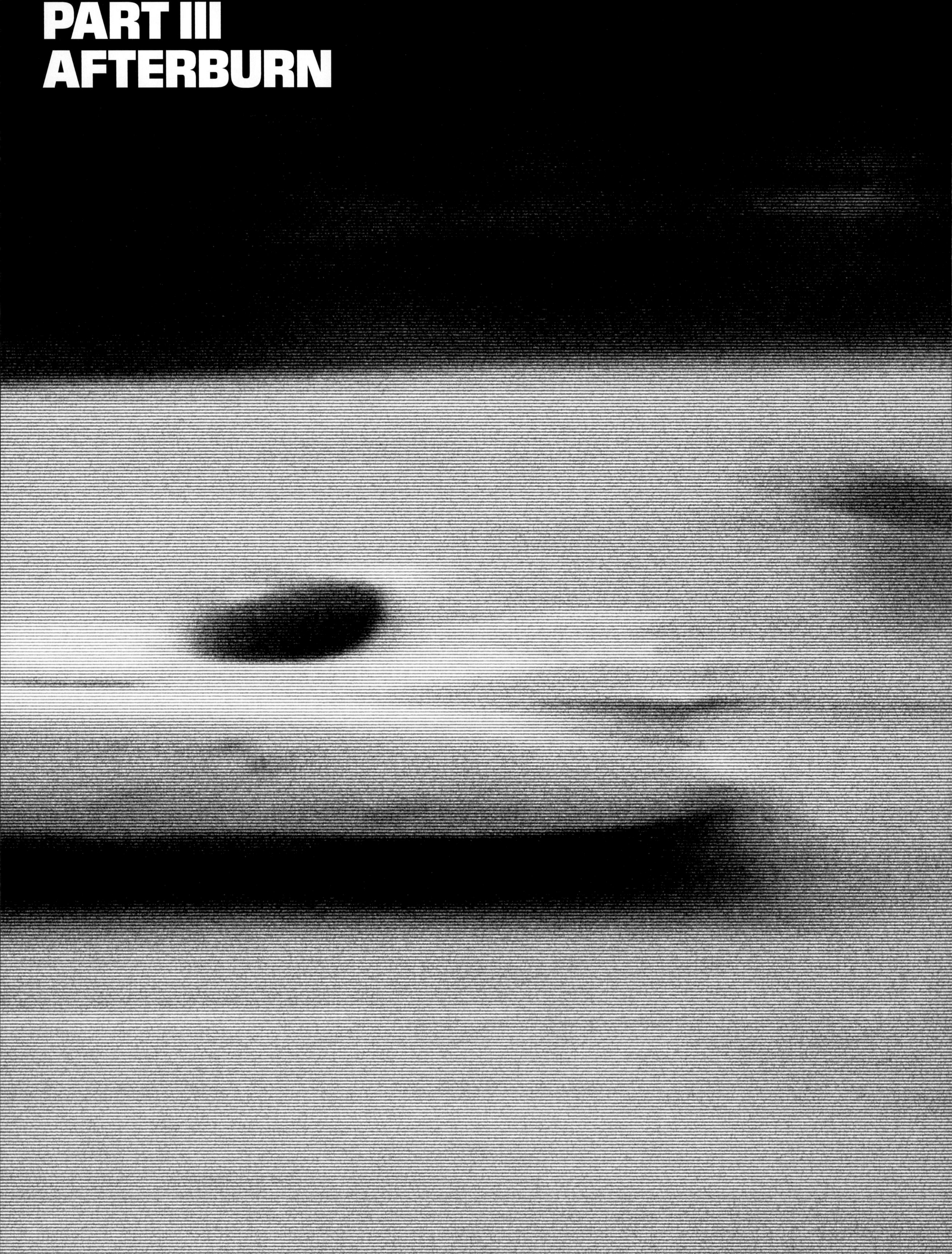
PART III
AFTERBURN

POSTCARDS FROM THE EDGE

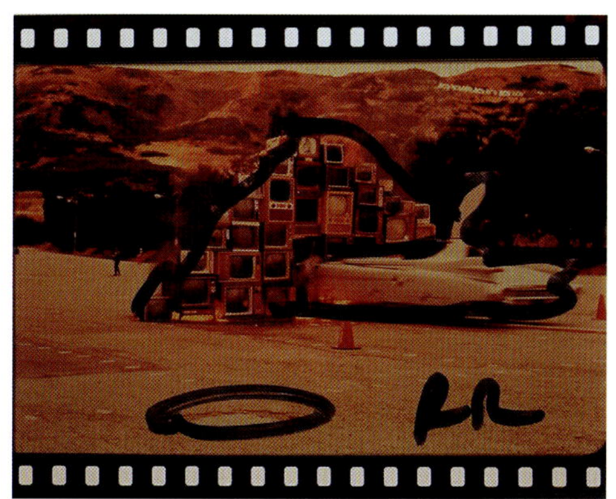

An enlarged film positive of John F. Turner's definitive collision photo used to make the postcards. The black markings designate alterations to the frame.

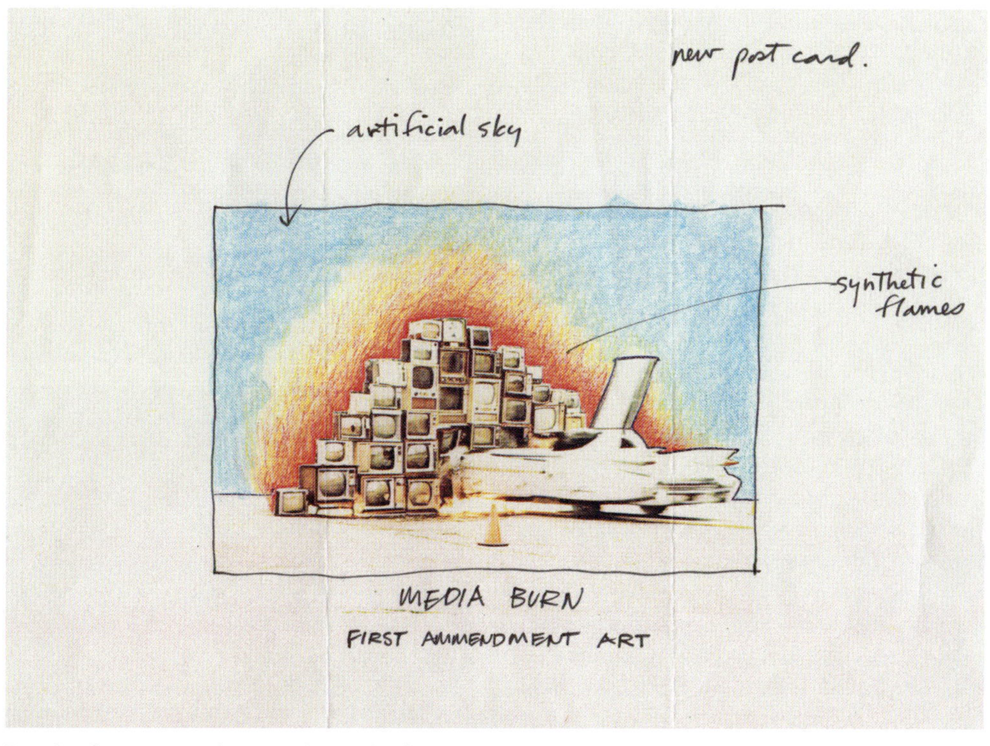

Drawing for a proposed postcard. Drawing by Doug Michels.

Following page: The three official *Media Burn* postcards. The top card is the unaltered original image. The remaining two have minor adjustments and coloration of the artificial sky.

Even the proto-punk petrol fury of *Media Burn* needed to be nurtured, tended, groomed, to prolong its potentially ephemeral life. As we have seen, within a few hours of the metal-mangling collision, a single image was plucked from a plethora of others and dispatched far and wide. The images circulated through the wire services, the art press, and hands-on marketing of Ant Farm. But two other vehicles carried forth the judicious circulation, the *Media Burn* videowork and the heavily reproduced postcards.

Less than three months after the July 4 extravaganza, the videowork had been mastered at the Synapse Video Center and distributed aggressively by Ant Farm, leading to dozens of screenings at art museums, cinematheques, and alternative spaces. Eventually both Electronic Arts Intermix (New York) and the Video Data Bank (Chicago), the principal distributors of video art, would pick up distribution rights—to this day *Media Burn* is an active rental/purchase title. As reported by VDB and EAI, the combined rentals and sales have reached approximately 2,500 copies of the work, principally to the educational market.[151] The Video Data Bank assumes that each copy is viewed by forty students in three classes, or 120 views; copies sold to campus libraries have an even higher view level. That puts the conservative number of pedagogical viewings at a quarter of a million.[152]

The postcard was another facet of circulation enhancement, a lesson learned from *Cadillac Ranch*. Several very successful postcards were issued following the well-earned popularity of Ant Farm's Amarillo-based sculpture. Riding high on seventies mail art and the last gasps of the postcard industry, eccentric, art-oriented, one-off postcards had become coveted and collectible. The local San Francisco publisher Quantity Postcards, with its upper Grant Avenue store, collaborated with Ant Farm to produce several big-selling *Cadillac Ranch* cards. But for *Media Burn*, Ant Farm dealt directly with the largest postcard press, Dexter, then based in upstate New York. Orders for cards, generally numbering 2,500 to 5,000, came off the press throughout the late seventies and eighties. Incomplete records make accurate counts impossible, but 125,000 postcards pinned to refrigerators, stationed on bookshelves, or traded and collected would be a cautious guess.[153] And we must recognize that these are *Media Burn* images embedded in daily life, regularly viewed, and domesticated.

The published postcards depict a departure from the iconic image captured by Diane Hall and dispatched to the press. That first "official" photograph

---

151   These figures were reported by Rebecca Clemens, Distribution Manager at Electronic Arts Intermix, and Abina Manning, Director of Video Data Bank via email in October 2017. Historically, VDB has covered the educational market with EAI having a greater impact on museums and galleries. The 2,500 copies rented or sold cannot be easily broken down but these informed estimates are useful nonetheless.

152   An interesting case study in multiple viewings would be the Ant Farm retrospective tour, organized by the Berkeley Art Museum. Beginning in 2004 at BAM, the tour traveled to more than six other museums (including the Yale University School of Architecture Gallery, ZKM in Karlsruhe, Germany, and the Blaffer Gallery at the University of Houston) with each site continuously exhibiting excerpts from *Media Burn* in the galleries. The combined patronage at the retrospective would be in the hundreds of thousands.

153   It should be noted that Chip Lord has some of these Dexter order forms filed away.

was replaced by one captured by another invited *Media Burn* photographer, John F. Turner, then a part-time editor for local news channels. Of the four *Media Burn* postcards released, three were modifications over time of Turner's single definitive shot.[154]

In the first card, we see the unaltered image of the wall of burning sets just penetrated by the Phantom Dream Car. Possibly enhanced flames crawl along the tarmac just beneath the auto's chassis. It is a clear Bay Area day. The hills behind the Cow Palace are fully evident with further framing provided by the tree line along the parking lot's border. It's a dramatic moment of impact with the pyramid of TV sets still retaining its vertical integrity. The inevitable fall will occur sometime later.

For the second postcard, the entire Cow Palace backdrop is removed, except for the asphalt lot. The tree line, hills, and sky are replaced by a fiery sunset and tumultuous clouds, suggesting some apocalyptic upheaval. This heavy alteration raises the ante of the image from firsthand document to secondhand cataclysm. The image's objective veracity is discarded in favor of a prediction of intensified doom. No longer just an act of defiance aimed at the mass media, the manipulated shot suggests nature in blazing revolt. Is this wishful thinking or an augury of things to come?

The final postcard follows the second in spirit, but further crops the framing and shifts the color toward the red spectrum. The effect is subtle: the very environment takes on a burnt tinge. As a collaborator, nature seems to cast its sympathetic pall over the high-octane proceedings. Or perhaps the entire globe is enveloped by the fury of road warriors in hasty smash-up. This expendable medium bore *Media Burn* forth, its meaning severed and circulated at 1/75th scale—reduced but resilient.

> "The event was only attended by maybe 300 people, including news media and friends of the artists," says John Turner. "But this postcard had a kind of life, an afterlife, and an after-afterlife …"[155]

154   The fourth postcard, published by Quantity Postcards, was of burning television sets with the backside caption, "The remains of a wall of burning television sets at Ant Farm's *Media Burn*."

155   Andy Wright, "Why is This Space-Age Car Slamming into a Wall of Flaming TVs?" *Atlas Obscura*, January 4, 2017.

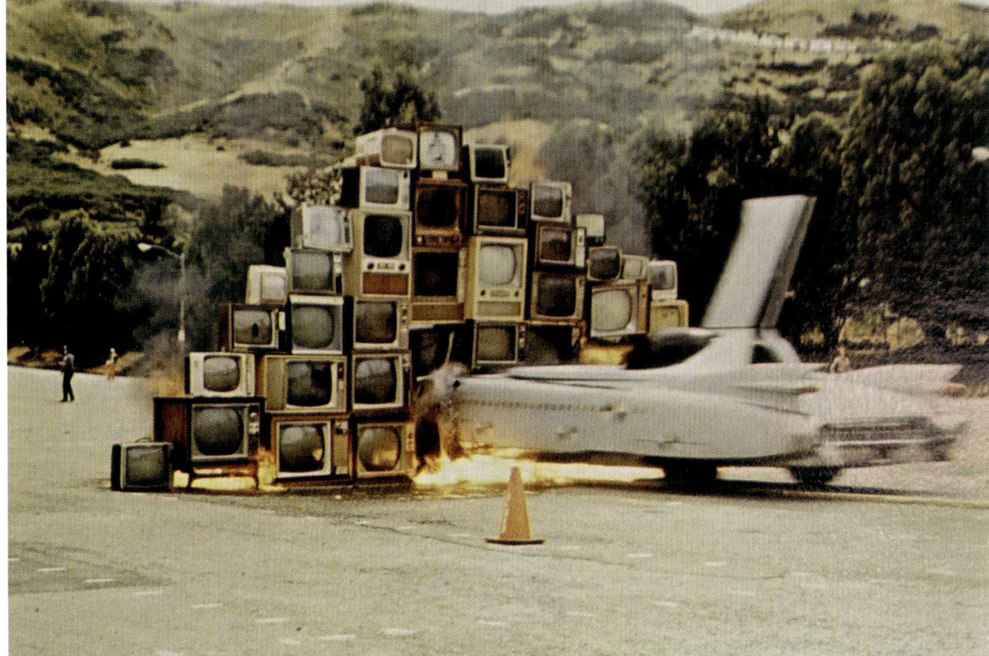

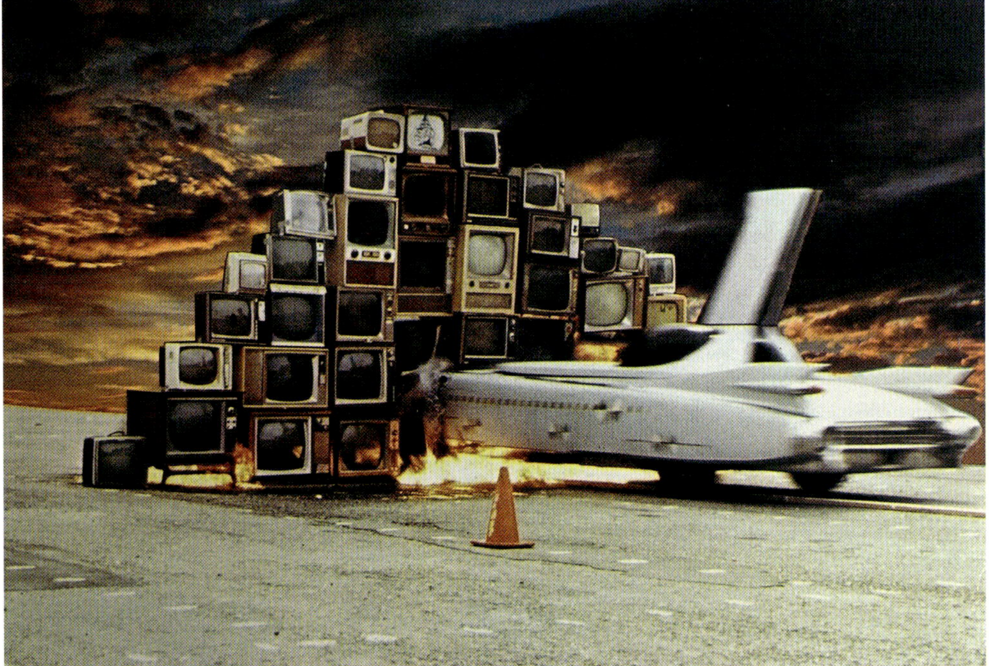

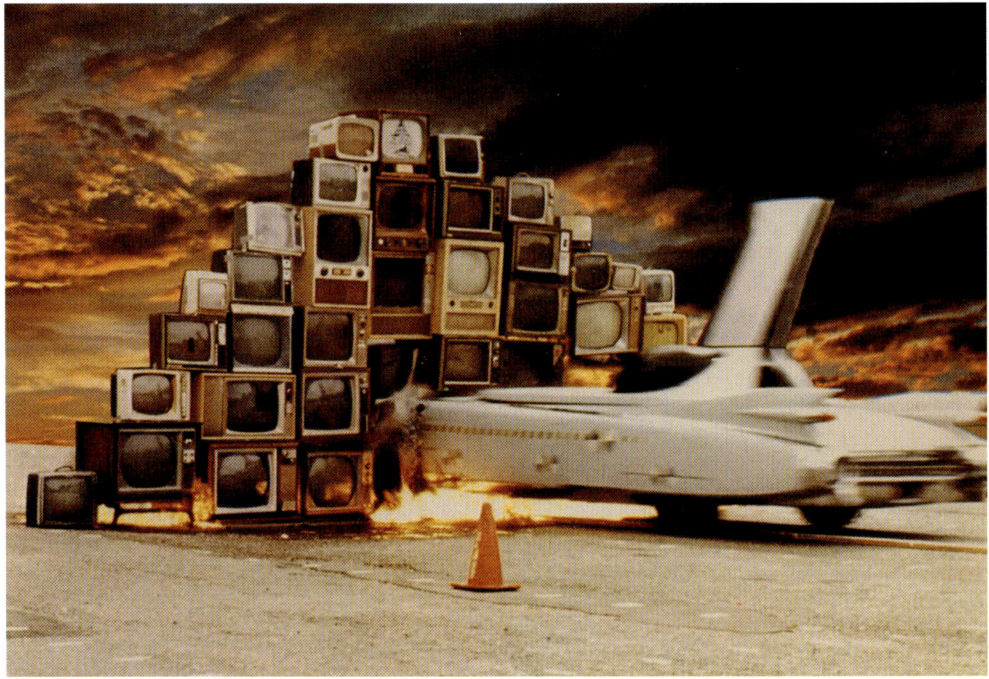

NATURE ABHORS A VACUUM TUBE

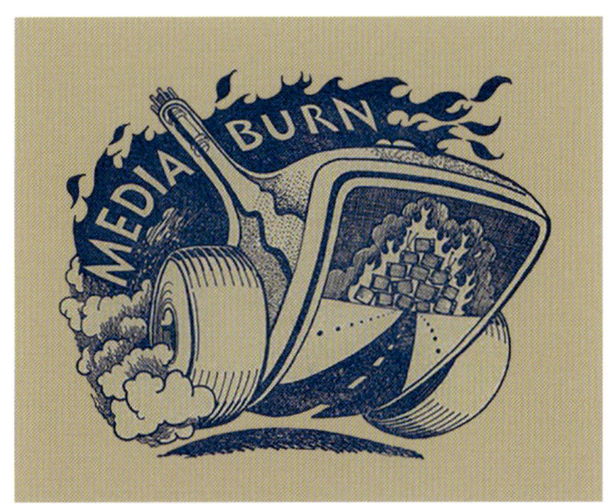

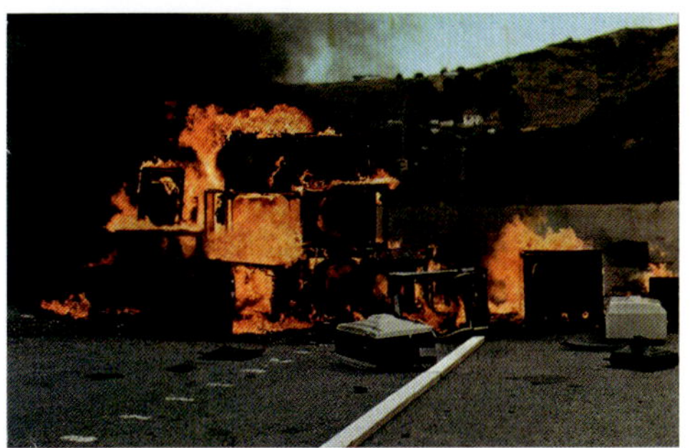

Top: The final rendering of the *Media Burn* logo as drawn by Curtis Schreier.

Bottom: A rare postcard showing *Media Burn*'s aftermath, issued by photographer John F. Turner. Published by Quantity Postcards in 1979.

On the periphery of the Ant Farm performance, a fire truck and crew sat at the ready. This was in case the actual burn, the forty-some television sets set aflame, got out of hand. Of course, it didn't—the vacuum implosions were minimal and, at worst, the asphalt lay scorched by the more flammable TV cabinets. Soon after the "media matadors" took their victory lap, the crowd moved in on the heap of smoldering TVs, further demolishing the smoky wreckage.

But what of the greater "media burn," the one that would consume all TV sets in its fiery protest, the one that would consume all CRTs in the heat of argument? "Haven't you ever wanted to put your foot through your television screen?" as the Artist-President queried. The anti-TV crowd constituted many feet, but not enough to kick in the entire output of the TV manufacturing industry, an industry at it since about 1940.

The principal inventor of television is debatable—whether it be John Logie Baird, the Scotsman, Philo T. Farnsworth,

the American, or Vladimir Zworykin, the thief—but by the mid-1930s, off-standard, do-it-yourself kits were available, though broadcast programming was not. This was to change in 1941 with the introduction of NTSC (National Television Standards Committee), the conforming requirements for black-and-white, 525-line television signals, adopted throughout much of the world. By 1953, a revised NTSC standard was introduced for color television.

World War II hindered the advance of the broadcast marketplace, slowing manufacture to a crawl, but by 1950, Americans had purchased 3.88 million TV sets, a total of nine percent of U.S. households. The number of television stations, a mere nine in 1945, rose to forty-eight within a few years and trebled the number of cities receiving broadcast signals. Soon the number of TV sets grew astronomically—a single decade, the 1950s, saw the number expand to 45.75 million, or eighty-seven percent of households. When *Media Burn* took place in 1975, ninety-seven percent of households could boast a TV, 48.5 million of them color. The total number of TV sets manufactured over the years is near impossible to calculate. Many TVs were replacement units and the average ownership per household continued to rise, clouding the real numbers. By 2006, 285 million television sets were owned by 298.4 million people, almost one per person, toddler, adolescent, or adult. (And this didn't include CRT computer terminals that numbered around 150 million.)

What did heavily impact TV purchases was a shift in technology that began in the late nineties with the introduction of the liquid crystal diode (LCD) flat screen. Those first forty-two-inch flat screens cost about $15,000. But with the standardization of High Definition TV (HDTV), old-school cathode-ray tubes were becoming giant paperweights.[156] When the Federal Communications Commission finally set

the date ending analog NTSC television—January 1, 2010—several hundred million CRT-based TV sets were put on the soon-to-be extinct list. Massive alterations to the new standardized signal—the resolution, the aspect ratio, the color map—made back-compatibility impossible. But this is really what the manufacturing industry had secretly sought, the complete and sudden irrelevance of almost 300 million home appliances and the need for their replacement.

In the roll-up to this mass extinction, disposal of the now-obsolete CRT televisions was not such a crisis. The lead-impregnated cathode-ray tubes, the phosphor coatings, the copper coils—these were all recyclable as raw materials for the next wave of TVs.[157] And even during those early years when plasma and LCD flat panels had begun to chip away at the market for cumbersome CRTs, countries like India and China still manufactured analog televisions for the local consumer. This sustained a market for sensible repurposing of CRT scrap. But now the complete move over to flat panel displays has ended the need for the toxic by-products, so the U.S. finds itself with as much as 660 million pounds of contaminated CRT glass stockpiled in warehouses (and banished from most landfills).[158]

Ant Farm's principal concern was not the toxic presence of electronic waste, but the malaise suffered by a television-addicted populace. In the *Media Burn* souvenir booklet, the statistical evidence of addictive viewing behavior is put forth, offering up a symbolic panacea for the "television generation": "At the moment of the impact, Admirals, RCAs, GEs, Sylvanias, Zeniths, and Hoffmans will fly apart in a cathartic explosion." But after the disciplinary boredom of mass media, after the proliferation of image culture, after the "cathartic explosion," came the disastrous environmental pile-up that, perhaps, Ant Farm never anticipated.

---

156 Toward the end of the tube era, Mitsubishi built a limited edition of sixty-one-inch CRT TV sets which were thought to weigh almost 750 pounds, making the television no longer a family room appliance, but an object of structural consequence.

157 Adi Robertson, "The Last Scan," *The Verge*, February 6, 2016.

158 "A Terminal Condition: The Cathode Ray Tube's Strange Afterlife," written by Josh Lepawsky and Charles Mather, *The Atlantic*, April 29, 2014.

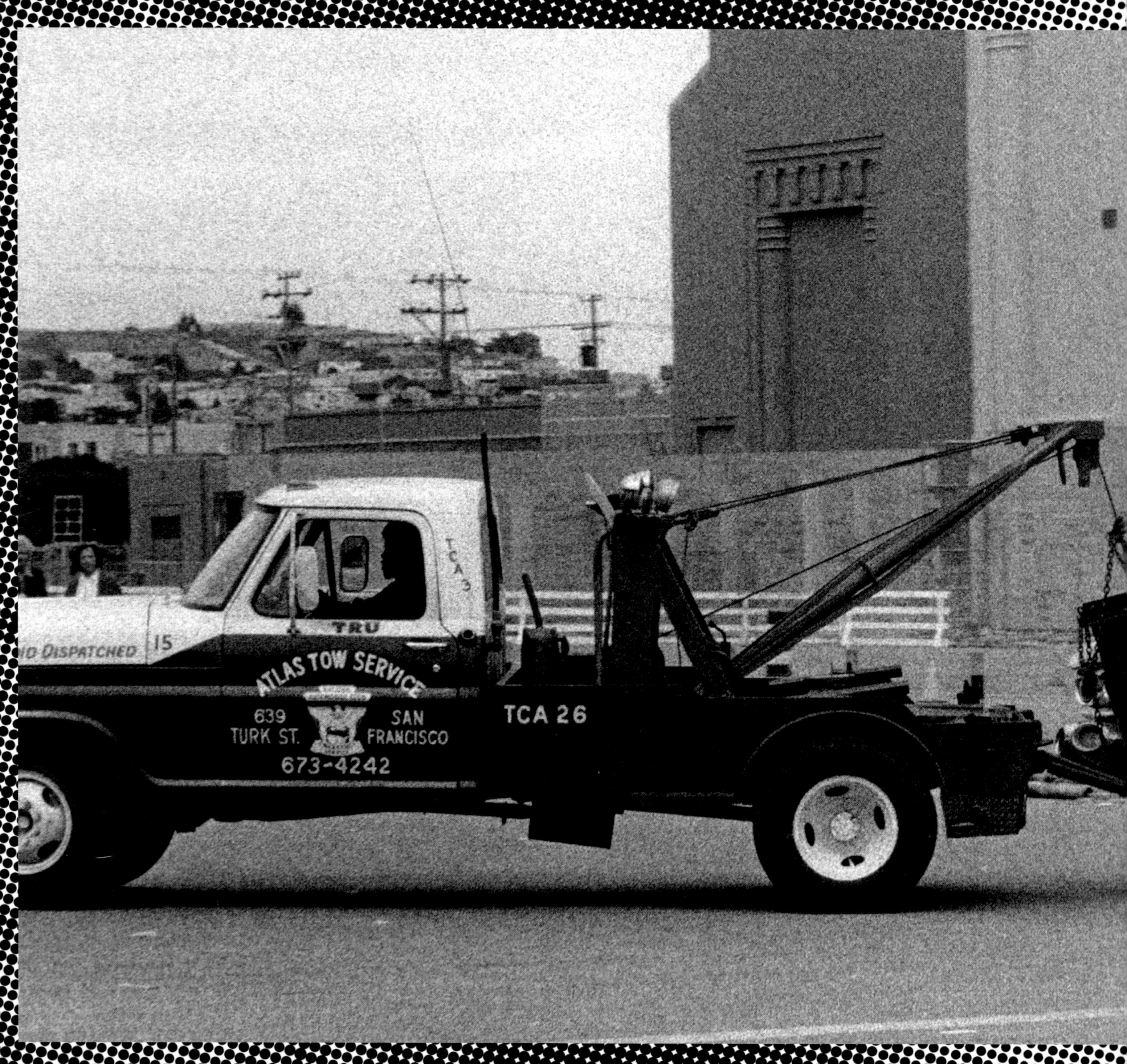

The Phantom Dream Car being towed. Note the missing vertical tail fin that had been knocked off during the collision.

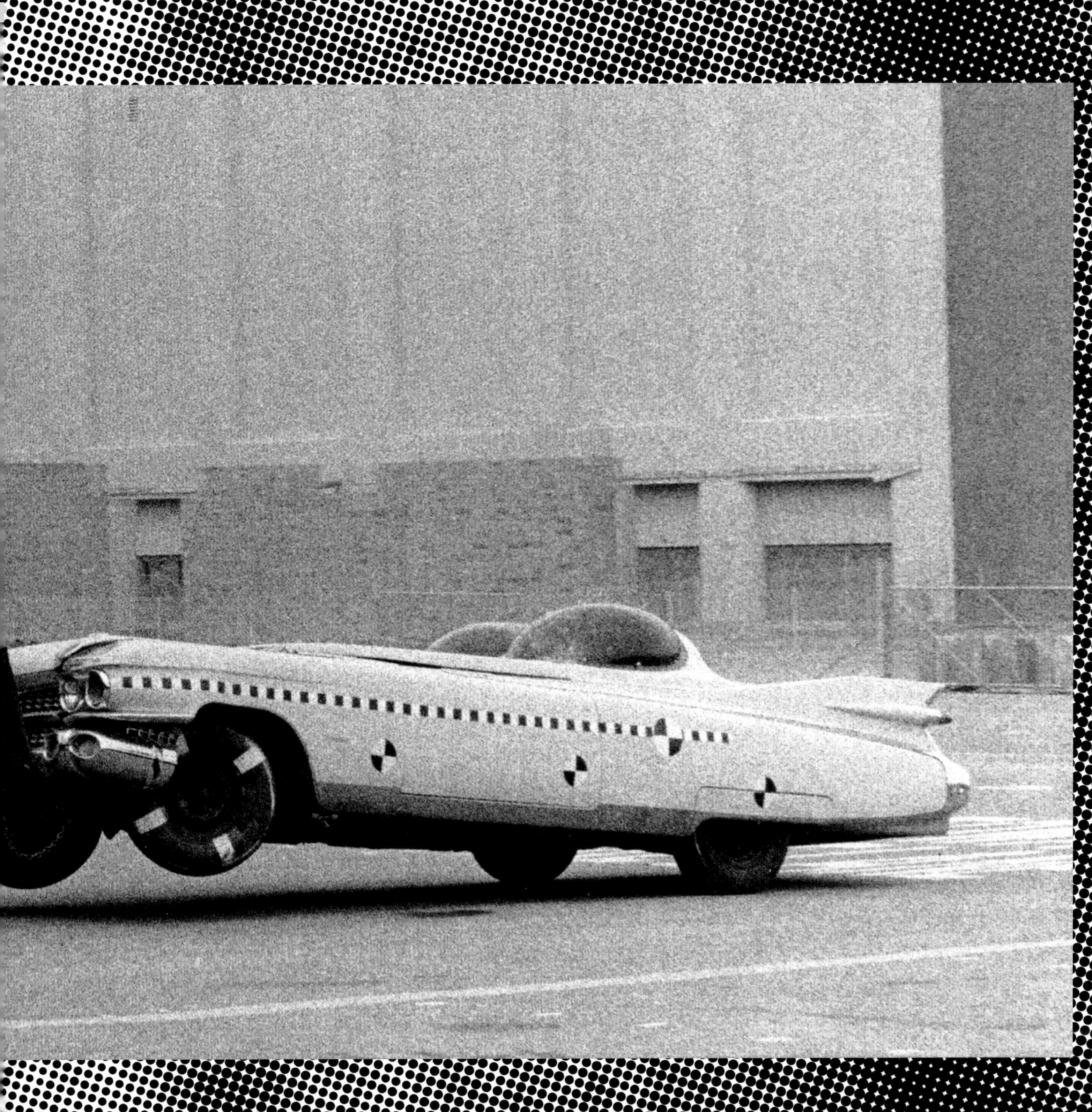

BURNT OFFERINGS

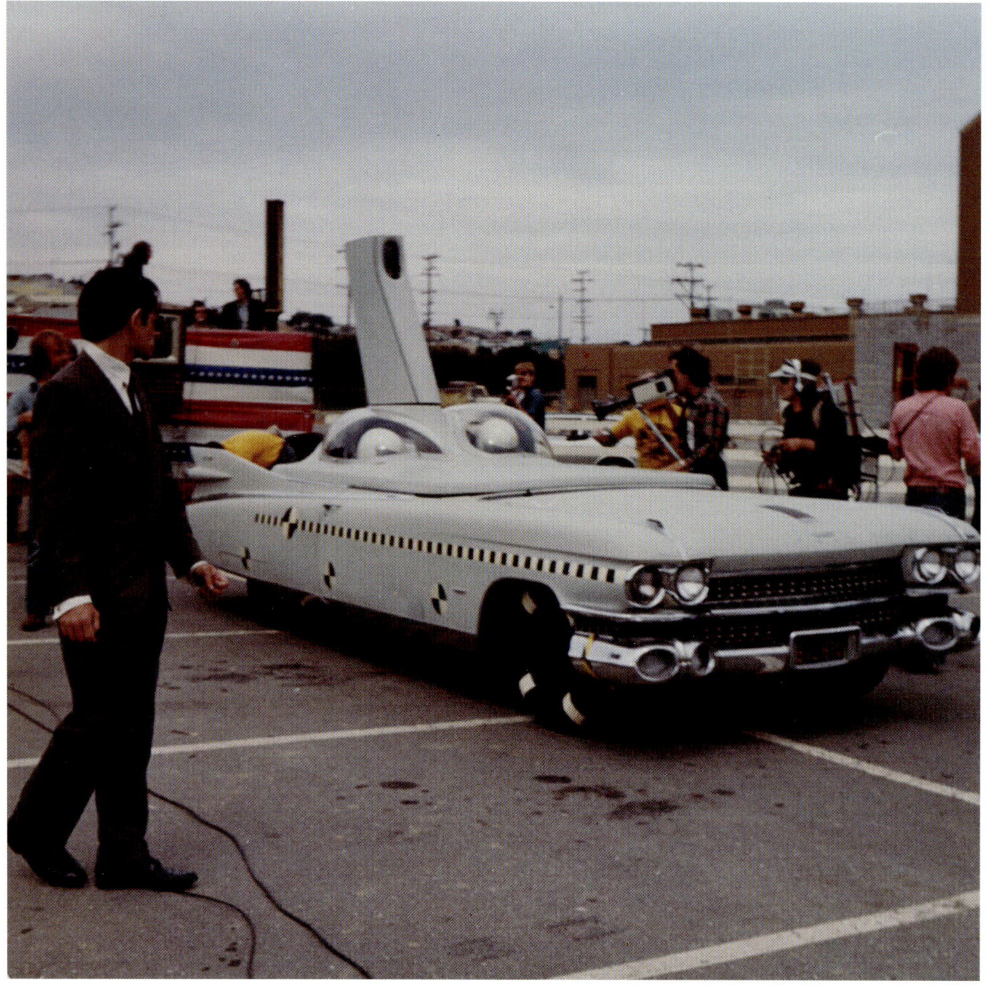

Another angle of the Phantom Dream Car before the bandstand. To the left foreground is Homer Flynn of the Cryptic Corporation in his role as a Secret Service Agent. Photograph by Phil Makanna. ©Phil Makanna.

There are at least two ways to think about *Media Burn*. First is as a blunt stunt in which a speeding vehicle expends some 10,000 pounds of brute force as it heaves obstacles out of its path. The stunt is gussied up with conceptual trappings impenetrable to the mainstream media, as they would divulge in their broadcast (and print) mockeries.[159] These ideas are not truly impenetrable, but the protective irony assumed by the press required they be perceived as such. Here, we observe the media ducking the blunt force trauma

of *Media Burn* in which, as one reporter states, "the message is for the media. Get it?"

This is *Media Burn* the publicity stunt, defused then neutralized for easy consumption. Through the use of ironic distance, curt commentary, and chronic belittlement, the mass media reinstitutes its rickety authority, winning over its audience whose cohort of "zombie-like Americans reach out to change channels as Walter Cronkite says, 'And that's the way it is ...'"[160]

But let's look at things differently, perhaps taking as our cue the words of another on-air reporter who said, "If

smashing a '59 Cadillac into a wall of old television sets is art, then the world may rest tonight with a new masterpiece." But *Media Burn* isn't a masterpiece in the sense of an extraordinary artistic achievement, fixed and unassailable; rather it's a forceful, prescient, and open-ended work that even anticipates (and attempts to guide) its afterlife.

If *Media Burn* fulfills a lifelong dream of driving a car into a wall of burning TV sets, as Lord and Michels have both attested, then what is the intended outcome? And further, if these two iconic images of American culture collide is it a fissionable event, a reordering of cultural mass and structure?[161] And what emerges? A synthetic icon rising from the discharged energy, rupturing consciousness like a tear in space?

The official Ant Farm press release sets the bar a bit lower: "It is a way of alleviating the frustration of watching television in America." A purgative, and one that would dispel angst in those firsthand participants. At one level, an artwork with a distinct goal, nowadays called a deliverable, *Media Burn* required an audience, even if on an invitation-only basis. Some 400 strong, the onlookers were being offered a sacrificial act, much like Burning Man would do years later, as an outlet for pent-up frustration.[162] The Artist-Dummies did not "do this for themselves, alone, but for all Americans." The gesture would spread beyond the 400 to the multitudes—a symbolic, participatory action. Amid the final wreckage, as the television sets smolder, a few fully alleviated souls would toss consoles with anarchic abandon.

But let us return to the "masterpiece." That, in a sense, was happening elsewhere. Like any significant and vital work,

---

159   The trappings referred to would be the particular choice of TV sets, the Artist-President's speech, the customization of the Phantom Dream Car, the carnival-like accoutrements (souvenir booklet, patriotic bunting, etc.), and the press and outreach materials.

---

160   Quoted from the "Television Addiction" section of the souvenir booklet.

---

161   For further reading on the icons, see Chip Lord's aforementioned *Automerica* (1976) and the catalog for *Receiver to Remote Control: The TV Set* (New York: The New Museum of Contemporary Art, 1990), a gallery exhibition about the mythology embedded in the television set.

162   In the case of Burning Man, two concurrent notions were afoot: one was the ritualized, sacrificial act; the other was pointing toward the formation of an alternative cultural movement.

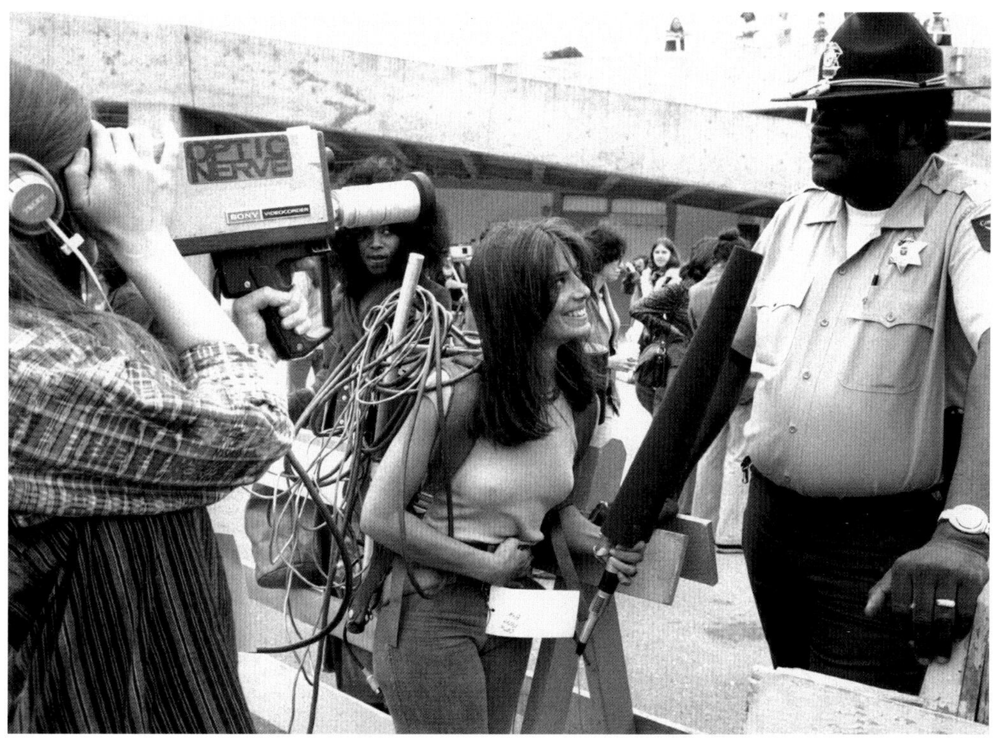

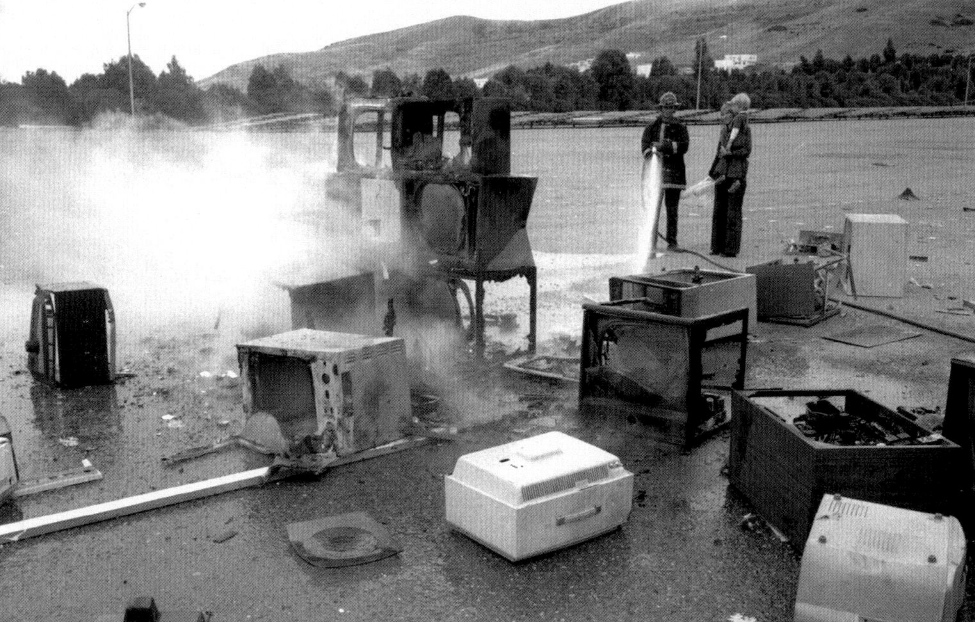

Top: Optic Nerve members Sherrie Rabinowitz (with microphone) and Mya Shone (operating the Portapak camera). Photograph by Lynn Adler.

Bottom: The smoldering remains of an epic undertaking get hosed. Photograph by Lynn Adler.

smoothing of an image, how its circulation through the mass media would rub off rough meaning, leaving a polished icon.[163] From a more implicit stance, the valuation of an autonomous object was also being challenged. The prismatic performance that was *Media Burn* was reduced to a sole image to meet the demand that art be a glistening and ineluctable thing to gaze upon. Though "the image created here" required this singularity, Ant Farm wanted it both ways: they wanted the singularity and they wanted to reinscribe meaning in the performance to rescue *Media Burn* from the vacuity of circulation.

Like a rediscovered palimpsest then, *Media Burn*, the videotape, reunited meaning with matter, returning the rich minutiae to its rightful place. The performative extravaganza had its layers of meanings, nuance, and temporality slathered back on like the strata of an upheaved geologic zone. Finally, Ant Farm's *Media Burn*, restored to its rad totality.

the meticulously staged spectacle was the refined essence of a complicated process of imagining, revision, and consummation. *Media Burn* isn't simply a consequence begun earlier with *Media Vision* and *Easy Money*. It is the thoughtful refinement of those earlier conceptions, guided by possibility and amendment. The earlier prototypes serve as studies, sketches, for the progressive detailing and design. Add to these the many other reworkings seen in the Artist-President's speech drafts, the corrected press materials, the revised souvenir booklet, the Phantom Dream Car modifications, the Secret Service agents, the paraphernalia of patriotism, the jump-suited Artist-Dummies, the forty-four television sets, no two alike.

On July 4, 1975, in a brief span of thirty minutes or so, all of these accumulated details, rethought and reappraised countless times, coalesced into a concerted performance, only to be jobbed out to a surrogate photographer, Diane Andrews Hall, who would condense the multitudinous event to a single image. In image-processing software, this function would be called flattening—to take all the layers of intervention and manipulation and reduce them to one seamless surface.

Through this reduction, Ant Farm was explicitly investigating the semiotic

---

163 This particular pursuit would be continued through *The Eternal Frame*, just one month later.

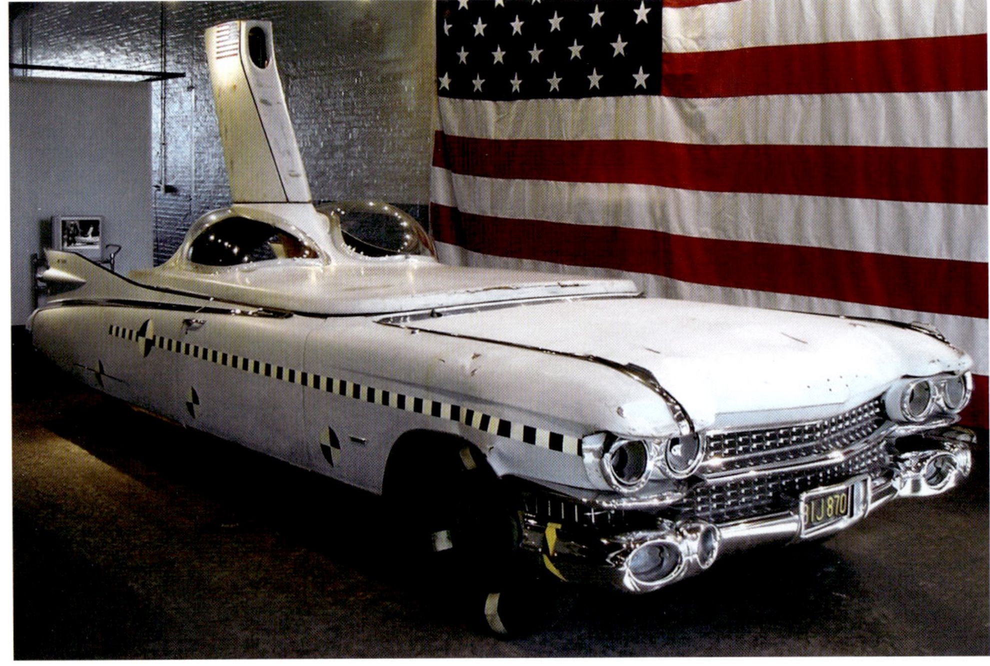

The Phantom Dream Car on display in the exhibition *American Dream: In Question* (2006–07), at the Belger Arts Center in Kansas City, MO. Photograph by Mo Dickens.

Flash forward forty-five years and we arrive at a time of entirely new social relations between the man-on-the-street and the media-in-his-hand. Even the simple question "Haven't you ever wanted to put your foot through your television screen?" is, now, more moot than ever. How indeed would you do it? Put your foot through your liquid crystal display with light-emitting diode backlight, that is. There'd be no boob tube to burst. No vacuum-filled CRT to implode. And, hey, that LCD screen might be smaller than your foot.

Gone too is the centrality of mainstream television (and the lesser gods like print media). This significance was destabilized then diminished a decade ago by the thorough entrenchment of the internet and its countless linkages—cell phones, tablets, WiFi nodes, Fitbit, the Apple watch, and other digital apparati. Connectivity securely soldered this matrix of media to the soul of the citizenry.

If mainstream media of yore didn't really want to hear from you, much less recognize a necessary dialogue that wasn't always about power and hierarchy, then the newly ubiquitized media changed the formula into one of exchange—as long as it was a transaction, the lines were open.[164] Brick-and-mortar fell to dust while data plans erected new superstructures of consumption. Instagram, Amazon, Vine, Spotify, Square, Twitter, Nest: every innovation, a pitch and a pitchfork.

Witness two people walking down the street in opposite directions, both with heads tilted downward as they gaze at their cell phones. They unwittingly collide, forehead-to-forehead. The new *Media Burn*? Or just two average Joes stuck in the nano-shaved present, never pondering consequence, never registering frustration, their blinders more encompassing than Oculus Rift.

And think too of this head-on collision as an everyday micro-disturbance in the field, a barely perceptible event occurring in limitless repetition, two bubble boys, sheathed in personalized media orbs, shearing bubble-to-bubble.[165] But where

Media Burn drew on the ire aimed at television (and mass media more properly), today's Phantom Smart Phone would be a discrete object of desire, a coveted appliance, not serving up alienation but an inverted access to sociability. The handy digital appliance is a portal to the phantasm of friendship, the frisson of global frolic, the ecstatic spasms of product and purchase. The medium is no longer the message, but it might be the text message.

The coy bit of seduction that we witness, in passing, is this—by discarding the monolithic one-to-many of past mass media, the hypermass media like the internet/cable/broadcast have perpetuated a con in which many-to-many feels like a rapturous plunge into a deep and shimmering pool of self-determined democracy. But in this case, democracy has been monetized. Every ripple in that shimmering pool is a transaction either directly as a commodity consumed or surreptitiously as behavioral data harvested.

In the nostalgic days of one-to-many, the media, in fact, had less sway over our lives and ultimately less power. We couldn't talk back to power, but as a result power was limited in its reach. Past media could noisily screech like a faulty PA system, but it couldn't pretend to listen. Now it assumes the guise of attentive listener, an algorithmic tastemaker posing as personable pal. But equations are not the same as equality.

If there was a point in which Ant Farm's far-reaching vision faltered it was in divining the future, accurately. No fault of their own: they weren't oracles or soothsayers, but artists toying with the nearterm. Considering their two major icons (the car and the TV console), they actually batted .500. The automobile continues to reign albeit with savvy adjustments in efficiency, design, and power source, but its symbolic value holds course, dragging independence and mobility in its slipstream. Autonomous autos may claim our attention, but fender benders still claim

---

164   Obviously, the issues have moved off into the infodrome, replacing traditional media with a more encompassing technologic conveyor.

165   The original "Bubble Boy" was suffering from severe combined immunodeficiency (SCID) and had to be isolated from an infectious environment. The contemporary equivalent would be severe involuntary human bonding (SIHB), an

---

ailment in which human contact is only bearable when mediated. *The Boy in the Plastic Bubble* (starring John Travolta) was released in 1976.

lives and fossil fuels no longer rule, but rue the day.

The TV set, though, has plunged in prominence as it has proliferated in presence. In 1975, Ant Farm's nemesis, the TV set, held dominion over "official" information and individual attention. The TV set but not the screen. As flat screens infiltrate every corner of culture, from the sports arena to the operating room, from the boardroom to the household appliance, the display landscape has gained in ubiquity and thinned out its prominence.[166] The prestige and power of "content" dilutes as the moving image comes to occupy every conceivable surface, domestic and otherwise.

The internet is the apotheosis of this tendency as images teem within its virtual space, then pour out through countless portals to ballyhoo our eyeballs. Ant Farm's intense interest in the circulation of images meets its match in this global network. *Media Burn* might be seen as an exercise in compression, a highly favored mode of digital culture. Rich in detail, iconic meaning, and logistics, the complex performance is first celebrated for its expansive mythic qualities through patriotic ritual and presidential address, then reduced to a single, purposeful image for its final entry into culture. This image is subsequently circulated through strategic media, screenings, and a heavily reproduced postcard, until its meaning is seared off, like the surface of a satellite re-entering the atmosphere.[167]

What Ant Farm anticipated is the notion of virality, but in reverse. Where Ant Farm assumed an image impregnated with meaning worn thin through circulation, the internet (as often as not) elevates the nonsensical image that accrues social meaning as it circulates. Each click, each like, each tag, a nano-node of affirmation. The now-collectible Ant Farm postcard featuring the incendiary collision from *Media Burn* foreshadows both the death of the visual signifier and its rebirth in the vacuum of the World Wide Web.

So how does the calamitous meaning of *Media Burn* bear any relevance to a culture in which mediating technology

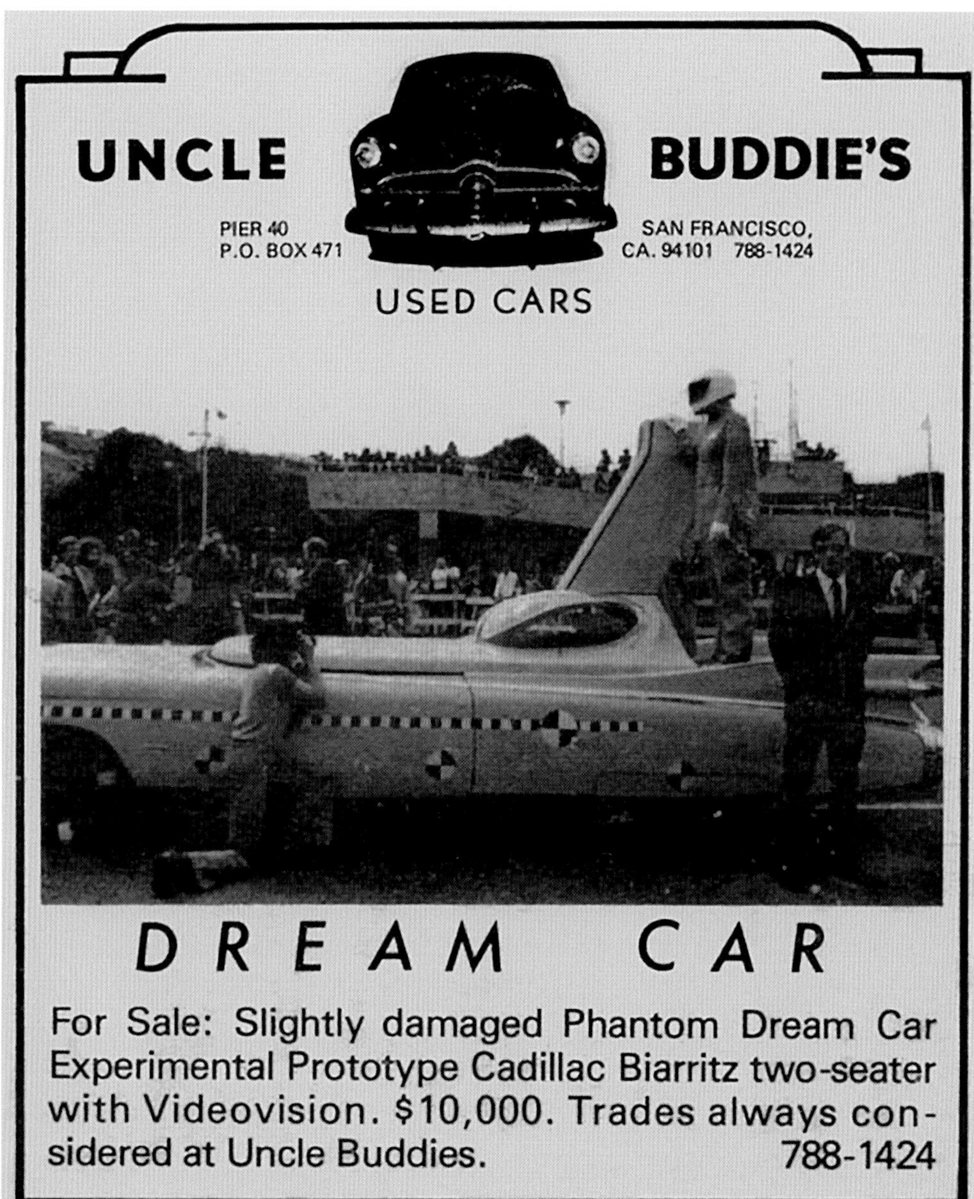

An "Uncle Buddie's" ad for the Phantom Dream Car. There were no takers until many years later.

Following spread: Framed by the American flag and the bold Cow Palace signage, the victory lap nears its end. Photograph by Phil Makanna. ©Phil Makanna.

has triumphed through its addictive necessity? The quick answer would be as a cautionary tale from across that great temporal divide when flat screens were *fat* screens—a cautionary tale, dystopic in nature, like an abbreviated *Hunger Games* for the fossil-fuel set.

Where resistance might now seem futile, we can enjoy the bravado of those mid-seventies "media matadors" as they suit up to assault their arch-nemesis, the mass media, having as their advantage a more identifiable foe, not the atomized adversary of the internet of everything. Yes, the enemy of yore has scattered; its trace is everywhere, but its corpus conspicuously absent. The Phantom Dream Car might still be able to turn its gas-guzzling engine over, but the point of impact is now pointless. And that final image (created here and now)? Forgotten in a frenzy of mandatory amnesia.

---

166   At this writing, the Microsoft Surface Hub offers an eighty-four-inch touchscreen with 4K resolution while Apple offers the iPad Pro with enhanced 2K resolution at under eleven inches.

167   This same notion would be pursued in Ant Farm's next work *The Eternal Frame* (1976) restaging the Kennedy assassination by reenacting the Zapruder footage. The veracity of the reenactment is judged solely by its similarity to the familiar footage. The meaning of this catastrophic political event is now thinner than the substrate of the 8mm film it was captured on.

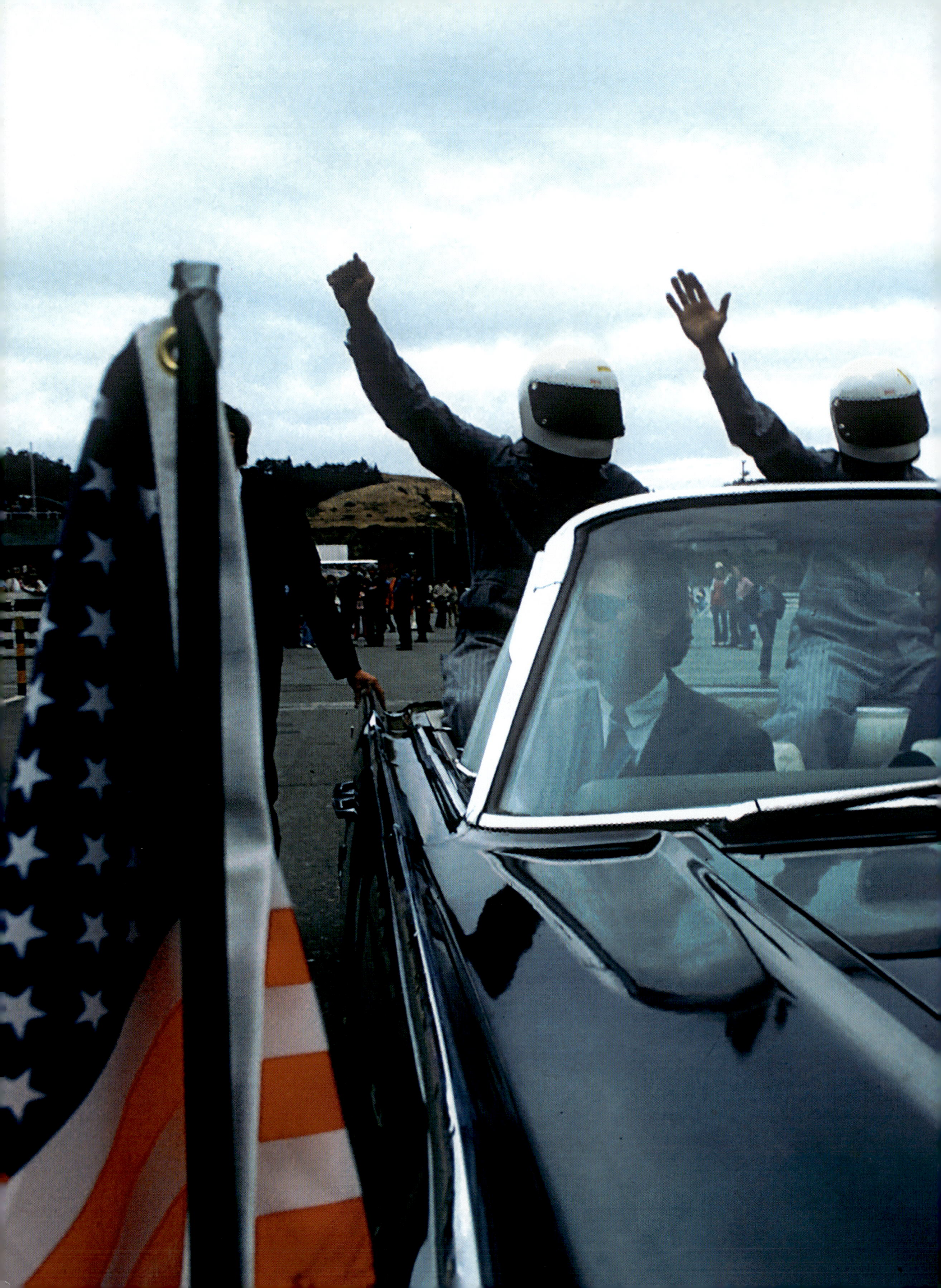

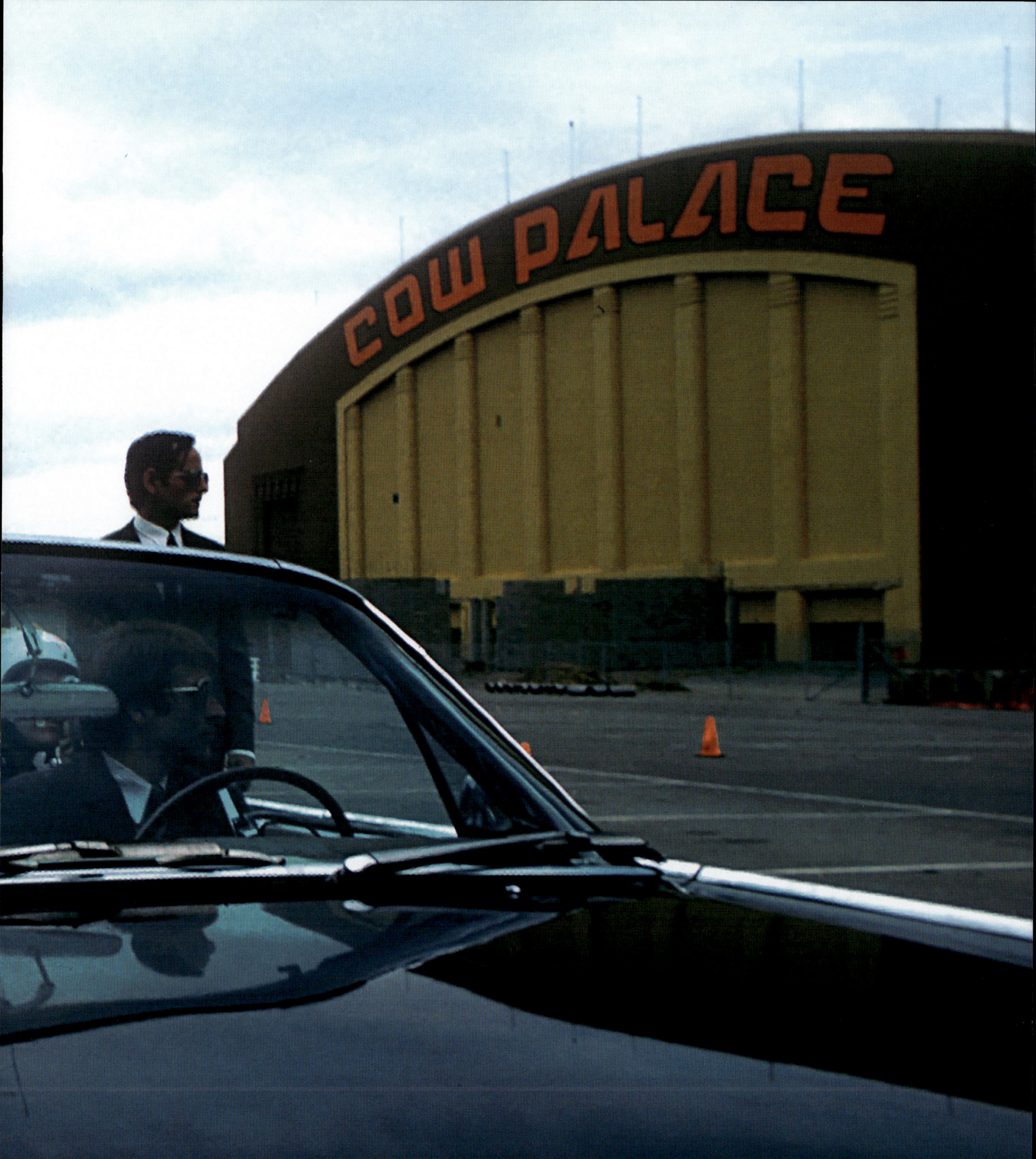

COW PALACE

ACKNOWLEDGMENTS

Media Burn is dedicated to Judy Bloch, who, more than once, singlehandedly pulled me out of the quagmire of language.

Much of the research for this book was made possible by extraordinary access to the Ant Farm archive held at the Berkeley Art Museum and Pacific Film Archive (BAMPFA) with supplementary materials held at the Pacific Film Archive Film Study Center. Special thanks are due to the archivists, especially Stephanie Cannizzo, not only for their open-ended cooperation, but for the finely organized state of the Ant Farm ephemera, and to Mona Nagai, Jon Shibata, and Michael Campos-Quinn (all BAMPFA) for their unerring cooperation.

I would like to single out Chip Lord and Curtis Schreier. They were bold enough to enact *Media Burn* and committed enough to nurture its historical memory.

I would like to highlight the photographers for having left behind such a great record of *Media Burn*, but also for their absolute generosity in providing access to their art: Lynn Adler, Kim Ecclesine, Diane Andrews Hall, Phil Makanna, John F. Turner, and the late Edmund Shea.

Much gratitude to the following: Burt Arnowitz, Eugenia Bell, Lisa Calden (BAM), Michael Couzens, Kari Dahlgren (SFMOMA), Shelley Diekman, Homer Flynn, Rudolf Frieling (SFMOMA), Diana Fuller, Ella Gold, Maureen Gosling, Jeff Gunderson (SFAI), Doug Hall, John Hillding, Randy Hussong, Lindsey Kouvaris (de Saisset Museum), Constance Lewallen, John Liikala, Tom Marioni, Jim Mayer, Allen Rucker, Jason Sanders (BAMPFA), Felicity Scott, Nathanael Seid, Beth Shippey, Starr Sutherland, Tom Weinberg, Megan Williams, Tanya Zimbardo (SFMOMA); and John Rewind and Glenn Walters, the Hoodoo Rhythm Devils.

Additional thanks go to Shelley Hayreh, Avery Architectural and Fine Arts Library, Columbia University.

I am deeply grateful to publishers Adam Michaels, Shannon Harvey, and Robin M. Wright, for recognizing the worth of this critical collision with art history.

Media Burn is partially funded by a grant from the Graham Foundation for Advanced Studies in the Fine Arts.

Media Burn:
Ant Farm and the Making of an Image
is published by
Inventory Press, LLC
2305 Hyperion Ave.
Los Angeles, CA 90027
inventorypress.com
&
RITE Editions.
San Francisco, CA
riteeditons.com

Editor: Eugenia Bell
Design: IN-FO.CO
(Adam Michaels, Ella Gold)

Printed and bound in Belgium
by die Keure

ISBN: 978-1-941753-35-4
LCCN: 2020941020

Distributed by
ARTBOOK | D.A.P.
75 Broad Street, Suite 630
New York, NY 10004
artbook.com

This book has been generously supported
by the Graham Foundation for Advanced
Studies in the Fine Arts.